SELF, NATION, TEXT IN SALMAN RUSHDIE'S *MIDNIGHT'S CHILDREN*

Self, Nation, Text in Salman Rushdie's *Midnight's Children*

NEIL TEN KORTENAAR

McGill-Queen's University Press
Montreal & Kingston · London · Ithaca

ISBN 0-7735-2615-3

Legal deposit first quarter 2004
Bibliothèque nationale du Québec

Printed in Canada on acid-free paper that is 100% ancient forest free (100% post-consumer recycled), processed chlorine free.

This book has been published with the help of a grant from the Canadian Federation for the Humanities and Social Sciences, through the Aid to Scholarly Publications Programme, using funds provided by the Social Sciences and Humanities Research Council of Canada.

McGill-Queen's University Press acknowledges the support of the Canada Council for the Arts for our publishing program. We also acknowledge the financial support of the Government of Canada through the Book Publishing Industry Development Program (BPIDP) for our publishing activities.

National Library of Canada Cataloguing in Publication

Ten Kortenaar, Neil
Self, nation, text in Salman Rushdie's Midnight's children/Neil ten Kortenaar.

Includes bibliographical references and index.
ISBN 0-7735-2615-3

1. Rushdie, Salman. Midnight's children. 2. India – In literature.
I. Title.

PR9499.3.R8M53 2003 823'.914 C2003-904456-4

Typeset in Palatino 10/12
by Caractéra inc., Quebec City

Contents

Acknowledgments

I would like to thank those who generously read the manuscript in its entirety and offered invaluable suggestions: Russell Brown, Chelva Kanaganayakam, Laura Moss, and, in particular, Alan Bewell. I am also grateful to Donna Bennett, Wendy Doniger, Judith Herz, Eyvind Ronquist, and Harish Trivedi for suggestions, comments, and answers to questions, and to Alan Bewell, Melba Cuddy-Keane, Linda Hutcheon, Garry Leonard, and Ed Pechter for advice. My students at the University of Toronto at Scarborough challenged me to refine some of my ideas, for which I am grateful. And I would like to thank Philip Cercone, Joan McGilvray, and Noel Gates at McGill-Queen's University Press for their generous and patient attention to this manuscript.

I am grateful to Lise McKean for permission to reprint the illustration of Durga from the Ekatmata Yajna souvenir volume of the Vishva Hindu Parishad, to the Tate Gallery for the print of Millais's "The Boyhood of Raleigh," to R.K. Laxman for permission to reprint three of his cartoons from the *Times of India*, and to Oxford University Press India for permission to quote from *The Collected Poems of A.K. Ramanujan*.

A version of chapter three originally appeared as "*Midnight's Children* and the Allegory of History" in *ARIEL*. I am grateful to the Board of Governors of the University of Calgary for permission to reprint it. Chapter 12 was published as "Postcolonial Ekphrasis: Salman Rushdie Gives the Finger Back to the Empire" in *Contemporary Literature* and is here reprinted with the permission of the University of Wisconsin Press. Chapter thirteen appeared, slightly modified as "Salman Rushdie and the Return of Inescapable Romance," in *The University of Toronto Quarterly* and is reprinted by permission of University of Toronto Press Incorporated.

SELF, NATION, TEXT IN SALMAN RUSHDIE'S *MIDNIGHT'S CHILDREN*

1

Introduction*

In 1993 Salman Rushdie's *Midnight's Children* was judged the best novel among all the winners of the prestigious Booker Prize in the twenty-five years of the prize's history. In the estimation of the Booker judges at least, *Midnight's Children* is the best novel published in the English-speaking world outside the United States in the last quarter of the twentieth century. It figures prominently in lists of the best one hundred novels of the century, even the best hundred books of all time, and has recently been reprinted in the Everyman's Library and the Penguin Great Books of the Century series. Certainly the story of Saleem Sinai, born at midnight, August 15, 1947, the precise moment at which India received its independence from Britain, has become the central text of Indian literature written in English. Anita Desai remembers hearing the then unknown Rushdie reading from *Midnight's Children* with "a voice that everyone present recognized instantly as being the voice of a new age: strong, original and demanding of attention" (Desai 1995, vii). The novel has had an inescapable influence on the succeeding literary generation, including Shashi Tharoor, Gita Mehta, and Arundhati Roy, whom Chelva Kanaganayakam has baptized "Midnight's Grandchildren." *Midnight's Children* also occupies a key place in the burgeoning academic field of postcolonial studies, where it is a staple of literature courses and Rushdie vies with Fanon as the epitome of the literary postcolonial. As Rukmini Bhaya Nair writes, "a contemporary mythos of postcoloniality has coalesced in the last decade or so around the 'devilish' figure of Salman Rushdie" (Nair 1999, 54).

* Throughout the text, references are to *Midnight's Children* (New York: Knopf 1981) except where otherwise stated.

The interest in Rushdie derives in part from his status as an immigrant in the metropole and, of course, in substantial part from the extra-literary notoriety that *The Satanic Verses* has earned him, but is primarily attributable to his condensation of the anxieties and concerns identified as postcolonial: how to imagine the nation-state and its history in a world of transnational migration and markets; how to locate oneself in a world of intersecting languages and cultures; how to be postmodern and write from the periphery; and how to make the English language express the needs of Indians. These themes Rushdie first stamped as his own in *Midnight's Children*, the novel which, Syed Manzurul Islam argues, includes so much of what he "would write as a writer" that his later novels, "despite their voluminous nature, appear as no more than minor elaborations of it" (Islam 1999, 125).

Not everyone is as taken with the novel, however. In particular, its status as a representation of India has been challenged. Some, like Harish Trivedi, have resented that Western critics and academics treat Rushdie as if he invented India or gave the continent a voice. Trivedi points out that *Midnight's Children*, far from the multilingual masala it is often claimed to be, is written for unilingual English-language readers for whom translations of Hindi-Urdu words are always embedded in the text. Trivedi has also established just how ignorant Rushdie is of Hindi-Urdu, of Hinduism, and even of Bombay cinema. Richard Cronin argues that Rushdie's hubristic project of encapsulating India proves that he is an outsider who thinks in English, inevitably closer in spirit to Kipling than to writers living in India, while Timothy Brennan attributes Rushdie's popularity among Western readers not to his Orientalist depiction of India, as Cronin and Trivedi do, but to his critique of nationalist ideology. Rushdie, according to Brennan, is a cosmopolitan intellectual who relies for his authority on his national origins but regards those origins with a detached, even cynical eye (Brennan 1989).

Brennan's explanation for the novel's popularity among Western readers – that it exposes the nation as an ideological construct – rings less true than Trivedi's: that its appeal lies in its depiction of Indian excess and grotesquery. But no explanation that hinges on the novel's depiction of otherness can account for the way readers have recognized in it their own experience. Whatever the limits of its purchase among people in India, *Midnight's Children* speaks to and for many inside India and out. Twenty years after its publication Rushdie can declare that "the delight with which Indian readers clasped the book to themselves, the passion with which they, in turn, claimed me, remains the most precious memory of my writing life" (Rushdie 2002B, 180–1). Nair feels Rushdie speaks "to all *postcolonials*," among whom she numbers herself (Nair 1999, 55). Patricia Mohammed invokes *Midnight's Children* in order to understand and to comment on the postcolonial politics of her native Trinidad. And I find Rushdie's novel addresses me although I am not Indian.

What is it that readers, male and female, identify with in the novel? We can begin to answer that if we ask ourselves why Rushdie's later novels (with the exception of *The Satanic Verses*, a special case) have not proven as popular or garnered as much critical attention. Rushdie himself regularly proclaims each new novel to be his best since the Booker Prize winner and, with each new title, announces that he is closing a cycle that began with *Midnight's Children*, as if he recognizes that the young man's novel represents a height the world-famous author must strive to regain. I would go so far as to say Rushdie has not yet equalled his achievement in the first half of *Midnight's Children*, and the closest he has come to doing so is in the second half of that same novel. Rushdie's career, with its early, seemingly unrepeatable, success, resembles that of another postcolonial cosmopolitan, V.S. Naipaul, however different the two authors insist they are from each other. Naipaul, too, has spoken of his desire to regain the youthful inspiration that went into the making of his *A House for Mr Biswas*, published when he was twenty-nine (Naipaul 1983A, vii); Rushdie was thirty-four when *Midnight's Children* was published. Naipaul's first real triumph, and his most realized novel, is set, like *Midnight's Children*, entirely in the land of the author's birth and ignores his status of an emigrant living in London. Naipaul followed *Biswas* with travel narratives and with *Mr Stone and the Knights Companion*, a novel set in England with only English characters. Rushdie actually started his career as a cosmopolitan fantasist, hiding his national origins in his first novel *Grimus*. Both *Grimus* and *Mr Stone* are the least successful products of their authors' careers. After their triumphs in writing about "home" and their failures in writing as Englishmen or citizens of the world, Naipaul and Rushdie went on to write important novels about the intersection of the national and the cosmopolitan in the figure of the migrant. It is a critical commonplace that Rushdie's great subject is the post-war wave of immigrants from the former colonies to the metropolis, who, by "tropicalizing" London, have challenged the cultural complacency of the erstwhile colonizers (Rushdie 1988, 354). Writing in his own person, Rushdie has celebrated the "translated man," inevitably hybrid in identification (Rushdie 1991E, 17), and has repeatedly denounced as retrograde the need some continue to feel for home and for belonging. His greatest book, however, is also the only one narrated by someone who has never left the subcontinent, (*Shame,* set entirely in a country resembling Pakistan, is narrated by a resident of London.) Naipaul's *The Mimic Men* and A *Bend in the River* are also less loved than the story of Mr Biswas, even by readers who might be expected to see in the international settings and mixed casts of characters of those novels a reflection or a refraction of their own experience. When not actively hated, the later books of both authors are more likely to be admired than loved. In something of a paradox, the national frames of *Biswas* and *Midnight's Children* prove more universal in appeal than the transnational frames of the later ones. Readers who are neither Indian nor West Indian actually require less background knowledge to understand those early novels than to understand *A Bend in the River* or *The Satanic Verses*.

If, in retrospect, *A House for Mr Biswas* and *Midnight's Children* feel inevitable, as if they had to be written, while the later novels of both authors bear ample testimony to the difficulty of the problems they were intended to solve, there is a ready explanation: both early novels can lay claim to central places in *national* literary histories. Readers know where to locate them. The authors fulfil critical expectations by representing (in both senses of that term) the people they "come from." We can draw the conclusion that, in the era of postcolonial migrancy, "imaginary homelands," as Rushdie has called them, or in Benedict Anderson's words, "imagined communities," (B. Anderson 1991) continue to matter, not least to those who have left them behind. At least as strong as the pull of deterritorialization, undermining the fixed meaning of geographical space, is the impulse to reterritorialize.

Rushdie, the migrant author always in pursuit of the metropolitan centre, has denounced as a lie the lesson that Dorothy affirms at the end of *The Wizard of Oz*: "There is no place like home" (Rushdie 1992, 57). Rushdie took his leave from "the East" in *Shame* (Rushdie 1983, 23), the novel that followed *Midnight's Children,* and he is still bidding it farewell sixteen years later, in *The Ground Beneath Her Feet* (Rushdie 1999A, 249) and in the screenplay to *Midnight's Children* (Rushdie 1999B). If he says good-bye so often, it can only be because he always dreams "A Dream of Glorious Return": "I wanted to get India back," he writes in the year 2000 (Rushdie 2002B, 180). The cosmopolitan author is also at some level a nationalist. The postmodern fabulist who declares that his artistic wellsprings lie in his exile – "To cross a frontier is to be transformed" (Rushdie 2002A, 353) – will also say, "This, perhaps, is what it means to love a country: that its shape is also yours, the shape of the way you think and feel and dream. That you can never really leave" (Rushdie 2002B, 180).

In *Midnight's Children* the nationalist cosmopolitan has invented a protagonist who may best be described as a cosmopolitan nationalist. Saleem Sinai's life is a fictional reworking of Rushdie's own experience as a child in Bombay, living in a house called Windsor Villa, located off Warden Road and overlooking Breach Candy Swimming Pool, with the significant difference that Saleem never leaves the subcontinent and eventually returns to the place where he was born. After adventures that carry him thousands of kilometres from the city of his birth, to Pakistan, Bangladesh, and Delhi, Saleem, unlike his creator, retires to Bombay, where a taste of the green chutney that his ayah used to make has restored the past to him. Saleem does not just remember the childhood self that he had thought long destroyed; he recovers that lost self and is able to do what is denied most children: return to the care of his ayah. The pickle factory his former ayah now owns provides him with all that he needs in order to pickle his memories and write his memoirs: a room of his own, free time, and an audience on whom to test his writing.

We can take the measure of the distance between cosmopolitan author and nationalist narrator if we consider what they each know. Linda Hutcheon writes that the novel's intertexts are "doubled": "They are, on the one hand, from Indian legends, films and literature and, on the other, from the west – *The Tin Drum, Tristram Shandy, One Hundred Years of Solitude* and so on" (Hutcheon 1989, 65). Dipesh Chakrabarty has taken Hutcheon to task for specifying only the Western references and leaving the Indian ones unnamed: "This ignorance, shared and unstated," he concludes, "is part of the assumed compact that makes it 'easy' to include Rushdie in English Department offerings on postcolonialism" (Chakrabarty 2000, 28). But Hutcheon and Chakrabarty are both wrong if they assume that the doubling of Rushdie's references is symmetrical. Hutcheon names only the intertexts that need to be identified because, while very conspicuous, they are left unstated by the novel itself. She leaves unglossed the references to the Quran and to Hindu mythology because they are already explicit: Ganesh and Mount Sinai, Gabriel and Kali are directly invoked by Saleem. The references that the novel does not gloss, which are all Western, do not belong to Saleem but to Rushdie. The implied author addresses cosmopolitan readers of Western literature who will hear in character names and plot devices allusions to E.M. Forster (Dr. Aziz), Rudyard Kipling and Shirley Temple (Wee Willie Winkie), Laurence Sterne (the business about noses and impotence, and the delay in getting to the hero's birth), and Günter Grass (Oskar). Saleem, usually eager to show off his historical and cultural knowledge, gives no sign of having read these authors. He has seen Hollywood films, has studied European plays in school, and has researched the history of Bombay and contemporary politics, but he does not read books. It would appear that newspapers constitute all his adult reading. Lest Saleem's repeated references to Cyrano de Bergerac (15, 95) appear out of character, Rushdie has him explain within parentheses that "We had done *Cyrano*, in a simplified version, at school; I had also read the *Classics Illustrated* comic book" (182).

Saleem is a bilingual Indian addressing cosmopolitan readers and, as Carmen Dell'Aversano points out, reassuring them that they will learn whatever they need to know about India (Dell'Aversano 1999). His English-language audience is aware of and interested in cultural difference, and willing to be educated about India. They are familiar with the names Nehru and Gandhi, Ganesh and the Quran, but must have Hindi/Urdu translated for them. For their benefit he is careful to explain that a "compound can be anything from a wasteland to a park" (36), a swastika is "not the Nazi swastika which was the wrong way round, but the ancient Hindu symbol of power" (75), "four annas" make a "chavanni" (134), and Ramzàn is "the month of fasting" (178). When Saleem makes allusion to things that are not Indian, for instance, to Karl Marx, Hollywood films, the *Arabian Nights*, or the Bible, he can do so because all these things may be found within India. The implied author, on the other hand, is an English-speaker addressing fellow cosmopolitans. When Rushdie alludes to European and Latin American literature, it is because he locates India in a larger world with all these things.

To some extent Brennan is right: Rushdie the implied author invites his readers to see around Saleem. Saleem the memoirist is also an allegorical figure for national history. The allegory presumes that the nation can be identified with its political history and that that history can be seen whole. This perspective is that of the non-resident Indian, who faces most acutely the question of what it means to be Indian and who must look to the map and to national history for an answer. Cronin writes that only in English is it possible to write about India as a whole in this way, because to write in Punjabi or Bengali or Hindi is to write for an audience smaller than the nation (Cronin 1999). This outside perspective on the state is something new, even in Indian literature written in English, which, before Rushdie, concentrated on the local and the domestic. Explicitly political novels, like *Kanthapura* by Raja Rao (Rao 1963) or *Waiting for the Mahatma* by R.K. Narayan (Narayan 1981), focus on the village or the town rather than the nation.

Rushdie, however, cannot speak directly in the novel; all readers hear is Saleem's voice. As Rushdie tells it, a first draft of the novel, narrated in the third person, changed completely when Saleem, at the time little more than an allegorical puppet, somehow acquired the divine spark of self-consciousness and became a real boy: "It was like a coup: he just simply took a deep breath and started talking, and 500 pages later he stopped" (Rushdie 1985, 2). The result is a glaring contradiction: a memoirist who is himself an allegory. Saleem will speak of "my India" (164), as if his was but one among many possible versions and his authority derived from his experience. At such points, he speaks like Rushdie, whose version of India, the product of his memory and his invention, this certainly is. Saleem, however, will also declare that he caused the death of Nehru (271) and that the Indo-Pakistani War of 1965 was fought with the sole purpose of wiping his family off the face of the earth (327). Saleem's partial perspective, based on limited experience and distorted by memory, is also a totalizing vision, inspired by the map and by national history. What is true of Rushdie's India, that memories tell us about the one remembering and about the world that produced him, is patently absurd in the case of a man who sees himself as an allegory of the nation: one might as well say that the perspective of a madman who declares he is Napoleon is as legitimate as any other. The memoirist who insists on his allegorical significance can only be a schizophrenic suffering delusions of greatness.

Saleem, a "Pinocchio" who has lost his strings (153), is an often absurd figure, a mimic man and a madman, who thinks differently from the way Rushdie does or wants his readers to think. Rushdie's other novels, *Shame*, *The Satanic Verses*, *The Moor's Last Sigh*, and *The Ground Beneath Her Feet* are all narrated by voices that share the author's opinions and sensibility. Even where, as in the last two novels, the narration is by a character in the story, there is no difference between what that character tells us and how we are intended to read it. In *Fury*, Rushdie's most recent novel, in which his literary imagination has followed the author to New York, the free indirect discourse is entirely without irony: what the protagonist, Professor Malik Solanka, thinks is what the novel thinks. Rushdie has put into each of these works all that he knows. In *Midnight's Children*, however, the distance between writer and narrator is both palpable and unstable. Rushdie has felt the need to speak out and cast doubt on Saleem's version, going so far as to suggest that "the entire book" be read as the narrator's "distortion of history, written to prove that he was at the middle of it," with the result that "the moment at which reality starts to face him it destroys him: he can't cope with it, and he retreats into a kind of catatonic state" (Haffenden 2000, 41). We can conclude, however, from the great lengths to which Rushdie has gone, both in the novel itself and after its publication, to ensure that he not be mistaken for his creation, that much of the ironic distance between author and narrator is filled with panic: the narrator furthest from Rushdie comes too close to him for comfort. The result is that only in *Midnight's Children*, where he has risked a significant distance between himself and the narrative voice, has the author been able to include more than he knows that he knows.

The great popularity of *Midnight's Children*, within India and without, suggests that readers feel a fascination, perhaps even a perverse identification, with Saleem that has nothing to do with madness – as a psychological case study, the novel is unconvincing – and everything to do with the novel's exploration of the links between the self of the citizen and the nation. Self-contradiction is a risk faced by all of Rushdie's books. In *The Satanic Verses*, the allegory about the ideological construction of otherness is fatally at odds with a sentimental fable about the existence of evil in the human heart. In *Midnight's Children*, however, the incompatible narrative impulses of allegory and memoir, to which we may add the self-conscious meditation on the nature of memory, writing, and identity, do not pull apart because, within each of these narratives, nation and self and text are intimately related. The novel's yoking of the conventions of allegory, centred outside the self on the nation and its history, and of memoir, focused on the self, its perceptions and memory, is best understood as a meditation on a more general condition. The nation-state itself is always a function of a double perspective, at once a projection of the self on the scale of the world and a means of locating the self within the world.

In most critical discussions the contradictions of Saleem's narrative are subsumed under the key postcolonial critical concepts of hybridity and mimicry, as well as under the postmodern terms, magic realism and metafictional historiography. These terms all imply a duality most often understood as self and other, India and England, a duality that, it is assumed, Rushdie transcends or contains. My study, however, will show that the duality in the novel has less to do with rival nations and the juxtaposition of incompatibles than with the oscillation between inside and outside. Saleem, the cosmopolitan nationalist, and Rushdie, the nationalist cosmopolitan, wage a struggle for control of the text, a struggle neither can win because the outside needs the authority of the inside and the inside the objectivity of the outside.

Inside and outside are usually cast in opposition to each other. In an American context, Martha Nussbaum has recently defended cosmopolitanism in the classical sense of world citizenship against what she sees as a dangerous resurgence of provincial nationalism (Nussbaum 1996). Michael Hardt and Antonio Negri, in a more radical context, champion a cosmopolitanism better able than reactionary nationalism to resist the global reach of what they term "Empire" (Hardt and Negri 2000). As one might expect, the debates between cosmopolitanism and nationalism take pride of place in the field of postcolonial studies, where Arjun Appadurai (1996), Kwame Anthony Appiah (1996), and Homi Bhabha (1994) deconstruct national essentialisms in the name of a more global awareness, while others, such as Brennan (1997), Neil Lazarus (1999), and Helen Tiffin (1996), defend the nation-state as a necessary bulwark against the tides of global capital, cultural imperialism, and a false universalism. To the latter critics cosmopolitanism looks like another version of cultural imperialism.

Rushdie, whose novel is at once nationalist and cosmopolitan, has something to teach us about the mutual imbrication of inside and out. Although cosmopolitans and nationalists caricature each other as detached and privileged or essentialist and parochial, each pays the other the compliment of critique. To Bhabha we owe the playful titles "Nation and Narration" and "Dissemi-Nation," while Brennan, a defender of nationalism, writes primarily about "Cosmopolitanism Now" and "Cosmo-Theory" (Brennan 2001). If both cosmopolitanism and nationalism seem to be currently enjoying a resurgence, there is also an increasing awareness that they are defined as not only opposite but also as complementary. According to Joan Cocks, a "new cosmopolitanism" delights "in the heterogeneity of peoples," and a "new nationalism" believes that the "care for place" requires people "to transcend the homogeneous nation-state" (Cocks 2001, 164). Cosmopolitans try to contain nationalists by asserting some combination of universal ideal and particular location called "cosmopolitan nativism" (Ramazani 2001, 48), "vernacular cosmopolitanism" (Bhabha 1996, Notes), the "cosmopolitan hearth" (Tuan 1996, 182), or "cosmopolitan patriotism" (Appiah 1996), while those who argue for the relevance of the nation-state defend "the possibility of the national-in-the-cosmopolitical" (Cheah 1998, 303).

In India the debate between cosmopolitanism and nationalism also rages but with a different inflection. The nationalism of secularists, such as Achin Vanaik (1997) and Dipankar Gupta (2000), is opposed not to cosmopolitanism but to the internal threat to the nation posed by communalism, while critics of Western influence, like Ashis Nandy (1994) and Partha Chatterjee (1986), are critical of the nation-state as itself based on harmful foreign models. A modernizing secularist, like Gupta, sees the nation-state as the field where the freedoms associated with citizenship are realized, and a critic of the modern, like Nandy, opposes the nation-state as an agent of cosmopolitan modernity. How can we explain that, in India, the cosmopolitan is also a nationalist and that opposition to globalization is primarily critical of the nation-state?

The Western-educated nationalists who fought for independence judged India according to the measure of other nations: they sought the sovereignty that others had on the grounds that India was a nation like others. The outsider's perspective, *pace* Cronin, has always played a part in the way the modern Indian nation-state (as opposed to Bengal, the Punjab, or the Bharat India of the Vedas) is imagined: the inside presumes an outside. Nehru's *Discovery of India* adopts a doubled perspective close to Rushdie's when he writes, "India was in my blood. [...] And I approached her almost as an alien critic. [...] To some extent I came to her via the west, and looked at her as a friendly Westerner might have done" (Nehru 1981, 50; cited in Needham 2000, 55). Nationalism, the modern movement which requires that everyone belong to a nation-state and which sees the world as completely apportioned among nation-states, is what Jonathan Friedman calls "a global system phenomenon," that is a characteristic of modernity found in every corner of the globe (Friedman 1995). In that sense nationalism is best understood as the first wave of globalization – Roland Robertson calls it the "universalization of particularism" (Friedman 1995, 72) – even as it poses the strongest resistance to the second, anti-national, wave of globalization currently engulfing the world. Nationalism, implying as it does a global framework in which the nation finds a place, is as large as the world. The debate between nationalism and cosmopolitanism is actually between rival forms of cosmopolitanism. Brennan assumes that, because Rushdie is a cosmopolitan writing for a Western audience, his national allegory is critical of the nation-state. *Midnight's Children*, however, is most often read, inside and outside India, as a triumphant celebration of the nation and as the first novel commensurate with India, because, in India, cosmopolitanism and nationalism are fully compatible.

In India nationalism and cosmopolitanism have both been opposed by another philosophy in the name at once of indigeneity and of universal humanity. A line of Indian thinkers from Rabindranath Tagore through Gandhi to Nandy and Chatterjee has denounced the nation-state, first, as derivative and Western, and second, as a dangerous, totalizing principle. Tagore, who in an essay called *Nationalism* defines the Nation as "the organised self-interest of a whole people, where it is least human and least spiritual" (8), suggests that nationalism is precisely to blame for imperialism: "When this engine of organisation begins to attain a vast size, and those who are mechanics are made into parts of the machine, then the personal man is eliminated to a phantom, everything becomes a revolution of policy carried out by the human parts of the machines, with no twinge of pity or moral responsibility" (Tagore 1976, 7). Chatterjee critiques anti-colonial nationalism because, "even as it challenged the colonial claim to political domination, it also accepted the very intellectual premises of 'modernity' on which colonial domination was based" (Chatterjee 1986, 30).

What we have here are rival versions of nationalism that are also rival cosmopolitanisms. Those subscribing to the anti-national, Indian-centred cosmopolitanism of Tagore and Chatterjee declare they are outside the nation-state and therefore able to appreciate the heterogeneity that the nation-state denies. The nationalist successors of Nehru, among which should be numbered Rushdie, also claim an outside vantage-point: outside what they regard as the dangerous will to homogenization of communal violence or the equally dangerous homogenization of globalization. Both forms of nationalist cosmopolitanism defend hybridity against the threat of homogenization; each seeks a vantage-point that will allow it to contain the other.

In upholding a version of Indian nationalism best described as Nehruvian, *Midnight's Children* claims to defend hybridity against purity, magic against realism, polyglossia against monoglossia. Yet, as I will show, it actually defends one form of cosmopolitan nationalism against a rival version. It defends one kind of hybridity from the threat, not of purity but of another kind of hybridity, good magic against bad magic, and a polyglossia that serves the self from a chaotic soup that threatens to engulf the self. The novel seeks constantly to balance inside and outside and to use one to uphold the other. It is haunted, however, by the potential of outside and inside to undermine each other.

PART ONE
Words and the World

2

Hybridity

Midnight's Children is commonly labelled "magic realism" to emphasize its juxtaposition of two normally incompatible frameworks. The events in the novel refer to the world outside the text and to a familiar narrative of history relying on conventions of verisimilitude, yet much that occurs is frankly fantastic, involving superpowers, a divinely mandated destiny, and a wildly implausible personal connection to the events of history. A critical consensus has it that magic realism is particularly well suited to the handling of materials from the Third World, where colonialism has resulted in the juxtaposition of cultural frameworks with different origins and where uneven development means that different modes of production exist side by side (Cooper 1998, 15). By this reading, magic realism, because it recovers or reclaims "cultural discourses dominated until now by the centralizing and suppressing impulses of an imperial culture in decline" (Lopez 2001, 210), is the literary expression of cultural hybridity, a favourite topos of postcolonial critics, associated in particular with Bhabha and Rushdie himself.

The common reading of *Midnight's Children*, which regards the magic in magic realism as indigenous (ibid., 172) and the realism as Western, finds ready corroboration in the narrative itself, where Roger Clark sees a "stereotypical polarity" between Indian spirituality and European worldliness (Clark 2001, 96). Amina, the daughter of a superstitious mother and a skeptical modernizing father, finds herself thinking, "this is still India, and people like Ramram Seth know what they know" (100). Her father, Aadam Aziz, imagines that "the hegemony of superstition, mumbo-jumbo and all things magical would never be broken in India" (67). The novel often pairs characters who reinforce this binary: Aziz, the Western-educated doctor, and Tai, the oral story-teller, together are "Tai-for-changelessness opposed to Aadam for progress" (107); Aziz the modernizer is married to Reverend Mother, the formidable bulwark of tradition; and Saleem, the English-language writer, reads his narrative aloud to Padma, his illiterate female companion who connects him "with that world of ancient learning and sorcerers' lore so despised by most of us nowadays" (191).

The problem with most critical discussions of hybridity, however, including Saleem's own, is that they assume India has an essence that can always be recognized, even when mixed with things derived from elsewhere. Alfred Lopez, for instance, assumes that levitation and clairvoyance belong to a neglected Indian wisdom that wells up to disturb the English-language text (Lopez 2001). In a careful study of creolization (a synonym for hybridity) in a Caribbean context, Chris Bongie has shown how expressions of mixed and hybrid identities inevitably hinge on fixed identities such as they purport to reject (Bongie 1998). To see England as linear, modern, and scientific and India as cyclical, traditional, and religious is to relegate India to a cliché of Orientalism. Trivedi, of course, has accused Rushdie of just such Orientalizing. Rushdie's own notion of hybridity frequently falls somewhere between two claims: the first, that India and the West have merged over time but they can always still be distinguished; and the second, that all identities everywhere are hybrid and mixed and there is no such thing as a pure identity. Neither claim is logically tenable, for the first bases the distinction between India and the West on essences that it purports to reject and the second provides no way of distinguishing between hybridities. When Rushdie (and Saleem) declare that they write magic realism because magic corresponds to an Indian worldview and realism to a Western one, they imply that there is such a thing as an Indian worldview that, however adulterated or attenuated, can always be pointed to. As Friedman reminds us, however, cultures are not essences of such a kind as "flow together and mix with each other" (Friedman 1995, 83). On the other hand, when Rushdie says, "this idea of a separation of cultures between the East and the West was certainly never the idea I grew up with," for "They were all mixed in together from the beginning" (Kadzis 2000, 217), he blurs all notions of difference. Twenty years after the publication of *Midnight's Children* he will go so far as to say that America and India should recognize themselves in each other because "they're both cultures made up of mixtures. They're both cultures made up of people who come from elsewhere, and who kind of transform themselves and make themselves again here. They're both mixed up people" (Rose 2000, 205). But if India and the world are both hybrid, what meaning does it have to distinguish between them? For that matter, if everything is hybrid, what value can accrue to hybridity?

It is relatively easy to tell England from India in *Midnight's Children*, but difficult to distinguish where India stops and Orientalism begins. How can one separate what in the novel finds its inspiration in Hinduism and folk religion from that which either caters to or parodies Western notions of Indian magic and superstition? How can we distinguish the absurdity that derives from Saleem's schizophrenia from the "ancient insanities of India" (250)? I will argue that we do not have to separate the genuine India from the projection of Orientalism for the text's hybrid magic realism does not mean what it appears to mean and what Rushdie declares it to mean. In spite of Saleem's and Rushdie's own comments, the blend of genres that produces magic realism does not result from a clash of meaning-systems. Rushdie's magic realism is not the combination of two different modes but a single mode that highlights its internal division.

Let me explain. Saleem himself declares that he patterned his narrative on the tales he heard from his ayah, Mary Pereira, as well as on the tales that old Tai the boatman used to tell Aadam Aziz, Saleem's grandfather. Mary Pereira passes on to her young charge the "rumours and tittle-tattle" she hears on the buses, according to which "the country was in the grip of a sort of supernatural invasion" harking back to the *Mahabharata*:

> Yes, baba, they say in Kurukshetra an old Sikh woman woke up in her hut and saw the old-time war of the Kurus and Pandavas happening right outside! It was in the papers and all, she pointed to the place where she saw the chariots of Arjun and Karna, and there were truly wheel-marks in the mud! Baap-re-baap, such so-bad things: at Gwalior they have seen the ghost of the Rani of Jhansi; rakshasas have been seen many-headed like Ravana, doing things to women and pulling down trees with one finger. I am good Christian woman, baba; but it gives me fright when they tell that the tomb of Lord Jesus is found in Kashmir. On the tombstones are carved two pierced feet and a local fisherwoman has sworn she saw them bleeding – real blood, God save us! – on Good Friday … what is happening, baba, why these old things can't stay dead and not plague honest folk? (238–9)

Here we have an example of narration that conforms to the usual critical interpretation of magic realism: Mary's brief account mixes the past of myth and the present of the news; the world of story, especially folk tale and religious myth, with the world of experience; divine characters and ordinary human beings. Chakrabarty argues that India combines "two noncommensurable logics of power, both modern," the first, the secular logic of the state institutions introduced by European rule, and the second, a system of hierarchical subordination that "continually brings gods and spirits into the domain of the political" (Chakrabarty 2000, 14). Mary's account is a good illustration of this second logic. We should note, however, the ways in which Mary's narration differs from that of Saleem, whose fascination with popular superstition and grand cosmology does not translate into an interest in spirituality, let alone into belief. Gods and mythological figures do not figure in Saleem's story except metaphorically (as when a criminal gang calls itself Ravana or Saleem compares himself to Ganesh).

Immediately after the *Satanic Verses* affair, when he felt he had to make concessions to religion, Rushdie declared that the fantasy in his fiction is an attempt to be faithful to a world where most people worship deities: "If one is to attempt honestly to describe reality as it is experienced by religious people, for whom God is no symbol but an everyday fact, then the conventions of what is called realism are quite inadequate. The rationalism of that form comes to seem like a judgement upon, an invalidation of, the religious faith of the characters being described. A form must be created which allows the miraculous and the mundane to co-exist at the same level–as the same order of event" (Rushdie 1991F, 376). Although of obvious relevance to *The Satanic Verses*, this is unsatisfactory as an explanation for the magic elements of *Midnight's Children*. If the magic in *Midnight's Children* actually represented religious belief, it would include theophany, divine intervention, and, possibly, reincarnation, as, for instance, Manil Suri's novel *The Death of Vishnu* does (Suri 2001), and not telepathy, amnesia, and an allegorical relation to the nation. The author of *Midnight's Children* is never himself tempted by religious belief, which he always depicts as belonging to others, especially to women and to the less educated. A later Rushdie, with reason to be hostile to religion, will explicitly locate his own magic realism in a hybrid genre that includes the films *The Wizard of Oz* and *Who Framed Roger Rabbit* (Rushdie 1992, 18, 33). He declares that *The Wizard of* Oz was a greater influence on him than Bombay cinema because of its secularism: "Good fairies and bad witches might superficially resemble the deities and demons of the Hindu pantheon," but the film's greatest virtue is the way it creates "a world in which nothing is deemed more important than the loves, cares and needs of human beings" (ibid., 12). *Midnight's Children* also creates such a world.

A more plausible inspiration than religion for the magic of *Midnight's Children* is oral story-telling. What stands out about Mary's story of supernatural events is its close relation to gossip, rumour, and the tall tale, which, according to Nair, are the models for Rushdie's novel as well. Another oral story-teller in the novel is old Tai, the Kashmiri boatman whose "magical talk," a blend of history and folktale (17), fascinates young Aadam Aziz at the very opening of the novel. In order to determine whether the narration of his life rings "true," Saleem does not consult his memory but asks himself, "Is this how Mary would have told it? [...] Is this what that fisherman would have said?" (79). Not for him any notion of a degree zero of writing, where writing would give transparent access to events. The truth of writing is instead a question of appealing to and imitating the well-springs of narrative in folktale and myth. By this reading, Saleem's magic realism is a hybrid of orality (folktale) and literacy (history).

Rushdie himself has declared his fascination with the figure of the story-teller who can gather around him an audience of thousands and hold them spellbound, sometimes over days. He tells how listening to one such story-teller in Baroda inspired him by "the shape of the oral narrative," "a very bizarre and pyrotechnical shape," to find "a written-down equivalent" (Rushdie 1988, 7–8). The thing to note, however, is how much Rushdie stands outside the scene of teller and audience that he describes, even as he imagines himself at the centre, in the position of the story-teller. The story-telling session took place in 1983, that is, years after he had published *Midnight's Children*. He does not tell us how the story-teller managed to address 600,000 at one sitting, what language he spoke in (or how much Rushdie understood), or what the story was about. Although he says, "Listening to this man reminded me of the shape of oral narrative" (ibid., 7), his own account suggests that the story-telling was not something he himself heard but something he heard about. It seems clear from both the details he gives and those he does not that what matters most to Rushdie about the Baroda story-teller is the confirmation he supplies of certain notions the author already has about oral story-telling.

Oral story-telling, in Rushdie's account, has a double appeal: the elasticity of the tale's spiralling structure and the story-teller's direct relation to his audience. To these we can add a delight in fantasy that is not permitted in realistic novels. These elements are by no means exclusive to orality nor are they unique to India: Mary, after all, is a superstitious Catholic whose stories are based on the Bible (247). The great, swirling narrative energy that Saleem claims to have learned from Mary and Tai, Rushdie has found primarily in the great compendiums of folk tale and myth: the Bible, the *Mahabharata*, and, especially, the *Arabian Nights*. Saleem explicitly compares himself to Moses (161), Ganesh (15), and Scheherezade (11, 25), the narrators or supposed writers of those books, (he compares himself to the Prophet as well [161], but the Quran, of course, does not display the same drive to narrative). The fantasy elements of Mary's stories, although derived from "rumours and tittle-tattle," have also made the transition to literacy ("It was in the papers and all," she says). Saleem himself readily acknowledges to his readers, who, he presumes, include non-Indians, that his own narrative represents "the kind of thing you're always reading about in the sensational magazines" (166). For an example of such "magic realism," a Westerner need go no further than the tabloids at the supermarket checkout counter: "HILARY CLINTON HAS AFFAIR WITH SPACE ALIEN! 'I THOUGHT SHE WAS GAY,' SAYS BILL."

If Saleem insists nonetheless that his models were Mary and Tai, rather than the *Arabian Nights*, it is because oral story-telling has a meaning quite apart from content and structure: orality appears primordial (the story as it was *before* there were books); it provides the middle-class writer with direct contact with the folk (by definition, those who are illiterate); and it supplies a model for community based on face-to-face communication and bodily presence that seems more real than the solitary activities of writing and reading.

The gossip so loved by Mary Pereira presumes a lore already common to many. This common lore, as propagated, for instance, by the ancients at the paan-shop (47), makes possible a community among strangers within particular spatial limits, say, a city. Although they do not know each other personally, the passengers on the bus and the readers of popular journalism do know the same things. Saleem claims that his own stories are just versions of what is already well-known: Mian Abdullah is "a legend of our times" (39); Reverend Mother's basilisk glare is "already becoming a legend" (43); and the women of Delhi high society regard Shiva "through the mist of his legend, coating their fingertips so that they touched him through the magical film of his myth" (394). Abdullah, Reverend Mother, and Shiva do not, of course, have an existence outside the novel, not even in legend. They are but modelled on figures of legend. And if Saleem must tell his readers how well-known these people are, it is because they are not already known to his audience.

As Saleem finishes each chapter, he reads it aloud to Padma, a worker in the pickle factory and representative of the folk. His "relationship to the oral narrative" is therefore, as Rushdie has suggested, "very direct" (Rushdie 1988, 8). However, Saleem's narrative spirals, supposedly borrowed from oral story-telling, frustrate the illiterate Padma who insists on "the banal chain of cause-and-effect" (287) and tries to squash Saleem's "attempts to put the cart before the bullock"

(327). Even in the world described by the novel, the oral narrative is embedded within a written narrative. Saleem directly addresses unnamed and unseen readers, whom he does not and cannot know personally, at least as often as he addresses Padma, and while these readers know everything about her, she knows nothing about them. These private citizens, isolated from each other yet united by their literacy, are invited to imagine a community based on more immediate oral communication and on a common lore. What is this community Saleem creates with readers, based on literacy but imagined as oral? The answer is the modern nation-state, which everywhere presents itself as the felicitous merger of the modern and the traditional.

In *Imagined Communities* Benedict Anderson shows that a national consciousness is the product of print literacy and therefore modern. It presumes an awareness of events unfolding simultaneously in different spaces and filling what Walter Benjamin calls "homogeneous, empty time" (B. Anderson 1991, 24). As S.M. Islam argues, the unidirectional "historical time of modernity" associated with the "colonial project" is represented in *Midnight's Children* by the ticktock of Lord Mountbatten's "English-made" clock (Islam 1999, 130). Certainly, the conception of empty time is modern in the sense that it did not always exist but can be assigned origins in eighteenth-century Europe (although Anderson disputes this and attributes it to colonial Spanish America instead). The modern sense of time is, however, by no means universal and everywhere encounters other modes of time, what Bhabha calls "the 'timeless' discourse of irrationality" (Bhabha 1994, 142). Anderson follows Benjamin in characterising the premodern sense of time as "Messianic," implying "a simultaneity of past and future in an instantaneous present" (B. Anderson 1991, 24). This time presumes that all time is one and all stories are versions of the same story, prefigured by the past and fulfilled in the present. This is the cyclical view of time, associated with the pre-colonial, that Saleem refers to when he says, "As a people, we are obsessed with correspondences" (291), and "no people whose word for 'yesterday' is the same as their word for 'tomorrow' can be said to have a firm grip on the time" (106) (the word he is referring to is *kal*).

While Anderson presumes that myth characterizes premodern and prenational communities, Saleem understands that the modern nation-state, however much it is based on homogeneity and simultaneity, everywhere continues to rely on myth. Methwold's English-made clock does not measure empty time, but counts down the days and minutes until midnight, the witching hour. As the subtitle of Brennan's study of Rushdie, "Myths of the Nation," reminds us, the nation – every nation – retains a strong component of the Messianic time supposedly left behind by modernity. Brennan does not use the term "myth" negatively: he believes that "any progressive vision today depends" on such "myths of national belonging" (Brennan 2001, 672). Such myths are necessary, for they provide an answer to Chakrabarty's question: "If the nation, the people, or the country were not just to be observed, described, and critiqued but loved as well, what would guarantee that they were indeed worth loving unless one also saw in them something that was already lovable?" (Chakrabarty 2000, 149). When Saleem speaks of the "national longing for form" (291), he uses "national" to mean "peculiarly Indian," but Brennan quite legitimately borrows the expression for a chapter title referring to a desire common to nations everywhere (Brennan 1989). India's longing for form is not a function of Indianness but of nationhood. Modern nation-states everywhere invoke both myth and history or, in the novel's terms, magic and realism. The magic and the realism in Rushdie's novel are mutually constitutive: they are both equally Indian and equally modern. They are not separate functions that Rushdie combines in a postcolonial hybrid but are each required in order to think the other and to think the nation. It is a mistake to divide magic and realism, myth and history, along national lines. Neither in the world nor in Rushdie's novel are England and India pure entities with characters that are stable and known in advance, and therefore always permit their presence to be detected and their essence to be recovered.

The defining element of Saleem's magic realism is less its hybridity than its self-consciousness. What the novel does when it juxtaposes the colonizer's culture and that of the colonized is to thematize culture. Rather than participating in oral modes of story-telling, Saleem thematizes orality. The novel opens with a memory of Aadam Aziz sitting at the feet of old Tai and listening to his stories. S. M. Islam regards Tai as "an embodiment of primordial India and a name for the 'anarchic' time of infinity" that survives in Saleem's modern nation (132). That is indeed what Saleem intends Tai to represent. Saleem's acknowledgement of his debt to Mary and Tai does not mean, however, that he shares their mental framework. Quite the reverse: when he models his own narrative on oral story-telling *because the latter is felt to be peculiarly Indian,* Saleem is participating in something larger than the world of oral story-telling. Tai's presence in the novel, intended as the marker of an irreducible otherness that disturbs the homogenizing project of modernity, constitutes a claim by the text to contain him. The figure of Tai marks Saleem's distance from, as well as his relation to, oral tradition. Saleem's echoes of oral tales, rumour and legend, are of a second order: self-consciously literate depictions of the oral.

Although Saleem explicitly patterns his narrative on the oral stories of Mary Pereira and Tai, he is also the self-declared heir of Aadam Aziz, who could no longer listen to Tai after he had returned from Germany. When Aziz returns from abroad, his scientific education prevents him from re-entering the timeless world of myth he had enjoyed as a boy and condemns him to live in the calendar time of history. As Roger Clark and Patrick Colm Hogan both suggest, Aadam is expelled from Paradise in a repetition of the original Fall (Clark 2001, 63–74; Hogan 2001, 531–4). However, this Fall is, from the novel's point of view, a *felix culpa*, or fortunate fault, since it makes possible all that follows. Aziz's new ambitions, to build a modern nation and to make history, are worthy ones, although they pose a direct threat to Tai, a Kashmiri Muslim who wants nothing to do with modern medicine or with India and Pakistan. Aziz has lost something, a loss which is figured as a hole within, but Tai has lost more. The old man rages at the betrayal by his youthful audience, ceases to wash, and becomes absolutely isolated. Tai, who had once seemed immortal, is killed, or so rumour has it, in 1947, when, hoping to give them "a piece of his mind," he came between the Indian and Pakistani armies in the Valley of Kashmir and was shot for his pains (37).

Saleem is careful to distance his own blend of myth and history from other blends that he regards as dangerously unselfconscious. For instance, he says that he borrows his narrative technique, "Matter of fact descriptions of the outré and bizarre, and their reverse, namely heightened, stylized versions of the everyday," from his dreaded rival, Shiva, as well as from Mary and Tai (214). It is difficult to imagine Shiva the hoodlum telling stories. The attribution of the narrative techniques of fantasy and hyperbole to the violent gangleader expresses an ambivalence on Saleem's part towards the very techniques he has made his own. In Shiva's narratives, Saleem tells us, the techniques are applied "without conscious thought, and their effect was to create a picture of the world of startling uniformity": "Death and defeat at rummy were all of a piece to Shiva" (214). Saleem's own deployment of the same techniques is, by implication, more valuable because self-conscious. In Saleem's case the "attitudes of mind" associated with hyperbolic and fantastic narrative are a pose, not in the sense of something false but in the sense of something self-consciously assumed (214).

Where might we look for an example of Shiva's narration, which Saleem abjures? A narration "without conscious thought" and "a picture of the world of startling uniformity" sound remarkably like the magic realism of Gabriel García Márquez (García Márquez 1991). *One Hundred Years of Solitude,* indifferent to national history and resistant to allegorical interpretation, provides, as Rushdie himself has said in an interview, "a village view of the world" (Pattanayak 2000, 18). It tells the story of national consolidation – the coming of the magistrate, the railway, the civil war, and the multinational fruit company – from the point of view of the resolutely unconsolidated Macondo, which has never learned to locate itself on the map of the nation. In magic realist works based on oral story-telling, such as *One Hundred Years of Solitude* and Ben Okri's *The Famished Road* (Okri 1992), although the reader perceives the flouting of realist conventions, the narrative itself betrays no awareness of incongruity. The narration is characterized by a naiveté or pseudo-naiveté that, apparently ignorant of novelistic conventions, does not distinguish between fantasy and non-fantasy. Saleem, on the other hand, is always acutely aware of the points at which his readers will have trouble crediting his narrative, and feels he must explain, apologize for, or at least comment on those aspects of it which defy verisimilitude and seem to belong to dreams or to madness. No García Márquez narrator would ever say, as Saleem does, "With some embarrassment, I am forced to admit that amnesia is the kind of gimmick regularly used by our lurid film-makers. Bowing my head slightly, I accept that my life has taken on, yet again, the tone of a Bombay talkie; but after all, leaving to one side the vexed issue of reincarnation, there is only a finite number of methods of achieving rebirth" (339). Saleem's narrative also differs from the Colombian novelist's in its explicit reliance on print literacy: the calendar, official national history, and Saleem's own experience of writing.

In its explicit thematization of moments in a larger historical narrative and of key historical relations such as orality and hybridity, *Midnight's Children* is closer to Ralph Ellison's *Invisible Man* (Ellison 1995), a novel that Rushdie pays explicit homage to in *Fury* (Rushdie 2001), than to *One Hundred Years of Solitude*. Ellison's unnamed hero, like Saleem, has a series of picaresque comic adventures that demand to be interpreted as allegories of larger historical events and political circumstances. The parallels to episodes in Rushdie are obvious. Bledsoe, the African American stooge who resembles one of Rushdie's mimic men, plays tricks on Norton, his white patron, who occupies a position not unlike William Methwold's. At the Liberty Paints factory Ellison's hero has trouble producing the required shade of whiteness; in Rushdie's India whiteness becomes a disease infecting the middle class. Like Saleem, Ellison's invisible man has had certain mental faculties removed on an operating table, loses his name, and remains strangely sexless. Both Saleem and the invisible man are tempted by communism and come to grief during communal riots. The glass eye that one of Mian Abdullah's assassins loses in the chapter "Hit-the-Spittoon" may even be a specific allusion to a memorable scene in Ellison's novel.

What matters most about Saleem and Ellison's invisible man is that they are writers, by definition outside the community and the world that they represent. Like the invisible man, Saleem thematizes his own writing. The two men live in severe isolation in small spaces removed from the world. The invisible man's hole underground, illuminated by 1,369 lightbulbs powered by an illegal feed from Monopolated Light & Power (Ellison 1995, 7), is an emblem at once of the camera obscura, the "little black box" which, as Peter Brooks notes, "figures both the experience of reading and the scene of writing" (Brooks 2000, 52) and of the African American writer's subversive appropriation of the master's tools. Saleem, too, retreats to a small space, in his case an office above the city that he writes about, where he sits in the "enchanted shadows" (121) cast by an Anglepoised lamp (20, 39), an allusion to the English language in which he is writing.

Midnight's Children is not so much hybrid as self-conscious. Indeed the opening scene makes literal the genetic implications of hybridity and imagines India as the product of sexual reproduction. Aadam Aziz, the modernizer returned from Europe, falls in love with and marries the young Naseem Ghani, representative of traditional India. Their descendant will be Saleem Sinai, the self-declared emblem of the nation. This is the marriage of modern and traditional as staged, for instance, by Tagore's novel *The Home and the World* (Tagore 1985). In Tagore's novel, published in 1915, the year in which Rushdie's novel opens, Bimala, a traditional Bengali wife, is forced out of purdah by her husband, Nikhil, and made to choose between her husband and his treacherous friend, who represent rival versions of modernity. Tagore was unable to imagine how the nationalist movement would reconcile modernity with what he felt were the universal values known to Hinduism, and his novel ends inconclusively and tragically. Gandhi returned to India from South Africa in that same year, 1915, with an answer to the dilemma that Tagore could not have foreseen. Saleem's own narrative, written with postcolonial hindsight more than sixty years later, approaches the union of tradition and modernity with the self-consciousness of parody. The union of Aadam Aziz and Naseem Ghani is a comical rendition of a topos that by 1978 had become banal. Although their marriage is almost as unhappy as Bimala's, the story of Aadam and Naseem is not a tragedy but a single episode in a mock-epic.

Brennan finds that Rushdie parodies the topoi of Indian literature in order to mock nationalism. Certainly there is a difference between Rushdie's self-conscious hybridity and previous Indian literature. Meenakshi Mukherjee explains that, although "nineteenth-century Indian writers were influenced largely by western concepts" and their "conscious models were Scott's and Thackeray's novels," their novels reveal "the unconscious influence [...] of the puranic tradition of oral narratives and the memory of episodes from *Ramayana* and *Mahabharata*" (Mukherjee 1985, 9). If the Indian novel has always been hybrid, everything changes when, as in Rushdie's novel, hybridity itself becomes a theme. This does not mean, however, that Brennan's criticism of the novel is wholly just and Rushdie's purpose is merely parodic. If Rushdie stands at a distance from the hybridity he describes, Saleem is directly implicated. In *Midnight's Children* the hybrid combination of elements (modernity and tradition, literacy and orality, West and East) implies a third position, outside and above hybridity. But this third position is also inside: what it contemplates is itself.

The Aziz-Ghani wedding stages and makes available for contemplation a division in the self that already exists. Aadam Aziz is not merely a Westernized modernizer, one half of a future hybrid: he is also the young man who falls in love with the traditional maiden. In other words, alongside his desire for progress, he already knows a nostalgia for tradition. When he falls in love with Naseem Ghani he is merely projecting his own desire onto the bedsheet held before her. Hybridity is part of his understanding of himself. The division of the world into the modern and the traditional is itself modern.

When Aziz left Kashmir for Germany to study medicine, he discovered secular humanism and lost his religious faith. He read *Vorwärts* and Lenin's *What Is To Be Done*, and his best friends, Oskar and Ilse Lubin, were anarchists (20). The exposure to other ways of seeing and doing "altered" how he thought about himself and the world (12). Having been "tainted by Abroad," he and others like him "will not easily go back to the old world" (34). However, like so many colonials in the metropole before him and since, Aziz also found that his newfound friends' progressive politics, deliberately internationalist in conception, had no room for his own difference. European radicals presumed they alone knew what the modern world required, and their confident modernity saw India itself as "the invention of their ancestors" (13). Aziz's dignity demanded that he reject their version of the world and reaffirm his self, a process that takes the form of return and recovery.

Aadam Aziz returns to Kashmir anxious to "re-unite himself with an earlier self that ignored" his German friends' influence (13). He finds it, however, as impossible to go back as it is to join his friends in their internationalism. When he tries to kneel and pray, he only smashes his nose on the ground. He cannot retrieve his religious faith and is left with a hole inside. Aziz, who rejects his German friends' anarchist humanism, reaffirms his own identity, but what is that identity? He is no longer a believing Muslim. His world is bigger than the Kashmir valley where he grew up. Yet he "does not feel Indian" (32). Eventually Aziz does find something to fill the hole left by his loss of faith: he finds "women and history" (4), a potent mix of desire and narrative that drives him to identify with the new nation of Gandhi and Nehru. As many, including Benedict Anderson, have pointed out, in modern times nationalism occupies the place in people's emotions formerly devoted to religion (B. Anderson 1991). Aziz learns to identify with a political state of his own, fully modern in the sense of secular and democratic, but in which he can see his own image and not that of his European friends.

Aziz's Indianness is just as modern as his experience of internationalism and depends on that experience. His Indianness does not precede his internationalism but arises in response to it. In Europe itself, Oskar and Ilse's internationalism appeared naive and doomed in 1915. As John Dunn says, socialism "has never looked the same since the parties of Engels and of Jaurès slunk into line and agreed to defend their fatherlands against the aggression of the largely proletarian armies of their foes" (in Guibernau 1996, 80). Saleem's German friend Oskar dies like a "comedian," while trying to convince a marching regiment of the futility of war (29), and Ilse comes to India to commit suicide. Anarchist principles, it would seem, are but a manifestation of what Saleem calls "optimism," a politics of high ideals that loses its wager on the direction of the future. Aziz's disillusionment with his German friends aligns him with the dominant historical current of the twentieth century which, in Asia as in Europe, has been nationalism.

The newly hatched nationalist participates in a larger global phenomenon, found in England as in India, a phenomenon which is not everywhere the same and is determined by local conditions and particular traditions, but whose manifestations are all related, wherever they occur. This global phenomenon puts a particular value upon the local, which it identifies with the nation. In that sense the global shapes how one sees the local, the inside presumes an outside. As is often declared and just as often forgotten, it is nationalism that creates nations. Nationalism, like capitalism, secularism, industrialization, democracy, and the other components of modernity, is part of the mental framework of many people living in India and, more importantly, has in turn shaped what it means to them to be Indian. This does not mean that nations are false or that they are all the same; only that they cannot be understood except in the larger international framework in which they all participate.

When Rushdie thematizes culture, for instance, by staging hybridity as a courtship, he implies a second level of culture: Saleem's hybrid identity is located within a larger mental framework in which it has meaning to declare oneself hybrid. It would be a mistake to look to Aadam Aziz's identity, his Indian self, in order to explain how he thinks. We must look instead at how Aziz thinks in order to explain his identification with India. Aziz's culture in the sense of identity is Indian and hybrid, but his culture in the sense of his mental framework is modern and necessarily larger than India. The novel does not suggest that nationalism is a form of false consciousness: only that it is more valuable if regarded self-consciously.

3

The Allegory of History

Saleem's narrative, which thematizes aspects of identity such as orality and hybridity, presumes a *"pre-text"* in which these aspects are already prominent. That pre-text is national history, not the history written by radical historians such as the Subaltern Studies group, who seek the traces and the empty spaces left in the archives by classes other than the middle classes and by groups other than intellectuals (Guha and Spivak 1988), but rather received history, the story of the nation as made by middle-class nationalist politicians, some version of which citizens are taught in schools and everyone knows. National history has a well-defined narrative form: established origins, turning points and climaxes, and an agreed chronology of significant events. We may find an example of such official history in Stanley Wolpert's *A New History of India* (Wolpert 1989), which David Lipscomb has shown that Rushdie had beside him when he came to write *Midnight's Children* (Lipscomb 1991). Catherine Cundy proves that Rushdie also read Larry Collins and Dominique Lapierre's popular history, *Freedom at Midnight* (Collins and Lapierre 1976; Cundy 1996).

Saleem was originally conceived as an allegorical figure with what he himself calls a "metaphorical" relation to the nation. As Brennan notes, "Narrative never follows the emotional logic of the characters' lives, but the brittle, externally determined contours of 'current events'" (Brennan 1989, 84–5). Saleem, however, insists that national history is as often an allegory of his life as his life is an allegory of national history. In an extended editorial passage reminiscent of *Tristram Shandy,* he draws a distinction between "active" and "passive" metaphorical relations, depending on whether it is he who mirrors the nation or the nation that mirrors him (232). The distinction is, of course, comical: what sense can it make to speak of national history as following the course of Saleem's life? His editorializing is as attenuated and ultimately unconvincing as any European Renaissance theological treatise on the two natures of Christ or political tract on the king's two bodies would appear to a modern reader. The example Saleem gives of a "passive-metaphorical" relation, "the unavoidable connection between the infant state's attempts at rushing towards full-sized adulthood and my own early, explosive efforts at growth" (232), assumes that his own increase in size did not arise from somatic exigencies but obeyed the external narrative pull of national history. When, on the other hand, what happens to Saleem is said to prompt what happens to the nation, he is like a voodoo doll, and the example he gives of an "active-metaphorical" relation is appropriately violent: "when I was detached from my fingertip and blood [...] rushed out in fountains, a similar thing happened to history, and all sorts of everywhichthing began pouring out all over us" (233). But why should Saleem judge the bloodletting both he and the nation suffer to be an integral part of his own story and only secondarily a part of India's? How does he know that this is not another example of the passive-metaphorical? When two mirrors face each other, how can we judge which is reflecting and which is reflected?

Saleem's editorializing does make an important point about national history. The construction that Saleem deploys to illustrate the "active-metaphorical" – "I was detached from my fingertip" – is symptomatic of a passivity characteristic of all such metaphorical connection: agency belongs not to the voodoo doll but to the one who sticks in the pins. If self and nation reflect each other, it is because agency belongs to something outside both: an implied writer or the demands of generic form or both. Self and nation do not share a narrative form because they each reflect the other; they appear to reflect each other because a narrative form mediates between them. Both self and nation can be said to be born, come of age, desire union with another, have potential that can be fulfilled, lose their illusions, and fail to realize their great expectations. In other words, both autobiography and national history take the form of a realist *Bildungsroman*, which Dubravka Juraga has argued is the form of *Midnight's Children* (Juraga 1999). National history is imagined in terms of a career marked by five-year plans, which is what makes it possible in turn for the curriculum vitae of the middle-class citizen to be related to national history.

Saleem's self-conscious thematization has the effect of heightening the events of national history and rendering them fantastic. Paradoxically, it does so, not by making the literal figurative but the reverse, by making literal the common metaphor implicit in national history of the nation as a person. Standard histories adopt a neutral, objective voice that claims to eschew metaphor altogether. The objective and the seemingly literal rely on dead metaphors whose figurative nature goes unnoticed. To understand Rushdie's text we must reverse the valences of metaphor and literalness: the genre of the fantastic, writes Tzvetan Todorov, "realizes the literal sense of a *figurative* expression" (Todorov 1975, 79). For instance, while a news report may speak of an "outbreak of optimism" in the tensions between India and Pakistan, in Rushdie's novel, the "optimism disease," both before and after independence, is quite literal. During the 1950s India might be said to have had a brief love affair with America ("In India, we've always been vulnerable to Europeans [...] Evie was American. Same thing" [182]), a fling that corresponds in the text to the youthful Saleem's infatuation with the American girl Evie Burns. India, the third-world nation, is "impotent," declares Saleem (179), and sexual impotence is a source of much of the novel's farcical energy. In Indira Gandhi's capital, "something smelled rotten," a state of affairs which Saleem's finely tuned nose can perceive (409). An Indian critic of Pakistan might say that its citizens are asked to forget all they know, and in a chapter in *Among the Believers* entitled "Killing History," Naipaul says just that: "The time before Islam is a time of blackness: that is part of Muslim theology" (Naipaul 1981, 134). Rushdie makes the metaphor literal by having Saleem suffer amnesia. Saleem's sardonic comment on his loss of memory: "To sum up: I became a citizen of Pakistan" (340).

Just as *Pilgrim's Progress* makes literal the metaphor of the journey crucial to Pauline Christianity, and *The Romance of the Rose* the metaphor of love as war, Rushdie's postmodern allegory thematizes the metaphors commonly deployed by historians to figure a totality. These are listed by Fredric Jameson in *The Geopolitical Aesthetic*: "The social totality can be sensed, as it were, from the outside, like a skin at which the Other somehow looks, but which we ourselves will never see. Or it can be tracked, like a crime, whose clues we accumulate, not knowing that we are ourselves parts and organs of this obscenely moving and stirring zoological monstrosity. But most often, in the modern itself, its vague and nascent concept begins to awaken with the knowledge function, very much like a book whose characters do not yet know that they are being read" (Jameson 1992, 114). The metaphors that Jameson says are used to figure the totality are precisely the metaphors that Rushdie's novel makes literal: the nation as a human body, history as the detection of an original crime, and historical knowledge and national consciousness as forms of omniscience that grant access to the thoughts of strangers.

The organic metaphor of the body that contains the members of the nation is central to *Midnight's Children*. Rushdie's novel is a complicated gloss on the received notion that India was "born" on August 15, 1947. Wolpert's standard history of India features more births than any multigenerational saga: the "cultural revival had given birth to violent revolutionary offspring" (Wolpert 1989, 261); British India was "severed as though by caesarian section to permit two new nations to be born" (ibid., 348); the Republic of India was "born" on January 26, 1950 (ibid., 356); and out of the ashes of the Bangladesh War, "the world's eighth largest nation had been born" (ibid., 390). What Rushdie has done is to take these metaphors literally by adding the pangs and screams, the forceps and midwives, that Wolpert implies but forgets. When a son is born to his wife Parvati at the same moment that Indira Gandhi declares a national emergency, Saleem explicitly relates the two events: "while Parvati pushed in the ghetto, J.P. Narayan and Morarji Desai were also goading Indira Gandhi, while triplets yelled push push push the leaders of the Janata Morcha urged the police and Army to disobey the illegal orders of the disqualified Prime Minister, so in a sense they were forcing Mrs Gandhi to push, and as the night darkened towards the midnight hour, because nothing ever happens at any other time, triplets began to screech it's coming coming coming, and elsewhere the Prime Minister was giving birth to a child of her own" (404).

The metaphor of birth is part of the larger metaphor of the nation as a person. Historians (and politicians conscious of making history that historians will record) speak of growth and maturity, as if the nation were a human child; of direction and progress and dangers, as if the nation were on a journey; of trauma and memory, desire and fear, as if the nation had a psychology. It is this personification of the nation that makes it possible to call Nehru the father of the nation and to speak, as Wolpert does, of the "legacy of communalism" (Wolpert 1989, 376). It is also what makes it possible to speak of the nation coming of age, the metaphor invoked by Indira Gandhi when she declared the state of emergency: "there comes a time in the life of the nation when hard decisions have to be taken" (cited in Wolpert 1989, 397).

The person has a body, and this, too, is a favourite metaphor of historians who will speak of the changing face of India or of the risk of dismemberment. Nehru, eventually reconciled to the Partition of India, quipped that by "cutting off the head we will get rid of the headache" (cited in Wolpert 347). Gandhi, on the other hand, continued to object to what he saw as "the vivisection of his motherland" (ibid., 347). Nehru feared that Gandhi was merely "going around with ointment trying to heal one sore spot after another on the body of India instead of diagnosing the cause of the eruption of the sores and participating in the treatment of the body as a whole" (Collins and Lapierre 1976, 104). In *Midnight's Children* the metaphor of the nation as a body is made literal and therefore comical: if India were a person it would be a grotesque such as Saleem, its paternity would be in dispute, and its ability to tell its story would be in question. The only thing more grotesque might be what Collins and Lapierre call "Jinnah's two-headed state" (150).

The second metaphor used for imagining the social totality is that of a crime and its detection. The historian, like the detective, argues back from effect to hidden cause. In *Midnight's Children* spilled blood calls on heaven to witness that the social order has been disturbed (when Saleem needs a transfusion, an analysis of his blood reveals that he is not the son of his parents). Many features of the detective novel are deployed: suspicious telephone conversations, spying on a secret rendezvous at the Pioneer Café, a cryptic anonymous warning, and a final confession. The original crime that holds the secret of Saleem's paternity is the exploitation by the retiring imperialist Methwold of the wife of a poor Hindu beggar. The clues that point to the truth are the centre-parting in Methwold's brilliantined hair and a rather prominent nose. However, the clichés of detection do not here make for narrative tension and resolution. The processes of detection are not themselves the story but are thematized within the story. The "smoking gun" in the Sabarmati homicide is not so much a clue dropped by the murderer as a means of directing traffic (255). The narrative is not so much a whodunit as a "Who am I?"

Even more central than the motif of detection is that of omniscience which, made literal, becomes the science-fiction cliché of telepathy. Saleem is able to eavesdrop on the thoughts of everyone and anyone, but only within the frontiers of the nation, a magical capacity he calls All-India Radio. The capacity to enter the thoughts of strangers, the means whereby, according to R.G. Collingwood, the historian participates in the events he narrates (Collingwood 1961), is here not constitutive of the narration but becomes part of what is narrated.

The novel opens with the image of a bedsheet stained with "three drops of old, faded redness," which Saleem says will serve as his "talisman" through the next 550 pages of the novel. The sheet inscribed in blood is a literalization of the common metaphor of history written in blood, the metaphor employed by Wolpert when he writes that in the "annals of Calcutta, Direct Action Day was to be written in blood as the 'Great Killing'" (Wolpert 1989, 344). Rushdie's novel asks just what kind of ink is involved here, what sort of pen does it flow from, and how should it be read.

The copious blood that flows in *Midnight's Children*, in massacres, riots, and wars as in schoolboy accidents, is, as one chapter title has it, "mercurochrome": it only looks like blood. It is like the rumoured "real blood" shed by flowers around the time of Gandhi's assassination (136) and not to be confused with the blood shed in non-metaphorical violence inflicted on real human bodies. In the case of the violence suffered by real bodies outside the text, however, shed blood still accrues significance that can only be described as metaphorical: it becomes the blood of sacrifice, a blood calling out for vengeance, or a baptism marking the coming of age. All these meanings presume that blood is shared, so that the blood spilled by some is the same as that flowing through the veins of others who have not suffered direct violence. The two, closely related, meanings of blood – "loyalties of blood motivated the Brass Monkey; and in the streets of the city, rioters spilled each other's blood" (221) – are invoked by the early nationalist Sri Aurobindo for whom the soil of India was "sacred land to be loved and defended, if need be, with the blood of her children" (Wolpert 1989, 262).

Saleem needs an emergency transfusion when he loses the top of his finger in a door, and an analysis of his blood performed on that occasion, in a chapter momentously called "Alpha and Omega," reveals that he is not the genetic son of Ahmed and Amina Sinai and not the brother of his sister. The implications determine all that follows. Rushdie's novel, by its literalization of metaphor, seeks to make readers aware again of the metaphorical nature of all bloodlines, of India's but also of Saleem's.

Saleem begins the story of his own life with the story of a grandfather. Aadam Aziz resembles Nehru in significant ways: both are from Kashmiri families, have been educated in Europe, have lost the faith of their fathers and uphold a secular ideal; and both were at Amritsar at the time of the massacre. Later we discover that Saleem carries none of Aziz's genes and, contrary to what we have been led to believe, has not inherited his outsized nose from that source. The revelation that Saleem is not the biological offspring of Ahmed and Amina (formerly Mumtaz) Sinai is a shock for the reader but is not what invalidates the previous family history. That history was always an invention and is not any more fictional because it lacks a biological base. Blood ties are a metaphor.

Chantal Delourme argues that *Midnight's Children* illustrates "the fictive character of every narrative of origins and its absolute otherness: to tell the story of one's origins is inevitably to appropriate those of another, or perhaps, inversely, to welcome those of another" (Delourme 1995, 28; my translation). Saleem's family tree was always already a fiction in the sense of being contingent and constructed. If Saleem had emerged from Amina's womb, he still would have had two grandfathers. The decision to tell the story of his mother's father and not that of his father's father is an arbitrary one. Why should one be more his grandfather than the other? Of course, to write about two ancestors would have made the narrative even more unwieldy than it is. But that is the point: it is the demands of the narrative and not some notion of fidelity to literal truth that determine the story. We could explain Saleem's privileging of his maternal line of descent by saying he never knew his paternal grandfather. Ahmed Sinai, whom Saleem accepts as his father, was an orphan at the time of his marriage to Mumtaz Aziz (66). But Aadam Aziz must also be invented. Saleem has to reconstruct the life of the young man who returned from Germany thirty-two years before he himself was even born and whose spirit no longer survives in the doddering, beaten-down old man whom he visits in Agra. Saleem privileges not just one grandfather over another but also the story of his grandfather over that of his grandmother, whom he has known just as long. One story is given more significance than the other because Saleem can identify with young Aziz and with his dreams of secularization and modernization. Put another way, we can say that Saleem invents a grandfather in his own image.

Even before the account of the baby switch makes nonsense of all genealogy, Saleem leaves temporarily undetermined his exact line of descent. For the space of some pages we are not told which of Aziz's children is Saleem's parent: "Meanwhile, in the old house on Cornwallis Road, the days were full of potential mothers and possible fathers" (52). Padma, Saleem's first audience, is impatient, and who can blame her? The suspense is entirely the result of narrative obfuscation. Suspense is, of course, always a function of the narration in the sense that the narrator knows the ending but withholds it from the readers. But in other narratives suspense corresponds to a past lived experience of mystery or not knowing, to a blank that was eventually filled in for the characters as it will be for the reader. Saleem's obfuscation is different because it corresponds to no blank in the past. Saleem only knew his grandparents because he already knew his parents.

The narrative tease suggests a point that Saleem is anxious to make: he speaks of "potential" mothers as if there had existed at any time the possibility that he could have been born to someone else. The implication is that Saleem was fated to be born to a child of Aadam and Naseem, but it was not certain to which one. This makes no conceptual sense if we think of Saleem as a flesh-and-blood human being, but it does make a kind of sense if we think of Saleem as India. Let us recall, as Saleem does, Nehru's words at the moment of independence: "A moment comes, which comes but rarely in history, when we step out from the old to the new; when an age ends; and when the soul of a nation long suppressed finds utterance" (115). India is imagined as a soul waiting somewhere off stage to be born and in search of potential parents, something like the "Soul of unborn Khusro" which, according to his publicity flyer, traverses "the BOTTOMLESS DEEPS of Celestial Space-Eternity, until by OUR LUCK! it came to our own Duniya (World) & lodged in Womb of a humble Parsee matron of Good Family" (260). The assumption is that a modern nation called India was inevitable, even if the circumstances of its creation were not.

History is written as if past events had to happen (and, from the perspective of the present, they did), but historians will present different interpretations regarding the causes of what happened. However much consensus there is on the ultimate origins of the nation – figured by the marriage of a Western-educated Kashmiri and his tradition-bound wife – historians will emphasize different direct causes: was Indian independence achieved by political action? Did it primarily serve a business class or a class of civil servants? Did India first have to be imagined by writers and artists? Rushdie's novel presumes that Saleem will be born, but keeps us guessing as to whether his parentage will be that of a military general, a film director, a politician, a civil servant, or a businessman.

At all times Saleem chooses his own line of descent. He takes the words of Mary Pereira's song, "You kin be just what-all you want" (370, 406), to mean he can invent himself by inventing his kin. The contingency of his choice is brought home by the asymmetrical treatment given to symmetrical circumstances. Both of Saleem's parents were previously married and divorced, but a whole chapter is devoted to his mother's unconsummated marriage to Nadir Khan and nothing to Ahmed Sinai's unsuccessful previous union (his first wife died when she was bitten in the neck by a camel [83]). Mumtaz's first marriage has significance for her offspring because Nadir Khan, the impotent idealist and later Communist, represents what might have been and perhaps should have been but what was also fated never to be. When Nadir is unable to hit the spittoon, the suppressed soul demanding utterance requires that Mumtaz find someone else to father her children. Underwriting the sequence of events is Lenin's metaphor of the "rendezvous with destiny," also invoked by Nehru in his independence speech: "Long years ago we made a tryst with destiny; and now the time comes when we shall redeem our pledge

– not wholly or in full measure, but very substantially" (115). When Nadir cannot help her redeem her pledge, Amina marries Ahmed Sinai instead, the representative of India's "other true faith," Businessism (384).

Mary Pereira's baby switch, of course, makes nonsense of this genealogy. When Saleem requires a transfusion, blood tests reveal to him and his family what readers already know: the falseness of the Kashmiri genealogy that accounted for the difference of his physical features, in particular his blue eyes, from those of the majority of the people around him. And what is the truth of Saleem's identity? The secret that Saleem discovers is that, like Kipling's Kim or Tagore's Gora, he has the blood of the colonizer in his veins (Tagore 1980; Kipling 1987). The corporeal signs of identity, Saleem's blue eyes and a large nose, that have been misread, can now, it would seem, be properly interpreted. Saleem tells us his genetic father was a profligate English hypocrite who had taken advantage of a poor Hindu's wife and then left when India achieved independence. This is a literalization of the metaphor used by Tariq Ali when he writes that the new state was "Indian in its colour, composition and make-up, but its pedigree was unmistakably British" (Ali 1985, 78). If Aadam Aziz embodies the established narrative of Indian history, this alternative genealogy expresses a dissatisfaction with national history and a rejection of the Indian nation-state itself as the bastard product of England's violation of the subcontinent.

If blood determined character, Saleem's bastard status and racial hybridity would explain why he has such an attraction to the English language and to things English. What appears to be mimicry on Saleem's part – his identification with Raleigh, his home in Buckingham Villa, his proud possession of a toy globe inscribed "Made as England" – would then not be mimicry at all, because, in his case, the colonizing other is discovered to be actually part of the self. The heterogeneous nature of Saleem's experience would not be, as it first seems, false to his self but would reflect a newly discovered, genetically hybrid self. Certainly, many critics have found it tempting to see in Saleem's genetic parentage the truth of his identity (e.g. Kamra 1996, 240), but to read genetic miscegenation as cultural hybridity, as is so commonly done in postcolonial criticism, is ultimately to misread. The truth is not in the blood. We know this because Shiva, the biological son of the middle-class Sinais, is deformed by the abject poverty in which he grows up and resembles in nothing the inhabitants of Methwold's Estate. The apparent coincidence of world and self in Saleem's case is just that: coincidental. Even though all the aspects of his identity appear to confirm that he is the son of William

Methwold, Saleem actually is who he is – an Anglo and an Indian – because he grew up in Methwold's Estate.

Saleem's alternative genealogy, from Methwold through Vanita, an apparent debunking of the standard narrative of Indian history, is but another invention. When Mary Pereira confesses the baby switch to the Sinai family, she explains that their son was the natural child of Vanita and her husband, the minstrel Wee Willie Winkie (272). Mary could not have known about Vanita's adultery with the Englishman Methwold. The account of the baby switch does not give us a final *true* version of events, but is itself another fiction. The alternative genealogy through Methwold advertises that, no less than the official genealogy, it is a rewriting of other fictions and itself a fiction. Saleem's legal grandfather, Dr. Aziz, is named after the main Indian character in Forster's *A Passage to India* (Forster 1979). Vanita's husband in the alternative genealogy, Wee Willie Winkie (not his real name [101]), is called after the English boy-hero in a story by Rudyard Kipling, later adapted for the screen as a role played by Shirley Temple. We are reminded that even the rejection of genealogical succession and of progressive history involves a choice of narratives. The radical stance that sees Indian history as a rape still depends on a metaphor.

David Birch writes that a "hundred pages or so after the start of the novel what appeared to be the family of Saleem turns out to be an illusion" (Birch 1991, 2). Birch reads *Midnight's Children* as a radically unstable postmodern allegory, a denial of the very possibility of meaning. However, what the first hundred pages draw attention to is not the impossibility of knowing but the conditions of knowing. What had seemed to be objectively true – Saleem as the grandson of Aadam Aziz – is revealed to be a fiction. But that the truth is actually a fiction does not mean that it is less true. Rushdie's point is not that there is no truth, but that there is no literal level of truth. The literal is always already a fiction. But the truth lies in fiction.

As we have seen, the line of descent from Aadam Aziz to Saleem would be a fiction even if Saleem had not been switched at birth: Saleem has chosen to claim descent from one grandparent and not from another. The fiction is not arbitrary but meaningful, and the meaning is not changed because later the baby switch is discovered. At the beginning of the novel Aadam Aziz is told by Tai the boatman that his protuberant nose is "a nose to start a family on, my princeling. There'd be no mistaking whose brood they were. Mughal Emperors would have given their right hands for noses like that one. There are dynasties waiting inside it [...] like snot" (15). The primary function of this passage is, of course, to mislead by suggesting a genetic link between Aadam Aziz and Saleem Sinai. But their noses *are* linked, even if later we learn the link is not genetic. Aziz feels an itching in his nose when history is about to be made, as at the massacre at Amritsar. This is a literalization of the common metaphor of the man who is sensitive to the "winds of history" (301) and the currents of change. Joseph D'Costa, Mary Pereira's Communist lover, is another who is sensitive to history; he sniffs the wind that comes from the North and it is full of dying (104). Amina also responds to "some irritation of her nasal passages" when she rescues Lifafa Das from a mob (76). Aziz's receptivity to history in the making foreshadows Saleem's telepathic sinuses. The modernizing grandfather is aware of history, the world of progress made by human beings, as is his grandson. That is why the grandson chooses to see himself as Aziz's heir (or, alternatively, why Saleem invents this particular grandfather.)

The reader is asked to recognize that it is always possible to see Saleem as Methwold's son rather than Aziz's grandson. At the same time it is also perfectly valid for Saleem to choose Aziz as an ancestor. There are only metaphors, but some metaphors are more equal than others. Saleem's father, Ahmed Sinai, invents a thoroughly mythical genealogical connection to the Mughals in order to impress Methwold, the Englishman whose house he is taking over but whose status he cannot equal even in his own eyes (109–10). This romantic genealogy, which comes complete with family curse, is mocked by Saleem's narrative. But if history is a fiction, why should one version be preferable to another? Why does Saleem have the "power of giving birth to fathers and mothers: which Ahmed wanted and never had" (108)? Saleem actually knew Aadam Aziz, his progenitor, while Ahmed Sinai's Mughal ancestors are invented whole-cloth. But that is not a sufficient answer, for that would mean one could never tell a history that extended beyond living memory. It is, after all, not illegitimate for Ahmed Sinai, as a Muslim, to claim some sort of connection to the Mughals. The real difference between Saleem's invented genealogy and that of his father, the reason the first is "truer" than the second, lies in their adequacy as explanatory narratives. Ahmed Sinai's romantic genealogy is harmful because it is nostalgic and self-glorifying and serves to "obliterate all traces of reality" (110). Saleem's genealogy, on the other hand, explains the world in a way that makes possible action in the present.

The novel makes a distinction between lies and fictions. Saleem hates lies. If the nation of India is to contribute to the self-definition of its citizens, Saleem says it must be a collective fiction, "a dream we all agreed to dream" (111). Pakistan, on the other hand, is governed by lies: "in a country where the truth is what it is instructed to be, reality quite literally ceases to exist, so that everything becomes possible except what we are told is the case" (315). Saleem is an Indian, not a Pakistani, and it would seem that fictions are what he himself believes, while lies are the unbelievable things that other people declare they believe. A more generous interpretation of the distinction, however, is that fictions retain a sense of other possibilities, while lies deceive by denying that the world could be imagined differently. When he suspects his mother of adultery (and that he himself may be a product of adultery), Saleem takes his revenge on Lila Sabarmati, whom he knows to be an adulteress. But once Mary has confessed to the baby switch, what had appeared to be a lie is revealed to be merely a fiction. Saleem's mother had not lied to her husband, and Saleem can therefore be accepted as their child. For Saleem, lies have to do with the betrayal of others' trust, fictions with the establishing of trust. Trust asks for another's free consent undertaken with full knowledge, while lies deny others the knowledge that alone would make their consent valid and meaningful.

The ruling Nehru-Indira Gandhi-Sanjay Gandhi dynasty, says Rushdie in his own voice, is a "collective dream," but a dream from which India must wake (Rushdie 1991C, 47). In both India and Pakistan the metaphor of the nation's bloodlines has been dangerously misappropriated and the history of the nation confused with the history of a single family: "These Nehrus will not be happy until they have made themselves hereditary kings!" exclaims Aadam Aziz, now an old and disappointed man (267). Rushdie admires Nehru, but not the political dynasty he unintentionally established. *Midnight's Children* offers a fictional alternative to the dynasty's lies: in the words of *Shame*, "the substitution of a new myth for the old one" (Rushdie 1983, 278). Rushdie's alternative genealogy, based on a Nehru-like figure and also descending through daughter to grandson, has as one of its virtues a self-consciousness about its own fictive status. What Indians must do is reject the literal Nehru-Gandhi bloodline (which is really a metaphorical bloodline) and accept that Nehru is a father only in metaphor. In this way they might avoid confusions such as that propagated by the election slogan "Indira is India and India is Indira."

Rushdie offers a countermyth to the myth of the Nehru-Gandhi dynasty, which exposes the naturalized metaphor on which the dynasty is built. But myth and countermyth are not alternative versions between which the reader is free to choose. The reader may accept or reject the countermyth, but the dynasty's myth must be rejected as a lie. Elsewhere Rushdie has argued that sometimes "it's better to counter myths with facts" (Rushdie 1991C, 52). In other words, the postmodern fantasist, who declares through Saleem that "what actually happened is less important than what the author can manage to persuade his audience to believe" (263), also believes that there exists a reality external to all myths that can be known and against which their adequacy can be measured. The "fact" is that family rule has damaged Indian democracy (Rushdie 1991C, 52). The "fact" is that Indira Gandhi has been too Hindu and not sufficiently national in her politics. The "fact" is that the dynasty is a threat to the survival of the nation.

For all the self-conscious questioning of the epistemological status of historical narration in *Midnight's Children*, some things are not left in doubt. We have no trouble judging Rushdie's Pakistan. Saleem is an impure soul in the Land of the Pure, and it is clear that he and Rushdie value impurity. The liberal novel is a cry for freedom against tyranny. The forces of tyranny include fundamentalist religious forces and communal chauvinism, but also death-dealing and coup-plotting generals, and Indira Gandhi when she declares the Emergency.

Rushdie's novel engages in the subversion of every form of convention and authority. It very nearly falls apart – but not quite. It must resist chaos even as it resists tyranny. Liberal freedom is under as much threat from the forces of anarchy, in the guise of language marchers, religious rioters, and the many-headed mob as it is from Indira Gandhi. These forces of chaos are embodied in Shiva, the genetic son of Ahmed and Amina Sinai who has been raised in extreme poverty and is now filled with a violent *ressentiment*, the bitterness that arises from inferior status. The two enemies, tyranny and chaos, are linked: Shiva becomes Indira Gandhi's henchman.

Liberal freedom, the novel suggests, is a perilous balance between the need for freedom from tyranny and the need for a centre that can withstand the threat of disintegration. History and sexuality, the twin sources of Saleem's identity, are "tightrope walkers" (95). They maintain the balance that Rushdie says Thomas Pynchon advocates as well: "freedom is chaos, he told us, but so is destruction, and that's the high-wire, walk it if you can" (Rushdie 1991I, 353). Only a liberal secular state, Rushdie believes, can permit the self both freedom and security. Brennan is right to argue that *Midnight's Children* is a plea for the liberal values of human rights and civil freedoms. It is also a plea for the secular state as the only political home for the individual self.

We can express this insight in a negative fashion: there is no self without the secular and democratic nation-state. An oppressive tyranny and a murderous anarchy both threaten the self. Indira Gandhi, Saleem, and Shiva are three figures of India, and their relations are those of superego, ego, and id. The ego must escape the tyranny of the superego, which threatens it with castration, but must not collapse into the id. Shiva is Saleem's dark shadow; he cannot be denied but cannot be fully acknowledged either.

Lipscomb assumes that Rushdie's citations from Wolpert's positivist history are parodic in purpose, that Rushdie's novel explodes "historical discourse's claim to singular authority" (Lipscomb 1991, 182). However, it is more accurate to say that *Midnight's Children* both undermines and presumes the possibility of history, and it does so in order to encourage a self-reflexivity in the reader. The novel does expose the fictionality of the nation and its history, but the denial of the possibility of literal truth does not deny the nation. Where there is no literal truth we must put our faith in fictions. All we have are fictions, but some fictions deserve our assent and others do not. This is Hutcheon's point in *The Politics of Postmodernism*: postmodern representation affirms only to subvert, but subverts in order to affirm (Hutcheon 1989). Rushdie's novel explodes the notion of the nation having a stable identity and a single history, then invites a sceptical, provisional faith in the nation that it has exploded.

In the screenplay that Rushdie later wrote of the novel he has Jamila sing "Make Believe," a tune from the Kern-Hammerstein musical *Showboat*: "Say, it's only a paper moon/ Sailing over a cardboard sea,/ But it wouldn't be make believe/ If you believed in me" (Rushdie 1999B, 208). Saleem's account of his genealogy ceases to be make-believe if we believe it. Once we recognize that Aziz is not literally Saleem's grandfather, we may accept the validity and the value of a line of descent through Aziz. So, too, the citizens of India, if they would honour Nehru's secular ideal, must recognize that his status as the Father of the Nation is merely a useful metaphor and that his ideal is betrayed by the ruling dynasty that claims descent from him. The point of the allegory is to allow readers to accept or to reject *and* to make readers aware of their choice. History is not meaningless, but its meaning requires an act of faith. That faith, however, must not be blind. Maureen Quilligan writes that all allegory works this way: "The reader is posed a choice and a choice, moreover, which defines the reader, not the book he is reading [...]. Whether one affirms a belief in belief, or a belief in doubt, both choices are ethical, and while the mere fact of choice is not truly action, the self-awareness induced by the recognition that one has, in fact, chosen, is the kind of experience which underpins action" (Quilligan 1979, 265).

Saleem offers the reader a choice between faith in the nation and doubt. It is because it is a real choice that it has proven possible to read the novel both as giving imaginative form to India – "It sounds like a continent finding its voice," reads Clark Blaise's blurb from the *New York Times* on the cover of the Picador paperback – and as a cosmopolitan text that exposes the false, ideological basis of the nation-state. We should note, however, that the freedom to decide for oneself is a liberal value not free of ideology. Rushdie concludes his account of Sandinista Nicaragua, *The Jaguar Smile*, by acknowledging that there are two possible Nicaraguas and two fearsome jaguars that Nicaragua may be riding: the jaguar may be either the powerful United States, which is "the 'leftist' interpretation," or it may be the Sandinista revolution itself. Rushdie feels that he must choose between interpretations: "Finally I chose between the two girls on the two jaguars. I tore up the picture that looked, well, *wrong*, and threw it away" (Rushdie 1987, 161). His decision was the right one, and it is admirable that Rushdie remains always aware of the other interpretation. It is also typical, however, that he should make this epistemological question an existential choice: as though the truth about the Sandinistas is less important than the possibility of defining himself by his choice of solidarity.

Because the choice in *Midnight's Children* is posed in terms of faith and doubt (and not in terms of competing faiths), it is actually weighted in favour of history and the nation. Rushdie goes out of his way to show that the opportunities for self-fulfilment that give the citizen a stake in the nation are a question not of merit but of the class into which one is born. Saleem does not deserve his central position because of anything he has done or anything that he is. Saleem's concern with order and meaning is a luxury that he owes to the circumstances surrounding his birth, and therefore a mere emblem of class privilege. There is no just explanation for why one person is born into wealth and another doomed to poverty and misery, and the reader is free to reject Saleem as a mirror of India. But the concern for order is valuable in and of itself, and we readers cannot but opt for order over chaos. There is no absolute reason to choose Saleem, but no reader will choose Shiva.

Just as Saleem's family continues to accept him as its son, so, too, Rushdie wagers on India. The novel treats its own faith with playful disrespect but is even more suspicious of any other. In a review of David Attenborough's cinematic biography of Gandhi, Rushdie says India defined itself by choosing between "Nehru, the urban sophisticate who wanted to industrialize India, to bring it into the modern age, [and] the rural, handicraft-loving, sometimes medieval figure of Gandhi" (Rushdie 1991B, 104). Rushdie criticizes the Attenborough film for avoiding the debate and making Nehru Gandhi's acolyte.

But his disgust at the film is out of proportion to the film's defects, large as these are. Rushdie wants the film to be more critical of Gandhi and non-violence than it is. Clearly it is more than the film *Gandhi* that provokes the author's ire.

In *Midnight's Children* India's choice is not between Nehru and Gandhi but between Saleem and Shiva. The violent and rage-filled Shiva has, of course, nothing of Gandhi about him, but he does occupy the position of counterweight to the secular nation that in other histories of India is occupied by the Mahatma. To substitute Shiva for Gandhi is as scandalous as to draw an equivalence between the Mahatma and his assassin. But that is precisely what Rushdie does. Almost the only episode of Gandhi's life that figures in Rushdie's allegory of Indian history is the news of his assassination. It is as though the assassination revealed the truth about Gandhi: that, as Collins and Lapierre suggest, by making "the freedom struggle a religious crusade" Gandhi aroused instinctive and irrational forces that the nationalist intellectual elite was unable to control (Collins and Lapierre 1976, 34).

The absence of a genuine alternative is the source of the great paradox of Rushdie's novel: *Midnight's Children*, characterized by nothing if not heteroglossia, the presence of many voices and many languages, feels narcissistic, as if we were locked into a single head. Michael Gorra, an admirer, complains that "The whole narrative of *Midnight's Children* remains so firmly under the thumb of his self-regarding style that at times I find it hard to distinguish between the writer's fantasies on the one hand and the Widow's on the other, between the book and the totalitarian world it purports to attack" (Gorra 1997, 145). Franco Moretti explains that, contrary to what Bakhtin himself thought, heteroglossia and dialogism do not accompany each other but are found in inverse proportion to each other: "if people don't speak the same language, after all, how is dialogue ever going to be possible?" (Moretti 1987, 194). Despite their exuberant polyphony, there is very little genuine dialogue among adults in Rushdie's novels. Certainly it is remarkable how little Saleem talks to anyone in the course of his life, and at the centre of his life is a secret he must keep from everyone he knows, and especially from Shiva. The memoirist reads his narrative aloud to Padma, of course, but even as the memoirist's volubility replaces the hero's taciturnity we are rarely allowed to hear a genuine alternative.

The absence of dialogue marks the difference between Rushdie's book and the majority of novels written in India. From Rabindranath Tagore's *Gora* (1980) and *The Home and the World* (1985) through Premchand's *Gift of a Cow* (1968) and Raja Rao's *The Serpent and the*

Rope (1987) to Anita Desai's *Clear Light of Day* (1995), Indian fiction has been characterized by debates pitting ideologies and personalities against each other, perhaps reflecting the practice of gathering socially in order to discuss and debate (Chakrabarty 2000, 180–213). Such debates, precisely because they reflect real issues of local import, do not always travel well and, after the passing of their historical moment, may not easily interest readers. *Midnight's Children* translates more easily across climes because the tension in the text is not between characters so much as within Saleem. Or rather the debate is not among different positions within a single field but rather between inside and outside. Rushdie's great theme is how faith in a thing makes it real.

4

Magic Realism

In the same editorial passage in which he distinguishes between active and passive relations, Saleem makes a distinction between two "modes of connection" that join himself to the nation, the "literal" and the "metaphorical" (232), a distinction obviously related to that between realism and magic. The connection that Saleem calls "metaphorical," which involves repetition across different scales, is based on a narrative form shared by self and nation. The connection that Saleem calls "literal" relies instead on causality, on unidirectional links unfolding in time between agents and contiguous receivers of actions. As terms of analysis, "literal" and "metaphorical" are, however, as unsatisfactory as "active" and "passive." Saleem declares that the "literal" is "the first, most significant" of the modes of connection (233), but why should he, of all people, judge relations of cause and effect more significant, and even more literal, than relations of similarity? After all, in his story sympathetic magic and causality are equally effective ways of acting upon the world, the one no less real than the other. The reason for the confusion is the two senses of the term "metaphorical," which means not only "a relation based on similarity" but also "merely rhetorical and not real." This second sense of the term is the one Saleem employs when he declares that, when he says that he is cracking up, he is not just speaking "metaphorically" but is "literally disintegrating" (38). Although relations based on similarity are just as real in Saleem's world as relations of causality, only the latter are called "literal." The misnomer is significant for it betrays Saleem's awareness that, in the world of his readers, sympathetic magic is considered to have only a verbal not a real existence.

We may better understand what Saleem means when he calls his relations to the nation "metaphorical" if we look at the structure of his actual metaphors, those discursive elements in his narrative that do not refer to things but are understood to have only a verbal existence, *even in the world of the novel*. When we look for metaphors, it is surprising how relatively few there are. Saleem prefers similes, which are found on almost every page. Similes draw attention to the verbal nature of the comparison and to the perceiver who makes the comparison. Saleem is less comfortable with metaphor, however, which asserts not just similitude but identity. He will often announce when he is about to employ a metaphor, in effect turning metaphor into a kind of simile. He will say, "Amina pictured herself as a convicted murderer in Mughal times" (100), "Suppose yourself in a large cinema" (164), or "I became a sort of radio" (164). Or he deflects metaphor into simile, as when he describes his father's frozen sex as "a woolly elephant in an iceberg, like the one they found in Russia in '56" (172). Amina patiently explains to Mary Pereira who panics when she hears that the government will keep an eye on Saleem, "It's just a way of putting things, Mary; it doesn't really mean what it says" (122). When he does use metaphors, Saleem deliberately alerts readers to their unreality: a young priest weighs his moral choices "in invisible scales" (105), and Jamila discards her brother in "the metaphorical waste-basket of Army life" (373).

What is significant about the occasions when Saleem uses full-fledged metaphors is the frequency with which they repeat a particular grammatical structure: the attribution of a physical object to an abstraction by means of the preposition *of*. Saleem writes of "a deafening wall of soundlessness" (54), a "bog of muteness" (54), and "the amniotic fluid of the past" (107). Amina is adrift in a sea that consists of "waves of excitement" and "hollows of fear" (112). The "battleground of their loves" (127) does not have a physical existence in the world of the novel, any more than do the "web of worries" (99), the "fever of a reckless scheme" (139), and "the long ladder of relief" (142), "the dark pearl of hatred" (143), "the shawl of genius" (161), or "the dark glass of my private despondency" (320). No literal bodies are attached to the "sudden fist of anger" (149), the "icy fingers of rage and powerlessness" (135), the "hot fingers of excitement" (162), or "the clutching hand of the explosion" (332). The "cold, waiting veins of the future" (14), "the insanitary bowels of the old wooden-house quarter" (16), and "the mouth of a long, snaking decline" (173) are equally disembodied.

In *Midnight's Children*, therefore, metaphor generally involves the attribution of physical attributes to abstract or inner entities. We can note two things about the imagery invoked by Saleem's metaphors: first, that it is banal sometimes to the point of cliché ("waves of excitement," "the Hand of Fate" [144]); and second, that the realm from which metaphors are drawn is coterminous with the world perceived by the senses. The radios, cinema screens, fogs, moths, and fingers that Saleem deploys in metaphor all belong in his world, filled as it is with actual radios, cinemas, and pointing fingers. When Saleem draws attention to his use of metaphor – "Suppose yourself in a large cinema" (164); "I became a sort of radio" (164); or "I seem to be stuck with this radio metaphor" (221) – the images invoked are likely to be technological. The metaphors that slip through his guard, as it were, are natural images: fluids, insects, and parts of the body. But whether technological or organic, the metaphors remain close to the life-world of the narrator. In Saleem's narrative there are no images borrowed for the purposes of metaphor from among the internal organs, from among large mammals, or from artistic or cultural practices.

Padma's jaw is "set in the concrete of a majestically unshakeable resolve" (428), but the images Saleem employs as metaphors are not usually so concrete. More commonly they evoke objects so insubstantial – for instance, "a hard cloud of determination" (54), "the fog of silence" (57), and "the ghost of an explanation" (135) – as to feel only partially present. Examples include the "veils of Musa's indecision" (112), "the insidious clouds of amnesia" (373), the "mist of expectancy" (151), and a "haze of anticipation" (152). In these cases the metaphors seem almost to capture the actual moment when the abstract condenses into the concrete. In Saleem's India, the tropical heat breeds inchoate dreams – "the exotic flowers of the imagination blossom, to fill the close perspiring nights with odours as heavy as musk, which give men dark dreams of discontent" – which then have the power to summon mobs into being: "the dream of Maharashtra was at the head of some processions, the mirage of Gujarat led the others forward" (165). Other metaphors that appeal to images too small to be seen – the "tiny seed of suspicion" (158), "the twin viruses of fame" (304), and "the soul-chewing maggots of pessimism futility shame" (349) – appear to record the microscopic origins of larger things.

Todorov hypothesizes that "a generating principle" of the fantastic as a genre is that "*the transition from mind to matter has become possible*" (Todorov 1975, 114). The child Saleem's fear of failure becomes a "shapeless animal" which still "champs and scratches" in the stomach of the adult (152). Alia's hatred of her sister and her husband "grew into a tangible, visible thing" and "sat on her living-room rug like a great gecko, reeking of vomit" (320). This "thing" on Alia's rug is midway between literal and metaphorical, as signalled by the simile of the gecko: Saleem can actually see and smell it, but he is the only one who can and he is unable to name it. Elsewhere, Alia and her mother give actual form to their emotions. Reverend Mother doles out "the curries and meatballs of intransigence," "the fish salans of stubbornness and the birianis of determination" (138); Aunt Alia invests the food she prepares and the clothes she makes with her emotions, producing "the baby-things of bitterness, then the rompers of resentment," and "the pretty flowered frocks of Alia's undimmed envy" (154). Saleem knows only too well "the bitter mittens and soured pom-pom hats of her envy" (298), and "the Datsun of her vengeance" (298). Aunt Alia's body itself is characterized by "the heavy-footed corpulence of undimmed jealousy," and "the thick dark hairs of her resentment" (298).

Saleem claims to be able to detect other people's emotions with his senses, especially by smell. His powerful nose can pick up "the heady but quick-fading perfume of new love, and also the deeper, longer-lasting pungency of hate" (298), "the fatalistic hopelessness of the slum dwellers and the smug defensiveness of the rich" (299), and the many other "perfumes of emotions and ideas, the odours of how-things-were" (409). Saleem smells on Padma's breath "the dream of an alternative (but impossible) future ... the bitter-sweet fragrance of hope-for-marriage" (372), and coming from his Aunt Sonia "the implacable odours of Civil Service jealousy" (378). He can even return to a past before he was born and discern "the acrid stench of his [Aadam Aziz's] mother's embarrassment" (20), "the whiff of things concealed mingling with the odours of burgeoning romance and the sharp stink of my grandmother's curiosity and strength" (52).

The many physical manifestations of abstract or mental phenomena in the novel operate, Patricia Merivale suggests (Merivale 1999, 126), as "objective correlatives," T.S. Eliot's term for "a set of objects, a situation, a chain of events which shall be the formula of [a] *particular* emotion; such that when the external facts, which must terminate in sensory experience, are given, the emotion is immediately evoked" (Eliot 1975, 48). Much of the inspiration for this particular magic surely derives from the fact that Rushdie left India at age fourteen, and the child registers smells and tastes more strongly than does the adult. The taste of chutney is different when one is six and when one is thirty. For Rushdie, India is the land of smells and tastes because it is forever the land of childhood. Saleem says that other people, "conditioned, from the cradle onwards, into recognizing the narrowest possible spectrum of fragrances" (298), have overdeveloped their sense of sight and allowed their other senses to atrophy. For the non-resident Indian in England, of course, India is also a map and a history, that is, an abstraction not present to the senses except in representations. The magic in *Midnight's Children* reflects this filtration of the abstract through a weave of vivid sense-memories.

When Saleem says his magical connection to the nation is "metaphorical," he is not commenting on its reality – for, as we have seen, in the world of the novel it is as real as the connection he calls "literal" – but referring to the structure of the relation. Saleem is forever relating two sets of events that occur at the same time, large-scale political history and private family history, by drawing a parallel between them. What makes this process "metaphorical" is the mixing of scales that is involved: the domestic becomes the concrete manifestation of the political realm, which remains abstract ("imagined" in Anderson's sense: B. Anderson 1971), because it cannot be directly perceived by the senses as bodies can.

At the end of the novel Saleem proclaims that his son's generation will forge its own fate "in the implacable furnaces of their wills" (431). The furnace of the will is a concrete image of the abstract that conveys how the abstract becomes concrete. Saleem's world is filled with people who seek to give physical manifestation to unseen inner emotions and desires, a process likened in another Rushdie novel, *Shame,* to psychosomatic manifestations such as blushing and disease, "the action of mind over matter" (Rushdie 1983, 132). In *Midnight's Children* the process is figured as the realization of private dreams in the public waking world. In the seventeenth century, the original William Methwold had a "dream of a British Bombay, fortified, defending India's West against all comers," which proved a vision "of such force that it set time in motion" (92). Indian independence, achieved at almost the same time as the creation of the state of Israel, is another "sort of dream" (117), one which Nehru and Gandhi have made real by getting others to share it: the nation, after all, is "a dream we all agreed to dream" (111). India "would never exist except by the efforts of a phenomenal collective will" (111).

Roberto Calasso finds in the Vedas the message that "To be sovereign of the whole earth, one need do no more than think of oneself as sovereign of the whole earth, one need do no more than celebrate the rite of him who is sovereign of the whole earth": "What is real in effect (actual sovereignty over the whole earth) is secondary and derivative with respect to what is of the mind, and to the rite that is its consequence" (Calasso 1999, 129). This is consonant with another, more modern magic: what Michael Taussig calls the Magic of the State (Taussig 1997). Theodor Herzl, the father of Zionism, declared at the turn of the twentieth century that "dream is not so different from deed as many believe": "All activity of men begins as dream and later becomes dream once more" (cited in Eksteins 1989, 4). Rushdie, speaking at Yale in 2002, sounds a similar note: "The creatures of our imagination crawl out from our heads, cross the Frontier between dream and reality, between shadow and act, and become actual." That is why "*In dreams begin responsibilities*" (Rushdie 2002C, 375).

The people immediately around Saleem have, for the most part, smaller dreams: Dr Narlikar "dreamed" of tetrapods to reclaim land from the sea (110); Ahmed Sinai about reordering the Quran (132); Hanif Aziz of being a film director (57); Major Zulfikar of a large modern house with a bath beside his bed (56); Emerald and Mumtaz Aziz of the men they hope to marry (56). All these dreams, part ambition, part prophecy, are realized with more or less completeness. The largest of these dreams, of course, is the "vision of bold headlines declaring 'A Charming Pose of Baby Sinai – the Child of this Glorious Hour!'" that rises before the eyes of Ahmed and Amina (99) and the "dream-world" that Mary Pereira "invented when she changed name-tags" in Dr. Narlikar's Nursing Home (272).

Not all dreams, however, are realized. Saleem describes Mian Abdullah, the leader, in the novel, of those Muslims who, before independence, hoped to avoid partition, as having the potential to project a dream outwards and to "shape the future by the sheer force of his will" (386). Abdullah is assassinated, however, and his dream goes unrealized. Deserving but unrealized dreams Saleem categorizes as "optimism." Dreams that are not realized *and do not deserve to be* Saleem labels "fantasies" (130). Such is "the fantasy of every island-dweller – the myth of conquering the waves" that possesses Ahmed Sinai when he funds Dr. Narlikar's pioneering land reclamation schemes (133). The Pioneer Café in Bombay is a "repository of many dreams," fantasies of film stardom, of Communism, or of love (211). Arguably, the Pakistani "dream" of Kashmir also involves "fantasies" (328). Elsewhere Rushdie has written that Pakistan itself is "a failure of the dreaming mind" (Rushdie 1983, 92) and has been "insufficiently imagined" (Rushdie 1991C, 387). As Jean Genêt recognized, "if the transmission of an invented self is seamless, successful, then it is accepted as the truth, whereas '*Mythomania*, a *waking dream*, *megalomania* are the words we use about someone who hasn't succeeded in correctly projecting the image he has formed of himself'" (E. White 1993, xliii). Saleem eventually decides that his own "dream of saving the country was a thing of mirrors and smoke; insubstantial, the maunderings of a fool" (399), and the reader may well wonder whether it constituted optimism or fantasy.

Alongside dreams that are not realized are others that are realized without deserving to be. Fears and nightmares, what Rushdie later has called "Imagination's monsters" (Rushdie 2002C, 375), have as much capacity to become real as desires and dreams. Evie Burns dreams of murdering a woman, perhaps her mother (188), and, once back in America, knifes an old woman and is sent to reform school (179). Saleem dreams Jimmy Kapadia's murder (241) and then blames himself when his classmate dies. Shaheed, a soldier in the Pakistani army, dreams his own death, "which took the form of a bright pomegranate, and floated in mid-air behind him, following him everywhere, biding its time" (341). The pomegranate fills his head "like a light-bulb," the way that ideas are represented in cartoons, just before, sure enough, a grenade (a word with the same etymology as "pomegranate") drops on him (364). Shaheed thus fulfills the destiny contained in the name his father gave him, which means "martyr."

Because their wombs are the prime site where the word becomes flesh, where potentiality is actualized and newness comes into the world, young women are particularly susceptible to nightmares. Amina Sinai has several nightmares symptomatic of her deepest fears: when she is expecting Saleem she dreams of being trapped in flypaper (109); before she conceives her daughter she has a guilt-filled dream of being impregnated by her former husband Nadir Khan (127); and pregnant once again, she dreams of giving birth to a monster child with a cauliflower for a brain (321). Her dreams condition her being in the world, surrounding her with a fog of guilt (127). The virginal Mary Pereira, too, is haunted by guilt-ridden dreams in which her dead lover, Joseph D'Costa, appears to her as a wolf, a snail, and a broomstick (169). The consequent "blurriness of her perceptions merged waking and dreaming into something very like each other" (201), and Joseph "managed to cross the blurred frontier, and now appeared in Buckingham Villa not as a nightmare, but as a full-fledged ghost" (201).

If, like dream, nightmare has the power to make the word flesh, it is a zombified flesh without spirit. Although it appears to make the word flesh, the power of nightmare actually works to unmake the world and reduce it to dream. Saleem and three fellow soldiers in the Pakistani army counter an "overdose of reality" during the 1970 war in East Pakistan by a "flight into the safety of dreams" (349). Once in the Sundarbans, the "jungle of dreams," the soldiers confront houris and snakes, the physical manifestations of their guilts, desires, and fears (356). However, "by giving them their heart's desire," the jungle "was fooling them into using up their dreams, so that as their dream-life seeped out of them they became as hollow and translucent as glass" (356). By making their dreams real, the jungle is making the soldiers' reality dreamlike. Saleem and his companions must flee the Sundarbans and return to the waking world.

Todorov writes, "If the fantastic constantly makes use of rhetorical figures, it is because it originates in them. The supernatural is born of language, it is both its consequence and its proof" (Todorov 1975, 82). Saleem likens the capacity to give abstract conceptions physical form to the creative work of the novelist, who sets down on paper what exists only in his head. Padma resents his "nocturnal scribblings as though they were the very flesh and blood of a sexual rival" (121). The novel opens with the words of the angel Gabriel to Muhammad recorded in Surah 96 of the Quran: "*Recite, in the name of the Lord thy Creator, who created Man from clots of blood*" (12). Saleem is making a claim to be receiving revelation and even more: to be creating, like God, a man called Aadam. This is the conceptualizing power – "I think, therefore it is" – that belongs to Grimus in the eponymous novel (Rushdie 1975, 230). Chimalker's Toyshop, Reader's Paradise, and Bombelli's the Confectioners are all "Names to conjure with" (Rushdie 1981, 94). By naming things the writer makes them exist. The word "Abracadabra," that Saleem's son speaks in the last pages of the novel, has the same magical power to bring things into being.

At its simplest the capacity of words to bring things into being involves what J.L. Austin calls the performative function of words (Austin 1962). By saying "*Talaaq*!" three times, a husband divorces his wife (62). Padma's phrase "Let us be married, mister" appears to have the force of "some cabbalistic formula, some awesome abracadabra" to release Saleem from his fate (428). Even more impressively, if the context is right and the speaker is appropriate, the word "*Hartal*" can bring a whole nation to a standstill. Gandhi's declaration of a hartal in April 1919, repeated in posters and leaflets (33), remakes the world in the image of his desire. Malik Solanka, in the later novel *Fury*, acknowledges that "words are not deeds," but knows also that "words can become deeds" and "If said in the right place and at the right time, they can move mountains and change the world" (Rushdie 2001, 66). The right words, spoken at the right moment by the man with the authority to do so from the walls of the Red Fort in Delhi, can even bring into being an independent nation.

Of course, the wrong words at the wrong time can be just as powerful: the "nine words of emptiness" in Gujarati that young Saleem recites for the Maharathi language marchers are "directly responsible for triggering off the violence which ended with the partition of the state of Bombay" (188–9). In *Midnight's Children* the capacity of words to become reality is, as often as not, sinister. When the bearer Musa denies the theft of the silver spittoon by calling down the curse of leprosy on his head, sure enough, he is struck down and hideously deformed (144). To explain why Jamila Singer sings from behind a chadar, her manager starts a story about her disfigurement in an automobile accident (304). Even though the story is not true, once planted in people's minds it takes on an existence of its own, and the image of her rotting face forever haunts Saleem (383). When, in order to avoid marriage to Parvati, Saleem tells Picture Singh that he cannot have children (390), the lie again quickly becomes the truth.

The atmosphere in Ahmed Sinai's office is said to be "so thin and abstract as to make breathing difficult" (199). The pun here turns on the two meanings of "atmosphere": air and mood. The second meaning, which we can call "metaphorical" in Saleem's sense, because it involves emotions and not physical objects, is here made literal and affects the act of breathing. But emotions do affect breathing. Words have a real effect on how the world is experienced.

The great of soul seem able to use words to mean what they want – "even language obeys the instructions of Gandhiji" (33) – yet the Mahatma himself finds that words resist their appropriation. A hartal, Saleem tells us, means "literally speaking, a day of mourning" (33), and in Amritsar in 1919 etymology will reassert itself. As in a fairy tale where spoken wishes are regretted as soon as they come true, "the Mahatma's grand design is being distorted" (35): when his call for a hartal is heeded, there is indeed a day of mourning – Brigadier Dyer's massacre – for which Saleem almost seems to blame Gandhi.

The words of Muhammad Ali Jinnah, the prime minister of Pakistan, have, like Nehru's, the power to bring a nation into being. Even as he proclaimed the new state of Pakistan, however, Jinnah lamented the "moth-eaten" territory (Wolpert 1989, 347) that it was awarded at Partition (Pakistan received only part of Punjab and of Bengal). "Moth-eaten" is also the cry of Aadam Aziz when he discovers what has happened to the perforated sheet in the old tin trunk: "You forgot to put in any naphthalene balls!" he shouts at his wife (111). In this case, the political realm does not just have a parallel in the domestic realm; the actual word used by Jinnah is repeated by Aziz. The effect is somehow sinister, as if the founder of the nation, like some sorceror's apprentice, has all his words realized, including those he intended only as figures of speech. Jinnah summons into existence not only Pakistan but also the "moth of unease" in Saleem's stomach (399), "the interior moths of despair" that plague Parvati (409), and perhaps even the "moths of excitement" in his guts when Padma proposes to Saleem (428).

Not all words, however, can make or unmake the world. When young Saleem and his sister intercept his phone call, Nadir Khan, their mother's lover, pretends to have dialled a wrong number and asks, "This is Shanti Prasad Truck Hire Company, please?" The Brass Monkey, ever mischievous, answers in the affirmative, and Nadir is forced to pretend to order trucks. Young Saleem wonders if the guy on the other end of the line ever asks himself why the trucks do not arrive, and the Brass Monkey, "wide-eyed, flutter-voiced," suggests that "maybe they *do*!" (158). Readers recognize the nonsense involved in falling for one's own lie. Sometimes it is a mistake to confuse words and things.

At times, rather than show the capacity of words to be realized, Saleem reverses the valences of abstract and concrete and describes the personal in terms borrowed from the political. At such times, instead of describing India in terms of a body or a genealogy, he will depict people's actions in terms of warfare or boundaries. The results are almost always unconvincing, and Saleem begins to seem mad or, at the very least, as embarrassing as someone who is forever making bad puns: "Far away the Great War moved from crisis to crisis, while in the cobwebbed house Doctor Aziz was also engaged in a total war against his sectioned patient's inexhaustible complaints" (26); "While Nasser sank ships at Suez, thus slowing down the movements of the world by obliging it to travel around the Cape of Good Hope, my sister was also trying to impede our progress" by burning the family's shoes (149); "While Commander Sabarmati was at sea on manœuvres, Lila and Homi were performing certain manœuvres of their own" (251); when the Indian army fled from the Chinese, Saleem and the Midnight's Children "retreated into private life"(290); when Tiger Niazi "surrendered" to the Indian army, Saleem "surrendered" to Parvati's embraces (362); and when the opposition parties' "people's front expanded," so did the "frontage" of the pregnant Parvati (402). The reason the parallels in the above examples fail to feel magical and seem *merely* puns (groan) is that the public sphere of the state is treated as concrete (boundaries, retreat, surrender, and explosion) and the personal or domestic as abstract. We might call this atrocious punning the metaphorization of the literal: instead of making the abstract immediate, the effect is to make concrete events seem unreal and *merely* a function of words.

In general, the first half of the novel is characterized by the magical literalization of metaphors ("active-metaphorical" in Saleem's terms) and the second by the bathetic metaphorization of the literal ("passive-metaphorical"). Saleem's insistence on his connection to the nation feels increasingly perverse as it comes to rely on forced puns and bad faith. His desperate quest to find relations leads him to reduce everything to the verbal. He will persist in drawing parallels even when there is nothing to compare: "the *status quo* was preserved in India; in my life, nothing changed either" (284). When no amount of insistence will yield a parallel, Saleem makes do with chiasmus: during the Indo-Chinese War of 1962, "public optimism about the war grew as fat (and as dangerous) as an overfilled balloon"; Saleem's "long-suffering nasal passages, however, which had been overfilled all their days, finally gave up the struggle against congestion" (290). Parvati returns to the ghetto "when Mr. L. N. Mishra, minister for railways and bribery, departed this world for good" (400). "Everything has shape, if you look for it," declares Saleem; "There is no escape from form" (221). But the reader may be forgiven for thinking that this prisoner of form is his own jailor.

Saleem's narrative is as filled with wordplay as advertising copy. He delights in zeugma, the use of a single word in two different senses. Reverend Mother does not "move" from her culinary ways even when her constipated husband's "movements become irregular" as a result (42). Having "learned to bare her face," she is "reluctant to lose any of it" (44). The name of a thing may suggest a punning metaphor. On either side of Saleem's forehead are temples like "bulbous Byzantine domes" (123); Ahmed Sinai becomes impotent when his testicles are "too frigid to hold" (135); and when Saleem's left hand receives a paper from Homi Catrack's right, he comments, "sinister paper, inserted by dexterous fist!" (240). Circumstances or events in the narration may also recall a common metaphor that in turn shapes the narration. When he comes to tell the story of the Accident in a Washing-chest, Saleem proclaims, "it is time for dirty laundry" (158). He invites his reader to "Find out about Mian Abdullah and his Convocations. Discover how we've swept his story under the carpet ... then let me tell how Nadir Khan, his lieutenant, spent three years under my family's rugs" (48).

Even as it effects a link between word and world, the bad pun emphasizes the wholly verbal nature of the world in the text: the only things literally in the text are words. Reverend Mother rebukes her daughter Amina for appearing in a photo in the newspaper: "when I saw your picture, you had become so transparent I could see the writing from the other side coming right through your face!" (138). Reverend Mother does not understand, as Saleem and his readers do, that the words and pictures in the newspaper are physical objects occupying space and are not the bodies that they represent. When Saleem says, "the dreadful murders of prostitutes [...] began to fill the gutter-press in those days (while the bodies filled the gutters)"

(214), the metamorphosis of the black print on the printed page into ditches filled with corpses is so callously inadequate that we are reminded of the text's incapacity to make bodies present. Violence in the novel bears the same relationship to violence in the world as the triumphant parade of the Indian army through the streets of Dacca does to the scenes of carnage which preceded it: the "human pyramids" of acrobats (366) echo the "pyramid of enemy soldiers" that Saleem encounters on a battlefield (361), and the jugglers' grenades and the female contortionists who swallow their legs up to their knees (366) recall the grenade that blows off Shaheed Dar's legs (364), but between the contortions of the entertainers and the mutilations of war there is a world of difference.

The metaphorization of the literal, by drawing attention to the "literal," in the literal sense of that term, that is, to words themselves, signals a distance between words and world. However mad it may appear, Saleem's metaphorization of the literal is a strategy to counter the negative power of curses and spells by restoring the distinction between dreams and waking, between the literal and the metaphorical, that he himself has blurred. Interested as he is in the capacity of words to bring a world into being, Saleem is also concerned with exposing the trick involved in that magic in order to put himself beyond the danger of words. He says the violence of Padma's words "would have wounded me, were I still vulnerable to words" (121). He pursues a two-pronged strategy, appropriating the power of words for himself and undermining that power when used by others. Saleem says, in effect, "My words are more powerful than those of my enemies, and in any case all any of us have are words."

Saleem's twin models in this regard are Dr Schaapsteker, of whom it is said that he had "the capacity of dreaming every night about being bitten by snakes, and thus remained immune to their bites" (137), and the magicians in Delhi's ghetto who never confuse their sleight of hand with reality. The latter are "people whose hold on reality was absolute; they gripped it so powerfully that they could bend it every which way in the service of their arts" (385). In this sentence the magicians' metaphorical "hold on reality" is made literal: they grip it and bend it. The literalization, however, draws attention to the metaphorical and verbal nature of the "hold" on reality. The reason the magicians are able to bend and change the world is that they appreciate the difference between words and world.

Where does the speaker stand when he declares his superiority to words? Every declaration of his has been made possible by words. Saleem's double relation to words – he wants their power for himself and seeks to render himself invulnerable to their power when it is wielded by others – is also his doubled relation to the nation-state in which, as we have seen, he puts his faith even as he deconstructs it. But where exactly does the self stand when it puts its faith in the nation? Only someone inside India is free to choose the nation; yet, for the choice to be meaningful, it must be possible for him or her not to be Indian. Is that indeed a possibility? The narrator of *Midnight's Children* wants his fellow citizens to join him at a vantage point outside the nation in order to see it whole. But they are his fellow citizens because he is inside with them. The next chapter will consider the novel as a *Bildungsroman* in which the young boy is taught to think of himself as Indian.

PART TWO
The Self and the World

5

Bildungsroman

Book One of *Midnight's Children*, a retrospective account of events before Saleem was born, depends on the narratives of others. Perhaps for that reason it lends itself well to the allegorical interpretation that I offered in Chapter Three. Once it turns to Saleem's memories of childhood, however, other inspirations inform the narrative. The story of the first fourteen years of his life, which forms the greater part of Book Two, the largest of the novel's three books, is based on Rushdie's own experience of growing up in Bombay. Rushdie, too, was born in 1947, and a family joke had it that, as soon as he was born, the British started packing their bags. The account of the previous marriages of both Saleem's parents, a circumstance I read allegorically in Chapter Three, is actually autobiographical in inspiration: Rushdie's parents also had both been divorced (Hamilton 1996, 92). Nadir Khan's sojourn under the carpet is based on the experience of the Urdu poet Faiz Ahmed Faiz, a friend of Rushdie's aunt (Rushdie 2002C, 371). Methwold's Estate, off Warden Road, is based on Westfield Estates, and Buckingham Villa on Windsor Villa, where Rushdie grew up. There, along with the house the Rushdies lived in, one can still find a clocktower, a house called Noor Villa (Rushdie 1981, 178), and a bookstore called Reader's Paradise. They have not been demolished, as their fictional equivalents have been, to make way for the Narlikar women's skyscraper. Saleem goes to Cathedral and John Connon Boys' School in the Fort district, just as Rushdie did.

In this chapter, I will reverse the critical judgement which argued that the novel's magic was a literalization of the metaphorical and will read the novel as a highly exaggerated and comic *Bildungsroman*, where Saleem's identification of the state with himself is but a rendering of the processes of identity formation that he undergoes along with Rushdie and millions of his fellow citizens (although by no means with all or even most who dwell within the frontiers of the Indian state). *Midnight's Children* is concerned not just with the nature of a collective history but also with what Lauren Berlant calls the "National Symbolic": "the order of discursive practices" by which "the accident of birth within a geographic/political boundary transforms individuals into subjects of a collectively-held history" (Berlant 1991, 20). In other words, I will read the novel as if the events of Book Two, the narrative of Saleem's childhood and adolescence, preceded those of Book One, as in a sense, of course, they did: Saleem located himself in relation to his parents before ever he learned how his grandparents met.

At least as important as the allegory which preoccupied us in the previous chapters is the impulse to allegory. The adult narrator with a history of India at his elbow is ever on the lookout for parallels he can draw between his own experience and national history. But even as a child, too young to read newspapers or know about politics, Saleem was already fully convinced of his own significance. Without any evidence, the young boy awaited a greatness which "at the appointed hour, would float down around my shoulders like an immaculate, delicately worked pashmina shawl" (155–6). When he does hear telepathic voices, he is not surprised. He has long been expecting such a sign that he is destined for great things.

The nine-year-old's conviction of his potential greatness is not the infant's sense of himself at the centre of the world. As a baby, Saleem did once manifest special powers – in particular, the power to give his mother luck at the racetrack by guiding distant events (140) – but these powers belonged to "Baby Saleem," referred to in the third person, and have long been forgotten by the schoolboy. The boy lost "the gifts with which every baby is born and which life proceeds to erode" (130) when he entered the world of speech and symbolic communication. Only Toxy Catrack, the twenty-year-old mentally handicapped and mute neighbour girl, retains the gifts of infancy, and her fate is an unenviable one.

Unlike the infant's sense of centrality, the boy's conviction of his latent greatness is something he has learned. His family, his experience at school, and the images and texts with which he is surrounded have all fostered in him this sense of his potential. The young Saleem is doted on by mother and ayah. His father, having imbibed too much, holds Saleem close and says, "Great things! My son: what is not in store for you? Great deeds, a great life!" (151). The adult narrator recognizes that, in their ambitions for him, his parents are not unique: all parents – and ayahs, too – dream of prodigies for progeny. Parents regard their children as an investment, says Saleem: they expect "the immense dividend of greatness" (155). They want their children not merely to replicate themselves but to be better than they are. The language of investment is significant: in the capitalist world that it presumes, change is expected and expected to be progress.

Saleem feels his own "special doom" (122), fostered as it is by the "beautifying mist" through which his mother has always seen him (124), as a "shimmering grey presence" (122), a "mist of expectancy" (151), and a "haze of anticipation" (152). The amorphousness of the greatness that is inside and in the future is, however, a source of fearful doubt. Greatness must have a form to be recognized. "Where do you get it?" Saleem despairs, looking down from his bedroom window at the pool in the shape of British India filled with European swimmers (152). "Where do you find it?" he pleads with the finger of the fisherman in the painting of "The Boyhood of Raleigh" on his wall (153). But the question is itself the answer: Saleem's greatness will take the form of the culturally sanctioned images of the nation and of the hero that interpellate him, at home, at school, and in the street.

As a child, Saleem regards everything as a sign addressed to himself. Of course, preadolescents often look for significance in the letters of their name and the date of their birth, and how much more might they do so if the latter coincided with a significant historical juncture like the moment in which the nation received independence. Saleem is encouraged in the conviction of his centrality by the clipping from the *Times of India* that proclaims his birth coincident with that of the nation and by the congratulatory letter from no less a correspondent than Prime Minister Jawaharlal Nehru, which declares that "We shall be watching over your life with the closest attention; it will be, in a sense, the mirror of our own" (122). Saleem is not wrong to read these documents as addressed to himself: his parents have mounted the clipping and the letter on his bedroom wall with the precise intention of inculcating a sense of greatness in their son. Beside the flattering mirrors of the newspaper clipping and the prime ministerial letter is another image the young boy is asked to identify with: a print of "The Boyhood of Raleigh" by the Victorian painter John Everett Millais, left by the retiring colonialist Methwold when he sold the house to the Sinais. Saleem's parents are quite happy to retain the painting for they hope that their son will take inspiration from its heroic theme. They see no incompatibility between the imperialist understanding of what constitutes a hero and the nationalist appeals to greatness implied by the newspaper clipping and Nehru's letter. Both the imperialist and the nationalist identify heroism with the nation, although the nations they identify with differ.

The painting features a sailor who points both Raleigh and the young male viewer in the direction of their destinies, thus assuring young Saleem that he has a destiny that can be pointed to. Millais's painting does not depict heroic deeds. It does not show what Raleigh did and Saleem must do to make history. It suggests instead, as do the clipping and the letter from Nehru, that greatness is already present inside the child and awaits only the fullness of time to be recognized. The boy Raleigh was already the hero he would eventually prove himself to be. Greatness is not a question of achievement but of the recognition by others of what was always present within. When his mother has decked him out in an ersatz-Elizabethan outfit inspired by the print and his grandmother gushes over him, Saleem wonders, "Was genius something utterly unconnected with wanting, or learning how, or knowing about, or being able to?" (155).

The formation of self requires the mediation of visual icons that reflect the boy back to himself. Saleem finds another such mirror in the comic-book and fairy-tale figures of "Hatim Tai and Batman, Superman and Sinbad" (152), and in the posters that he sees from the window of the bus on the way to school. Soaring above the city, the focus of all eyes, are the images of the Air-India Rajah ("See you later, alligator! I'm off to London on Air-India!") and of the Kolynos Kid, "a gleamtoothed pixie in a green, elfin, chlorophyll hat," proclaiming "the virtues of Kolynos Toothpaste" (152) (an uncertain number of years later, in Suri's novel *The Death of Vishnu*, the Air India Rajah still floats above Kemp's Corner, but now he advertises flights to New York: "Uncle Shyam wants you!" [Suri 2001, 241]). Saleem is certain these figures, too, are signs addressed to him, as of course they are, even if he is confused about how to emulate them. To Rushdie, as a boy, such iconic figures may have presaged his future as an advertising copy-writer in London, but they leave young Saleem confusedly wondering if he is not "a comic-book" borrowed from the library (234) or a mansized tube of toothpaste, progressively squeezed as he grows up (235). The lesson these outsized icons impart is an identification with a scale much larger than the physical body, an expansion of self that makes it possible to imagine hopping to London or looking down on the city from above.

Saleem is not alone in his conviction of his own merit, though the nature of the greatness he imagines for himself, requiring as it does uniqueness, is to make him feel alone. His friends may not have been exposed to Millais's painting, but they also live in Methwold's Estate among things left behind by the colonizer, and travel every day beneath the signs of the Air-India Rajah and the Kolynos Kid. One house over from Saleem's, in Sans Souci, Sonny has posters of Spanish bullfights on his bedroom walls (208). Others find a shape for their ambitions in the cinema, and, like Evie Burns, Rashid the rickshaw boy (49), and Shiva (217), dream of being cowboys. Or they dream of being spies (Saleem), detectives (Saleem), or gangster bosses (Shiva). One-eyed Eyeslice plans to be a test cricketer, Saleem's best friend, Sonny Ibrahim, a bullfighter (152). We can safely assume that all Saleem's classmates – "yes, all of us, future bullfighters and Navy chiefs and all" (180) – guard the secret of a special destiny. His sense of his own unrequited merit is precisely what Saleem shares with others.

Along with a sense of potential greatness, his parents' optimistic dreams for him inculcate in Saleem a fear of failure. The boy picks up from his parents the idea that at all costs he must not be like them. The language of investment presumes progress but also risk. The very images that promise significance threaten insignificance. When his mother and ayah dress him up as Raleigh, "in frilly collar and button-down tunic" (122), Saleem is conscious of how absurd he looks (155). The world outside the home, far from according him the recognition he feels he deserves, is an experience of humiliation. In particular, the discipline of school life fosters a painful self-consciousness. His classmates mock his nose, comparing it to Everest (154) and calling him Pinocchio (153). Saleem shuns the "furious, interrogating eyes"of his teachers (169), especially "the mad eye of Mr Emil Zagallo, and the steelier gaze of a framed Spanish conquistador" in a print on the classroom wall (165). When the geography master stabs a finger at the conquistador, a "stern, sweaty soldier in a pointy tin hat and metal pantaloons," and proclaims that this New World conqueror "eez civilization!"(224), he is not holding him up, like Millais's Raleigh, as a model for the boys but as a standard by which they can be measured and inevitably found wanting. Mr Zagallo pulls Saleem up before the class to make his ugliness an object lesson in human geography.

Saleem seeks corroboration of his greatness in the world around him but does not know where to look. Everything seems to conspire to deny that greatness. Could it be that he has misread all along and that the fisherman's finger in the painting is held up in rebuke? Small wonder that Saleem begins to look inward and feels he must hide his true self. The last thing the schoolboy wants is to draw the attention of others. Saleem seeks only anonymity: he pushes away his father's drunken embraces, objecting, "Everyone will *see*!" (151). Until such time as it is ready to be recognized, the promise of greatness must be hidden inside, where it becomes a source of anxiety, the "shapeless animal" which "champs and scratches" in Saleem's stomach (152). The boy who sees himself reflected in the Kolynos Kid and the Air-India Rajah and who plays football with a tin globe soon comes to feel that a nose the size of Everest is too big and needs to be hidden. His body actually comes to feel too large. In order to evade others' eyes Saleem seeks to be smaller than his body: he shrinks to a point where he can comfortably fit into the private womblike space of a washing-chest.

The result is a division of the self between inner and outer: the oversized superhero hides behind the self-effacing exterior. My point is that both selves, the captain of a team of superheroes and the demure, awkward mask of the schoolboy, have been learned. The inner and outer Saleems do not represent authentic self and false mask of humility. Saleem has learned to identify with "mild-mannered Clark Kent" well before his superpowers manifest themselves (153) and he always retains more of the mild-mannered reporter than of Superman. Again he is not unique in this regard. Cyrus Dubash plagiarizes from Saleem's own *Superman* comics and, under the direction of his mother, the religious fanatic, becomes a rich and famous guru (262). His mother dresses him up in "brocade skirt and a turban" (262), much as Saleem is dressed up by his mother and his ayah to resemble Raleigh. Like Saleem, Cyrus is divided into inside and outside: he sits "quiet as genius" on the schoolbus until the moment when his identity as Lord Khusro Khusrovand can be revealed (153). At that point he successfully reverses the inner and the outer selves and displays the great guru while hiding the quiet genius, but inside "the faintly-smiling, benediction-scattering boy ... in a place which was forever hidden by his mother's frighteningly efficient shadow [...] there lurked the ghost of a boy who had been my friend" (262).

The fact that Saleem must hide his greatness is a source of doubt but also, paradoxically, constitutes its own proof: as the perforated sheet at the opening of the novel teaches us, concealment plays at least as large a role as disclosure in the creation of significance. Saleem is not surprised when eventually he does receive confirmation of vast inner resources. From the ages of eight to fifteen (that is, the years of growing up in Bombay that Rushdie himself remembers), Saleem, like the Prophet, hears voices in his head. In the privacy and security of a washing-chest and later of a clocktower, Saleem acquires and develops the telepathic powers that allow him to travel anywhere within the frontiers of the nation-state. The voices he hears are in part a restoration of the powers associated with infancy, and Saleem believes Toxy Catrack made them possible (130). The powers were not already his, however, except potentially; they have had to be acquired or found.

The voices Saleem hears belong, he insists, to people who exist outside himself and in the present. However, with the exception of Parvati, he never lays eyes on any of the strangers whom he meets telepathically. Saleem organizes the children born at the same hour as himself, the moment when India received its independence, into a Conference of superheroes, but most of the Midnight's Children go unnamed, and almost none have their speech directly reported. For all intents and purposes, their only existence is within Saleem's head. This does not necessarily mean his head has something wrong with it. Thirty years before, his grandfather, Aadam Aziz, was visited by presences that behaved in much the same way as Saleem's voices: "Heidelberg invaded his head; here was Ingrid, briefly his Ingrid, her face scorning him for this Mecca-turned parroting; here, their friends Oskar and Ilse Lubin the anarchists" (13). Memory and imagination make absent people present. Each of the agemates with special powers who meet in the Midnight Children's Conference behind Saleem's brow reflects some facet of himself. For instance, the child who travels at will across the land by passing through mirrors resembles Saleem the telepathic tourist. The "blue-eyed child" from Kashmir who can change sex (195) is like Saleem in appearance and in sexual ambivalence (about which I will have more to say). The "sharp-tongued girl" who can inflict wounds with words is like the memoirist we have already met who wants to do things with words (and is herself a literalization of a metaphor) (195). Just as Saleem embodies the nation, so do "the Siamese twins with two bodies dangling off a single head and neck – the head could speak in two voices, one male, one female, and every language and dialect spoken in the continent" (195). The girl who can fly high above events and the boy who can travel through time, "thus prophesying the future as well as clarifying the past" (196), have powers similar to those of Saleem the writer. The Midnight's Children represent aspects of their fearless leader, and "their heads were full of all the usual things, fathers mothers money food land possessions fame power God" (223), the very things that preoccupy Saleem himself, fathers and mothers topping the list. Together they form a club of friends of his own age to compensate for Saleem's exclusion from Evie Burns's "gang" (203).

Shiva, the one member of the club whom Saleem knew before his discovery of his special powers, is, of course, a special case. But he, too, is very much a part of Saleem's psyche, present even when forgotten. Saleem's lone act of direct violence, when he knees in the groin two schoolmates who have taunted him before the pretty Masha Miovic, is inspired by the "image of two irresistible knees" floating into his head (228). Despite his frantic desire to keep Shiva out, Saleem carries him within himself.

Like sexuality, the power to hear voices must be kept secret. When Saleem proudly announces to his family that "Archangels have started to talk to me," his enraged father hits him over the head, and he crashes through a glass tabletop: "having been certain of myself for the first time in my life, I was plunged into a green, glass-cloudy world filled with cutting edges, a world in which I could no longer tell the people who mattered most about the goings-on inside my head" (162–3). Saleem learns that, in "a country where any physical or mental peculiarity in a child is a source of deep family shame" (167), uniqueness, the prerequisite of greatness, arouses deep ambivalence. Although his greatness is no longer latent, Saleem resolves to keep it hidden, fearful as he is of a "withdrawal" of his parents' love (165).

Saleem's experience is shared with many. The young boys who attend Cathedral and John Connon Boys' School with Saleem in the first decades after independence grow up to be the sophisticated young Bombayites who frequent the Midnite Confidential Club in the 1970s. These children of privilege also experience the contraction of the outer self to fit into a small private space and the concomitant expansion of the inner self to the scale of the world. The nightclub offers the "secrecy of midnight darkness" in which patrons are able to indulge romantic fantasies. The "world without faces or names," "that place outside time, that negation of history" (437), sounds very much like the washing-chest that Saleem retreats to as a child, which is also "a hole in the world, a place which civilization has put outside itself, beyond the pale" (155). Just as in the washing-chest Saleem catches sight of his mother undressing and mysteriously acquires the power to eavesdrop on strangers in the far corners of the nation, so, too, in the sexually charged atmosphere of the Midnite Confidential Club patrons are aroused by the presence of strangers, catch their "soft, amorous susurrations," "the chink of glasses held by twined arms, and gentle brushings of lips," and imagine "all manner of new stories and beginnings, of exotic and forbidden loves, and little invisible contretemps and who-was-going-too-far" (437). The thrill is inseparable, however, from a vulnerability: every night a roving spotlight seeks out one of the couples and reveals "them to the hidden eyes of their fellows" (438). When he returns to the city of his birth, the thirty-year-old Saleem, who remembers writhing under "the relieved eyes of my fellow-pupils – *thank God it's him not us*" (225), finds himself standing "illuminated in a cellar while Bombayites tittered at him from the dark" (438). The desire to see and not be seen is inseparable from the nightmare of being seen without being able to see.

In young Saleem's volatile combination of isolation and self-aggrandizement we have an explanation for the novel's allegorical identification of self and nation that starts not from national history but from the experience of the young citizen. The distinction between the vulnerable present, a time of secrets, and the triumphant future, when greatness shall be recognized, is also a distinction between the world of family and schoolmates, from whom greatness must be kept secret, and the world of a larger public, to whom it will be revealed. As we have remarked, his withdrawal from the people immediately around him is precisely what guarantees the young boy's centrality: he is confident he does not belong among these people. The newspaper clipping and the official government letter on his wall not only promise Saleem greatness but supply the stage for that greatness, the abstract yet public field of the nation-state. The pointing finger of Millais's fisherman, which Saleem reads as a sign of his own "inescapable destiny" (122), also locates significance in a larger public history. Charles Taylor writes that the modern self seeks to escape from the mediations of others, but avoids "the individualism of anomie and breakdown" by projecting future and larger mediations (Taylor 1998, 197–8). One is freed from the claims of family, sect, and immediate community by "imagining oneself as belonging to ever wider and more impersonal entities" (ibid., 198), in particular to the nation-state.

The modern nation-state, as Tom Nairn argues, has two faces: even as its combination of individualism and homogenized mass makes possible the penetration of capitalist modernity into every sphere of human activity, the identification it invites with something larger than the individual provides the emotional and psychological compensation necessary for the self to cope with the forces threatening its dissolution. We need not go as far as Fredric Jameson and see "all third world texts" as national allegories (Jameson 1986) in order to appreciate that, in the postcolony, where the state has only recently achieved sovereignty, the modern individual's identification with the state acquires an extra charge. Sanjeev Kumor Uprety explains the particular power of nationalism for the colonial subject: "Nation becomes that imagined space where the fractured and alienated third-world subject finds a wholeness of form with which he can identify. Like the child before the mirror in the Lacanian schema, the third-world subject recognizes itself momentarily in the image of the nation" (Uprety 1997, 179). Frantz Fanon also accounts for colonial subjectivity in terms of fracture and incompleteness and by appealing to Lacan: "the colonized subject becomes a part-object, or 'amputation,' to himself, without a nation to be 'sheltered behind.' National identity provides, then, a translation of the historical subject into an 'Imaginary' realm of ideality and wholeness, where the subject becomes whole by being reconstituted as a *collective* subject, or citizen" (Berlant 1991, 24; italics in original). If in national allegories the private is a figure for the collective, as Jameson would have it, it would seem that the collective is also a projection of the private.

Saleem, alone in his clocktower, is isolated from others but connected to the whole. The visionary in the washing-chest and later in the clocktower has something about him of what Quentin Anderson calls the "imperial self" of Emerson and Whitman: "Both men are pinned Gullivers, submitting to the totality of experience on the one side and titans filling all space on the other; the measure of submission dictates the measure of assertion" (Q. Anderson 1971, 146). What is lacking in the imperial self, which is at once apart from the world and able to contain it, is an awareness of "reciprocal roles, the middle ground of life, in which we fall in love, change the diapers, call each other names, and are bounded by other people, as well as by our nature and our reveries and dreams" (ibid.).

Anderson believes the imperial self, which is also the adolescent self that refuses to grow up, had its origins in nineteenth-century America but is now found throughout the world. Saleem's fantasy of personal destiny and his fear of purposelessness are but extreme examples of a stage of development common to protagonists in other novels. Martine Hennard Dutheil reminds us that one of the things that seems most magical in Rushdie's novel, its fairy tale opening – "I was born in the city of Bombay…once upon a time. No, that won't do, there's no getting away from the date: I was born in Doctor Narlikar's Nursing Home on August 15th, 1947. And the time? The time matters, too. Well then: at night. No, it's important to be more specific … On the stroke of midnight, as a matter of fact. Clock-hands joined palms in respectful greetings as I came" – is actually an echo of *David Copperfield*, the most prominent of Victorian *Bildungsromans*: "Whether I shall turn [out] to be the hero of my own life, or whether that station will be held by anybody else, these pages must show. To begin my life with the beginning of my life, I record that I was born (as I have been informed and believe) on a Friday, at twelve o'clock at night. It was remarked that the clock began to strike, and I began to cry, simultaneously" (cited in Dutheil 1998, 215). Saleem, who identifies with Moses and Muhammad (161), is akin to Balzac's Lucien de Rubempré who also "soars above the Sinai of the prophets"

(Balzac 1976, 53; my translation). The boy who is certain everything conspires to prove and reward his merit is related to Dickens's Pip (Jamila Singer who hates the notion of love bears more than a passing resemblance to Estella, while Shiva is like Orlick, the violent apprentice who is Pip's rival and wicked alter ego) and to Joyce's Stephen Dedalus who also "in secret ... began to make ready for the great part which he felt awaited him, the nature of which he only dimly apprehended" (Joyce 1964, 62).

Along with his ambition, Saleem is acquiring a painful self-consciousness, like that suffered by Dostoyevsky's man from underground more than a hundred years earlier: "But whether I despised them or thought them superior I dropped my eyes almost every time I met anyone. I even made experiments whether I could face So-and-so's looking at me, and I was always the first to drop my eyes. This worried me to distraction. I had a sickly dread, too, of being ridiculous, and so had a slavish passion for the conventional in everything external" (Dostoyevsky 1960, 217). Saleem has so internalized the judgement of others who see only his grotesque, outsized, and ever-running nose and his misshapen face stained with birthmarks, that the mental picture he later sends of himself to others on his telepathic broadcasts inspires fear in all who receive it (Rushdie 1981, 214). Again he sounds like no one so much as Dostoevsky's underground note-taker: "It is clear to me now that, owing to my unbounded vanity and to the high standard I set for myself, I often looked at myself with furious discontent, which verged on loathing, and so I inwardly attributed the same feeling to everyone. I hated my face, for instance: I thought it disgusting..." (Dostoyevsky 1960, 216).

On the other side of the world, in colonial Trinidad, Ralph Singh, the narrator of Naipaul's *The Mimic Men*, was convinced as a boy that "a celestial camera" tracked his movements: "I was marked; I was of interest; I would survive. This knowledge gave me strength at difficult moments, but it remained my most shameful secret" (Naipaul 1969, 94–5). George Lamming's *In the Castle of My Skin* describes a similar self-consciousness among Barbadian schoolboys and teachers, who are surprised to learn they all feel that "there ain't no other man like yourself, that you is you, so to speak, an' there can' be any other you. An' that everybody else is different from you. You start to believe you see things nobody else see, an' you think things nobody else think, an' that sort of thing can take you far, far, far" (Lamming 1983, 143). Lamming's protagonist, like Ralph Singh and Saleem, desires invisibility for his glorious individuality because "The eye of another was a kind of cage. When it saw you the lid came down, and you were trapped" (ibid., 73). He finds it a painful experience to walk down the aisle in a lighted cinema, under all those eyes. Better to wait until the lights have come down: "There was something absolutely wonderful about not being seen" (ibid., 74).

Saleem and the heroes of these other *Bildungsromans* share a conviction of their uniqueness, a fear that their worth will not be recognized, and a desire for anonymity as preferable to being misrecognized. The desire for recognition springs from a culture that values self-determination and individuality. The desire for anonymity derives from the equally strong tendency towards normality and socialization. In all these novels, identity is something inside and in the future to be kept secret and protected from the eyes of others in the present. This is a recipe for the replication of passivity. As John Ball notes, Saleem "is much more convincing as 'the sort of person *to whom things have been done*' than as the central, determining influence on Indian history that he sometimes claims to be" (Ball 1998, 68). In this, however, he is no different than the young would-be gentlemen, artists, and heroes of Dickens, Balzac, Flaubert, Joyce, Kureishi, Naipaul, and Lamming; they also, in spite of, or rather because of, their sense of their own yet-to-be-recognized greatness, wait for things to happen to them.

To what can we attribute this experience of individuation shared across miles and across more than a century? All these young men have two things in common: first, they belong to the first generation in their families to experience standardized education designed to form citizens; and second, the society that their education is designed to prepare them for is characterized by a complex division of labour into very specialized tasks. The division of the young boys into outer and inner, which are also present and future, results from the common discipline that education subjects them all to and the promise held out by that same education that they will be distinguished from each other by the career paths they take. Add to this combination of standardization and specialization the loss of ascriptive professions and status, and we have the beginnings of an explanation for the split into present anonymity and future greatness. The song that Mary Pereira, his ayah, sings to Saleem – "Anything you want to be, you can be:/ You can be just what-all you want" (126) – is a hymn to social mobility. In the world in which Saleem grows up, it is no longer the case, as it may once have been, that professions and status are inherited. Class and status are now something to be acquired at particular elite schools (see Srivastava 1998). The boy can be what all he wants because who he is is not fixed. Because he only sees their outer selves, his classmates do not seem to Saleem to suffer the agonies he does: "one-dimensional, flattened by certitude, they knew what they were for" (153). Saleem is sure Glandy Keith Colaco will run his father's cinemas and Fat Perce Fishwalla his father's jewellery business, Hairoil will follow his father into the navy, and Cyrus the Great will be a nuclear scientist like Mr Dubash. None of these professions, however, are passed down within families the way caste professions were. Aadam Aziz did not follow in his father's gemstone business, and Fat Perce will not necessarily follow his father in his (and the surname Fishwalla suggests that the jewellery business has not always been the family occupation). Saleem's classmates do not know, any more than he does, what the future holds for them. Social mobility, however, is the experience only of those who already belong to a certain class. Shiva, who has not been to school, has no reason to separate who he will be from what he actually does. He also feels no reason to hide anything.

The voices that fill Saleem's head and that represent the awakening of a national consciousness are explicitly compared to those heard by Saint Joan in the Bernard Shaw play put on at his school (161). Shaw explains in his preface to the play that what Joan heard was the new force of nationalism, stirring in Europe (Shaw 1924). The voices Saleem hears are also already in the air, waiting to be heard, before he ever picks them up. But Saleem is not the isolated prophet Joan was. His voices are inseparable from the experience of school, which channels the conviction of centrality and heroism in adolescent boys into an identification with the state. Saleem's narcissism and identification with the nation are but extreme forms of identity formation experienced by many. Not every young child in India can boast a letter from the prime minister, nor can there be many whose bedrooms, like Saleem's and Rushdie's own, overlook a swimming pool in the shape of British India, but all schoolchildren learn a map and a national history with which they are asked to identify. "God knows what they teach you boys these days," bemoans Tai the boatman (18).

The desire for anonymity, coupled with expansion to the scale of the world, that the young boys first learn at school is also the experience of capitalists in the modern economy. Ahmed Sinai who invests in Dr. Narlikar's grandiose land-reclamation schemes has learned from the freeze imposed on his assets "to draw as little attention to himself as possible" (173). Like his son in the washing-chest, he retreats to a "sunless office" (271), where he cuts off ties to the world and succumbs to "abstraction" (198). Just as from the privacy of his clocktower, Saleem travels mentally "the length and breadth of the country" (203), so, too, from "the abstract sanctum of his office" (246) Ahmed maintains telephone contact with the market, an entity that, like the nation, can only be represented and never made present. Ahmed is entertained in his office by young secretaries, but they do not so much arouse his desire – his assets have long ago been frozen – as flatter his ego. His relationship to them is like Saleem's to Padma in the small office in which he is writing his memoirs. Ahmed's desire is directed instead to an abstract realm: he reacts to the market's "emotional, unpredictable shifts and changes the way a lover does to his beloved's slightest whim" (199), which is also the way Saleem relates to the nation. Saleem characterizes his own relation to the nation as that of an "unseen hand" (284), a metaphor borrowed from the capitalist market that suggests both invisibility and mastery.

In his "steady divorce from reality" (199), Ahmed neglects wife and family and becomes rich. Even as his own dreams of greatness and fear of failure are what make him most like Ahmed Sinai the speculative investor, Saleem desperately wants to avoid ending up like his father. The deepest wellsprings of the self are shared by all males of a certain class, but the result is not solidarity but rather isolation, rivalry, and suspicion. Like his father, who wants to outdo the "Dawoods, Saigols, Haroons" (302), Saleem is surrounded by others who, precisely because they have received a similar socialization, are his sworn rivals. Some, like his cousin Zafar and Mutasim the Handsome, Saleem defeats. Those whom, like Shiva, he cannot defeat, he casts in the roles of usurpers and imposters. When Cyrus the Great achieves the recognition that eludes him, Saleem feels, "It should have been me" (262). Perhaps the message of the Kolynos Kid is not his transcendent freedom high above the city, but his competition with the Air-India Rajah for attention. Even in the print of Millais's "The Boyhood of Raleigh" young Raleigh has to compete with a second boy (more about him in a subsequent chapter). This is the challenge faced by the narcissist who imagines himself on the scale of the nation: what to make of all his fellow citizens?

6

Parts and Whole

From infancy Saleem has been programmed to undertake what Judith Butler describes as the Hegelian project of becoming "a self-sufficient subject for whom all things apparently different finally emerge as immanent features of the subject itself" (Butler 1987, 6): "This subject's desire is structured by philosophical aims: it wants to know itself, but wants to find within the confines of this self the entirety of the external world; indeed its desire is to discover the entire domain of alterity as a *reflection* of itself, not merely to incorporate the world but to externalize and enhance the borders of its very self" (ibid., ix-x). As long as Saleem remains in his clocktower, telepathically roaming the nation, he can imagine himself as whole. When, however, Saleem leaves home and enters a space more commensurate with the collective that he identifies with, the public sphere of his supposed greatness, he comes into contact with others, from different classes and with different interests, who are also necessarily part of India. The young middle-class boy is regularly confronted by bodies, especially, as Jean Kane points out, "female and poor bodies" (113) and, I might add, the bodies of Hindus, in which he does not see reflections of his own.

What is he to make of these many others who inhabit the same world that he does, the world he would like to imagine as himself writ large? Saleem cannot want his fellow citizens all to identify with the nation and so to resemble himself. One scenario where every citizen has identical features proves a nightmare when India is filled with gangs of Sanjay Gandhi clones, all with plump stomachs, oily curls, and fleshy lips (382). What Saleem values about the nation is precisely that it permits his own individuation. Nor can he wish that his fellow citizens all be individuals like himself. The sheer vastness of the numbers involved would make nonsense of uniqueness: "Five hundred million still alive. And only one of me…" (241). Somehow Saleem must contain all these others and not allow himself to be swallowed.

Saleem undertook his memoirs to prove how intimately linked his fate has been to that of the nation. As he brings his project to a close, however, he renounces his claims to be a mirror of the nation and defines himself as a private individual who has been made by all his experiences and his choices: "Who what am I? My answer: I am the sum total of everything that went before me, of all I have been seen done, of everything done-to-me. I am everyone everything whose being-in-the-world was affected by mine. I am anything that happens after I've gone which would not have happened if I had not come" (370). He is no longer the mirror of the nation, single and sovereign, who resists his dissolution in the many, but is now a pluriform and contingent self made up of many. In his own terms, he now defines himself by his literal connections (based on causality) rather than on his metaphorical ones (based on putative similarity). Reality has been badly damaged and it is necessary "to put it together again" (405). The narrative in which Saleem performs this magic is an assemblage of thirty chapters, each one called a "piece" (245, 258). His narration frantically assembles "shreds and scraps"; the "trick," Saleem explains, "is to fill in the gaps, guided by the few clues one is given" (412) and so to piece "the story together" (394).

To discern the "sum total" of all the relations Saleem has ever had with others involves, however, tracking an impossible number of links, past, present, and future, conscious and unconscious. He contains multitudes, "six hundred and thirty million particles of anonymous, and necessarily oblivious dust" (38). The impossibility of accounting for these multitudes explains both the gigantism and the porousness of Saleem's narrative. He always remembers something else that he must include and must relate to every other thing:

> How many things people notions we bring with us into the world, how many possibilities and also restrictions of possibility! – Because all of these were the parents of the child born that midnight, and for every one of the midnight children there were as many more. Among the parents of midnight: the failure of the Cabinet Mission scheme; the determination of M.A. Jinnah, who was dying and wanted to see Pakistan formed in his lifetime, and would have done anything to ensure it […]; and Mountbatten with his extraordinary haste and his chicken-breast-eater of a wife; and more and more – Red Fort and Old Fort, monkeys and vultures dropping hands, and white transvestites, and bone-setters and mongoose-trainers and Shri Ramram Seth who made too much prophecy. And my father's dream of rearranging the Quran

has its place; and the burning of a godown which turned him into a man of property and not leathercloth; and the piece of Ahmed which Amina could not love. To understand just one life, you have to swallow the world. (108)

Saleem's strategy for "swallowing" the multiplicity of the world is to compile catalogues. From his infancy, when he drained his mother's breasts of milk (124), and even before, when still in the womb, he has been engaged in ingesting and absorbing everything around him: "I move on [...] ingesting thumb-and-forefinger, swallowing the moment at which Aadam Aziz did not know whether he was Kashmiri or Indian; now I'm drinking Mercurochrome and stains the shape of hands which will recur in spilt betel-juice, and I'm gulping down Dyer [...] growing larger now, floating in the amniotic fluid of the past, I feed on a hum [...] Through my umbilical cord, I'm taking in fare dodgers [...]Amina's assiduity seeps into me" (107–8). Of course, this ingestion did not actually occur *in utero* – Saleem never was in Amina's womb – but is performed in the present as the retrospective narrator records these events. Already as an infant, however, paraded by his ayah around Methwold's Estate, he claims to have been aware of the "teeming," "manifold," and "multitudinously shapeless" things that fill the world (126), and since even "a baby is faced with the problem of defining itself" (129), the future memoirist coped by compiling lists:

So here is old man Ibrahim, dying with worry because, back in Africa, governments are nationalizing his sisal plantations; here is his elder son Ishaq fretting over his hotel business, which is running into debt, so that he is obliged to borrow money from local gangsters; here are Ishaq's eyes, coveting his brother's wife, though why Nussie-the-duck should have aroused sexual interest in anyone is a mystery to me; and here is Nussie's husband, Ismail the lawyer, who has learned an important lesson from his son's forcep-birth: "Nothing comes out right in life," he tells his duck of a wife, "unless it's forced out." [...] And, moving across to Versailles Villa, here is Mrs Dubash with her shrine to the god Ganesh, stuck in the corner of an apartment of such supernatural untidiness that, in our house, the word "dubash" became a verb meaning to make a mess" (129).

If a catalogue were actually to include everything in the world, it would need to expand to the point where each element in the catalogue was but a dot. The apotheosis of the catalogue is to count numbers. When one of his classmates dies, Saleem has a nightmare of "annihilation-by-numbers": "Jimmy is dead; five hundred million still alive. I start counting: one two three. Numbers march over

Jimmy's grave. One million two million three million four. Who cares if anyone, anyone dies. One hundred million and one two three. Numbers march through the classroom now. Crushing pounding two hundred million three four five. Five hundred million still alive. And only one of me ..." (241). As the catalogue begins to approach infinity, it suggests not a whole that contains all the constituent elements, but the impossibility of such containment: "ten million (like all numbers larger than one thousand and one) refuses to be understood" (346). The impossibility of the catalogue renders the ambition farcical, the narrator unreliable, and the narrative at once urgent and hopelessly dilatory.

By its randomness the catalogue suggests its openness and gestures towards infinity, but in *Midnight's Children* the seemingly random always suggests a larger pattern. In the list of neighbours at Methwold's Estate, quoted above, the boy brings order to his dubashed world by drawing vectors of genealogy, money, or sexual desire between the discrete elements. The synchronous, all that coexists in a particular field at a particular time, is assumed to be related by causality. Of course, cause and effect still have a distressing propensity to overdetermination and openendedness. How to begin to list "everything done-to-me" and "everyone everything whose being-in-the-world was affected by mine"? Effects do not, it seems, ever have single causes. Who can know, for instance, the origin of Musa the bearer's resentment of the Sinai family? "What remnants of guilt fear shame, pickled by time in Mary's intestines, led her willingly? unwillingly? to provoke the aged bearer in a dozen different ways [...]? What tiny grain of grit, in the sea of old age now washing over the old bearer, lodged between his lips to fatten into the dark pearl of hatred [...]?" (143). A consideration of causality must include motivations: was Musa's resentment provoked by Mary? by his servile status? or by Ahmed Sinai (143–4)? Etiology must also take into account necessary conditions and even those forces that militate against alternative outcomes. Saleem would never have found his way back to India from Pakistan "if Yahya Khan and Z.A. Bhutto had not colluded in the matter of the coup of March 25th , [...] if ten million had not walked across the frontiers into India, [...] if it were not for the Mukti Bahini" (362). The search for links always points to more things that need to be included. Even as it ostensibly asserts order, causality works to open the text up to yet more possibilities.

Causality suggests everything is related and therefore forms a larger whole to be called "the historical moment" or "the nation," but it leaves the shape of that whole perilously plastic. Saleem counters the threat of infinite elasticity by surreptitiously importing into his catalogues a principle of homology. Saleem's catalogues of the synchronous rely on recurrence on a scale that "would stagger even C.G. Jung" (193). The following passage is typical: "While astrologers make frantic representations to Congress Party bosses, my mother lies down for her afternoon nap. While Earl Mountbatten deplores the lack of trained occultists on his General Staff, the slowly turning shadows of a ceiling fan caress Amina into sleep. While M.A. Jinnah, secure in the knowledge that his Pakistan will be born in just eleven hours, a full day before independent India, for which there are still thirty-five hours to go, is scoffing at the protestations of horoscope-mongers, shaking his head in amusement, Amina's head, too, is moving from side to side" (109). "While" and "meanwhile" are favourite words of Saleem's, liberally used to relate things belonging to different scales and registers. Here the personal and the political, unfolding at the same time, are further linked by similarity (both Amina and Jinnah are moving their heads) and by a buried metaphor: Jinnah's defiance disturbs the sleep of everyone in the subcontinent because the nation is "a dream we all agreed to dream" (111). The implication is that, whether or not we believe that the shape of things is written in the stars, all that exists under the same skies is related by similarity.

Compare Oskar Matzerath's practice of linking the political and the personal in *The Tin Drum*: "While history, blaring special communiqués at the top of its lungs, sped like a well-greased amphibious vehicle over the roads and waterways of Europe and through the air as well, conquering everything in its path, my own affairs, which were restricted to the belabouring of lacquered toy drums, were in a bad way. While the history-makers were throwing expensive metal out the window with both hands, I, once more, was running out of drums" (Grass 1962, 252). And again: "While V-1 and V-2 rockets were winging their way to England, my voice winged its way over Langfuhr and along the file of trees on Hindenburg-Allee, hopped over the Central station and the Old City, and sought out the museum in Fleischergasse" (ibid., 365).

It may not be possible to account for all the bits that make up Saleem and into which he is disintegrating; in practice, however, he does not have to do so. He can assume he is made up of "(approximately) six hundred and thirty million particles of anonymous, and necessarily oblivious dust" (38), not because he has worked out "the sum total of everything that went before me, of all I have been seen done, of everything done-to-me" (370), but because he already knows that the number will coincide with the population figures of the national census. In other words, Saleem knows in advance that the others he meets form a totality and what shape that totality takes: it coincides with the nation, which is a mirror of himself. The reliance on the literal as opposed to the metaphorical that Saleem asserts at the end of the novel does not represent a new humility: he assumes that others are all a part of him – he speaks of "each 'I', every one of the now-six-hundred-million-plus of us" (370) – but he alone corresponds to the whole. To imagine that all those with whom he has ever come in contact, who have influenced him or been influenced by him, add up to the nation is conveniently to forget that his experience includes non-Indians – Pakistanis, Bangladeshis, Englishmen, Eastern Europeans, and Americans – with whom he does not share an identity. Moreover, the people he has affected and who have affected him, though certainly too numerous to count, are unlikely to number six hundred million, even when his telepathic rambles are included.

Saleem assumes that the two ways of relating to the world outside the self, similarity and causality, or, in his terms, the "metaphorical" and the "literal," correspond to each other. As we have already noted, the term "literal" is a solecism, since events in the magical world of the novel are fully as likely to be determined by similarity as by causality. The relation called "literal," based on causality, is no less figurative than the "metaphorical" and is better termed "metonymic" to highlight its basis in language. The relation called "metaphorical" is, in turn, best called "synecdochical" to indicate that it is not more figurative but merely a different verbal configuration. In synecdoche the part is a microcosm of the whole, with which it shares a shape or essential quality. William Methwold's reference to his fellow colonialists as "old India hands" (96) is a synecdoche: the essence of the colonial workforce is the strength they put at the service of the administration, a strength which can be said to lie in their hands. In metonymy, on the other hand, the relation between part and whole is not based on the qualities they have in common but on the relation of the part to all other parts (H. White 1973, 35). Aadam Aziz's mother deploys metonymy when she blames young Naseem Ghani's ill health on the "absence of a mother's firm hand" (25): the hand can represent loving discipline because it is an instrument of the heart and the will and but one part of what makes a mother. Saleem is speaking metonymically when he says he wants "the ears of Ministers": he wants to convince them to put their hands and minds at his disposal (376). It must be pointed out that, as the above examples of the old India hands and the firm hand of the mother suggest, a single body part, the hand, can be either a synecdoche or a metonym depending on its presumed relation to the whole. The distinction between the two relations, which will be of great importance in the discussion that follows, is that a metonym is one part among many different parts and a synecdoche is an essential part that shares the character of the whole. The wholes implied by metonymy and synecdoche can also be distinguished: the first is the sum of many interconnected parts, and the second has an essence that is the same all the way down, no matter how small the parts into which it is divided.

Saleem's is first and foremost an allegorical imagination. He sees synecdochical repetition between part and whole everywhere: in vultures "whose bodies are as hooked and cruel as their beaks" (84); in the fisherman's finger pointing out a window to a city that itself resembles "an outstretched, grasping hand" (92); and in "the relieved eyes of my fellow-pupils" (225), the last a synecdoche that works by punning. A Delhi muhalla, where a Sindi and a Bengali Muslim live on either side of a Hindu on whom they rain "multilingual abuse," functions as a microcosm of the subcontinent (73). Even as Mian Abdullah's eloquence woos members to the tents of the Free Islam Convocation, his powerful hum induces erections and the audience find their own "members made tents under their robes" (48; Heffernan 2000, 481). The principles of similarity that link parts to the whole also link them to other parts: for instance, "the bosomy contours of Padma's cheeks" (335). A pointing finger reminds Saleem of "another, long-lost finger" between his legs (121), like the "eleventh finger" that Grass's Oskar develops when his ten fingers prove inadequate for making love (Grass 1962, 273). Saleem's nose, that "rampant cucumber" (124; 18, 340), resembles his penis, "the useless cucumber hidden in my pants" (121; 18), and when he loses his memory, he himself becomes "a vegetable" (340).

Saleem's body, the synecdoche of the nation, suffers from a surfeit of form. Not only the body but the face, too, is imagined as replicating the nation: "Fair skin curved across my features – but birthmarks disfigured it; dark stains spread down my western hairline, a dark patch coloured my eastern ear," stains that correspond to the location of East and West Pakistan on the map (123). The ugliness only seems discordant: it actually serves the repetition of form and so is significant. Even Saleem's ever-running nose echoes the shape of the subcontinent, with Ceylon dripping from the end (226). The nose in the face, the face in the body, the body born at the same time as the nation: synecdoche within synecdoche. The result recalls the comic-book convention of drawing a series of congruent shapes of varying size, each within the other, in order to suggest rapid shrinking or expansion.

No wonder Saleem identifies with Ganesh, the elephant-headed god, whose nose is too big for his head and whose head is out of proportion to his body.

The series of synecdoches can be further extended: Saleem is hybrid like Bombay, the city where he lives, which is in turn a microcosm of the multicultural nation-state. Saleem, in spite of his remonstrations, is literally a "monster" (117), that is, something put on display to *demonstrate* an object lesson in "human geography" (225). During his exile at Uncle Hanif and Aunt Pia's Saleem plays "an increasing number of bit-parts" (235), the "most treasured bit-part of all" being that of son (237), but the most appropriate being that of "the Faithful Body-Servant" (235). The pun on "bit-part" reminds us that Saleem understands himself as a body that faithfully serves a larger whole.

Saleem's sense of his own centrality is threatened, however, by his awareness of the many others who surround him and who could legitimately point to him and ask, with Ahmed Sinai, "where am I in that face" (230). As a result of his identification with the nation, Saleem can look down, as from a great height, on the multitudes, characterized by numbers too large to count. These millions are frequently compared to insects. In 1919 Aadam Aziz looks down from his hotel window on the excrement that clogs the streets of Amritsar and on the people who "swarmed about, too, mirroring the motion of the flies" that "buzzing gaily from turd to steaming turd, celebrated and cross-pollinated these freely-given offerings" (33). In 1956, the young Saleem looks down from the hillock of Methwold's Estate on the language marches which form an "endless ant-trail of language" (187). And in 1978, at the time of writing, Saleem can see from his office window the "yellow-and-brown local trains" that pass in front of the factory and the "Human flies" that "hang in thick, white-trousered clusters" from them (206). Saleem's response to the swarming multitudes is not that of the "Jain in a face-mask," who brushes "the pavement before him with a twig-broom, to avoid stepping on an ant, or even a fly" (33). Instead, their number and individual insignificance fill him with horror. Saleem, like Resham Bibi, has ants in his brain (374). The swarming multitudes, the "numbers marching one two three, four hundred million five hundred six," like so many ants, will trample poor Saleem into as many "specks of voiceless dust" (446).

When the Russians invade Grass's Danzig, Oskar's narration focuses on "a military highway" laid out by ants and he judges "the life of my times by their industry" (Grass 1962, 385–6). So, too, in a Bangladesh weary of war, Saleem notes how red and black ants fight over a cockroach, as in the streets "antlike people were emerging, preparing for peace" (364). The metaphorical relation between the two sets of ants is also, in Saleem's terms, a literal one: Shaheed, a soldier in the Pakistani army, kills ants and licks them off his palm (357), and they in turn find him when he is wounded and eat him, so that he becomes the victim "of not one, but two wars" (365). The ants and "the antlike," making a meal of each other, perform a grotesque parody of Saleem's active-passive relation to the nation.

An anthill, as Eugene Marais was the first to teach, can be imagined as a single body where each class of members, workers or soldiers, fulfils the role of an organ (Marais 1937). The whole comes under the control of the queen who, alone in a cell deep underground, acts as the brain of the colony. If she dies, the other ants cease to perform their functions, congregate in excited groups, and die. Saleem, like the queen ant, sits by himself in the confined space of the clocktower from where he imagines "that I was somehow creating a world; that the thoughts I jumped inside were *mine*, that the bodies I occupied acted at my command" (172). He feels himself "capable of acting-at-a-distance and shifting the tides of the world" (172). And when Saleem loses his telepathic power over the whole, order collapses in the world around him as well.

The pickle factory in which Saleem holes up in order to write his memoirs resembles an anthill in its division of labour. Factories are, of course, the preeminent site where labour is divided so that parts may be assembled. A pickle factory, however, is not just any factory: when Saleem describes the specialized tasks at the Braganza pickle factory, he uses organic rather than mechanical imagery. Saleem acts as the factory's eyes "which can see corruption beneath citrus-skin; fingers which, with featheriest touch, can probe the secret inconstant hearts of green tomatoes; and above all a nose capable of discerning the hidden languages of what-must-be-pickled" (443), while the actual labour of stirring the pickle vats is done by the hairy arms of the female workers (164). Padma, "all ears" (46) at Saleem's elbow (39), serves as his "necessary ear" (149). The division of labour in the pickle factory is imagined in terms of a single human body in which Saleem performs the function of the organs of perception and the women of the labouring limbs and the ear. What this body looks like is suggested by the "winking, saffron-and-green dancing figure of the neon goddess Mumbadevi" perched above the factory (179; 38, 439). The body of which Saleem is now the eyes, nose, and fingers, is explicitly feminine.

Where once the Kolynos Kid and the Air India Rajah had loomed over Saleem's childhood, encouraging him to project his self on a transhuman scale, as he grows older he comes to desire an assembled body that will complement rather than mirror his own. There is a general movement within the narrative from an identification with the male body that is the self writ large to an allegiance to a female body that is the sum of many parts. Saleem's desire has been whetted by his classmate Cyrus Dubash's "lecture on the Parts of a Wooman's Body" (sic), which makes use of a nude statuette belonging to Cyrus's physicist father (262). His desire is realized at the end of the novel, when Mumbadevi has become the "benign presiding influence" above the narrator (92), displacing not just the Kolynos Kid and the Air India Rajah, but also the equestrian statue of Sivaji (93) and "the plaster effigies of the god" Ganesh, hurled into the sea in order to make the monsoon possible (93).

We might expect the two bodies, the male one that is the self writ large and the female one that is the sum of many parts, to complement each other in the vaguely sexual way in which the protuberances at Saleem's temples fit into the hollows on either side of Sonny Ibrahim's head, thereby confirming that "everything is for a reason" (184). It is the accidental bumping and interlocking of the friends' heads in midair that first makes Saleem aware of the voices of the Midnight's Children and of his special relation to the nation to which he is joined "(so to speak) at the hip" (373). In practice, however, instead of complementing each other, the assembly of parts into a single feminine whole threatens the projection of the masculine self onto that same whole.

Saleem's magical allegorical relation to the nation asserts form, but the assembly of parts into a female whole threatens a collapse into chaos. Criticism of *Midnight's Children* has emphasized the magical relation of Saleem to the nation and has underestimated the extent to which the novel relies on metonymy to tell its story and imagine the whole. Body parts litter Saleem's narrative, as they do his world. If he tries to imagine who is calling his mother on the telephone, it is "a finger" that "reaches towards a dial" (159). Pupils in a classroom are so many "hands" flying in the air (225). A crowd of demonstrators are "heads feet bodies" (188).

The novel is a compendium of every English-language idiom referring to the body that Rushdie can think of. Just a sample: Tai tells Aadam Aziz to follow his nose (19); his mother tells him to "see the nose on your face for once" (27); Ahmed Sinai, however, can't "follow his own nose" (73), Dr. Baligga "can't see what's under his nose" (66), and neither can the Delhi magicians (389). Naseem Ghani does not "flaunt her body under the noses of strange men" (24). The Mughal

Emperors, who regarded big noses as a mark of nobility, would have given "their right hands for noses like" Aziz's (15). Padma swallows what Saleem tells her "easily enough" (46), even though, or perhaps because, the story has her "by the throat" (39). Mian Abdullah created the Free Islam convocation "almost single-handedly" (46) with the help of Nadir Khan, his "right-hand man" (50). The East India Company "got its hands on the island" of Bombay in 1668 (93), but in the twentieth century the colonial administration's "old India hands" lost "their stomachs for India" and "washed their hands" of the place, leaving Methwold "holding the baby" (96). Methwold accuses Ahmed Sinai of pulling his leg (109). The newlywed Naseem Aziz does "not turn a hair" at the sight of her husband covered in blood (37). Homi Catrack urges Ahmed Sinai to fight the freezing of his assets "tooth and nail" (134). When Rashid and Nadir Khan come upon each other in the night, they "both turned tail and ran" (50). The city and young Saleem both grow at "breakneck speed" (93, 136); Dr Schaapsteker makes "no bones about" the risks of the medicine he administers (147); the stories of Kalidas Gupta can make "your head spin" and "your ears burn" (240); and Evie and the Brass Monkey give "the thumbs-down" to their suitors (183). Dr Narlikar wants to get the importance of birth control "through people's thick heads" (114). Partition "reared its head" (218); Saleem keeps his head (281); but Mutasim falls "head-over-heels" with Jamila's eyes (311). Saleem takes "to his heels" (32); Aadam Aziz digs "in his heels" (141); and the Pakistani soldiers spend time "cooling our heels" (344) before returning to base "empty-handed" (347, 357). Saleem reflects that "tipped off by a nose, I could have taken to my heels" during the Emergency but also recalls that the last time he fled he "only escaped by the skin of my teeth" (409). Saleem retreats to "the bosom" of his family (377), where Aunt Sonia declares that he has "a cheek" (380) and wants to throw him "out on his ear" (381). When the magicians' slum, "the putrid underbelly" of the city (376), is destroyed, the official version is that "an eyesore was being removed from the face of the capital" (415). As Saleem gets older, he is different parts in turn – a "private eye" (202), a "forked snake's tongue" (254), and an "unseen hand" (284).

Body parts do not just figure in familiar idioms; they also regularly perform or suffer clichéd movements: eyes regularly widen in astonishment (29, 158); teeth are "gritted" (68) and lips are pursed (32, 150), sealed (161, 167), or bitten (237); mouths and jaws are set (99, 428), and throats are cleared (19, 20, 106, 114–5). Policemen and soldiers slap lathis or swagger-sticks against their legs (144, 337).

Mary tears her hair out (147); the Brass Monkey jumps "half-way out of her skin" (152); fear makes "the downy hairs on their arms stand on end" (280); and the sight of beauty brings lumps to throats (94, 355). Psychological burdens press upon backs and shoulders (99, 157, 163). Lies are told "with a straight face" (147) or a "poker-face" (343). In these clichés, body parts appear to follow the dictates of language, which prefers to flow in familiar channels, rather than the wills of the characters to whom they belong. Occasionally the narrative makes such clichéd actions ludicrous by making them literal. When a Sikh's hair stands on end, his turban is pushed off (40). Saleem reports that Aadam Aziz passes a green trunk to his newly married daughter in the train "with his own hands" (66). The pleonasm strikes Saleem as comical, and he repeats variations on it in the same paragraph: Aziz "lifted his daughter (with his own arms)" and "walked (with his own feet) along the platform" (67). Later, at a climactic moment, Saleem "hears, in his ears," his mother call her lover's name and "through ice-blue eyes I see a slip follow the sari" (159–60).

The apparent autonomy of body parts, especially those belonging to women, is further suggested by making them the subjects of absolute phrases. "Lips clamped; eyes squeezed; a single violent No from the head," the new Mrs Aziz refuses to accompany her husband for a walk (35). "Thick of waist, somewhat hairy of forearm," Padma flounces, "her right hand slicing the air updownup in exasperation" (25). Her hand later repeats the slicing gesture (32). When she first met Saleem, she planted herself before him, "arms akimbo, hair glistening with perspiration on the forearms" (440). Amina stands before Ramram Seth the fortune-teller, "her palm slanted outwards towards the advancing palmist, her eyes wide and unblinking as a pomfret's" (86). Parvati-the-witch stands on the steps of Delhi's Friday Mosque, "hands folded calmly over her swollen belly, long rope-of-hair blowing gently in the crystal air" (399). Such absolute phrases suggest a bodily disconnection which in certain circumstances must feel literal: "spine curving, eyes popping," Vanita heaves and strains in the throes of childbirth (113); a drunk Ahmed Sinai sways upstairs, "whisky-bottle in his hand, his eyes rimmed with blood" (274–5), and hungover, comes down to the breakfast table, "his eyes red, his head throbbing" (131). Mouths, in particular, escape the control of the self: Amina's "mouth made fish-motions" (158); the Brass Monkey falls asleep "with her mouth still working silently" (166); Ahmed plays chess with Dr Narlikar, "his tongue (as well as his game) made somewhat loose by djinns" (173); and Dr Narlikar is cast into the ocean, "his mouth opening in a voiceless A" (174).

Not content with the semi-autonomous status they achieve in absolute phrases, body parts acquire minds or at least emotions of their own: the "rage" of Tai's "sweeping hand" dismisses literacy and literature (17); Aziz's sphincter is "astonished" (53); Ahmed's toe is "unaware of its coming doom" (101); Mary's eyes wonder what the government knows (122), and her "conscious or unconscious lips" give Musa a hint of his dismissal (143). People pour their confessions into Amina's "long-suffering" ear (157); during Ramzàn the children are shaken awake "by my mother's assiduous hand" (178); and the Brass Monkey's "furious heels" crush her brother's tin globe (259). Amina's hands "without any conscious instructions," "press down, hard, upon her womb," and her lips mutter "without her knowledge" (112). Aadam Aziz feels "his feet begin slowly, as though encased in boots of lead, to turn" (23). Before she married and became Reverend Mother who could maintain silence for three years in protest, young Naseem's "tongue was getting freer all the time" (29). Her father starts to tell her to mind her tongue but then bites his own when it is clear she has not caused offence (28).

From here it is but a short step to the demand for full sovereignty. Body parts become the subjects of their own sentences, usually with absurd results. Aadam Aziz's "eyes – which were, like the rest of him, twenty-five years old – saw things differently" (12). And "In the garden of Buckingham Villa, my father's big toe strolled (with its nine colleagues) beside and beneath the centre-parting of William Methwold"(101). Saleem finds that his "nose has been playing tricks on" him (164). Sometimes one body part plays the role of another: when they bury an umbilical cord on the site of a future home, the Sinai family are "watched by the eyes of a team of labourers and the beard of a mullah" (300). At other times the one and the many are strangely blurred, as when "the city was poised, with a new myth glinting in the corners of its eyes" (111) or "The workforce giggles behind its hands" (164). The following sentence with its juxtaposition of superabundance and lack, and its ambiguity about who exactly is involved, is typical: "Six hands are waving but Jimmy's ear is in danger of coming off" (225).

Assigned the task of assessing the health of Naseem Ghani from glimpses of parts vouchsafed through the perforated sheet, the first thing that Dr.Aziz asks to see of his new patient is her stomach (24): he will mentally attach the other parts to that. Rarely, however, does Saleem, who faces the similar task of assembling parts into a narrative whole, focus on the torso. The unpleasantly squashy bellies of Nadir Khan, Ahmed Sinai, an Uttar Pradesh landlord (171), and Sanjay Gandhi are not as prominent in the text as they are in profile.

The "swelling balloon" that is Amina's pregnant belly is soon deflated (99). The body parts that figure most in Saleem's narrative are extremities such as feet, hands, or heads, joints such as knees, appendages such as fingers and toes, and protuberances such as ears, and noses. Internal organs are almost completely ignored. Blood receives much attention but only when it pours out of the body.

Saleem's focus on the external and the physical differs from that of other Indian nationalisms, which, as Chatterjee shows, assume the essential India to be "inner" and spiritual in contrast to materialist Europe (Chatterjee 1993, 6). The novel's most prominent image of the internal, the hole left in the centre of Aadam Aziz's body by his loss of religion, reflects an assumption that the inside is indeed more spiritual and closer to the self but also that it has been emptied and the subject must now seek outside itself to fill the vacuum.

The emphasis on the physical and on the partial also betrays the narrative's overweening reliance on sight. If smell is the sense associated with Saleem's magical powers and, in particular, with the literalization of metaphor, the metonymic assembly of physical detail relies primarily on the visual. Saleem the voyeur hides and watches, and the narrative often presents the severely restricted view afforded by a hole in a bedsheet, the crack of a door (254), the wire-netting of a door screen (378), or the cracks of a basket. Saleem has a friend who is called Eyeslice because he has been blinded in the right eye (128) – or is it the left (361)? – but the name could as easily be applied to Saleem himself, whose eye is forever slicing the world. As he watches Evie Burns making advances to his friend Sonny, the split-bamboo slats of the chick-blind, a screen that can be rolled up or down to cover the window, dismember the object of the gaze: "did Evie's hand (sliced lengthways by the chick) not reach out toward my electoral agent? – and weren't those Evie's fingers (the nails bitten down to the quick) touching Sonny's temple-hollows, the fingertips getting covered in dribbled Vaseline?" (183).

Saleem's last name, Rushdie tells us, is pronounced "See-nigh" (Rushdie 1999B, 89), and he often deliberately prefers a restricted focus to the wide-angle panoramic shot. When Evie pushes him out of her way to get a better view of demonstrators in the street below, Saleem focuses on the "Finger, chewed off nail and all," which "jabs down in the direction of the language march" (187). He offers a "Close-up of my grandfather's right hand: nails knuckles fingers all somehow bigger than you'd expect. Clumps of red hair on the outside edges. Thumb and forefinger pressed together, separated only by a thickness of paper. In short: my grandfather was holding a pamphlet" (33). When Saleem is struck by his father, he sees "my father's hand, which stretched out suddenly, thick-fingered, heavy-jointed, strong-as-an-ox, to fetch me a mighty blow on the side of my head" (163). For Rushdie, who left at age fourteen, India is forever the land of childhood, and much of the narrative's magic derives from the child's sense of living in a world of giants.

Just as the "Unblinking pupil" that "takes in upside-down image of sari falling to the floor" reports to the brain which inverts the image to the way it should be (160), so, too, the brain must accept the partial perspectives supplied by the eyes and put them together into a picture of the whole. The reader, too, is invited to "tie up a few loose ends" (52). Saleem runs parts together – "thumb-and-forefinger" (225) and even "thumbandforefinger" (78) – hoping thereby to suggest the essential links between parts: "teeth tongue roofofmouth gums" (167), "chest shoulders arms" (350). The insistence on parts, however, has the opposite effect of suggesting that there is no viable whole to which the parts add up. It would require an acupuncturist to explain how "ears jaw penis" (45) and "knee-joints elbows neck" (408) are related. The often repeated close-up shot of a thumb and forefinger pinching together – Aziz's hand with pamphlet (33), chaprassi-hand holding urchin-ear (33), Aziz's hand with *maulvi*'s ear (43), Amina's hand and her son's ear (161), Emil Zagallo's hand and Saleem's nose (225) – comes to suggest that the disciplinary gesture has an autonomy of its own. So, too, the insistent pointing of fingers, performed by Millais's fisherman, but also by Tai (17), Amina (99), Dr. Narlikar (132), Evie Burns (187), and even by betel juice stains (45) and dead fish (135), may suggest that fingers in Saleem's world are more closely related to each other than to the bodies they belong to.

Saleem compares reality to a cinema screen: seen from a distance, the projection convinces of its reality, but closer up, "the stars' faces dissolve into dancing grain; tiny details assume grotesque proportions" (164). Having seen the many parts from close up, he himself, it would seem, can no longer see the projected whole. What is the whole that can accommodate both the labia-lips of his rival Sanjay Gandhi (can there be a more literal image of the vagina dentata!) and Saleem's Shandean nose? In a story called "Yorick" Rushdie writes of a banquet featuring "boar's heads, sheep's eyes, parson's noses, goose-breasts, calves' livers, tripes, fish-roes, venison haunches, pig's trotters," and imagines that, if the dishes were "assembled into a single edible beast, a stranger monster would lie here than any hippogriff or ichthyocentaur," with "antlers on its giant turkey's head, and hooves set weirdly down beneath its scaly belly and its hairy shanks" (Rushdie 1994, 72–3). If, as we have seen, the nation that is a projection of the self resembles elephant-headed Ganesh, then the nation that results from metonymic assembly is best compared to many-headed Ravana, "multi-limbed Kali" (355), "multi-limbed" Devi (422), or Skanda of the six heads. The crowds filling the streets at independence are a "many-headed monster" (114). The Midnight Children's Conference itself is "manytongued" (160), "a sort of many-headed monster, speaking in the myriad tongues of Babel" (223).

The businessman Mr Kemal dreads what he feels is "the many-headed many-mouthed rapacious monster that is the public, which, if given its heads, would force prices so low in a time of abundance that godfearing entrepreneurs would starve while the monster grew fat" (71). His fear echoes the European Renaissance idea of the mob as a Hydra whose snakelike heads grow again and even multiply when they are cut off. The actual threat to the businessman's property comes not, however, from the public but from the extortion racket called Ravana, "a brilliantly-conceived commercial enterprise" (72). Saleem's mother, who visits Chandni Chowk, the slum behind the Friday Mosque in Delhi, understands that the "terrible monster, a creature with heads and heads and heads," is but the projection of the propertied classes (81). Amina stifles her fear of the masses and of those other monsters she encounters – the "men with broken arms, women with feet twisted backwards at impossible angles" (83) – and tells herself that the poor and the broken represent a "power of some sort, a force which does not know its own strength, which has perhaps decayed into impotence through never having been used" (81–2). Her wisdom is that expressed in V. Shantaram's film *"Do Ankhen Barah Haath"* ("Two Eyes, Twelve Hands"; 1957), about a jailor who tries to rehabilitate a group of six dangerous criminals. The jailor is "slender in body and has a soft voice and a pleasing appearance, while the ex-prisoners fulfill all the stereotypes of 'brutes,' having heavy bodies, bushy eyebrows, unkempt hair, loud voices, and uncouth manners"(Chakravarty 1993, 144–5). They are the twelve "hands" of the film's title who learn to channel their energies by submitting to the moral force represented by the two eyes of the jailor.

It is not excess in the other that terrifies Saleem, who, after all, takes a perverse pride in his own grotesque appearance and in his outsized text which can feel as overfull as Dr Narlikar's apartment taken over by a crowd of women, "their elbows sticking out of the windows and their behinds overflowing on to the verandah" (175). He delights in the comedy of incongruous transplants, like the dream figure of Sindbad Mengal in Rushdie's novel *Shame*: "all joined up in the wrong way, so that the dead man's head was in the middle of his stomach and his feet stuck out, soles upward, like asses' ears from his neck" (Rushdie 1983, 302). Saleem is "a headful of gabbling tongues" (161), but finds himself "tongue-tied in the face of Evie Burns" (182), whom he calls the "Adam's-apple of my eye" (179). Sanjay Gandhi's labia-lips are a confusion not just of sex, like Tai's "woman's lips" (17), but also of bodily orientation (the lower stratum replaces the upper and the vertical becomes horizontal). In this case, the grotesque is also a pleonasm ("labia" are "lips" in Latin). Occasionally, as in David Cronenberg's film *The Fly,* not all the parts that Saleem reassembles are human. The young Saleem who follows his mother to a tryst with her lover is "a pocket-sized sleuth with the nose of a bloodhound and a loud drum pounding in the place where my heart should have been" (211).

No, what frightens Saleem is not excess or incongruity but rather the probable lack that excess can imply. Two related fears in particular possess Saleem: that a part should become autonomous and independent of the whole and that the key part that will bring the whole together should be missing. Saleem's metonyms, unlike his metaphors, tend to remain figurative. At first the autonomy of the many limbs and appendages and their violent gestures of jabbing, striking, and grasping are only a matter of perception and expression: "Wrist smacks against forehead" (25); "Ten-year-old hand is swallowed up by film magnate's fist" (240); and "Index fingers entered ear-holes and seemed to lift Emerald out of her chair" (61). At other times, however, the violence is real enough but the autonomy of the body parts is rhetorical: "Thumb and forefinger closed around the maulvi's ear" (43); "her husband's foot was applied to the divine's fleshy parts" (43); and the hairs of Reverend Mother's moustache are "ripped off by a sharp, violent hand" (266). The monumental battle between Evie Burns and the Brass Monkey is described in terms of cartoon violence: "Shrouded in the dust of the circus-ring they rolled kicked scratched bit, small tufts of hair flew out of the dust-cloud and there were elbows and feet in dirtied white socks and knees and fragments of frock flying out of the cloud" (220). At still other times, however, the metonym expresses a quite literal lack of self-control, and Saleem even refers to himself in the third person: "Saleem's hand is tightening into a fist; the right hand, despite mutilated finger, contemplates violence" (310). Although the novel never goes as far as Gogol, who has a nose leave a face and become a civil servant (Gogol 1957), the metonyms do become increasingly literalized. A seemingly contrite nine-year-old Saleem takes his ayah's injunction literally and washes his mouth out with "the sharp foul lather of Coal Tar Soap" (167). The most striking such literalization of a metonym is the "bodiless hand" (166), picked up from a Parsi Tower of Silence by a vulture and dropped, that delivers a cosmic slap in the face to Ahmed Sinai (90).

William Methwold's power resides in his hair, and more particularly in his centre-parting, a part which parts. When he says goodbye to the Estate that bears his name, Methwold reveals that the hair which has seduced another man's wife is not his own but a wig. The sentence in which the revelation is made suggests that other parts of his body also have an independent existence: "White hand dangled above brilliantined black hair; long tapering white fingers twitched towards centre-parting, and the second and final secret was revealed, because fingers curled, and seized hair; drawing away from his head, they failed to release their prey" (113). This collection of autonomous parts that goes under the name Methwold recalls the "complete gentleman" in Amos Tutuola's *The Palm-Wine Drinkard* who rents body parts from other people to disguise the fact that he is no more than a Skull (Tutuola 1961).

Rushdie's characters, and especially his villains, are, in the words applied to Dickens' grotesques by Dorothy van Ghent, relentlessly "'thinged' into one of their own bodily members or into an article of their clothing or into some inanimate object of which they have made a fetish" (cited at Harter 147, n16). Two of Saleem's childhood friends are known only by the nicknames of Hairoil and Eyeslice. His knees are what make Shiva Shiva. Pakistan's generals constitute a "fabulous array of moustaches, swagger-sticks, gimlet-eyes, medals and shoulder-pips" (279), and when plotting a coup, "Gongs-and-pips assume stern, statesmanlike expressions" (280). Some parts of some bodies, such as the fisherman's finger, Shiva's knees, and the Widow's hand, loom so large that they acquire the force of synecdoches.

The dedication of villainous characters to a single limb or bodily appendage is a sign that something important is absent. Autonomous body parts are to be feared because they lack a rational self and merely obey their natures. The takeover of the characters by a single limb or organ betrays an unswerving single-mindedness on their part. Shiva is an eternal principle (290). There is no reasoning with his knees ("Behind me, as I run, come the pumping knees of my doom" [415]) nor with Indira Gandhi's hand ("the Widow's hand comes hunting hunting the skin is green the nails are black towards the corner hunting hunting while we shrink closer into the corner our skin is green our fear is black and now the Hand comes reaching reaching" [204]). The Widow's Hand is later revealed to be a female lieutenant who executes Indira Gandhi's orders, a literalization which makes possible the unlikely sentence "The Widow's Hand had rolling hips" (424). When Saleem's sister succumbs to "the exaggerations and simplifications of self which are the unavoidable side-effects of stardom," she is reduced to her voice, which she dedicates to the service of religion and nation (304).

Moretti attributes the panoply of grotesque, exaggerated characters in Dickens, who are exactly what they are forever, to a nostalgia for childhood and for a precapitalist world where everyone knows their place: "It is a device that makes us see society like a gigantic Foucaultian *tableau*, where an implacably detailed and yet conspicuous taxonomy confines every individual to his slot for life" (Moretti 1987, 193; italics in original). Vedic Hinduism teaches that caste society was created from the primeval sacrifice and dismemberment of the cosmic giant *Purusha*. As one of the late hymns of the *Rig Veda* puts it, "When they divided the Man, into how many parts did they disperse him? What became of his mouth, what of his arms, what were his two thighs and his two feet called? His mouth was the brahmin, his arms were made into the nobles, his two thighs were the populace, and from his feet the servants were born" (O'Flaherty 1975, 28). In *Midnight's Children*, however, the whole assembled from parts is always at risk of collapsing back into its parts.

While aggressors are identified with a single part that has taken over the whole, their victims are dismembered. At first this, too, is but figurative, as when "bearded" coconuts are "beheaded" (93) or, in a display of sharpshooting skill, Evie Burns shoots "the heads off the kings" in a pack of cards (180), but the dismemberment is soon all too real. The pie-dogs that attack Mian Abdullah's assassins – "some without legs, others lacking hair, but most of them had some teeth at least" – leave a trail of "bones and dung and bits of hair" (48). Wee Willie Winkie tries to cripple his son, for, as beggars know, "you get more if you're all broken up" (216). Ayub Khan's would-be assassin has "his teeth pulled out one by one, [...]his nails set on fire," and "burning cigarette-ends [...] pressed against the tip of his penis" (323). During the Pakistani occupation of Dacca, Shaheed Dar's life is "bisected" when his legs are blown away by a grenade (364), and men "in spectacles with heads like eggs" suffer the fate that the shape of their heads suggests (363). There is no other way to make an omelette, the generals might insist.

In a demonic parody of the whole made up of manifold parts that Aadam Aziz had projected onto the bedsheet more than fifty years before, Saleem comes across a pyramid in an East Bengal battlefield with "six feet and three heads and, in between, a jumbled area composed of bits of torso, scraps of uniforms, lengths of intestine and glimpses of shattered bones" (361), in which he can identify the not-quite-dead remains of his three childhood friends, Eyeslice, Hairoil, and Sonny. Saleem's laconic comment: "Ants were crawling over it, but it was not an anthill" (361).

7

Lack and Desire

In her study of Indian cinema, Sumita Chakravarty observes that "A notable feature of the male-dominated romantic drama of the post-sixties era is that while the identity of the villain is fixed and self-evident, the proof of the hero's heroism is that he can change identities at will, if only temporarily and often playfully" (Chakravarty 1993, 212). In *Midnight's Children*, too, while the villains are grotesque monsters, the protagonist changes character several times. This is, in part, the source of his virtue, in part, an index of his passivity and ineffectuality. Saleem and his family and friends are moral beings and more complex than his enemies, but their psychological integration remains unfulfilled. They therefore seem smaller and weaker than the enemies they encounter, who subordinate everything to the service of a single part.

The "will" with which Shiva is said to espouse his profligate lifestyle (394) refers to his innate predisposition to violence, power, and promiscuity. Ill will, in the novel, is strong because it follows its nature. It does not debate, suffers no doubt, cannot even be said to choose. Good will, on the other hand, is not an innate propensity but involves judging and choosing. People of good will in Saleem's world must make choices and, as often as not, make the wrong ones. Worse, they waver and backtrack. Because they are free agents, it is possible for them to change their minds, to be of two minds. Ahmed Sinai can do what Shiva never can, that is, change: late in life the lonely philandering speculator discovers his love for his wife. But his freedom is also a measure of his weakness: he cannot follow his nose, and his career is a series of wrong turnings. Saleem admires Mian Abdullah and Picture Singh for their power "to shape the future by the sheer force" of their wills (386). He feels Padma, who wants to marry him, may be able to alter the ending of his story "by the phenomenal force of her will" (428), and he proclaims that his son's generation, unlike his own, will not look "for their fate in prophecy or the stars" but forge "it in the implacable furnaces of their wills" (431). Mian Abdullah, Picture Singh, and Padma, however, all fail to realise their dreams. Because they are free to act, they can make mistakes. Because they respect the freedom of others to choose, their capacity to realize their intentions is limited. Saleem applauds the "singleness of purpose" of his uncle Hanif who, when he plays rummy, never lays down "a hand" unless it is all hearts: "Always hearts; all the hearts, and nothing but the hearts" (240). This is a kinder, gentler version of the dedication to a single organ characteristic of Shiva or Indira Gandhi. Hanif's hearts are, however, nowhere near as effective as the villains' knees or hand: he loses at cards as he does at love. Eventually he commits suicide.

The villains in the novel are ruled by a single part, which is a mark of their strength but also of a dangerously self-sufficient partiality. The good guys, on the other hand, are doomed to remain incomplete. Aadam Aziz has a hole in the centre, and his mother tells him he always was "heartless" (23); Nadir Khan is "the spineless one" (48); Ahmed Sinai, he "of the jutting lip and squashy belly" (113), wants a sense of direction (73). Others also have imperfect bodies. Many, like Tai the boatman (16), Aadam Aziz (267), Tai Bibi (309), Resham Bibi (375), and even Mary Pereira (442), are conspicuously missing teeth and unable to obey the Kolynos Kid's injunction to "Keep Teeth Kleen and Keep Teeth Brite" (234). The general opinion of old Tai is that his "brain fell out with his teeth" (16). Saleem never gets his wisdom teeth (154). Most of Saleem's family and friends have parts that elude their full control. Amina's cheeks regularly betray her: in spite of her blackness, "the fever of a reckless scheme flushed her cheeks" (139), and "politics and emotions" turn them scarlet (212). Disbelief provokes a tic in Padma's cheek (263); excitement in the presence of power does the same to Emerald (279). Parvati's lips assume a pout that "neither muscles nor wizardry" can remove from her features (389).

We can express this perceived lack of control another way: while the villains are unself-conscious, the good guys, by contrast, suffer from a debilitating self-consciousness. When Roshanara Shetty pours her poison into Shiva's ears – she whispers to him that the women who fall "into his arms" (395) are laughing "behind his back" (396) – the war hero suddenly learns to think of himself in terms of how others perceive him. At age thirty he begins to acquire some of the condition that drove Saleem to the washing-chest at age ten. Symptomatic of this condition is a clumsiness expressed in constructions in which he appears uncharacteristically passive: "food flew off his plate on to priceless Kelim rugs and belches broke from his throat with the roar of a train emerging from a tunnel" (396). Self-consciousness is not a gain but a lack. Shiva's knees are no longer for crushing but for kneeling (396). It is from this time on that Shiva becomes susceptible to control by Parvati.

What consciousness is *conscious of* is a lack of full control. When Saleem is born and before he has acquired a self, his eyes remain preternaturally open. Calasso, in his meditation on Hindu mythology, explains, "Only what is conscious blinks, only what is inhabited by a mind" (Calasso 1999, 400). In order to see if he is really keeping his eyes open or is merely blinking at the same moment as they do, Amina the new mother and Mary the new ayah keep careful watch, their "eyelids opening-and-closing alternately" (125). By force of effort they assert control over a sign of consciousness that is so natural as to be unconscious. Eventually Amina takes "matters into her own hands" and closes her son's lids for him (125). Then she and Mary take it in turns to open and close his eyes. Unlike the immortals, Saleem learns to blink, and with that knowledge enters the world of time: "anything that blinks dies," says Calasso (Calasso 1999, 43); "nobody can face the world with his eyes open all the time" concludes Saleem (125).

Long before the threat of violent amputation is realized in the Widows' Hostel, Saleem has felt he is missing something. The moment when he and the other Midnight's Children have their testicles and wombs excised during Indira Gandhi's State of Emergency is but the fulfilment of a series of castrations he has suffered since childhood. His earliest memory is of his circumcision at the age of two months: he swears he can still remember "the grinning barber, who held me by the foreskin while my member waggled frantically like a slithering snake; and the razor descending, and the pain" (126). He begins his narrative at a moment before he was even born, with an account of how his grandfather lost his faith and was left with "a vacancy in a vital inner chamber" (12). In the beginning was the wound. Calasso explains, "As long as there is only mind, intention is action. But, as soon as there is something outside mind, Time slips in between intention and act. And then one escapes forever from the mental universe through a breach that is still open, like an open wound, in Prajāpati's groin" (Calasso, 45).

In Saleem's case, the original wound of the first progenitor (Prajāpati) is a hole created by the loss of faith. When Aadam Aziz, returned from abroad, makes an effort to pray, "his hands, guided by old memories, fluttered upwards, thumbs pressed to ears, fingers spread, as he sank to his knees" (13). The autonomy of the body parts in this description suggests a dangerous automatism. The kneeling scene is twice more repeated, each time at a moment of death, as the hole in the body precedes the genuflection. When Ayooba Baloch, a Pakistani soldier in the Bangladesh War, shoots a man, "slowly slowly the arms of a peasant rise up as though in prayer; knees kneel in paddy-water, a face plunges below the water-level to touch its forehead to the earth" (348). The scene is presented with an emphasis on distinct parts and in the present tense, the narrative equivalent of slow motion. Later, when Ayooba's fellow soldier Farooq Rashid is shot, death again is described in terms of prayer: "somebody drops to his knees; somebody's forehead touches the ground as if in prayer" (360–1). If death looks like prayer, it is because religion, in its loss of self, is like death. The integrity of the self demands that Aziz reassert his control over the parts of his body. Of course, when Aziz resolves "never again to kiss earth for any god or man" (12), he is left with a hole. To have a self is paradoxically to be missing something.

Saleem who fears unmeaning more than anything else remembers a self that has always been shadowed by the threat of unmeaning. The self is a function of the fear of losing that self. Butler explains that "Castration could not be feared if the phallus were not already detachable, already elsewhere, already dispossessed; it is not simply the spectre that it will become lost that constitutes the obsessive preoccupation of castration anxiety. *It is the spectre of the recognition that it was always already lost, the vanquishing of the fantasy that it might ever have been possessed – the loss of nostalgia's referent*" (Butler 1993, 101; italics in original). Saleem eventually loses the tip of his finger, his special powers, and even his memory. The climactic loss of self that is Saleem's mutilation at the hands of Indira Gandhi was foreshadowed long before she came to power. Just because they are after you does not mean you are not paranoid.

The ancient seer Yājñavalkya once said that man was composed of himself and a void: "Hence that void is filled by woman" (Calasso 1999, 187). Aadam Aziz's own hole leaves "him vulnerable to women and history" (12). After losing his faith, he promptly falls in love with Naseem Ghani, whom he perceives in parts through a hole in the bedsheet. Sexual desire, however, is potentially even more of a threat to the self than religion. Aadam Aziz's feelings of love for Landlord Ghani's daughter soon acquire "a life of their own" (27). Desire, which seeks to fill a void, actually foments the autonomy of body parts and fosters a sense of lack. *Midnight's Children* is filled with examples of private parts asserting their independence from the self under the incitement of sexual desire, examples that are always suitably comic. Mian Abdullah, the Hummingbird, is able with his constant hum to set teeth on edge and induce erections: his unfortunate secretary, Nadir Khan, suffers in consequence: "ears jaw penis were forever behaving according to the dictates of the Hummingbird" (46). Amina Sinai can wheedle money from her husband by stroking him with caresses and sweet words until "something moved in his pajamas" (70). When Methwold's hair seduces Vanita, Saleem's biological mother, she "found herself approaching him, fingers outstretched, felt fingers touching hair; found centre-parting; and began to rumple it up" (107).

Saleem recounts his own adolescent discovery of sexuality in the third person and present tense. The young voyeur "finds his eye looking through a chink in dirty washing" (190); his mother's "son's right eye peers out through the wooden slats" (190–1); and he cannot close it: "Unblinking pupil takes in upside-down image of sari falling to the floor" (191). When a distraught Aunt Pia later invites the ten-year-old Saleem to her bed to console her, "a hand flutters at her heart; her chest heaves… Tragedienne's arms, flying outwards towards me… …The arms close around me, tightertighter, nails digging through my school-white shirt… hips pushing up towards me" (243). Saleem finds himself "in the grip of a strength greater than my strength" for "something has started twitching below my S-buckled belt" (243). Saleem tries to keep his mutilated hand free of the action, but gets carried away with excitement: "I have forgotten my finger, and when it touches her breast, wound presses against skin…" (243). His cry of pain breaks the spell, and Pia delivers a resounding slap to his "left cheek" (244).

The rebellion of private parts is comic – Mary Pereira jokes about baby Saleem that "His thing has a life of its own!" (126) – but the threat to the self is real enough. Sexual ecstasy threatens the obliteration of the self in the jungle of the Sundarbans, where Saleem and three companions, who have abandoned their assigned duties as soldiers in the Pakistani army, meet four girls without names or selves. The sexual ecstasy here is inseparable from the sinister religious variety: the four girls provide a foretaste of the perfumed gardens where Muslim men who are faithful will be rewarded with "four beauteous houris" and women with "four equally virile males" (329). When the lovers come together "eight eyes stared into eight, saris were unwound and placed, neatly folded, on the ground; after which the naked and identical daughters of the forest came to them, eight arms were twined with eight, eight legs were linked with eight legs more" (355). The multiple linked bodies that meet "below the statue of multi-limbed Kali" are best understood as forming a single body (355). Unlike Mumbadevi, however, the goddess who benignly presides over the pickle factory, this multi-limbed deity is to be feared. To count the eyes and legs of several people together is to ignore and dispose of the integrity of the individual self. Saleem and his companions discover to their horror that the houris are succubi or apsaras to whom they are losing their selves.

The distinction between the merger with an other that completes the self, such as Aadam Aziz seeks, and the merger with an other that obliterates the self, such as the soldiers find in the Sundarbans, is the distinction between love and sex. Sex in Saleem's world poses a danger to the integrity of the self. Love, on the other hand, both preserves the self and completes it. Nadir, like Aadam Aziz, first falls in love with a body part he glimpses beneath a veil, "an ankle that seems to glow with graciousness" (61). Then "he finds his eyes straying upwards, up along delicate sandals and baggy pajamas and past loose kurta and above the dupatta, the cloth of modesty, until eyes met eyes, and then" (61). Whereas sexual desire in the novel is voyeuristic – it involves seeing and not being seen – genuine love involves the meeting of eyes. Love, however, would seem to preclude physical union. The novel's most significant image of true and abiding love is unconsummated: Nadir and Mumtaz Aziz (later Amina) provide the novel's one example of a happy marriage, even though, after two years, she remains a virgin.

The marriage of Amina and Nadir is not allowed to survive. Their divorce not only drives them asunder but results in a split in Amina's own self. When, years later, having remarried and become a mother, she arranges a secret tryst with her first husband, her son spies on the lovers through a dirty window and describes their behaviour as an intricate series of hand gestures reminiscent of bharatanatyam, except that in this case the right hand pretends not to know what the leftover hands are doing: "But now hands enter the frame – first the hands of Nadir-Qasim, their poetic softness somewhat callused these days; hands flickering like candleflames, creeping forward across reccine, then jerking back; next a woman's hands, black as jet, inching forwards like elegant spiders; hands lifting up, off reccine tabletop, hands hovering above three fives, beginning the strangest of dances, rising, falling, circling one another, weaving in and out between each other, hands longing for touch, hands outstretching tensing quivering demanding to be – but always at last jerking back, fingertips avoiding fingertips" (212). Saleem also reports that "there are feet beneath the table and faces above it, feet advancing towards feet, faces tumbling softly towards faces" (213), which makes it sound as if there were more than two bodies present and no selves at all. The figurative autonomy of Amina and Nadir's hands at the Pioneer Café suggests not the obliteration of the self, as in sexual ecstasy, but the mutual withholding of two selves, each painfully aware of incompleteness but unable to risk surrender.

Sexual desire operates by the metonymic assembly of dispersed parts. That is how Aadam Aziz falls for Naseem Ghani and later how Amina learns to love her new husband: "Each day she selected one fragment of Ahmed Sinai, and concentrated her entire being upon it until it became wholly familiar; until she felt fondness rising up within her and becoming affection and, finally, love" (68). The assembly of parts is inevitably accompanied, however, by the threat of disintegration: disintegration of both the self and the object of desire. Before leading the young doctor to his patient, Ghani shows him a picture of Diana the Huntress who, to punish him for glimpsing her nakedness, transformed Actaeon into a stag (19). Actaeon was then torn to pieces by his own hounds. Aziz, however, ignores the warning, as Ghani knew he would, and his marriage to Naseem Ghani is unhappy. Amina, "try as she might," finds there is one part of Ahmed Sinai she cannot learn to love "although it was the one thing he possessed, in full working order, which Nadir Khan had certainly lacked" (90). The adult Saleem comes close to falling in love with a list of Parvati's features, "Saucer-eye, rope-like pony-tail, fine full red lips," but "the face, the sick decaying eyes nose lips" of his sister Jamila Singer, with whom he had previously been in love, get in the way (387). Everywhere he looks Saleem sees the "horribly eroded physiognomy" of Jamila (409), like the suppurating face of Émile Zola's Nana, symbolic of the rot at the heart of the French nation at the onset of the Franco-Prussian War (Zola 2001).

The rotting body, no less than the idealized body, reflects something within the observer, a fundamental incompleteness. Just as Aziz projects his desire onto the bedsheet, the decaying and mutilated face that comes between Parvati and Saleem is actually a narcissistic projection of the latter's feelings of guilt: the "rancid flowers of incest blossomed on my sister's phantasmal features" (383). Other lovers are also haunted by images of disintegration, notably the virginal Mary Pereira to whom the ghost of the man she loved, Joseph D'Costa, appears in a state of advanced decomposition: "bits of it were missing: an ear, several toes on each foot, most of its teeth; and there was a hole in its stomach larger than an egg" (246). Joseph tells Mary that the decomposition his body suffers is punishment for her crime of switching the babies (246). The "occult leprosy of guilt" which has Joseph in its grip (383) links him to the leper Musa who has also lost "fingers and toes" (272). When Aadam Aziz sees Musa, "holes in hands, perforations in the feet," he imagines he sees Jesus Christ, complete with stigmata, come to charge him with "culpability in the affair" of his son Hanif's suicide (268). The other in whom the self seeks a mirror of his own wholeness instead reflects his sense of his own incompleteness.

The grotesque disorder that threatens the body from without is already within: "O eternal opposition of inside and outside! Because a human being, inside himself, is anything but a whole, anything but homogeneous; all kinds of everywhichthing are jumbled up inside him, and he is one person one minute and another the next. The body, on the other hand, is homogeneous as anything. Indivisible, a one-piece suit, a sacred temple, if you will. It is important to preserve this wholeness. ... Uncork the body, and God knows what you permit to come tumbling out" (230–1). The phrase "The body, on the other hand" in the above passage, so typical of Saleem's narration, confuses the relations of whole and part by putting them side by side. The discrepancy in scale between the rhetoric and what has actually occurred at this point in the narrative (Saleem has lost a bit of his finger in a door) makes for comedy. The violence in *Midnight's Children,* as in all Rushdie's fiction, is always as much farce as horror. Farce, however, as John Carey points out, "is only nightmare of which we are no longer afraid" (Carey 1973, 97). Saleem's fear that the absence of a key part spells the dissolution of the whole is broadly drawn but nonetheless real.

The finger whose loss threatens Saleem's self is a fetish, what Lacan would call the phallus. The finger is arguably a displacement for another organ, but the phallus, the emblem of the self and guarantee of its wholeness, is not necessarily to be identified with the penis, as is made clear by Saleem's experience in the Pakistani army when he is reduced to a tracking dog. There his virile organ performs as never before but he has lost his memory, his name, and his very self. A finger, a nose, or a navel-string can perform the role of phallus and anchor the self as well or better than the penis does. For instance, William Methwold's power resided, "Samson-like," in his hair (113). Saleem revels in all that is excessive about his nose. His grotesqueness is what he has in common with the fabulous world of India, and, at the same time, what distinguishes him from his fellows. He says with pride, "if one wishes to remain an individual in the midst of the teeming multitudes, one must make oneself grotesque" (108).

The navel string that once linked Saleem to his mother and that is preserved intact in a pickle-jar is potentially another phallus. It is accorded the same respect as that given to the person and more:

"While the newly-hired ayah, Mary Pereira, made her way to Methwold's Estate by bus, an umbilical cord travelled in state in the glove compartment of a film magnate's Studey" (123). As Saleem changes, grows bigger, acquires powers and loses them, his body bears the scars of his forced accommodation to the world: his damaged ear, his missing hair, his cut finger, and worse. His umbilical cord, however, remains "unchanging in bottled brine, at the back of a teak almirah" (123), a reminder of an identity prior to consciousness that survives the horror of experience. The cord is eventually buried in Karachi on the site where the Sinais intend to build a home, thus providing a link between blood, earth, and self. Through everything the cord remains intact, mystically connecting the person to the soil and giving birth to a house that, like the one sought by Naipaul's Mr Biswas, is intended to accommodate and express the self.

Saleem's umbilical cord is repeatedly introduced in answer to a question. At the beginning of Book Two the cord is "What was sealed beneath rubber, preserved in glass, concealed in manila" (123). At the end of Book Two, it is "What, pickled in brine, sat for sixteen years in my father's almirah, awaiting just such a day? What, floating like a water-snake in an old pickle-jar, accompanied us on our sea-journey and ended up buried in hard, barren Karachi-earth? What had once nourished life in a womb – what now infused earth with miraculous life, and gave birth to a split-level, American-style modern bungalow?" (300). The cord is not, however, a final answer. There are always more questions: in particular, as to whether "what-was-left-inside" the jar is actually Saleem's or Shiva's (300; 123). If the cord represents the self, it is the wrong self, the Pakistani self: "buried like an umbilical cord in every Pakistani heart" is "the fear of schizophrenia, of splitting" (341). Saleem says, "The city of Karachi proved my point; clearly constructed on top of entirely unsuitable cords, it was full of deformed houses, the stunted hunchback children of deficient lifelines" (300). The house that the Sinais build on Korangi Road in Karachi is fated, like Mr Biswas's, to be unfinished: "although the foundations were dug very deep, they would not prevent the house from falling down before we ever lived in it" (300).

The truth of the phallus is that it is always lost. Saleem and Rushdie regularly mock other people's fetishized obsession with missing parts. The theft of the hair of the Prophet from the Hazratbal Mosque in Srinigar (269) and the toe bitten off the mummified corpse of St Francis Xavier in Goa (273) generate great excitement. Uncle Puffs' mouth is filled with gold teeth – "I keep my cash where it's safe" (302), he explains – just as Tai the boatman is supposed to keep a hoard of gold teeth (16). The self, however, is not a commodity nor the body a "safe-deposit box" (307). Uncle Puffs goes toothless when the war effort demands that citizens contribute their gold.

Saleem defines consciousness as "the awareness of oneself as a homogeneous entity in time, a blend of past and present, ... the glue of personality, holding together our then and our now" (341) and as a "white dot" that, "like a wild flea," jumps about within the "pell-mell tumble of a brain, in which everything ran into everything else" (210). The self does not, however, actually hold anything together. Instead it is generated by its obsession with the single physical emblem that would guarantee integrity and completeness had it not just gone missing. When Saleem the amnesiac recovers his memory and reclaims everything, "all of it, all lost histories, all the myriad complex processes that go to make a man" (353), what he actually remembers are absent parts, "monk's tonsure, finger-loss, one-bad-ear, and the numbing, braining spittoon," or deformed ones, "cucumber-nose, stain-face, bandy legs, horn-temples" (358). Which part acts as a fetish to anchor the self depends on which part is absent and therefore a focus for anxiety. With headmaster Crusoe, Saleem is forever crying, "And the bit, has anybody got the *bit*?" (229).

At the end of Book Two Saleem suffers amnesia and literally loses name and self. Although the memory is gone and the body of the amnesiac seems but an empty shell, the self must be imagined as somehow persisting since it is, in principle and in Saleem's case, recoverable. So where is it located during its absence? The externalized emblem of this self, lost yet not dead, is the silver spittoon that Saleem carries around with him, the only link "connecting me to my more tangible, historically-verifiable past" (417). He is "Spittoon-brained" in both possible senses of that term (335): in falling and hitting him on the head, the spittoon has robbed him of his memory and has replaced his brain. It is both what gave him his "war wound" and compensation for it (339). The spittoon is a "talisman" (415), just as the perforated sheet is (11), the equivalent of the token of identity carried around by the hero or heroine of a romance. Saleem carries "it everywhere like a love-token" (339). The spittoon, "catching the light of the moon" and "silver as moonlight," is also "a piece of the moon" (332), the nickname given Saleem by his mother. Saleem apostrophizes the spittoon, which has been in the family since before he was born, thus: "Elegant in the salon of the Rani of Cooch Naheen, it permitted intellectuals to practise the art-forms of the masses; gleaming in a cellar, it transformed Nadir Khan's underworld into a second Taj Mahal; gathering dust in an old tin trunk, it was nevertheless present throughout my history, covertly assimilating incidents in washing-chests, ghost-visions, freeze-unfreeze, drainage, exiles; falling from the sky like a piece of the moon, it perpetrated a transformation. O talismanic spittoon! O beauteous lost receptacle of memories as well as spittle-juice! What sensitive person could fail to sympathize with me in my nostalgic agony at its loss?" (432). It drives Saleem wild when people try to get his spittoon away from him (338). The spittoon allows Nadir Khan who appears in a dream to recognize Saleem as Mumtaz's little boy (413). And, like a golden bough that allows him to return from the underworld, it again saves Saleem when he enters Parvati's basket of invisibility and almost loses his hold on the world of the living (369).

The spittoon is the phallus, the site where the self and its authority are securely located. Deshmukh, the corpse-robber, offers a radio "almost working order" for the spittoon (360), radios being the standard exchange item offered for phalluses in Rushdie's India (Deshmukh's name, which means "a district head" in Hindi-Urdu and sounds like the Yiddish-derived slang "the Schmuck," is a cleverer and more appropriate interlinguistic pun than the "buddha"). The spittoon is the phallus but does not represent the penis. On the contrary, the spitting contest called hit-the-spittoon, which Nadir Khan and his wife Mumtaz play in their underground lovenest, suggests that it represents the vagina. The spittoon originally belonged to the Rani of Cooch Naheen, whose name means "princess of nothing" and whose home Aadam Aziz frequents when his marriage has soured (41). The Rani used to invite her fellow members of the Free Islam Convocation to her home to play: "I have a superb silver spittoon, inlaid with lapis lazuli, and you must all come and practice. Let the walls be splashed with our inaccurate expectorating! They will be honest stains, at least" (45). The Rani gives the spittoon to Mumtaz Aziz and Nadir Khan as a wedding gift, and they enjoy playing with it. He is, however, unable to hit the spittoon. The phallic spittoon that Saleem carries around therefore actually represents feminine virginity.

Northrop Frye explains the obsession with virgin-baiting in romance as follows: "Apart from the idealizing of the pre-sexual state, there is a sense in which virginity is an appropriate image for attaining original identity: what is objectively untouched symbolizes what is subjectively contained, so to speak" (Frye 1976, 153). The spittoon represents an original identity that must be preserved. It may seem strange to put Saleem in the company of the Nawab of Kif's daughter, who resolves "never to reach puberty" so that she does not have to consummate her marriage to the bed-wetting Zafar (315), and of Jamila Singer, who hates the very thought of love and eventually enters a convent, but it is fitting nonetheless. At the end of the novel Saleem returns to a pre-sexual state, explicitly feminized and inseparable from his post-sexual condition. Saleem is able to do what is denied most young men: return to the care of his beloved ayah. When his son is born, Saleem giggles "like a schoolgirl," and Picture Singh is scandalized to see him "tittering hysterically" (405). His son's nurse offers to let Saleem suckle alongside his son: "and afterwards maybe you"ll start thinking straight again" (430). When eventually Padma proposes marriage, Saleem protests "like a blushing virgin" (428).

Saleem's virginity, unlike his sister's, is one that is forever being lost. As Sara Suleri writes, "the eros of the nation cannot but represent, for the subcontinental psyche, a somewhat titillating induction into the idiom of perpetual separations, or the perpetual repetition of loss" (Suleri 1992, 194). Saleem loses his innocence at least as often as his manhood. Twice bitten by snakes, Saleem finds "the cobra which lay coiled within myself" (251). When he discovers the sexual nefariousness of adults he declares that childhood is "murdered" (250). The nurse who prepares him for the drainage of his sinuses and the loss of his special powers tells him not to be "a baby" (294). When he and his three soldier companions become involved in the wanton rape and murder that characterized the Pakistani takeover of the East Wing, once again "Innocence had been lost" (347). Innocence, it would seem, like religious faith or like Rushdie's own relationship with "the East" (Rushdie 1983, 23), is forever being lost because loss is what gives it its meaning. The "badge of sexual innocence" is always worn "fraudulently" (237). The narrator in *The Tin Drum* says something similar of himself: "Oskar lost his innocence more than once and recovered it or waited for it to grow again; for innocence is comparable to a luxuriant weed" (Grass 1962, 490–1).

What is most striking about Saleem's many returns, first to India, then to Bombay, and finally to his ayah, is how much they each involve a recovery of innocence. A spittoon can, it seems, always be knocked "back into shape" (63). While Pakistan is the land of perversion, where each perversion – promiscuity, prostitution, incest, bestiality, and succubism – is a degree closer to narcissism, we should remember that Saleem never has sex of any kind in India. Precisely because his memory and self are restored to him, his desire for Jamila Singer continues to stand in the way of his ever achieving sexual union with his wife Parvati. And the novel ends before he is married to Padma. The next chapter will examine Saleem's desexualization, at once feared and strangely desired.

8

Women

Saleem's relations to women are every bit as disastrous as his grandfather's. The Widow, Indira Gandhi, and her lieutenant, the Widow's Hand, who performs the sterilizing operations on the children of Midnight, are but the culmination of a series of women who threaten Saleem with the loss of his manhood: Evie Burns pushes him and the bicycle he has learned to ride in order to impress her down a hill and into a crowd of language marchers; Jamila Singer disowns him and consigns him to the demeaning role of a tracking dog in the Pakistani army; and houris in the Sundarbans threaten to sap him of his life. "Women have made me; and also unmade," Saleem tells Padma (391).

Saleem has reason to fear his "too-many women" (392). In *Midnight's Children* women destroy, men are destroyed. The novel is filled with descriptions of the violent deaths of men. It is no exaggeration to say that every male character either dies violently – Dr Narlikar, Uncle Zulfikar, Homi Catrack, Hanif Aziz, Ayooba Baloch, Farooq Rashid, Shaheed Dar, Hairoil and Eyeslice Sabarmati, Sonny Ibrahim – or like Dr. Schaapsteker, Aadam Aziz, Ahmed Sinai, and Picture Singh, is reduced to an empty shell of himself as a prelude to physical destruction. On the other hand, a woman who is shot, like Lila Sabarmati, will survive. Women who are murdered, like the prostitutes who are strangled, probably by Shiva, die offstage as it were: Saleem only reads about them. It is strongly hinted that he has invented them in order to slander Shiva. The women raped by Pakistani soldiers in Bangladesh are not only officially denied but left anonymous in Saleem's text as well. Amina, Zohra, Pia, Reverend Mother, Alia, and Emerald all die in bombing raids during the 1965 Indo-Pakistani War, along with Zafar, the Nawab of Kif, Major Alauddin Latif, Ahmed Sinai, and Mutasim the Handsome, but the bombs are so sudden and noiseless that they register more as narrative conveniences than as images of horror. Parvati disappears in the vicious slum clearance led by Sanjay Gandhi, but Saleem is more concerned about the loss of his spittoon. None of the deaths of women compare in intensity to those of Shaheed Dar, whose legs are blown off and who is eaten by ants, and of Dr Narlikar, pushed into the sea as he clings to one of his tetrapods.

Sexual humiliation is as common a fate of men as violent death: witness Aadam Aziz, Commander Sabarmati, Hanif Aziz, Ahmed Sinai, cousin Zafar, and even Shiva, who comes to believe that the middle-class women he sleeps with are all laughing at him. A woman who is sexually humiliated may cause a great scene, like Aunt Pia, or exact revenge, like Alia, or retreat into motherhood, like Amina Sinai and Mary Pereira, but she will survive, whereas the men who humiliate women suffer violent deaths, like Homi Catrack, Joseph D'Costa, and even, Saleem imagines, Shiva. The misogynists Dr Narlikar and Dr Aziz both die violently after rebuking lingam-worshipping women (174, 270).

Saleem, it would seem, has every reason to fear and mistrust women, yet he is never happier than when in their company. In the pickle factory, where he is writing his memoirs, the workers are all women. The owner, none other than his former ayah, the virginal Mary Pereira, hates "the mens" since her betrayal by Joseph D'Costa and admits no males except Saleem and his baby son "into her new, comfortable universe" (443). Here Saleem can count on Padma's undivided attention. For Saleem this represents a return to the happy period of infancy when two doting mothers competed in spoiling him. The fear that women inspire in Saleem can, it seems, be relieved by eliminating the presence of men.

We cannot escape the conclusion that what Saleem fears is not women so much as being male in a world divided along gender lines. From childhood Saleem is surrounded by women and confused about the extent to which he belongs among them. He senses that the attention lavished on him by his mother and ayah has to do with his maleness. His "two-headed mother" (124) makes much of his circumcised penis (126). The same maleness that the maternal figures appreciate, however, will require Saleem to leave their company. His Aunt Pia pushes the adolescent Saleem out of her bed when her maternal closeness arouses a sexual response from him.

Saleem wants to stay among women but cannot risk being mistaken for a woman. Amina and Mary dress him up in a frilly collar and tunic like Walter Raleigh in the picture, but he feels mortified when Lila Sabarmati exclaims, "Look, how *chweet*!" (122). At a school dance Glandy Keith Colaco and Fat Perce Fishwala insult Saleem in the presence of Masha Miovic, the "champion breast-stroker" (227). In a "budding spirit of sexual mischief," she challenges Saleem, "*What are you? a man or a mouse?*" and Saleem responds by kneeing both his classmates in the groin and decking them (228). When, however, they pick themselves up and pursue him, Saleem abandons "all pretence of manhood" and flees (228). The result of the chase is an accident with a closing door in which Saleem loses a finger. Saleem had agreed "hands off" when he was trying to convince Masha to come outside with him (228), but this is not what he had intended.

As Sudhir Kakar reminds us, if we need such reminding, "a cut on a finger ... has behind it the 'primitive' idea of being a woman" (Kakar 1990, 130). If not a man, measured in the competition with other men for the attentions of women, the boy risks being reduced to the abject position of a woman. Butler explains that the undesirable, subordinate position of women is inevitably figured in the imagination of men as their own castration, their loss of the emblem of authority and integrity. What has already happened to women is always almost about to happen to men (Butler 1993, 205). "Woman," exclaims Bilquis's father in *Shame,* who is himself known as Mahmoud the Woman, "Was there ever such a broad-backed and also such a dirty word?" (Rushdie 1983, 62–3).

Masha Miovic does not ask Saleem if he is a man or a woman, but if he is a man or a mouse. Naseem Ghani had asked her fiancé exactly the same question (29), and later, as Reverend Mother, she proclaims that "women must marry men," "Not mice" or a "worm" (62). The boy must display masculinity just to be acknowledged as human. Posted as a guard in the Rann of Kutch, where the border posts between India and Pakistan have deliberately been left "unmanned" to facilitate smuggling (325), Saleem's "cocky cousin" Zafar (266) wets himself in fear. The pun involved when the young man who "mans" the border posts shames himself suggests that to be "unmanned," in the sense of failing in virility, is to leave an empty space, to have no one at the helm.

In India, Saleem lives among women. As long as he remains a small boy, he is safe among them and he wants to return to that safety. But a crisis occurs that can be variously dated by the onset of puberty and the donning of long trousers, by his fatal intervention in the adulterous affair of Lila Sabarmati and Homi Catrack, or by the operation to cure him of his Sinai-sitis, inflicted by his parents who feel that the running nose and perpetual sniffing of the child can no longer be tolerated. This crisis precipitates his departure for Pakistan, where his voice deepens and he starts shaving. His experience of

Pakistan is of a world of men, especially of soldiers, whose narcissism excludes women and who challenge each other to displays of virility. Saleem allies himself with military generals and their violent plans for a coup, and later he forms part of a tyrannical army of occupation in East Pakistan.

The Karachi to which Saleem moves with his family is a version of Nighttown, replete with prostitutes and secret incest. In Rushdie's *Shame* Karachi is "the great whore-city" (Rushdie 1983, 157). There Saleem takes on something of the role that his changeling alter ego Shiva performs in India. There is nothing attractive about the sex in Karachi; all bodies seem tainted by the city's own "misshapen lumpiness of a gigantic dwarf" (299). At the same time, the sexlessness which characterizes Saleem in India becomes in Pakistan the property of his cousin Zafar, the bedwetter, whose rightful place in his father's affections Saleem usurps. The Pakistani generals who gather around Uncle Zulfikar's table in Rawalpindi extend an invitation to Saleem and Zafar to stay among them after the women have left and to join in plotting a coup. General Ayub Khan, the coup-leader, says, "The little men should stay. It is their future, after all" (280). The coup is the boys' future because it will determine the fate of the country, but also because it provides a model of masculinity to which the boys will have to conform. The challenge is too much for Zafar, who wets his pants and is dismissed from the room by his father, crying, "Pimp! Woman! [...] Coward! Homosexual! Hindu!" (281). On that occasion at least Saleem, anxious to show his worthiness as a son, is able to prove he belongs.

As the scene around the dinner table suggests, to be a man among men is to participate in a hearty camaraderie. But the manhood shared with some also presumes a competition in which others, the losers, suffer a sexualized humiliation. When the coup leaders depose Iskander Mirza as President of Pakistan, he is bundled naked out of bed, "gun-barrel pushed between the cheeks of an overfed rump" (282). A similar fate is later meted out to the Bangladeshi leader Sheikh Mujib, who is arrested and conducted to the airport, "where Ayooba stuck a pistol into his rump" (346). To be a man among men, you must prove you are more of a man than other men. Farooq Rashid the soldier is worried that, when he and his comrades return to base with long "woman's hair" after their sojourn in the Sundarbans, they will be put up against the wall and killed dead (357).

Homosocial camaraderie makes it possible for Tiger Niazi and Sam Manekshaw, the Pakistani and Indian generals who came through the British Army together, to be reconciled immediately after fighting a war with each other:

> "I say, Tiger," Sam Manekshaw said, "You behaved jolly decently by surrendering."
> And the Tiger, "Sam, you fought one hell of a war." (367)

The reunion of these mates who call each other "old boy" and "old man" (367) has come at the cost of millions of deaths. The same war also brings about the grisly reunion of Saleem with his own boyhood friends from Methwold's Estate. Sonny Ibrahim greets him with "Hullo, man" before dying (361). The lesson Saleem learns is that, if the world of men is his future, that future is cold and hard. Just because you're paranoid does not mean they are not after you.

Those who succeed in the unforgiving world of adults accentuate a brutish masculinity, promiscuous, exploitative, and violent. None is more successful in the competition for women than Saleem's nemesis, Shiva. He has thousands of lovers on whom he fathers offspring. His possession of women is as close to hate as it is to desire, however, and Saleem accuses him of the serial murders of prostitutes (214, 221). Rumour has it that "they" put Saleem in the Army "to make a man of him" (338), but the army is actually where soldiers lose their humanity. Saleem's metamorphosis into a dog, no more than a nose and a penis, is an extreme form of a fate suffered by all in the Pakistani army. Their participation in an unjust war makes the Pakistani soldiers "dogs of war," "wolfhounds" that "sink fierce teeth into their prey" (346).

The sympathies of Saleem, who says, "guns have never appealed to me" (184), are with those, like his grandfather Aadam Aziz, his uncle Hanif, and Nadir Khan, who abjure the competition among men. Saleem adopts a series of fathers whose qualification for paternity seems to be their impotence. Aadam is henpecked and browbeaten; Nadir is forced to divorce Mumtaz when her continued virginity after two years of marriage is made public; and Hanif commits suicide when deprived of the funds provided by his wife's lover (263). The last father that Saleem adopts is Picture Singh, the snake-charming leader of the magicians's slum. Picture Singh, unlike Saleem's other fosterfathers, is a man of some willpower, a power symbolized by his fetishized "umbrella of harmony beneath which men and women would gather for advice and shade" (429–30). Leading the resistance to Indira Gandhi's army juggernaut and its dreaded "tent of vasectomy," Picture Singh brandishes "a furious umbrella, which had once been a creator of harmony but was now transmuted into a weapon, a flapping quixotic lance" (414). But the last glimpse Saleem has of his friend, before he is carted off, is of a bearded giant, running "wildly before the advancing bulldozers, clutching in his hand the handle of an irreparably shattered umbrella, searching searching, as though his life depended on the search" (416). When Saleem finds his friend again, Picture Singh is minus the umbrella and, having married the virago Durga the washerwoman, "seemed to be shrinking daily" (430). He still has it in him to win a crucial snake-charming contest for the title of the Most Charming Man In The World, but "the efforts of his struggle had broken something inside him"; "his victory was, in fact, a defeat" (439).

Given the brutish nature of this male-dominated world, actual fathers are perceived not as models but as betrayers. Wee Willie Winkie tries to smash his son's knees so that he will be better fitted to be a beggar, but Shiva catches the hammer-wielding wrist between his knees and breaks it (216). Uncle Zulfikar gives his son Zafar one more chance to "prove you're not a woman" by joining the army (283). However, posted to the Rann of Kutch and scared out of his wits by the presence of ghosts, Zafar fails the test. The supposed ghosts turn out to be smugglers operating under his father's orders, and Zafar returns to slit the throat of the father who undermined him (326). As Oskar Matzerath says of his own presumptive son, "Perhaps he, too, could express only by homicide the childlike affection that would seem to be desirable between fathers and sons"(Grass 1962, 397). Ahmed Sinai is described in effeminate terms as having lank hair that curls over his ears and a squashy belly, traits he shares with Nadir. At Saleem's birth, his father broke his toe (115). When his assets are frozen by the government, his testicles become ice cubes and Saleem describes him as "frigid" (134). He takes to his bed and pays no attention to his mother-in-law's injunctions to "Be a man" (137). Ahmed's impotence does not, however, make him a better parent. Unlike Nadir Khan or Hanif Aziz, sufferers of impotence who are genuinely the victims of others, Ahmed has only himself to blame. He accuses his family of "emasculating him" (287), but his emasculation is actually the consequence of his own incapacity to love and his retreat into abstraction.

Or is it? Readers may be forgiven for sensing "an overly-harsh taste" in Saleem's presentation of his father (443), who stands convicted of both impotence and infidelity. When extortionists burn down his godown, the businessman receives a further slap in the face from a human hand dropped by a vulture flying overhead (90). The narrative perspective throughout Book One is close to the bird's – "high-in-the-sky" (74), "pulling away in a long rising spiral from the events," "flying across the city," and "winging towards the Old Fort district" (102) – and the reader may be forgiven for feeling that the hand that delivers the slap is Saleem's own (and Rushdie's), reaching into the text to strike at his father. Ahmed recalls looking up and seeing the hand drop, "which – now! – slapped him full in the face" (90), and the "now" refers not only to the time of the slap and to the frustrated moment of sexual intimacy with his wife when he relives the slap, but also to the present moment of the reader.

Saleem's fear of masculinity explains his attraction to strong, self-sufficient women who do not require men to be men because they do not require men at all. "European" women, in particular, are ready to assume the power associated with masculinity – "Evie was American. Same thing" (182). Evie Burns identifies with Robert Taylor and the Lone Ranger, just as Saleem and his mates do, but she can ride better, shoot straighter, and drink more coconut milk than any of the boys in Methwold's Estate (180). She gets no argument from them when she declares herself the "new big chief" (180). The only person ever to "get on top of her" is Saleem's sister, the Brass Monkey (178), herself a tomboy better than her brother at bike-riding, at street-fighting, and at mischief. Among the other European women in Saleem's experience are the "beefy" members of the Walsingham School for Girls swim team, who allow the Brass Monkey "to fool around with them and pinch their bulging musculatures" (202). From these friends Saleem's sister learns a hostility to heterosexual roles that will eventually land her in a Catholic convent.

Women who do not need men attract Saleem, but fill him with fear as well. He falls in love first with Evie Burns and then with Jamila Singer, and in each case suffers a disastrous humiliation. Evie Burns's second name, Lilith, is an allusion to the apocryphal first wife of Adam in Jewish and Islamic tradition. Lilith proved too strong for Adam to control, and she was replaced by Eve and her story excised from the Bible. In Islamic tradition, she slept with the devil and gave birth to the djinn. In later legend she became a succubus who steals and kills children. Saleem's American neighbour is both Eve and Lilith, an object of desire and of fear. It is not just men that Evie threatens: after her return to America, she knifes an old woman and is sent to reform school (179). The character that she most resembles is Shiva, the suspected murderer of prostitutes, who is called "a second, and more potent, Evelyn Lilith Burns" (215), a comment not intended to cast aspersions on his masculinity.

Saleem continues to seek out women with lots of muscle or with hair on their arms, but after his experience with Evie, he is also wary of them. The Brass Monkey and her "superbly muscled" swim team friends are dangerous: they strip her suitor, Sonny, on the street (182). Padma, Saleem's faithful listener, has strong thighs filled with "Padma-muscles" (286), arms "which could wrestle mine down in a trice" (263) and "hairy forearms" (286). In his new home, the pickle factory, Saleem is surrounded by the reassuring presence of an "army of strong, hairy-armed, formidably competent women" (164). "Competent," however, is a word that, when used of women, expresses Saleem's fear. The "formidable competence" of the pickle workers (443) recalls the "sea of giant, noisy, omnicompetent women" who flow into Dr. Narlikar's apartment like a "stream of outsize womanhood" (175). The Narlikar women are "grossly competent" (258), and something of their "awesome competence" leaks into Cyrus Dubash's mother (262), where it manifests itself as religious fanaticism and a sinister control of her son. "Competence" is clearly a synonym for a "self-sufficiency" that the male feels as desirable (he does not have to prove his own virility) and as a threat (he is entirely superfluous). The threat is illustrated by Padma who mocks him: "Arm extended, its hairs glowing in the lamplight, she jabbed a contemptuous index finger in the direction of my admittedly non-functioning loins; a long, thick digit, rigid with jealousy, which unfortunately served only to remind me of another, long-lost finger" (121).

Women who prefer the company of women, like the Narlikar women or the Walsingham swim team, are feared, but so are spinsters, like Alia and Jamila Singer, or widows, like Mrs Dubash, Indira Gandhi, and Reverend Mother. Such women are described as witches: rumour has it that the Rani of Cooch Naheen is a "singing witch" (47); Reverend Mother is an "old hag" (59) with enormous moles "like witch's nipples" on her face (41); Evie is "a witch on wheels"(180); two of the Midnight's Children can "bewitch fools young and old" into falling in love with them (248); Pia has "bewitched" Saleem (235), who also suffers the "bewitchment" of his spinster sister (388); and Parvati is literally a witch, able to make people disappear or do things against their will.

The ambivalence towards strong women that the narrative expresses reflects a chiasmic reversal in gender roles repeatedly performed in the novel. In courtship the male appears to have agency and the female occupies what seems to be a more passive role, but in Saleem's world, power switches sides after marriage. The most obvious such reversal is the courtship with which the novel begins, that of Aadam Aziz and Naseem Ghani. The doctor returned from Europe falls in love with the demure young maiden of whom he is vouchsafed tantalizing glimpses through a small hole in the centre of the white bedsheet modestly held before her. Aziz is, as Saleem will be, cast in the role of voyeur who desires to possess the object of his gaze. His marriage to Naseem is, however, despite its romantic beginnings, destined to be an unhappy one: "as though their marriage had been one of those mythical unions in which succubi appear to men as innocent damsels, and, after luring them into the matrimonial bed, regain their true, awful aspect and begin to swallow their souls" (266). The woman who will be Aziz's wife is "unified and transmuted into" a "formidable figure" (41), much closer to the three servants, each "with the biceps of a wrestler," that hold up the sheet than to the phantasm of a partitioned woman that the doctor projects onto the sheet (23). Naseem Ghani, having become Reverend Mother, expands in size and presence as her husband declines in stature; she acquires a moustache (266), while he is reduced to "another shrivelled, empty old man" (185) and becomes more and more like a child (266). A similar fate awaits Saleem's hero, Picture Singh, when he marries Durga the washerwoman, "whose biceps bulged" (429). Durga, too, is a "succubus" and "A bloodsucker lizard in human form!" (429). She gains in energy and her voice grows louder, as she flattens Picture Singh the way she does the shirts she smashes on stones, "until at last she reminded me of Reverend Mother in her later years, when she expanded and my grandfather shrank" (429–30). In the world of Saleem's nightmares, women become hairy: Alia grows a beard (320) and hair sprouts on Amina's face as on their mother's before them (322). Male-female relations appear as doomed to unhappiness as the relations between men, and for the same reason: they are fierce struggles for domination. Bano Devi, a female wrestler who fights only men, has never lost a match because she threatens to marry anyone who beats her (126).

There is, however, another kind of power available, one particularly associated with the feminine, although not deployed by all women and not limited to women. To be unmanned, after all, is not to be without power, as Saleem proves by filling six hundred pages with the narrative account of his sexual humiliations. Let us consider yet once again the scene where Aadam Aziz falls in love with an image projected onto the bedsheet. The projection is not independent of the screen onto which it is projected. Agency belongs not solely to the male voyeur but perhaps even more to the seemingly passive woman behind the sheet. Naseem Ghani, with the connivance of her father, controls the representation of her body, and her calculated partial and gradual self-exposure is as responsible as the doctor's narcissism for awakening his desire. She is what Peter Brooks calls in a very different context "the scenarist of her own body" (Brooks 1993, 271). Viewer and viewed are part of a "circulatory system" of desire, in which the man's desire creates the woman but she creates his desire (ibid., 274). Women are to be feared if, like Evie Burns, they take over from men and reduce males to women, but are even more to be feared if they appear passive and feminine, as Naseem Ghani does. The same subordinate location which would destroy a man if he were to occupy it is one in which women can find a source of power.

In Saleem's narrative women are not happier or more whole than men. In this patriarchal world, the competition among women for men is no less fierce than that among men for power. Mumtaz Aziz (later Amina) takes Ahmed Sinai from her sister Alia; cousin Zohra in turn threatens Amina's hold on Ahmed Sinai; Alice Pereira steals Joseph D'Costa from her sister Mary and later Ahmed from his wife; and Lila Sabarmati takes Homi Catrack from Pia Aziz. Yet, all these female rivals are distinguished both from the men and from the strong women like Evie Burns and Reverend Mother by their seeming lack of power. What then does this women's power consist of? Saleem's nose can smell what is hidden from sight, but Lila Sabarmati's nose possesses equally tremendous powers: "a wrinkle of nasal skin could charm the steeliest of Admirals; a tiny flare of the nostrils ignited strange fires in the hearts of film magnates" (252). These women conceal in order to arouse curiosity and desire. They reveal in order better to conceal. They confess their sins in order to be forgiven. They submit to changing their names in order to change the natures of their husbands.

Amina brings some of the powerful passivity that is the source of this feminine strength to her marriage to Ahmed Sinai. She employs "the techniques of street beggars" – "strokes and 'Janum, my life, please …' and '… Just a little so that I can make nice food and pay the bills …'" – to get whatever money she wants from her husband who likes "to have it wheedled out of him" (70). Parvati, the Child of Midnight most loyal to Saleem, also has a great deal of power, not all of which is magical. When her magic summons Shiva to come to her in the ghetto, he "cannot have known what force impelled him to come" (394). When she hops onto the back of his motorcycle, he believes she is obeying his irresistible masculinity. Parvati takes off his boots, presses his feet, oils his moustache, and caresses his knees. They live happily until the day that Parvati, kneeling at his feet and "fully aware of his views on the subject," tells him she is expecting a child (397). He then drags her by the hair back to the ghetto, where he dumps her, "just as she had planned" (398). Parvati's pregnancy invalidates Saleem's only excuse for not marrying her (his lie that he cannot have children) and forces him to come to the assistance of the seemingly helpless single mother. In this version of events (very much Saleem's own), Parvati's victim status is a role played to con Shiva into giving her a child and Saleem into fathering it. The hypermasculine Shiva has been played on by a woman before. Roshanara Shetty, whom he also abandoned when she became pregnant, gets her revenge by playing Iago to Shiva's Moor and filling his ears with bitter lies that make him doubt all his masculine triumphs. She makes him see the world with different eyes: where before he had basked in the adulation of women, now he sees only their contempt for him (396).

Saleem himself becomes expert at using the feminized power that lies in abjuring power. When enraged by his mother's infidelity, he exacts revenge on the known adulterers Homi Catrack and Lila Sabarmati, not by doing battle "on horseback, with fiery eyes and flaming sword" but by "imitating the action of the snake" (252). He writes a cryptic and anonymous note to Commander Sabarmati, and "snake-like" slips it into a pocket of the officer's uniform (253). He feels "the delight of the snake who hits its target, and feels its fangs pierce its victims's heel" (253).

What is it that women want (or rather, that Saleem and Rushdie think they want)? Saleem never shows us the view from the other side of the bedsheet and is not close to his grandmother, even though it is from her that he has learned about Tai, the Hummingbird, and the Rani of Cooch Naheen (267). We can assume that the sheet serves Naseem Ghani as both a position of power and a screen protecting the self from the other. When she becomes Reverend Mother, she lives within "an invisible fortress of her own making," "a system of self-defence so impregnable that Aziz, after many fruitless attempts, had more or less given up trying to storm her many ravelins and bastions, leaving her, like a large smug spider, to rule her chosen domain" (41). She creates the physical equivalent of this space in kitchen and pantry, "her inalienable territory" to which she denies her husband admission (41). Other women also seek a room of their own. The veil with a small hole in the centre held up before Jamila Singer when she gives concerts is the source of her mystique and isolates her from all around her. She eventually retreats behind the "blind wall" with a single opening that is the convent of Saint Ignacia (306). Lady Mountbatten retreats in similar fashion to the lavatory in order to eat the chicken breasts that had been prepared for her dogs, unable to countenance such a display of profligate luxury (65). When they are unhappy in love, Aunt Pia retreats to her bedroom and Amina Sinai to the washroom.

The privacy afforded by the veil or the washroom resembles the small, dark spaces to which men retreat in order to hide from the eyes of others: the washing-chest in which Saleem curls up as a schoolboy, the clocktower where he convenes the Midnight's Children's Club in his head, and the room above the pickle factory in which he writes his memoirs. Other examples are Nadir Khan's refuge in another large old laundry-chest (53) and his hideaway under the carpet, Dr. Schaapsteker's room, and Ahmed Sinai's office. The difference between the male and female need for privacy, however, is that, as we saw in Chapter Five, the men seek a vantage point from which to range over the world and even control it – they want to see without being seen – while the women in their lonesomeness want to share their space with another. Aunt Pia in her bed and Amina Sinai in the washroom call lovers to them. Parvati in her shack conjures up Shiva. After her husband has died, Reverend Mother finds fulfilment sitting in a small "glass confessional" at a petrol station on the Rawalpindi-Lahore Road, listening to people tell her their problems (318). She bathes "in the blessed oblivion of other people's lives" (318). Men want a centre from which the self is free to roam far and wide, and women a space for the self that they can share with another.

These complementary desires are effective for reproduction but are not, it seems, well suited for mutual understanding or love. As we have already noted, the closest the novel comes to portraying a happy marriage is that of Nadir Khan and Mumtaz Aziz. Aadam Aziz hides Nadir, fleeing the assassins of Mian Abdullah, in a room in the basement, where he falls in love with the Aziz daughter who brings him his meals. After Nadir and Mumtaz are married, they remain in their basement room, which they think of as their own Taj Mahal, not a mausoleum such as Shah Jehan built for the original Mumtaz but a private retreat. True, their marriage is never consummated, but the couple's relations are not less sensual for not being genital. Kakar might almost be describing Mumtaz when he identifies as "the profound yearning" of an Indian wife "the intense wish to create a two-person universe with the husband where each 'finally' recognizes the other": "In contrast to much of popular Western fiction, the Indian "romantic" yearning is not for an exploring of the depths of erotic passion, or for being swept off the feet by a masterful man. It is a much quieter affair, with the soul of a Mukesh-song, and when unsatisfied this longing shrivels the emotional life of many women, making some go through life as mere maternal automatons" (Kakar 1990, 22–3). Padma declares, "love, to us women, is the greatest thing of all" (190).

Mumtaz and Nadir's marriage, which offers private fulfilment in the present, is intolerable to her parents and sister, concerned as they are with family honour and the reproduction of the family line. But even after her family forces him to divorce her, Mumtaz's erotic fantasy continues to dwell on her first husband's features, his lank hair and squashy tummy. It is hard not to feel that the absence of sexual consummation is precisely what makes that marriage ideal: a union where two meet on equal, respectful terms because both are feminized.

It is in voluntary feminization, the abdication of the superior position accorded to masculinity and the meeting of the other on common ground, that the self can find itself in Rushdie's novel. When Mumtaz Aziz gets remarried, the "painstaking magic" of her love acts upon Ahmed to change him into someone she can love: under her analytical gaze, his hair thins and curls behind his ears and his belly becomes squashy like Nadir's (69). Evie Burns is more attracted to Sonny Ibrahim than to Saleem, and the reason seems to be the hollows on either side of his forehead made by the forceps when he was born: "Girls (Evie, the Brass Monkey, others) reached out to stroke his little valleys" (118). While his mother nurses Sonny, "her fingers move, absently stroking his hollows, up and around, down and about, in a steady, unchanging rhythm" (134). Later Evie's fingers repeatedly touch those hollows, "the fingertips getting covered in dribbled vaseline" (183, 187). What women want in *Midnight's Children* is, it would seem, best represented as mutual masturbation. Mutual masturbation is, of course, not permitted to the male characters: the Brass Monkey takes revenge on Sonny by falsely reporting that she saw him and Cyrus "behind a bush, doing such funny rubbing things with their soo-soos!" (151).

Saleem's own understanding of the relations of power and sexual desire begins at an early age. At eight years old he witnesses a version of the Freudian primal scene, not parental copulation, but, more in keeping with the theme of sexual frustration in the novel, his mother masturbating with her lover's name on her lips. Saleem, hidden in the dirty laundry in a washing-chest, unintentionally spies on Amina in the washroom, after she has received a phone call from Nadir Khan: "And her hands are moving. Lost in their memory of other days, of what happened after games of hit-the-spittoon in an Agra cellar, they flutter gladly at her cheeks; they hold her bosom tighter than any brassières; and now they caress her bare midriff, they stray below decks […] hands which held telephone now hold flesh, while in another place what does another hand do? To what, after replacing receiver, is another hand getting up?" (159). The metonyms here are part of a configuration by now familiar: Saleem's partial view of the scene focuses on discrete parts of mother's body, while, in Amina's lonely approximation of sexual union, parts of the body are made love to by other parts, hands assume a memory of their own, clutching breasts, midriff, and cheeks as if they (the antecedent deliberately left imprecise) belonged to another.

Saleem who involuntarily catches a glimpse of his mother's buttocks, the "Black Mango," occupies the male position of voyeur that was once his grandfather's, also vouchsafed a view of a "celestial rump" (27). Saleem, however, feels guilt rather than desire. The sight of Amina masturbating conjures up for her son what Kakar identifies as the two most dreaded figures in Indian male psychology: the sexual mother and the unfaithful mother (Kakar 1990, 143). Saleem refers to these as the twin "miseries of maternal perfidy and paternal decline" (222). The son who spies on his mother's adulterous longings identifies with the moral position of his father. Amina's desires are a direct challenge to her husband's masculine pride and so to her son's identity. Saleem cannot forgive her and ultimately exacts revenge from the adulteress Lila Sabarmati, hoping thereby to warn his mother (254). Saleem, however, also blames his father. He associates his own unwanted vision of naked female buttocks, "framed in laundry and slatted wood" (160), with the "godknowswhat rot" that fills the head of his father when he mentally undresses his secretary, "crisscross marks all across her rump" from "sitting stark naked on a cane-bottomed chair" (168). As Saleem says himself about his complicated motives, he hates Homi Catrack when he seduces his Aunt Pia and even more when he discards her (243).

The evidence of his mother's sexuality arouses in the boy what Kakar would diagnose as an anxiety about his own adequacy to fulfil women's sexual desires (Kakar 1978, 96). Saleem has retreated to the washing-chest, his private "hole in the world" (155), precisely in order to protect himself from the terrifying demands made on him by the world, prime among which is the need to prove his manhood. Saleem's defence against that anxiety is, however, to renounce his masculinity and take on the femininity of his mother. In a curious hermaphroditic transformation, Saleem the voyeur identifies with the object of his gaze. In the washing-chest, a pajama cord, "snake-like harbinger of doom" (159), which normally hangs harmlessly down from the waist, has inserted itself up Saleem's nose, described in the third person as if detached from himself: "shattered by two-syllabic voice and fluttering hands, devastated by Black Mango, the nose of Saleem Sinai, responding to the evidence of maternal duplicity, quivering at the presence of maternal rump, gave way to a pajama-cord, and was possessed by a cataclysmic – a world-altering – an irreversible *sniff*" (160). The mother's desire is communicated to the son much as germs are: the flutter of hands in one small space provokes the paroxysm of a sneeze in another. The resulting sneeze is a comically displaced figure for penetration and orgasm: "But other things are rising, too: hauled by that feverish inhalation, nasal liquids are being sucked relentlessly up up up, nose-goo flowing upwards, against gravity, against nature. Sinuses are subjected to unbearable pressure … until, inside the nearlynineyearold head, something bursts. Snot rockets through a breached dam into dark new channels" (160).

The Shandean confusion of noses and penises is a running joke throughout the narrative. The boatman Tai tells Aadam Aziz that dynasties are waiting inside his nose like snot (15), and Saleem's father suspects that the size of his nose has to do with masturbating: "Whoever got a nose like that from sleeping?" (154). The scene in the washing-chest reminds us, however, that noses are orifices as well as protuberances. Saleem's sinuses are the only internal body parts, aside from the hole in the centre of Aadam Aziz, to feature in the novel, and they, too, are hollow cavities to be filled with elements from outside the body. The accident with the pajama string, involving as it does both penetration and ejaculation, blurs the active and the passive (male and female in the novel's terms). It is a comical literalization of one of the worst imprecations in the English language, one only ever urged of others, never actually performed, and indeed so metaphorical as to be practically unimaginable.

The boy in the washing-chest who feels such terror and confusion when he discovers sexuality also experiences an unexpected access to power. The accident with the washing string is an irreverent version of "the Hindu theory of sublimation," which Kakar explains as follows: "Physical strength and mental power have their source in *virya*, a word that stands for both sexual energy and semen. *Virya*, in fact, is identical with the essence of maleness. *Virya* can either move downward in sexual intercourse, where it is emitted in its gross physical form as semen, or it can move upward through the spinal chord and into the brain, in its subtle form known as *ojas*" (Kakar 1990, 118–9). As a result of an "internal ejaculation," which releases something like the "self-contained, enlightening energy of yogic kundalini power" (Alter 150), young Saleem experiences a bizarre parthenogenesis and becomes a telepathic receptor open to the voices of all the people who live within the frontiers of the state, a kind of All-India Radio. This is a reprise of the power now lost that he once had as an infant when Toxy Catrack used to send her thoughts to him as she stood at a "barred" window, "stark naked, masturbating" (129). Sexuality is related to national consciousness because both are experienced as surges of power that expand the range of the self. As we shall see in the next chapter, national identity is inevitably configured in terms of gender and desire.

Sexuality is also related to narrative and to writing, two other great engines of desire. The two small dark spaces where Saleem first awakens to sexuality and to the nation, the washroom and washing-chest, are, like the office where he writes his memoir, versions of the camera obscura, the little black box which, as we have already noted in Chapter Two, figures the experience of both reading and writing. Amina, like a writer, alone in the only room she can call her own, imagines an absent lover. In her moan, "Nadir. Nadir. Na. Dir. Na" (159), we can hear an echo of the *"fort-da"* that, in a famous incident recounted by Freud, marked one child's first awareness of the continued existence of things in their absence and of the capacity of language to make absent things present. Saleem, like the reader, hidden in his even smaller space, watches Amina giving free rein to her imagination and, incongruously, experiences in his own body a violent parody version of her experience.

Saleem combines the desires we have identified as masculine and feminine: the desire to range over the world without himself being seen, and the desire to share his privacy with another. His life is a succession of small cells, even of cell within cell. As a boy, he retreats inside the washroom, and inside "a white wooden washing-chest, within the darkened auditorium of my skull" (160). Later, the washing-chest and the clocktower become sites from which he can roam the world. Parvati-the-witch smuggles him in her basket of invisibility from Bangladesh into India. Still later, Saleem is imprisoned by the Widow in a cell, where his nightmare takes the same form as his dream: in a parody of his earlier convocations of the Midnight Children's Conference, he whispers to the other children, now also prisoners, through the walls that separate them. This combination of narcissistic retreat and hubristic expansion may legitimately be called masculine. Saleem ends his active life and begins his narrative in a small office in a pickle factory where Padma joins him. On the surface, the office resembles Saleem's other cells. He explicitly compares the writing in which he is currently engaged to the headful of voices he discovered as a child. Both the child in his clocktower and the adult memoirist in his private office are able to contain multitudes: "Then as now, someone was awake in the dark, hearing disembodied tongues" (165). From the small space of his desk illuminated by an Anglepoised lamp, the memoirist must "send these words into the darkness," "afraid of being disbelieved" (165). The writer appears as but another version of Quentin Anderson's Imperial Self (Q. Anderson 1971).

Saleem's writing is a contest configured in sexual terms. Every night Saleem reads Padma what he has written and then sleeps with her (263). He thinks of the relation of story-teller and reader as a contest for mastery. He uses the tautness of the muscles in Padma's hairy arms and thick thighs as a guide to her boredom or her interest (263). Writing, however, is also a sublimation of sexual desire, Saleem's compensation for being unable to get his "other pencil" to work and the only way he has of reproducing himself. Padma berates him for having his "nose in paper" (190), a valid description not just of the act of writing but of his whole project. As a writer, Saleem's strategy for coping with Padma's sexual demands is to abdicate his masculinity and assume the power that he associates with women. Saleem deliberately compares his story-telling to Scheherazade's, to his mother's masturbating that conjures up Nadir, and to the perforated sheet that brought about the original union between his grandparents. He casts the muscular, hairy-armed Padma, whose attention he seeks to capture and retain, in the position of the hapless Aadam Aziz: "'Condemned by a perforated sheet to a life of fragments,' I wrote and read aloud, 'I have nevertheless done better than my grandfather; because while Aadam Aziz remained the sheet's victim, I have become its master – and Padma is the one who is now under its spell'" (141). As Nancy Batty points out, Saleem also teases readers with his many "trailers" of events to come (Batty 1999), just as Naseem Ghani teases Aadam Aziz with incomplete revelations of her body. If Saleem has learned anything, it is that the abdication of authority is not merely a way of protecting the self but a source of power in its own right. The feminine position of passivity and seeming weakness is not a renunciation of power, but a different kind of power. As Sukeshi Kamra writes, Saleem strategically occupies "the marginalized world of the feminine, a world in which power is gained only through sexual/textual performance" (Kamra 1996, 240)

Saleem's sexlessness is in part a defence mechanism to forestall a potentially catastrophic challenge to his manhood. His explicit feminization is not, however, as it might appear, disempowering. In *Midnight's Children* the feminized have an alternative power of their own, a power that is inseparable from their abdication of masculine power. By detaching itself from a virility which, if lost, would mean the self's destruction and by deliberately adopting a position associated with women, the self is able to preserve itself and win the trust of others. This was a lesson first learned by Saleem's friend and "first mentor" (97), Cyrus the Great. The self-styled expert on the Parts of a Woman's Body "played girls' parts in school plays" and the pun on "parts" suggests both identification and metonymic assembly (97). His most successful appearance on stage, "playing a female part as usual" (161), is that of Saint Joan in Shaw's play.

Saleem, however, has unwisely boasted of being able to arouse Padma's love by the power of his tale: "Sitting in my enchanted shadows, I vouchsafe daily glimpses of myself – while she, my squatting glimpser, is captivated, helpless as a mongoose frozen into immobility by the swaying, blinkless eyes of a hooded snake, paralysed – yes! – by love" (121). As a reader of Kipling would know, the mongoose is the one creature that can resist the snake's fascination and kill the snake. Saleem has overestimated his own powers. He wonders if it is not he himself who has fallen in love (164) and Padma who controls him. Padma is not just his audience but also his muse: it is she who commands him to write – "Enough. Start. Start now" (286) and "Begin [...] Begin all over again" (336) – and he obeys.

Saleem's text is ominously associated, not just with masturbation, but also with impotence and with defecation. Saleem shares his vocation as a writer with his uncle Hanif, the "only realistic writer working in the Bombay film industry" (237). Realist screenwriter and magic-realist memoirist resemble each other in their obsession with the labour of pickling: Hanif's last project is an epic about a pickle factory, which is arguably a description of Saleem's project as well. Uncle and nephew are also alike in their impotence. Hanif's writing is inseparable from his cuckold status: he is forever breaking pencils in his nervousness. Yet young Saleem says, "Hanif mamu has taught me to hold the pen differently, so I can write okay" (244). Hanif's childless and unfaithful wife Pia hates the film scripts that fill their apartment, "so that you had to pick them off the toilet seat before you could lift it" (238). She stands in the doorway, "her hand slicing air," and accuses her husband of creative impotence – "So much talent, a person cannot go to the pot in this house without finding your genius" (242) – and the text draws an explicit parallel to Saleem's relation to his own scornful muse: "'But what is so precious,' Padma demands, her right hand slicing the air updownup in exasperation, 'to need all this writing-shiting?'" (25).

Of course, in a world where mutual masturbation represents the truest possibility of fulfillment and where feminine passivity represents a power possibly greater than that of masculine violence, impotence and even defecation may be sources of power of their own. In what is almost the last scene in the novel, a man with an umbrella like Picture Singh's defecates outside Saleem's window and challenges him with the size of his turd, fifteen inches in length: "How long can you make yours?" Saleem claims victory by ducking the contest. He responds, "Once, when I was more energetic, I would have wanted to tell his life-story; the hour, and his possession of an umbrella, would have been all the connections I needed to begin the process of weaving him into my life, and I have no doubt that I'd have finished by proving his indispensability to anyone who wishes to understand my life and benighted times; but now I'm disconnected, unplugged, with only epitaphs left to write. So, waving at the champion defecator, I call back: 'Seven on a good day,' and forget him" (440). Saleem cannot match the stranger's prodigious length, but his words allow him to contain and dismiss him nonetheless. He does not need to compete for he has the text he is about to finish.

PART THREE
The Nation and Its Others

9

The State

In Chapter Five I suggested that Saleem's identification with the nation, the source of much the novel's magic, is best understood as a refracted form of the national consciousness fostered in modern bourgeois subjects everywhere. Saleem himself identifies with the whole and not with a part, as though, like absolute monarchs in Renaissance Europe, he was two bodies at once: a physical body and, in its image, the spiritual collective body of the state. The collective that Saleem imagines in his own image and in whose image he imagines himself resembles the figure of the sovereign in the original frontispiece of Hobbes' *Leviathan*: a giant towering over his dominions, his body composed of the lilliputian figures of his subjects (Fig. 1). Carole Pateman explains that, in the modern story of the social contract, "Men give birth to an 'artificial' body, the body politic of civil society; they create Hobbes' 'Artificial Man, we call a Commonwealth,' or Rousseau's 'artificial and collective body,' or the 'one Body' of Locke's 'Body Politick'": the result is "a social body fashioned after the image of only one of the two bodies of humankind, or, more exactly, after the image of the civil individual who is constituted through the original contract" (Pateman 1988, 102). In Hobbes, only the sovereign can embody the whole; in modern republics, however, as Balzac says, every citizen now feels himself a king. Balzac's comment on Lucien de Rubempré's youthful egoism – "Nowadays we all say, more or less, with Louis XIV: *L'État, c'est moi*!" (Balzac 1976, 62; my translation) – applies with at least equal validity to Saleem.

The expansion of the self to the scale of the nation implies not just the centrality of the self but also the personalization of the nation-state. According to Chatterjee, the development ideology that inspired Nehru and his generation was premised "upon a *rational* consciousness and will, and insofar as 'development' was thought of

Fig. 1 Frontispiece of Thomas Hobbes's *Leviathan*, showing the king, whose body is made up of his subjects, surveying his lands.

as a process affecting the whole of society, it was also premised upon *one* consciousness and will – that of the whole" (Chatterjee 1993, 204). The nation is a single sovereign individual, not itself part of a larger society.

The cover of the Ekatmata Yajna souvenir volume, published by the Vishva Hindu Parishad (World Hindu Council), shows the map of India filled with masses of people all headed in the same direction, towards a giant figure of the goddess Durga (Fig. 2). The imagery here is Hindu and the central figure is female, not male. Love of nation involves worship rather than identification. This version of the nation is therefore different from Hobbes's image of the state. In the traditional story of the creation of Durga, the emphasis is not on the sovereignty of the whole but on the assembly of many parts. The male gods, faced by the menace of the buffalo demon, combined their energies to create the goddess:

> from the combination of these energies a certain woman appeared: her head appeared from the energy of Shiva, her two arms from the energy of Vishnu, her two feet from the energy of Brahma, and her waist from

Fig. 2 Cover of the Ekatmata Yajna (Sacrifice for Unity), souvenir volume of the Vishva Hindu Parishad (World Hindu Council), showing the goddess Durga, sacrificial fire, ritual pot, and masses of participants. From Lise McKean, *Divine Enterprise: Gurus and the Hindu Nationalist Movement* (Chicago: University of Chicago Press, 1996).

the energy of Indra; her hair was made from Yama's energy, her two breasts from the moon's energy, her thighs from the energy of Varuna, her hips from the earth's energy, her toes from the sun's energy; her fingers were formed by the energy of the Vasus, her nose by Kubera's energy, her rows of teeth from the energy of the nine Prajāpatis; her two eyes arose from the energy of the Oblation-bearer; the two twilights became her two brows, and her ears were made from the energy of the wind; and from

> the incredibly fierce energies of the other gods other limbs were made for the woman who was the supremely radiant Durga, more dangerous than all the gods and demons. (O'Flaherty 1975, 241; orthography regularized to conform to Rushdie's)

David Kinsley explains that "The subcontinent is sown with the pieces of Sati's body, which make the land especially sacred. The myth also stresses that the numerous and varied *pithas* and goddesses worshipped at them are part of a larger, unified whole. Each *pitha* represents a part of Sati's body or one of her ornaments; taken together, the *pithas* found throughout India constitute or point towards a transcendent (or, perhaps better, a universally immanent) goddess whose being encompasses, underlies, and unifies the Indian subcontinent as a whole. In short, the Indian subcontinent *is* the goddess Sati" (Cited at Monti 1999, 79).

Let us look again, however, at the VHP picture of Durga. As in the image from Hobbes' *Leviathan*, two bodies are imagined as coinciding: the sovereign self of the nation is complemented by the sum of its many constituent parts. The emphasis in both images, however, is not on the relation among parts but on the sovereign whole that contains them. Louis Dumont explains that whereas, in traditional, hierarchical societies, the individual and the society are both composed of many related parts, "in modern times the society or nation is conceived as a collective individual, which has its 'will' and its 'relations' like the elementary individual, but unlike him is not subject to social rules" (Dumont 1970, 10). Durga in the VHP image is closer to the Hobbes version of the nation than to the Hindu mythology it derives from. Tagore, for one, abhorred the attribution of absolute sovereignty to the nation, and by extension, to the individual as citizen of the nation. Nationalism's promise of sovereignty seduces Bimala, the protagonist of his novel *The Home and the World*, who declares, "I am only human. I am covetous. I would have good things for my country. If I am obliged, I would snatch and filch them. I have anger. I would be angry for my country's sake. If necessary, I would smite and slay to avenge her insults. I have my desire to be fascinated, and fascination must be supplied to me in bodily shape by my country. She must have some visible symbol casting its spell upon my mind. I would make my country a Person and call her Mother, Goddess, Durga – for whom I would redden the earth with sacrificial offerings" (Tagore 1919, 38). Tagore saw that modern nationalism could transform the Goddess into the emblem of the nation's sovereignty, and he believed that nothing could come of centring morality on the self, even the transindividual self of the nation, except violence and disaster. Nandy, who follows Tagore in this regard, argues that Hindu fundamentalism is, in fact, a modern phenomenon, a recasting of Hinduism in the shape of Western-derived nationalism (Nandy 1994). Hobbes and the VHP offer contrasting images of the nation, one modern and male, the other explicitly traditional and female, but the images may be covertly the same.

As we have seen, Saleem also imagines two bodies for himself, the first a projection onto the scale of the nation of a body like his own and the second a composite of the bodies of all his fellow citizens. The body of the nation as imagined by synecdochical identification and that figured by metonymic assembly are gendered differently. The sovereign whole, figured as the Kolynos Kid or Ganesh, is masculine; the assembly of metonymic parts is, like the statue of Mumbadevi above the pickle factory, feminine. The two bodies do not, however, conveniently coincide, as they do in the versions of Hobbes and the VHP, where the sum of many parts is the same as the sovereign whole. Instead their relationship is charged with desire and anxiety.

Young Saleem becomes a sort of All-India Radio, receiving the voices of strangers who share a national identity with himself, at the moment when, at the age of nine, he catches a glimpse of his mother's nakedness. The adolescent's developing national consciousness is intimately associated with a burgeoning and confused sexuality. Among the many perspectives to which Saleem's newfound telepathy gives him access are two inspired by the voyeuristic circumstances in which he first discovered his power: a lascivious fisherwoman "whose sari was as tight as her morals were loose" and an adolescent village boy embarrassed in the presence of the erotic sculptures at Khajuraho "but unable to tear away my eyes" (171). Sexuality and national consciousness both have to do with identity and with desire: both grow well "in the heat" (165).

It would seem that the nation-state can be imagined either as an ideal version of the male self or as a beautiful female who will complement the male nationalist. As we might expect, it can also be a mutilated version of the male self or a terrifying female with desires of her own who threatens the male self with emasculation. But how can the nation-state be two bodies at once? The answer is that the nation-state is not gendered absolutely, but always involves two principles defined against each other, principles labelled masculine and feminine, neither one, however, being limited to men or women. We must keep in mind the hyphenated nature of the nation-state, at once nation and state. The state is defined by a territory, an official history, and institutions of administration and control. A nation is a people united by fellow feeling and identifiable by a common language, religion, or story. State and nation can be distinguished but, at least in nationalist conception, cannot be thought apart from each other. A collective proves itself a nation if it can successfully demand a state in its own image. Without such a state, a group united by language or religion or common interests remains perforce subnational and the enemy of the nation. At the same time, in order to legitimize itself, a state must summon a nation into being by appealing to shared interests and propagating symbols and narratives with which people can identify. Unless it becomes a nation, the state's legitimacy is always open to challenge. The two processes of nation and state formation are symmetrical but their intersection frequently brings conflict, as can be seen in the creation of India, where a colonial territory claimed to be a nation and therefore entitled to sovereignty, and Pakistan, where a self-declared nation based on religion sought a state in its own image.

It is tempting to read the different roles played by state and nation in *Midnight's Children* in terms of gender, to read the Indian state as male and the nation that it courts as female. Saleem describes Sonny who courts Evie Burns on his behalf as a politician wooing a female electorate (183). As we have seen, the projected body that Aadam Aziz falls in love with through the bedsheet can fill the hole in his own centre because it is a female body, explicitly unlike his own. When the young Dr Aziz, who is beginning to think of himself not as a Muslim but as an Indian, falls in love with a traditional Kashmiri Muslim whom he glimpses only in fragments, he is in the figurative position of the Western-educated nationalist who rediscovers and lays claim to a folk-nation untouched by colonialism. Anti-colonial nationalists, like Aziz and like Nehru, seek independence for a modern state in the name of the nation, the repository of tradition and of authenticity which predates colonialism. The nation, of course, like the "phantasm of a partitioned woman" (26), is a projection of the male nationalist's desire. As Anne McClintock writes, "Women are represented as the atavistic and authentic body of national tradition (inert, backward-looking and natural), embodying nationalism's conservative principle of continuity. Men, by contrast, represent the progressive agent of national modernity (forward-thrusting, potent and historic), embodying nationalism's progressive, or revolutionary, principle of discontinuity. Nationalism's anomalous relation to time is thus managed as a natural relation to gender" (McClintock 1996, 263).

The marriage of the modern and the traditional is not, however, where Rushdie's novel ends but where it begins. The male nationalist who needs female tradition to complete himself must also awaken the traditional nation to the need for modern politics. Aziz falls in love with a projected image of traditional womanhood, but wants to remake his bride into a modern woman such as "his Ingrid," whom he has known in Germany (13). Naseem Ghani's purdah is what aroused her suitor's desire, but her husband wants her now to uncover her face. As he burns her veils, Aziz urges his wife to "Forget about being a good Kashmiri girl" and "Start thinking about being a modern Indian woman" (35). On their wedding night the modern doctor urges Naseem to move "like a woman" (34), invoking a model of womanhood that purports to be universal and that his wife feels as a violation.

This is the contradiction of modern nationalism: the nationalist wants a nation different from and at the same time like all others. In a single sentence Saleem characterizes India as an ancient land that in its "five thousand years of history" had "invented the game of chess and traded with Middle Kingdom Egypt" and as a new "nation which had never previously existed" (111). In *Nationalist Thought and the Colonial World* Chatterjee describes such modernizing nationalism, which he associates with Nehru, as a ruse: tradition is but a mask worn by the modernizer (Chatterjee 1986). Rushdie depicts it not as bad faith but as a paradox at the heart of desire and identity.

The modern nationalist's synthesizing desire for a whole greater than the sum of its parts is explicitly male. The inadequacy of this "derivative discourse" manifests itself, according to Chatterjee at least, in the resistance it faces from the true folk tradition. The women who are the objects of desire, like the folk communities they represent, have desires of their own that do not necessarily coincide with those of the modernizing nationalists. Naseem, the woman behind the perforated bedsheet, refuses Aadam's interpellation. At his insistence she does give up the veil, but she is stronger than he is. Reverend Mother, as she becomes known, is not remade in the image of her husband's desire. She never becomes an Indian but remains a Muslim and eventually moves to Pakistan. It seems that loving in fragments was a "mistake" (41).

The nationalism of Aadam Aziz is itself but a form of "optimism," a lost wager on the direction of the future. The future lies not with a united India but with Partition and with subnational allegiances. Of course, "Prophets are not always false simply because they are overtaken, and swallowed up, by history" (296). While the state that seeks a nation loses the opening battle with the nation seeking to be a state, Saleem's and Rushdie's sympathies clearly lie with the self-deluded optimist Aziz, rather than with the self-sufficient Reverend Mother.

Saleem, like his grandfather before him, identifies with the state that Nehru and the Congress Party wrested from the British, conceived of in terms of a mapped territory and an official history made by political leaders, and imagined as a body like his own. This state seeks to marshall the tremendous powers associated with industrialization, state capitalism, and mass education for the benefit of the hundreds of millions of its nationals. The Nehruvian state is best described as a "project," with all the connotations that word has acquired in the twentieth century of progress, hubris, large-scale mobilization, and mass participation. *Midnight's Children* is a nationalist manifesto by a Muslim who does not identify with a particular minority but with the totality. His India is a modern, secular state, defined against Britain, the imperial power, but also against Pakistan. It is intended to win the allegiance of readers, even, paradoxically, when these are not imagined as Indians.

Saleem has lived, however, to see women not only resist the state but successfully take it over. The Widow, Indira Gandhi, quite literally threatens men with the loss of their manhood, first, in the form of forced sterilizations, and then in the form of castrations performed on all the Midnight's Children, when Saleem and his peers, male and female alike, are reduced to "women." Saleem declares that the "too-many women" in his life are all "aspects of Devi, the goddess," "who is Kali Durga Chandi Chamunda Uma Sati and Parvati" (393). But Indira Gandhi in the novel is not a figure of traditional society: she mobilizes the powers associated with modern Weberian rationality, the powers of mass propaganda and surveillance, in order to bolster her own rule. The emblems of this new tyranny are slum clearance and mass sterilization, perversions (but also, arguably, the logical outcome) of the great Nehruvian projects. The Widow, like Durga in the VHP image, is not essentially different from the male sovereign that Hobbes portrayed. It is the state, once the ground of Saleem's psychological integrity, that now directly threatens that integrity.

As a record of growing up in the conditions promulgated by capitalist modernity, *Midnight's Children* inevitably becomes an anti-national satire. When Saleem is unmanned, he ceases to be the hero of his own story. He abandons his identification with the state, now usurped by the Widow, and comes to regard himself and the other Midnight's Children (with the significant exception of Shiva) as the state's victims. He identifies instead with the poor and dispossessed, and with alternative ways of being such as communism, in short, with the nation rather than the state.

The two modes of metonymic assembly and synecdochical identification in *Midnight's Children* correspond to the two processes that

Crawford Young identifies as crucial to the formation of national identity in postcolonial states: "the collectivization of people as a nation and the personalization of the state as the nation-state" (20). The state defines a sphere of public action and exchange filled by organizations, institutions, and media, whose participants by their interaction with each other and with state institutions constitute civil society. The state brings civil society into being by interpellating the people within its borders as citizens and setting the limits of the arena in which people make their careers and debate issues. Civil society, in turn, demands accountability from a state that it creates by consensus and contract. As Young explains, "The state protects and provides while it dominates and extracts," and civil society "responds with exit, voice, or loyalty," that is with rejection, a demand for full participation, or identification (222). In Young's description, the state performs the stereotypical male roles of providing and dominating, while civil society, because it includes the private and the domestic spheres, "relates to the 'domestic kingdom,' where women and feminine virtues are said to prevail" (McCrone 1998, 91). In Rushdie's novel the state may not always be male – it may fall into the hands of the Widow, a modern Durga – but civil society is always feminized.

When the state becomes an enemy, Saleem learns to identify with the nation, not, however, the nation of tradition, as once represented by Reverend Mother, but the nation of civil society. Gupta points out that in India civil society is generally regarded as inimical to modernity, as lying "in traditions and customs that are either before the state or outside the state" (Gupta 2000, 165). Saleem deliberately revises that definition so that civil society comes to mean a public sphere brought into being by the state and therefore modern, but also victimized by and opposed to the state. The movement from the state to the nation, by transforming the state into the nation-state, actually rescues the state from insignificance. Saleem learns that the institutions of state are inherently violent. They cannot be justified by their triumph over foreign or internal rivals. The victim of the state in the first instance is Shiva, doomed by the baby switch to a life of poverty, who represents those for whom the state represents at best an irrelevance and at worst an unmerited loss. But Saleem and Shiva reverse roles and Saleem becomes the state's victim. Unlike Shiva, this victim neither rejects the state nor seeks to usurp its power but remembers the state as it promised to be and calls it back to its better self. This victim takes the state for granted and wants only to redeem it.

There is a sense in which Saleem's disastrous castration is merely a literalization of a lack that has haunted his consciousness ever since he first became conscious. From the start, he has declared that India, the third-world nation, is "impotent" (179). His telepathy, called All-India Radio, recalls not only the transistor radio that the memoirist has beside him while he writes but also "the notorious free-transistor sterilization bribe" (165). Saleem himself is unusually sexless, at least as long as he is in India (in Pakistan, as we have seen, his sexuality is a different story). Indira Gandhi, it would seem, did not take anything from him that Saleem had not already renounced.

Saleem is not, in the final analysis, a Captain India figure at all, but rather an Indian Everyman, or perhaps a Shri 420, the hero of the 1955 Raj Kapoor film of that name. At the end of the novel, Saleem reduces his claims to significance: rather than the agent or the catalyst, he has merely been a witness to terrible events much larger than himself, someone like the figure of the Common Man in the cartoons of R.K. Laxman (Figs. 3, 4, 5). In his Introduction to *The Best of Laxman,* Volume Two, the cartoonist describes how "when our struggle for independence from imperial domination began to gain momentum, the enslaved masses were symbolized by a sorrow-struck Bharat Mata – a semi-divine being adorning (sic) a crown with flowing black tresses wearing a carefully draped saree" (Laxman 1993). However, it would have been "anachronistic" to prolong her appearance after independence. In his introduction to Volume One, Laxman tells how he developed the figure of the Common Man:

> In the early days I used to hurriedly cram in as many figures as I could to represent the masses. Gradually my efforts narrowed to fewer and fewer figures. These my readers came to accept as representative of the whole country. Finally, I succeeded in reducing my symbol to one man: a man in a checked coat, whose bald head boasts only a wisp of white hair, and whose bristling moustache lends support to a bulbous nose, which in turn holds up an oversized pair of glasses. He has a permanent look of bewilderment on his face. He is ubiquitous. Today he is found hanging around a cabinet-room where a high-powered meeting is in progress. Tomorrow he is among the slum-dwellers listening to their woes or is marching along with protesters as they demand the abolition of the nuclear bomb (Laxman 1990).

Laxman's Common Man, without power himself, is nevertheless privy to all that happens in the state, which he regards with clear-sighted irony. He represents both the nation and the reader.

Midnight's Children teaches us, however, to be wary of the supposed powerlessness of abdicating power. When he first sits down to write, Saleem, mutilated and much reduced, still insists on his

Fig. 3 Laxman cartoon showing Congress Party infighting upon the supine body of Nehru who had just announced his desire to retire (2 May 1958). The Common Man is being strangled by the speaker. *The Eloquent Brush*, p. 19.

identification with the state of India. Indeed, the narcissistic child had never appreciated his intimate link to history; it is the adult memoirist who, looking back, finds all the parallels between autobiography and national history, and who insists on the grandiose meaning of his life. Only as he brings his writing to an end does Saleem concede that such megalomania has no future. This humility is not the lesson that his life has taught him – it is, after all, the conviction of his own significance that inspires him to pick up pen and start to write – the newfound humility is instead the calculated conclusion to the narrative, the way Saleem actually guarantees his significance and ends up meaning something. The narration moves from an identification with the state, as extreme as that of the ten-year-old who convened the Midnight Children's Conference, to a disillusioned disengagement from the state, and presents this as the lesson of Saleem's life. The implication is that the state cannot anchor identity, but the nation can.

Fig. 4 Indira Gandhi (17 December 1974). *The Eloquent Brush* p. 111.

By abjuring the masculine trappings of state power and joining an all-female working-class community, Saleem succeeds where his grandfather failed: he secures his own and the reader's allegiance to the nation-state, and makes it seem inevitable. Of course, Saleem who abjures power is relying on another, more subtle kind of power, one that denies that it is power, the power that Scheherazade had over the Sultan. But this does not mean his achievement is merely a ruse, an underhanded way of reinstating statist ideologies. It can also be read – and I would attribute part of the novel's popularity to the fact that it has been read – as transforming a comprador regime into a popular nation-state. When he suffers at the Hand of the Widow, Saleem shares a bond with all the other victims of the state. Together they constitute a nation. At the end of the novel, the identity of India is no longer in question: India is made up of all who have suffered at the Hand of Indira Gandhi. It might not be too much to declare that Saleem the memoirist (as opposed to Saleem the hero) is the child of that second Midnight, the hour when Indira Gandhi arrogated dictatorial powers to herself with the declaration of a State of Emergency

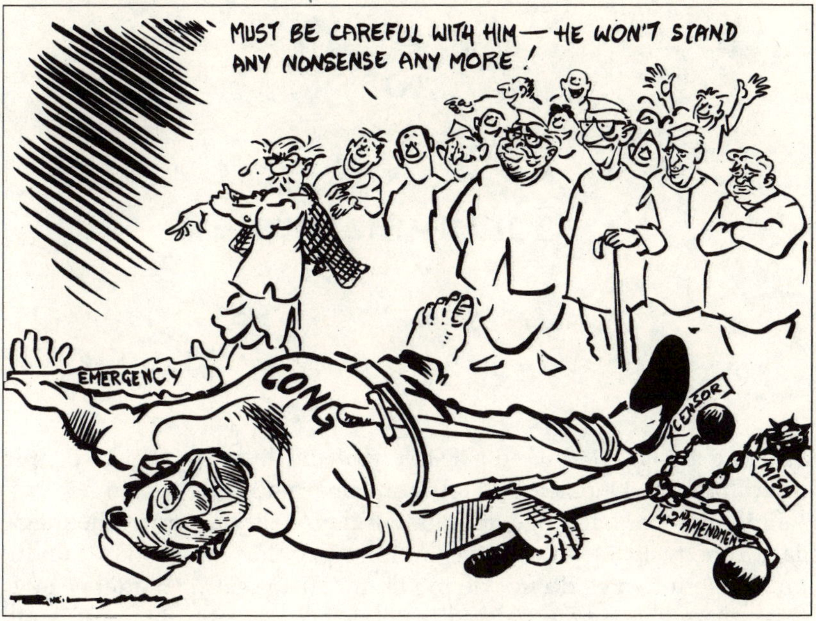

Fig. 5 The Common Man's victory over the Congress Party (29 March 1977). *The Eloquent Brush* p. 137.

10

Communalism

Growing up in Methwold's Estate, Saleem lives alongside people called Ibrahim, Dubash, Catrack, and Sabarmati, whose primary self-definition is not language, religion, or nationality. Later, in the magicians' ghetto in Delhi, he lives among people whose Sikh, Hindu, and Muslim names do not define them. Historically, Chatterjee suggests, there has always existed in the subcontinent a mode of being in the world that denies "the centrality of the state in the life of the nation" and appeals instead "to the many institutions and practices in the everyday lives of the people through which they had evolved a way of living with their differences" (Chatterjee 1995, 126–7). According to this view, "the true history of India lay not in the battles of kings and the rise and fall of empires but in this everyday world of popular life whose innate flexibility, untouched by conflicts in the domain of the state, allowed for the coexistence of all religious beliefs" (ibid., 127). Chatterjee contrasts the peaceful acceptance of difference, characteristic of the everyday, with the multicultural ideology of the state. Hogan makes a similar contrast between "practical identity," which is "a matter of being able to do things with people here and now" (519), and "categorical identity," "the hierarchized series of categories that one takes as definitive of one's self" (517). Saleem, however, runs the two kinds of hybridity together. His nostalgia for Methwold's Estate and the Delhi ghetto, both destroyed, is also his nostalgia for the unfulfilled promise of the Nehruvian state.

The India that Saleem identifies with is many-headed, polyglot, and multicultural. Its vibrant hybridity is best suggested by the catalogue. When, as the result of an accident in a washing-chest, Saleem first acquires a national consciousness, he becomes a kind of "supernatural ham radio" (369) catching the voices, "as profane, and as multitudinous, as dust" (166), of all who live within the frontiers of the state:

> at first, I was no more than a tourist, a child peeping through the miraculous peepholes of a private "Dilli-dekho" machine. Dugdugee-drums rattled in my left (damaged) ear as I gained my first glimpse of the Taj Mahal through the eyes of a fat Englishwoman suffering from the tummy-runs; after which, to balance south against north, I hopped down to Madurai's Meenakshi temple and nestled amongst the woolly, mystical perceptions of a chanting priest. I toured Connaught Place in New Delhi in the guise of an auto-rickshaw driver, complaining bitterly to my fares about the rising price of gasoline; in Calcutta I slept rough in a section of drainpipe. By now thoroughly bitten by the travel bug, I zipped down to Cape Comorin and became a fisherwoman whose sari was as tight as her morals were loose ... standing on red sands washed by three seas, I flirted with Dravidian beachcombers in a language I couldn't understand; then up into the Himalayas, into the neanderthal moss-covered hut of a Goojar tribal, beneath the glory of a completely circular rainbow and the tumbling moraine of the Kolahoi glacier. At the golden fortress of Jaisalmer I sampled the inner life of a woman making mirrorwork dresses and at Khajuraho I was an adolescent village boy, deeply embarrassed by the erotic, Tantric carvings on the Chandela temples standing in the fields, but unable to tear away my eyes ... in the exotic simplicities of travel I was able to find a modicum of peace. (171)

Saleem's new national consciousness is the tourist's itinerary of clichés: he "hops," "tours," "zips" through, and "samples" a collection of Viewmaster scenes. When travelling the country during the election campaign of 1936–7, Nehru himself developed a mental "Indian album, a repertoire of turning images" (Khilnani 1997, 170). Charles Taylor explains that in the modern conception of society, "the search for a truer and more authoritative perspective than my own does not lead me to centre society on a king or sacred assembly, or whatever, but allows for this lateral, horizontal view, which an unsituated observer might have – society as it might be laid out in a tableau without privileged nodal points" (Taylor 1998, 199).

If all perspectives are equal, how do any acquire meaning? Jean-Paul Sartre makes a distinction between the "series" which is an ensemble of people connected by nothing but their relation to an external object, like people waiting for a bus, and a "group" in which members recognize reciprocal relations with each other (Tomlinson 1999, 202–3). The series is incapable of acting together; its members even find it difficult to speak to each other. Saleem seeks to convert the *series* of people living within the state's frontiers into a *group* of citizens by establishing relations among them.

Saleem explicitly compares his new national consciousness to the "Dilli Dekho" ("See Delhi") peepshow of Lifafa Das, who before independence wandered the streets of the capital, offering picture postcard views not just of Delhi but of the nation, including the Taj Mahal and Meenakshi Temple (75). The Dilli Dekho peepshow is at once a collection of metonyms, a synecdoche (because an image of the nation in miniature), and a metonym itself (because a symptom and perhaps a catalyst of a growing national consciousness). It thus functions as what Lauren Berlant, following Walter Benjamin, calls a "dialectical image," "an image that functions like a montage in which objects are made part-objects by their relation to a larger simulacrum of wholeness" (Berlant 1991, 24). All-India Radio, to which Saleem also compares his telepathy, is another such dialectical image. The national broadcaster announces itself with the words "Yé Akashvani hai" (Rushdie 1981, 198), literally "Here is the voice from the sky."* This singular voice addresses a plurality of listeners who, while they will never know each other, hear the same broadcasts at the same moment (and at the same hour: India sprawls across a single time zone). The nation consists of all who follow the same events in politics, sports, and popular culture, especially music and film. In his telepathic travels, Saleem boasts, "I learned the truth behind the *Filmfare* gossip about the dancer Vyjayantimala, and I was at the crease with Polly Umrigar at the Brabourne Stadium; I was Lata Mangeshkar the playback singer and Bubu the clown at the circus behind Civil Lines" (171). If imagining himself with entertainers and sports heroes were all that Saleem's telepathy amounted to, the only thing to distinguish him from other listeners of All-India Radio would be that he does not require batteries nor is he subject to power cuts. Saleem's telepathy, however, allows him intimate access not just to the people featured on All-India Radio but also to the many worlds of its listeners. Saleem can travel on the telepathic airwaves to explore the minds of "a landlord in Uttar Pradesh, my belly rolling over my pajama-cord as I ordered serfs to set my surplus grain on fire," of a two-month-old child "starving to death in Orissa," of voters for different parties, and even of Nehru himself (171–2).

* I am grateful to Harish Trivedi for translating this for me. Trivedi also points out that Rushdie's Urdu is poor and the phrase should be written with "yeh" (singular) not "ye" (plural).

Saleem quickly tires, however, of eavesdropping on strangers: he abandons All-India Radio for the satisfactions of the Midnight Children's Conference. The children represent a single age grade, linked not by blood but by the moment of birth. They are mirrors of Saleem as well as of the nation: they are all the same age and have special powers just as he does. Saleem receives their transmissions from the four corners of the state, but their messages are identical: "From far to the North, 'I.' And the South East West: 'I.' 'I.' 'And I.'" (166–7). In Saleem's imagination the Midnight's Children represent the hope, however illusory, of the nation as it should be.

In the best scenario, the nations represented by All-India Radio and the Midnight Children's Conference would complement each other. Saleem is a hybrid self in Bombay, the Indian capital of cultural hybridity, built by the British and home to every language and religion in the subcontinent. Precisely because it is made up of so many parts, Bombay can be a synecdoche of the hybrid nation: not just one part among many, but the part that expresses the whole. This vision of the city as a synecdoche of the whole is expressed in the titles of recent twin volumes edited by Sujata Patel and Alice Thorner: *Bombay: Metaphor for Modern India* and *Bombay: Mosaic of Modern Culture* (Patel and Thorner, 1996). Self, city, and nation repeat each other: self is to city as city is to nation. This is the notion of sovereignty that, according to Hardt and Negri, characterizes the modern nation-state: "the people representing the multitude, the nation representing the people, and the state representing the nation" (Hardt and Negri 2000, 134). As Jonathan Rée puts it, the logic of nations "is one not of linkage, but of substitution": "By a kind of dialectical conjuring trick, they make it seem as if nature, politics, and subjectivity could all be translated into each other without remainder" (Rée 1998, 84–5).

Saleem's nationalism does not just make room for difference but requires difference. He defines India as "a mass fantasy shared in varying degrees by Bengali and Punjabi, Madrasi and Jat" (111), a formula that suggests that the nation is the sum not of all its citizens but of a series of collective identities. Saleem's words are an echo, deliberate or not, of the judgement passed by Sir John Strachey: "That men of the Punjab, Bengal, the North-Western Provinces, and Madras, should ever feel they belong to one great nation, is impossible" (cited in Embree 1980, 17). According to Chatterjee, British Orientalism saw the identification with insular rival communities as an "irredeemable racial characteristic" of Indians, proof that India could never be a modern nation (Chatterjee 1993, 223). Saleem disagrees with Strachey the colonial administrator about the subcontinent's capacity for nationhood, but does assume that the nation is an assembly of distinct subnational identities.

Let us look again at the catalogue that expresses Saleem's national consciousness. In order to suggest the "multitudinous realities of the land" (172), Saleem's catalogue of voices and perspectives must be "random" (171) and include as much diversity as possible. At the same time, as with all Saleem's catalogues, the apparent randomness is controlled by relations of complementarity: the extreme south is "balanced" against north, the Taj Mahal against the Meenakshi Temple, the outsider Englishwoman against the insider priest, the sea against the mountains, the landlord against the starving peasant, the Congress supporter against the Communist. For the metonyms that make up the whole to be all related to each other, their meaning must be immanent: the voice from the south must represent the south; the priest must represent Hinduism. The metonyms in Saleem's catalogue are therefore all potential synecdoches of groups smaller than the nation. The Taj Mahal and the Meenakshi Temple represent Moghul and Hindu India respectively. The bigbellied landlord and the starving child, the primitive tribal, and the mystical priest are Indian clichés. In the India that Saleem tours, Englishwomen are fat and suffer from the runs, poor fisherwomen are always hitching their saris "brazenly up between their legs" (as they do repeatedly: 94, 262, 443), and what else do auto-rickshaw drivers do but complain about gasoline prices (see also 432)? Each seemingly random perspective in Saleem's telepathic tour of India does not just point to the larger whole that contains them all but also to a smaller whole, based on class or language or religion, with which it shares an essence. If the people Saleem visits telepathically had names or were allowed to speak to him, they might become individuals, but then the representative nature of the sample would be compromised. Chakravarty notes a similar "tendency within the Bombay film to both identify and nullify marks of (intercultural) difference" which "allows national identity to surface as so many styles of the flesh" (Chakravarty 1993, 200). This reproduction of stereotypes of gender, class, race, and religion is inevitable: there is no other way of imagining the bodies of strangers whom one has not met.

Compare the vision of a self as big as the world that Lyndall has in Olive Schreiner's *Story of an African Farm*:

> When my own life feels small, and I am oppressed with it, I like to crush together, and see it in a picture, in an instant, a multitude of disconnected unlike phases of human life – a medieval monk with his string beads pacing the quiet orchard, and looking up from the grass at his feet to the heavy fruit-trees; little Malay boys playing naked on a shining sea-beach; a Hindoo philosopher alone under his banyan tree, thinking, thinking, thinking, so that in the thought of God he may lose himself; a troop of

> Bacchanalians dressed in white, with crowns of vine-leaves, dancing along the Roman streets; a martyr on the night of his death looking through the narrow window to the sky, and feeling that already he has the wings that shall bear him up ... an epicurean discoursing at a Roman bath to a knot of his disciples on the nature of happiness; a Kaffir witch-doctor seeking for herbs by moonlight, while from the huts on the hill-side come the sound of dogs barking, and the voices of women and children; a mother giving bread and milk to her children in little wooden basins and singing the evening song. I like to see it all; I feel it run through me – that life belongs to me; it makes my little life larger; it breaks down the narrow walls that shut me in. (Schreiner 1993, 228)

The principles in this catalogue are the same as in Saleem's: a collection of stereotypes is meant to suggest the whole of which others are all parts but which only the self, somehow outside the whole, can contemplate. While Lyndall and Saleem are complex, many-sided composites characterized by a negative capability that allows them, in Saleem's words, "to look into the hearts and minds of men" (196), those whose thoughts they look into are simple and fixed. Other people are part of the complex, many-sided whole, by virtue of their knowability, their capacity to be reduced to a single known quality.

Although both Lyndall and Saleem are explicitly opposed to empire, their visions express what Quentin Anderson has called the Imperial Self (Q. Anderson 1971), able to swallow the world because it is at once as large as the world and outside it. There is a difference, however, between Lyndall and Saleem: her catalogue is of the world, while his is of the nation, an entity smaller than the world but big enough to feel like the world. Hers is of all recorded history while his is of the present moment. We can account for the difference by considering their locations. Lyndall speaks from a colonial frontier about a world that has been made one by empire. Saleem, on the other hand, locates himself not on the periphery of empire but in a national centre, a rival of the imperial centre.

The difference between regionalist identities and a national one, in Saleem's view, is that the former are undifferentiated, made up of individuals that are "aggregable" because identical (B. Anderson 1998, 44) – all Bengalis are Bengali – while the nation constitutes a healthier whole precisely because it is made up of distinct elements that can be listed: India includes Bengalis and Punjabis and Jats. Saleem assumes that Bengal (only West Bengal?), the Punjab, Tamil Nadu, and the Jat caste are more real somehow than the nation – "The word Indian doesn't really mean anything," Rushdie tells David Brooks, "Bengali means more than Indian; India, if it means anything, means plurality" (D. Brooks 2000, 67) – but he also feels that subnational identities are more limiting and less desirable as identities because they are inherited and ineluctable, while India is freely chosen ("a dream we all agreed to dream," 111). In other words, Saleem and Rushdie imagine that the culture called Bengali functions as a second nature, rigorously determining how members think and act, while India relies on a different notion of culture altogether, culture as the realm of human freedom wrested from the necessity of nature.

Saleem's hybrid self claims to be able to contain the many pure but incomplete selves associated with language and religion. In effect, he makes his identity congruent with his world by saying, in effect, "I am as large as the many things I know." In his experience, communal selves, by contrast, make their selves smaller than the world or, even worse, insist on reducing the world to the size of their selves. In their homogeneity, subnational identities resemble autonomous organs such as Shiva's knees and Indira Gandhi's hand, whose strength derives from their partiality: they obey no reason but merely follow their nature. Identity that involves natural predilection is stronger but of less value than an identity freely chosen. Language and caste, it would seem, exist before the self – "old regionalist loyalties and prejudices" represent "atavistic longings" that threaten to crack "the body politic"(239) – and have therefore to be transcended by the rational self, which only finds expression in the hybrid nation.

Identities based on religion or language inspire dangerous mobs. A violent mindlessness, which is also single-mindedness, characterizes the language marchers and communal rioters prepared to kill Lifafa Das and Dr. Narlikar. When Dr Narlikar is killed by demonstrators demanding the break up of the Bombay Presidency on linguistic lines, his killers are described metonymically: "The ears of the language marchers heard the roughness of his tongue; the marchers' feet paused, their voices rose in rebuke. Fists were shaken; oaths were oathed" (174). In a later episode, also involving demonstrators, Saleem on his bicycle hurtles "down into the mouth of the march, heads feet bodies": "Hands grabbing handlebars as I slow down in the impassioned throng. Smiles filled with good teeth surround me" (188). The language marchers have "eyes," "ears," "feet," "fists," "hands," and even a "tail-end" (174), but no selves, not even grotesque selves, to which these parts are subordinate. They resemble the autonomous body parts we saw in chapter seven, dangerously partial in their self-sufficiency. The mob's demand to break up the polity is symptomatic and emblematic of its own lack of wholeness.

These poorly differentiated collections of eyes and ears and hands, lacking selves of their own, threaten to swamp the selves of any they absorb. The psychologist Kakar describes how "The individual is practically wrapped up in the crowd and gets continuous sensual pounding through all avenues that his body can afford. The consequence is a blurring of the body image and of the ego, a kind of self-transcendence that is reacted to by panic or exhilaration as individuality disappears and the 'integrity,' 'autonomy,' and 'independence' of the ego seem to be wishful illusions and mere hypothetical constructs" (Kakar 1995, 57). Saleem is insensible to and suspicious of the ecstatic pull of crowds and acutely aware of their power to crush the individual who seeks to maintain his integrity: "I am being buffeted right and left while rip tear crunch reaches its climax, and my body is screaming, it cannot take this kind of treatment any more" (445).

Kakar distinguishes the "physical group" of the crowd, "represented in the bodies of its members rather than in their minds," from "the cultural group" of the imagined nation, which remains perforce an abstraction (Kakar 1995, 56–7), and Rushdie's novel implies a similar distinction between the dangerous mob representing linguistic or religious identities and the valuable collective that is the nation-state. The nation-state may be a crowd but it is not a mob. Rushdie declares that "To my mind, the defining image of India is the crowd, and a crowd is by its very nature superabundant, heterogeneous, many things at once" (Rushdie 1991E, 32). This is "the many-headed monster of the crowd" that, at the moment of independence, celebrates in the streets of Delhi and receives a transfusion as "the new myth courses through its veins, replacing its blood with corpuscles of saffron and green" (114). The crowd that represents the nation may suffer violence but is not itself violent. "Swept along" by the "many thousands of Indians" who fill Jallianwala Bagh on April 13th 1919, Aadam Aziz enters the "mouth of the alley" and "penetrates the heart of the crowd" (36). After Brigadier Dyer's massacre, he is crushed under the bodies of the crowd, but because they have assembled in the name of the nation, he does not lose himself but finds himself.

We must conclude that the distinction between a crowd and a mob is the distinction between the nation-state and the subnational grouping based on language or religion. For the individual to be a whole requires not indiscriminate blending but a proper balance among parts. In the mob the self is lost; in the nation, however, it is confirmed. It is not subordination that Saleem fears but improper subordination.

I want, however, to emphasize how much hybridity, rather than being a faithful description of Saleem's identity, is a valorized description of self. Hybridity allows Saleem to contain others instead of excluding them. All societies and all selves are hybrid, and while it is arguably more valuable to recognize this than to deny it, it can be but a rhetorical move to claim superiority on the basis of hybridity. In practice, the hybrid self, no less than the pure self it opposes, relies on the exclusion of some things: in this case, on the exclusion of purity. Its claim to contain others relies on two senses of containment: making room for others but also seeing around them.

Saleem's notion of the nation-state as a collection of representative minorities appears more democratic and more respectful of difference than are the subnational groupings that make it up. However, the apostle of hybridity and impurity is still what Rogers Brubaker terms a "groupist": one who "sees the population as composed of definable, bounded, internally homogeneous blocs," albeit "located not in *physical* but in *social* and *cultural* space" (Brubaker 1998, 295). In order to be thought, the hybrid consensual nation that Saleem and Rushdie celebrate requires the essentialist subnational constituents that it transcends.

We may better understand Rushdie's nation if we contrast it with several other versions of India. G.N. Devy, for instance, argues that pre-colonial India has always been characterized by two contending modes of being, the *mārga*, the Great Tradition, associated with Sanskrit and encompassing the whole of the nation, and the *deśî*, the Little Traditions associated with the different Indian languages and their literary traditions. To identify India only with the former is to suffer, Devy says, from colonial amnesia (Devy 1992).

Sunil Khilnani, on the other hand, argues that the subnational and regional identities are neither atavistic nor primordial but "only came into being as people tried to define a larger 'Indian' community": "The belief that Indian nationalism had subsequently to unite and subordinate these regional identities is thus a curious misreading of the relationship between nation and region in India. In fact, a sense of region and nation emerged together, through parallel self-definitions – and this point is essential to any understanding of the distinctive, layered character of Indianness" (Khilnani 1997, 153). Federal elections, central to the development of an Indian national consciousness in Khilnani's account, inspire subnational identities based on language or caste: "Democratic politics seems to require that identities and perceptions of interest be stable; but political identities and interests do not have a pre-political existence – they have to be created through politics. Thus, paradoxically, democratic politics must itself produce the very identities and interests which it presupposes in order to function in the first place. And this process of identity creation is a dangerous business, more akin to conflict than competition" (ibid., 49). Chatterjee, too, observes that federal elections have come to rely on appeals to "vote banks" which translate "forms of social power based on landed proprietorship or caste loyalty or religious authority" into "'representative' forms of electoral support" (Chatterjee 1993, 213): "Thus, a particular interest, whether expressed in terms of class, language, region, caste, tribe, or community, is to be recognized and given a place within the framework of the general by being assigned a priority and an allocation relative to all the other parts" (ibid., 214–5). By this reading, the same forces that bring the nation-state into being also promote an awareness of its constituent parts. The census and the electoral rolls classify people by caste and race and language and religion, making citizens of the nation aware of their majority or minority status in the larger whole.

The movement for linguistic provinces in the fifties, which Saleem (and Rushdie) remember as a dangerous nostalgia for purity, actually "found their fervour in the metaphor of popular participation" (Gupta 2000, 125): "The proponents of this movement did not ask for linguistic provinces to diminish the aura of the nation-state, but as good Indians," for, they argued, "India would be better governed as a democracy , if democracy functioned in the languages of its people" (ibid., 239). Read in this way, the disintegration Saleem so fears is greatly exaggerated: Gupta points out that secession from the federation, a respectable topic before Independence, became almost impossible to imagine, and its espousal "a criminal offence," after Partition had "consecrated territory and seared it into India's consciousness" (ibid., 119).

Sanjay Srivastava, more radical than Gupta, writes that the violent manifestations of fundamentalism and communalism "are not *aberrant* acts of 'backward' populations, they are part of the functioning of a larger system": communalists recognize that their enemy is the self-declared modern elite that, in turn identifies with the whole and justifies its control of state instruments by its own rationality, which they defend against the "irrationality" of the backward classes (Srivastava 1998, 211). Citing Nandy, Srivastava concludes "that there do not exist discrete realms of the (liberal) good and the (fundamentalist) bad and that savagery is not elsewhere" (ibid., 210).

We do not have to go as far as Srivastava, who views the whole as a deplorable system that he somehow manages to stand outside, in order to see that Saleem's presentation of communal mobs is incomplete. Saleem's writing is a race between two opposing forces, one that would contain others and one that must preserve itself from the threat posed by others. Saleem has "swallowed" all the people and events that he has ever known, "Letting no blood escape from the body of the tale" (59), and they grow inside him until he is prepared to give birth to them by writing them. At the same time "what-gnaws-on-bones" is also within, beneath the skin and beyond the powers of doctors to discern, threatening him with disintegration (372). The centripetal feeds the centrifugal, and anything added to the one produces an equal and opposite supplement to the other. Saleem's India is not a self-validating whole betrayed by those who wish to tear it apart. Its integrity, like that of Saleem himself, can only be understood in terms of its potential for fragmentation: India is that which may fall apart.

Saleem's fear of the centrifugal is not misplaced: he recognizes his enemy. Where he is mistaken is in assuming that communalism is primordial or premodern. The nation is constituted by the struggle, Saleem by that which he opposes. The nightmare vision of disintegration with which *Midnight's Children* concludes does not mark the end of either the self or the secular Nehruvian nation, but is their necessary condition. As Lopez writes, Saleem's India "is itself composed of the discourses of multiplicity and cultural entropy" (Lopez 2001, 178). When will the postcolonial nation be whole? The answer, if we are discussing Rushdie's secular India, is "never."

If, as Uprety suggests, nationalism is psychological compensation for colonial amputation, it is also always the site of that amputation. In *Midnight's Children*, the desire to recover wholeness is as much a function of loss as of memory. When Aadam Aziz, Saleem's grandfather, witnesses the massacre at Jallianwala Bagh in Amritsar in 1919, he suffers a bruise that never heals. It is "the shape of that hurt"* that first prompts Aziz's identification with India the nation. He says, "I started off as a Kashmiri and not much of a Muslim. Then I got a bruise on the chest that turned me into an Indian" (40). The nation with which the postcolonial subject learns to identify continues to bear the traces of colonial dismemberment that were its original inspirations. Born as he is at the moment of Indian independence, Saleem has no direct experience of colonialism. We might expect him to inherit only the image of wholeness and not the bruises or amputations inflicted by colonialism. Yet, if not bruised exactly, he is "Stained by the bruise of a Heidelberg bag's clasp" (107). The identification with the nation's wholeness is always haunted by the amputation that the wholeness is supposed to remedy. National consciousness is a "ceaseless throbbing" not of a heart but of a pain (107).

---

* I borrow this expression of Anthony McNeill's from the title of a collection of essays by Gordon Rohlehr (Rohlehr 1992).

11

Pakistan and Purity

Unlike his fellow citizens, all of whom he imagines as parts of a larger whole, Saleem is able to stand outside of and identify with the whole. Indeed, he is terrified of being identified with a particular part. He feels his ability to represent the whole is at risk when his body is claimed by and marked by the subnational (and transnational) community of Islam. Saleem "remembers" the moment of circumcision, when his body was literally inscribed as a Muslim's, not as an affirmation of his belonging to a larger body but as a castration: "I still swear that I can remember the grinning barber, who held me by the foreskin while my member waggled frantically like a slithering snake; and the razor descending, and the pain" (126). Saleem the adult narrator reads in the circumcision a foreshadowing of the "ectomies," the ghastly castrations performed on himself and the other Midnight's Children by the Widow, Indira Gandhi, during the State of Emergency. If he is a Muslim, and so but a part of India and not a mirror of the whole, then he is somehow incomplete and missing a crucial part.

The minaret of a mosque repeatedly casts its minatory shadow over the places Saleem lives in. While he is in Delhi this shadow can be "a protective, unmenacing penumbra" (299), the negative adjective "unmenacing" suggests how much Saleem expects the shadow to be sinister. He has "never lost my Karachi-born view of mosque-shadows, in which, it seemed to me, I could sniff the narrow, clutching, accusative odour of my aunt," the spinster Alia (299). The latent fear of Islam may have something to do with the Indian Muslim's fear of guilt by association, or it may reflect the expatriate Rushdie's sense of nationality. Whatever the motivation, it is certainly the case that, while Saleem finds in Islam a source of imagery and cultural reference, he has no interest in the spiritual dimension, in Urdu, the language associated with Islam in the subcontinent, or in the communal identity that religion and language together mark and create.

The partiality that Islam represents is best illustrated by Saleem's depiction of Pakistan, which is to his India as singleness is to multiplicity, purity to hybridity. At stake are not merely rival states but incompatible definitions of nation and statehood. In the struggle for independence, the Congress Party of Nehru and Gandhi sought to represent all communities in the subcontinent, explicitly including Muslims. They defined India against Britain. The vision of a single India was sabotaged, however, by the Muslim League of Muhammad Ali Jinnah and his rival theory that Indian Muslims and Hindus constitute two nations which can only be accommodated in separate states. The League rejected Congress's right to represent all Indians; Congress disputed the League's claim to speak for all Muslims. Jinnah's two-nation theory, whose triumph resulted in the Partition of the subcontinent, continues to pose a challenge to India's self-definition as a multicultural secular state. "To accept the idea of India," writes Shashi Tharoor, "you had to spurn the logic that had divided the country" (Tharoor 1998, 51). Pakistan, which declares that Muslims constitute a separate nation, and India, whose flag is saffron and green because it includes both Hindus and Muslims, cannot both be right. One must be wrong.

Which side Saleem favours is clear. He consistently deplores Partition. He reminds readers that millions of Muslims, including his grandfather, supported Congress and "loathed" Jinnah's Muslim League (46): "If you don't believe me, check. Find out about Mian Abdullah and his Convocations. Discover how we've swept his story under the carpet" (48). As far as I can make out, in spite of his challenge to the reader to "check," Saleem has invented the Free Islam Convocations, supposedly led by Mian Abdullah the "Hummingbird." Uma Parameswaram suggests that Mian Abdullah is based on the Kashmiri Muslim leader Sheikh Abdullah, "the Lion of Kashmir" as Saleem calls him (253), who formed the National Conference in 1939 to fight for democracy in the predominantly Muslim princely state and for accession to Nehru's India (Parameswaram 1988, 23). Sheikh Abdullah, however, was not assassinated, and he always identified with Kashmir in preference to India. The Free Islam Convocations may be fictions; it remains true, however, that many, probably most, Muslims within the frontiers of India hoped for unity. Those hopes were crushed, Rushdie suggests, by mob-style intimidation, such as is responsible for the Hummingbird's assassination.

In Saleem's narrative, India and Pakistan are not merely distinct states, rivals for his allegiance, but differ qualitatively. India is filled with magical occurrences, and these are assumed to be true if not real. In Pakistan there is also much that appears unbelievable – "Nothing was real; nothing certain" (Rushdie 1981, 329) – but what looks like magic is merely a lie. The ghosts who so terrify the Pakistani soldiers in the Rann of Kutch turn out to be smugglers. The sky is filled with mirages and mysteries, but these are French fighter jets (330). The truth of Saleem's Pakistan, when known, is prosaic, ugly, and dangerous.

In *Midnight's Children* Pakistan represents a dark underworld where the hero is always at risk of losing his identity. India, for all its magic and wonders, is the land of consciousness, located above Pakistan, the land of illusions and nightmares. Only in India can Saleem be Saleem; in Pakistan he loses his powers of telepathy, his memory, and his very humanity. Even the identity of narrator and hero asserted by the use of the first-person pronoun comes under threat in Pakistan. In an extended fairy tale about the land of Kif, in the chapter called "Jamila Singer," set in West Pakistan, Saleem appears in the third person as the villainous brother of the heroine and the incestuous rival of Mutasim the Handsome. This narration, close to the perspective of the Nawab of Kif's court, is full of irony – Saleem is described as "an unfortunate fellow with a face like a cartoon" (312) – which signals not only his own but also the reader's distance from what is being narrated. The title of the next chapter, "How Saleem Achieved Purity," is the first to refer to the protagonist in the third person. After a bomb has levelled the house where the Sinai family is staying, he suffers amnesia and "all the Saleems go pouring out of me" (332). Third-person narration in the first two chapters of Part Three, set in East Pakistan, marks Saleem's thoroughgoing loss of self. The entity that survives the loss of name and memory becomes "the buddha," a tracking dog in the Pakistani army, retaining of Saleem only his wondrous sense of smell. (When Siddhatta Gotama, the Buddha, achieved enlightenment under the bodhi tree, he also referred to himself in the third person, crying out "It is liberated" [Armstrong 2001, 85]).

We have already noted how important vision is to Saleem's perception of the world. Bombay is full of colour: "the livid green of the waters of the Mahalaxmi Temple 'tank,' the stark black-and-white of the traffic policemen's sun umbrellas and the blue-and-yellowness of their uniforms; but most of all the blue blue blue of the sea" (Rushdie 1981, 288). Karachi, on the other hand, is distinguished by its smells: "the mournful decaying fumes of animal faeces in the gardens of the Frere Road museum, the pustular body odours of young men in loose pajamas holding hands in Sadar evenings, the knife-sharpness of expectorated betel-nut and the bitter-sweet commingling of betel and opium" (307). Saleem's national consciousness has been established through the gaze and the mirror, but smell, the sense that dominates in Pakistan, brings the perceiver close to something before and below the self.

Time does not move the same way in India and Pakistan. For the most part it is speeded up in Pakistan. Independence came at midnight, as it did in India, but is celebrated on August 14, and the clocks run half an hour ahead (79). In travelling from Bombay to Karachi Saleem has the feeling of "having moved directly from an overlong and dribbling childhood into a premature (though still leaky) old age" (276). Whereas it requires nine chapters to cover the two years from the age of nine to the age of eleven spent in India, three chapters cover thirteen years in Pakistan. Many years spent in Pakistan are not covered at all. Saleem has the excuse of amnesia to explain why there is nothing in his narrative between 1965 and 1971, but no excuse except the nature of Pakistan for the "Four years of nothing" between 1958 and 1962 (283). No wonder that Saleem and his companions in the Pakistani army feel "Time lies dead in a rice-paddy" and "they have murdered the hours and forgotten the date" (348). Whereas India is marked by a countdown to a birth, which has the effect of delaying time and building suspense, in Pakistan a countdown to death actually speeds things up (331). The pages of a calendar are torn off one by one as India counts down to independence and the suspense builds up (91); in Pakistan the fluttering of a calendar's pages suggests the passing of five years (336).

India is repeatedly described as a dream, that is, a desire that is projected outwards and inspires action in the world. There is, to be sure, a distinction to be made between the dream and its actualization: think of the almost unbridgeable distance between the woman projected onto the bedsheet by Aadam Aziz and the reality of Naseem Ghani, or between the Midnight Children's Conference and the many-headed monster in the streets. That distance between idea and reality is fearful, but also healthy. The need to accommodate one's dream to the world of others is precisely what generates consciousness and self in the novel. Rushdie's Pakistan, on the other hand, is a nightmare forcefully realized. The Pakistani army believes it can exercise its will on a passive world. When the generals plot a coup, they translate the movements of pepperpots on the table directly into military actions in the larger sphere. Whereas in India the bodies and wills of others present obstacles to the realization of dreams, nothing gets in the way of the generals' will.

Passive constructions fill the chapters set in Pakistan, as if Saleem were watching a film in which he can distinguish what is happening but not what it might mean. When General Zulfikar seizes President Mirza at gunpoint, "the tip of the gun is forced mmff between the man's parted teeth," "My uncle's pistol is extracted from his mouth" and "gun-barrel pushed between the cheeks of an overfed rump" (282). These passive constructions make for a sense of slow motion; others, however, imply the acceleration of time-lapse photography, as in the following passage in which the Sinai family builds a house in Karachi: "and now a pickle-jar was produced. Brine was discarded on the thirsty ground; and what-was-left-inside received the mullah's blessings. After which an umbilical cord [...] was implanted in the earth; and at once, a house began to grow" (300). Given the passive voice with which Saleem describes it, it is perhaps not surprising that the house was never to be finished.

There is a pattern of chiasmic reversal in Saleem's experience of the two states. In Pakistan his sister, now called Jamila Singer, takes over his role as mirror of the nation and enters "fully into her kingdom" (285). Where he was once All-India Radio, his sister becomes the "Voice of Pakistan," the name of the Pakistani government broadcaster (329). As Jamila tells him, "looks like from now on I'll just have to be the good guy, and you can have all the fun" (247). In Bombay the Brass Monkey had been the animal – Mary says she "Should have been born with four legs!" (150) – and her place had been the figurative "family doghouse" (167, 247), but in Pakistan it is Saleem who is literally relegated to the kennel: "while she rose into the clouds, I fell into the gutter" (306). Indeed, in Pakistan Saleem takes on, however uncomfortably, the brutish, hypermasculine role played by Shiva in India. The "spoors of Karachi streets" among which the adolescent Saleem prowls on his Lambretta motorcycle are explicitly compared to Shiva's "whoring trails" in Delhi (397). Later, as an actual tracking dog, Saleem enjoys a free sexuality, not unlike Shiva's promiscuity in India. Saleem the memoirist refers to his amnesiac canine self as "he (or I)" (339), which echoes how he had previously referred to himself and Shiva (222).

Saleem recovers his memories and his self, when he is transported "back" to Delhi in Parvati's magical basket. Saleem was conceived in Delhi (as an idea of his parents, if not as an embryo), but has never actually been there. Such is the magic of the nation, however, that his journey there for the first time is nonetheless a return. The shape of Parvati's basket recalls both the womb and the washing-chest in which he first saw his mother's nakedness and became aware of himself as Indian. India is clearly the hero's true home and Pakistan a false one.

When seeking completion and sovereignty, how does the colonial know which nation to identify with? There are two possible answers: to identify with the colonial territory in which one finds oneself and thus make of the state a nation (Saleem's solution and the form of nationalism almost universal in the decolonizing world) or to identify with a particular group and seek a state for it (Jinnah's solution and the nationalism endemic to twentieth-century Europe). Pakistan is almost unique among non-European states in following the second course to independence. Iqbal argued that "the Muslims of India are the only Indian people who can fitly be described as a nation in the modern sense of the word" (cited in Wolpert 1989, 317). The successful prosecution of the case for Pakistan resulted in that rare phenomenon: the drawing of national boundaries which were not first colonial boundaries. Whereas, at regular intervals throughout the twentieth century, maps have had to be redrawn to accommodate European nationalism, territorial borders in the Americas, Africa, and West, South and East Asia have remained static; in general, only the names and the colours have changed. The only other examples of a colonized people united by language or religion who seek a state in their own image that does not correspond to a colonial territory (Quebec, Biafra, Kurdistan, Tamil Eelam) are exceptions that, by their failure, prove the rule. Zionism, of course, successfully carved out a West Asian state for a particular nation the year after Pakistan did the same in South Asia, but Israel was arguably the creation of European people.

Jinnah's solution has the attraction of consistency; it promises to abolish the struggle between rival definitions of self based on religion and citizenship. Such consistency is, however, illusory: appeals to homogeneity merely paper over difference, which is certain to resurface. Twenty-four years after independence, the Bengali-speaking East wing of the new Pakistani state waged a successful war of separation. During that war Saleem and his mates go AWOL from "the main body" of "the West Wing forces" (357), a phrase that summarizes just what is wrong in the war. The quest for consistency has the further disadvantage, from Saleem's point of view, of requiring a denial of one's own experience. Amina declares that the move to Pakistan is a "new beginning": "Inshallah, we shall all be new people now" (300). But such a "noble" desire is "unattainable" (300). There is no such thing as a "new people": "What you were is forever who you are," says Saleem, recovering from amnesia (356). For the Bombay dweller to move to Sind in the name of recovering wholeness is to forget the self that she has been and the world that has made her. To be a citizen of Pakistan, says Saleem, is to be "emptied of history" (340).

To be Indian, however, requires just as much forgetting. Saleem's India is also "a nation of forgetters" (38) and an "amnesiac nation" (443). In order to be Indian the first thing that Saleem must forget is that he could ever have been anything else. As we have seen, Uprety accounts for the colonial's identification with the nation in terms of compensation for the psychic damage inflicted by the experience of colonialism: "Nation becomes that imagined space where the fractured and alienated third-world subject finds a wholeness of form with which he can identify" (Uprety 1997, 179). Uprety provides an answer to the question "Why the nation?" but not to the question "Why this nation?" After all, as a Muslim, the young boy in Bombay is explicitly interpellated by another state, in which he is entitled to claim citizenship, where he has relatives, and to which his own parents eventually emigrate. If a Muslim in the subcontinent were to imagine a state of which he or she could be the synecdoche, why should it not resemble Pakistan rather than India? As Khilnani recognizes, "The impulse ascribed to Muslim 'separatists' was no different from that which animates all modern political sensibilities: a desire to reduce the impersonality of the modern state" (Khilnani 1997, 202). Why should Saleem identify with his Kashmiri grandfather in Agra, who has learned to be an Indian, instead of with his Kashmiri grandmother in Karachi, who is first and foremost a Muslim?

The question is raised in acute form by the presence in the novel of another child who grew up, like Saleem, in a bedroom where a picture of a fisherman's finger points at a swimming pool in the shape of British India. Saleem's sister, the Brass Monkey, shares his blue room (152) and, predictably, she too is "possessed by her need to place herself at the centre of events": "she was my sister, after all" (149). Mary Pereira even sings to her the little ditty "Anything you want to be [...] you can be. You can be just what-all you want" (246). Unlike Saleem, however, the Brass Monkey comes to identify with Pakistan and even wins the title of Voice of the Nation for her patriotic songs.

The second thing that Saleem, the mirror of India, forgets is Bharat India, the India that extends from the Indus to the Sundarbans and that Nehru and Gandhi fought for. Breach Candy Swimming Pool, outside his window, is in the shape of British India, and Saleem imagines that his own physiognomy is a map of the entire subcontinent, explicitly including Pakistan (123). Yet, the telepathic powers that allow Saleem to eavesdrop on any of the six hundred million people in India, from the poorest malnourished peasant to the richest of landlords, have as absolute limits the newly established frontiers, "arbitrary" and without historical foundation as they are, of one of the two (later three) successor states to the British Raj (193). These powers give Saleem access to perfect strangers, many who speak languages he does not know, and even to an Englishwoman touring the Taj Mahal, but they do not extend to the members of his own family who have emigrated to Karachi or Rawalpindi. The limits of Saleem's national consciousness respect the Partition, as if Pakistan were indeed a separate nation as well as a separate state. Post-Partition India is the whole of Saleem's world, and until he arrives in Pakistan, he is not even aware that "somehow the existence of a frontier 'jammed' my thought-transmissions" (275).

If India includes Muslims, as Nehru and Gandhi insisted, then it implicitly includes Pakistan. Yet, in retrospect, Saleem characterizes the pre-Partition Muslim opposition to Pakistan as so much "optimism," that is, as admirable but self-deluding. In 1978, the year of writing, Saleem accepts Partition as, however deplorable, perhaps inevitable and certainly irreversible. It would seem that the new state of India, in its amputated form, calls into being a nation of its own, one that claims identity with the India originally proclaimed by Gandhi and Nehru but that is defined against Pakistan rather than against Britain. Gupta points out "There has never been any significant demand in India to capture Pakistani territories" (Gupta 2000, 122). The nation that bases itself on a given territory can, it seems, learn to accommodate itself to new definitions of borders.

A third thing that Saleem deliberately ignores is the "mass blood-letting" (111) that accompanied Partition, leaving citizens of both states with traumatic memories. Saleem decides to "avert my eyes from the violence in Bengal" (111), and only mentions in passing the trains burning in the Punjab (114). Later, in 1965, Saleem loses his parents and most of his family to bombs dropped by the Indian armed forces on Karachi and Rawalpindi, but that devastation leaves him with no bitterness against India. The deaths are not remembered as trauma or even repressed, but are wholly and conveniently passed over: all those people had come to the end of their stories anyhow. As we have seen, Saleem's psyche is haunted by images of amputation, which it is hard not to associate with Partition. The imagery of amputation, however, has surprisingly little to do with Pakistan. The greatest threat to Saleem's bodily wholeness (as opposed to his memory) comes from Shiva and Indira Gandhi. Partition would register as an amputation if the whole that the self identified with included both Islam and India. The cleavage of Islam from India would then be felt as a cracking within the Indian Muslim. But, as we have seen, Islam is not part of Saleem's self that has been excised, but itself represents a threat of amputation in the form of circumcision.

Saleem's Indian identity appears to himself inevitable, at once the product of his experience and freely chosen. Pakistan, however, looms as a larger presence in Saleem's life than he is prepared to recognize. It occupies six chapters, a fifth of the book and more than a quarter of the story of Saleem's life since his birth. Moreover, the number of chapters does not do justice to Saleem's ties with Pakistan. He has spent almost half of his thirty-one years, from the age of eleven to the age of twenty-four, outside India: first in Rawalpindi, then in Karachi, and finally in East Bengal. Pakistan casts the same kind of a shadow over the narrative as Shiva does; it, too, was born at the same moment Saleem was and poses a continual challenge to his legitimacy. Pakistan is what he must forever deny.

It is not sufficient explanation for Saleem's identification with the state of India to say he was born in Bombay on the day of India's independence and not, say, in Karachi the day before. His sister, the Voice of Pakistan, was also born in Bombay. The magic ascribed to the midnight hour is a pseudo-explanation, the equivalent of the secret identity ascribed to blood or birth, deflecting attention from the need to account for the identification with one polity rather than another. I do not mean to imply that Saleem *should* identify with Pakistan: either identification must be accounted for.

Pakistan's name, the Land of the Pure, insists that an abstract essence is embodied not just by the collective but by each of its members. Where each is a synecdoche of the whole, there are, by definition, only mirrors of the self. The poet Iqbal, the laureate of Pakistan, had desired a state where all are brothers. *Midnight's Children* makes Iqbal's dream uncomfortably literal: where all are siblings, the only kind of love possible is incest. In Pakistan Saleem falls in love with his sister in whom he sees an image of "new wholeness" (306) that can complement and complete his own sense of fracture: "What I could smell, Jamila could sing. Truth beauty happiness pain: each had its separate fragrance, and could be distinguished by my nose; each, in Jamila's performances, could find its ideal voice. My nose, her voice: they were exactly complementary gifts" (306). Saleem who desires the Voice of the Nation participates directly in the national fantasy. The converse is also true, however: Rushdie associates the fantasy of Pakistan with sister-sleeping, one of the worst imprecations in many non-English languages, including Urdu.

Saleem has always feared exogamous sexuality and the challenge that genetic admixture poses to the replication of the self. He feels an incestuous desire for his "subcontinental twin sister," India, "which was not only my twin-in-birth but also joined to me (so to speak) at the hip" (373). In Saleem's Bombay, however, incest is relatively rare and itself a mark of otherness attributed to Parsis: the imbecilic Toxy Catrack is "the product of years of inbreeding" (130). In India Saleem falls in love with women from groups other than his own: first with Evie Burns, and later with Parvati and with Padma. In Pakistan, however, where everyone is supposedly a synecdoche of the whole, there is no room for others and reproduction can only be incestuous.

Jamila rejects Saleem as a lover because, even though it has been demonstrated that they do not share genes, she cannot think of him in any role except that of brother. When Saleem insists he is sufficiently distant to be her lover, she has him consigned to the demeaning role of a dog in an army tracking unit. What Jamila feels towards him can be gauged if we remember that she has always hated dogs, ever since a rabid one bit her as a child (151). It would seem that, if he is not her brother and so a version of herself, Jamila cannot recognize Saleem's humanity at all. Where the only humanity acknowledged is an image of the self, sexual relations with others are limited to a choice between incest or bestiality. Such a dilemma Marc Shell sees as the inevitable consequence of identifying a universalist religion with a particular nation: the citizens represent a single family, and non-citizens are perforce not human (Shell 1993).

Why is Saleem not a Pakistani? A Pakistani, in *Midnight's Children*, is one who pretends the part is the whole. His is a nationalism without other nations, undifferentiated both within (where all are siblings) and without (where all are infidels). Such a nationalism resembles nothing so much as the sinister autonomy of the body part, Shiva's knees or the Widow's Hand. Saleem requires a nation that accepts difference within (Punjabis and Bengalis and Jats) and that exists in a world of difference (India and England and America). Such a nation will have room for his own difference, and at the same time he will be able to transcend it and see it from outside, as it were.

The India that Saleem identifies with has room for Muslims as well as Hindus; that is why he can identify with it. In this India one can imagine potential fellow citizens who are not related to one by blood and yet are still human. It therefore becomes possible to imagine the exogamous unions of Saleem the Muslim and Parvati the Hindu (at least, Parvati can imagine it), of Saleem and Padma, or even of Saleem and Evie Burns. We must remember, however, that none of these loves is consummated. Doris Sommer argues that in Latin American literature the problem of imaginatively incorporating the other in the self is solved in terms of sexual desire: the union of the colonizing male self with the native female other produces a hybrid offspring that can claim native status (Sommer 1990). As we have seen, the courtship of Naseem Ghani by Aadam Aziz represents just such a national romance. The difficulty with hybridity as a concept, however, is that, if Indians are produced by the intermarriage of Hindus and Muslims, then neither Hindus nor Muslims are yet Indian until they combine with the other. Indianness would always be something deferred, and the national romance would require renewal with every generation. Saleem, however, wants to insist that as a Muslim he is already Indian. If he is already Indian, there is nothing hybrid about his marriage to an Indian Hindu. Indianness is not a matter of sexual reproduction.

An early Hindu nationalist, Bhudev Mukhopadhyay, quoted approvingly by Chatterjee, has a fictional character pose the dilemma of the Muslim in India in terms of family: "Although India is the true motherland only of those who belong to the Hindu jāti and although only they have been born from her womb, the Muslims are not unrelated to her any longer. She has held them at her breast and reared them. The Muslims are therefore her adopted children. Can there be no bonds of fraternity between two children of the same mother, one a natural child and the other adopted? There certainly can; the laws of every religion admit this. There has now been born a bond of brotherhood between Hindus and Muslims living in India ..." (Chatterjee 1993, 111; also cited in Chakrabarty 2000, 232). In spite of the hand it ostensibly holds out to Muslims, this passage is a good example of the dangers involved in conceiving of identity in terms of blood: individuals are distinguished as natural children or as foster children according to the subnational communities they are identified with. Bhudev cannot ever see the Muslims in India as sons of the soil because the Muslim community is personified as a foster child in an eternal, transindividual family. In every generation, Muslims will have to be adopted anew, which poses the risk that at some point they will not be.

Saleem's response to such thinking is to suggest that adoption is more significant than blood and that, in fact, all filial relations are forms of affiliation. Insofar as Saleem's marriage to Parvati and his engagement to Padma are successful unions – the one produces a child who represents the future and the other produces the text that we are reading – it is not in spite of but *because of* their lack of consummation. Saleem's text is his means of competing with Shiva, the only one of the Midnight's Children to have children. The rivals both have a claim on Parvati's son, Aadam, who was engendered by

Shiva and born at the moment Indira Gandhi declared a State of Emergency, but named by Saleem. While Shiva litters India with his offspring, Saleem writes the novel for his son. While it may be true that "nobody ever married a book" (64), the novel, with its plethora of invented parents, represents "a form of reverse fertility beyond the control of contraception, and even of the Widow herself" (237). Because the narrative is all we readers have, it inevitably appears a more successful claim on the next generation than Shiva's.

Affiliation poses difficulties for identity, however: is it ever possible not to choose the nation? Saleem defends the superiority of adoption over blood as grounds for belonging, but India is not just what he chooses; it is also felt to be the right choice. It is not the act of choosing that makes a choice right. India is Saleem's true home and Pakistan is false for reasons that are pre-existent to the act of choosing. Even to consider Pakistan as a home, as Saleem must do when his family moves there, is to put the self at risk. The moment of choice is a moment of danger. For Saleem, Pakistan represents adolescence, a time of choices and journeys that in principle allows the self to define what it will become but that in practice takes the self away from its true identity, defined in childhood. India, on the other hand, represents the truth of childhood which must be returned to. At the end of the novel, Saleem returns to his ayah and the very spot where he lived as a child. He can declare, like Dorothy at the end of *The Wizard of Oz,* that "there is no place like home." Rushdie the immigrant author will later declare that Dorothy's lesson is a lie – "Once we have left our childhood places and started to make up our lives, armed only with what we have and are, we understand that the real secret of the ruby slippers is not that 'there's no place like home', but rather that there is no longer any such place *as* home: except, of course, for the home we make, or the homes that are made for us, in Oz: which is anywhere, and everywhere, except the place from which we began" (Rushdie 1992, 57) – but a national identity such as Saleem claims seems almost to require such a principle.

Here we have a contradiction: the nation is freely chosen, and therefore superior to identities based on language and religion and ultimately on blood. At the same time Saleem must recognize the truth of his Indianness and the falseness of his Pakistani experience. As Chakravarty writes, "Indian identity would have it both ways: to be a composite and yet claim a prior and more significant status" (Chakravarty 1993, 204). In other words, Saleem must choose what is already his. This contradiction hides the fact that the nation is neither freely chosen (it has made Saleem what he is) nor inevitable (it still has to be imagined).

12

England and Mimicry

Saleem's hybrid identity blends not just Hinduism and Islam, but also India and England. The novel implicitly makes the claim that English is now an Indian language. India does not, however, include England in the same way it includes Islam. Saleem is at once Muslim and Indian; he is not and cannot be English. Even to say India combines India and England is to raise the question of how India can be both part and whole. The way that Saleem's India includes England is more akin to imitation and contamination than to containment.

The nationalists who assumed power at independence took over a parliament and a state administration based on English models. The inevitably imitative nature of nationalism everywhere is Benedict Anderson's thesis in *The Spectre of Comparisons*: modern nations measure their nationhood against that of others (B. Anderson 1998). We might call this process whereby the nation is created in its performance of nationhood "imperso-nation," a term borrowed from Chakravarty (Chakravarty 1993, 4), whose use, however, is different from my own. Saleem is Indian the way an Englishman is English, and his India is a nation in the same way England is a nation.

Anderson's thesis that nationalism is a process of imitation of other nations is not a critique. Nations are not false because they are not original. Yet, paradoxically, nationalism denies imitation in the name of authenticity. In that sense, nationalism can appear, as it does to Ernest Gellner, a form of false consciousness (Gellner 1997). Indeed, among nationalists, imitation has an entirely negative connotation: to imitate is to betray one's truest self and to grant the superiority of another. Rushdie exploits the satiric potential of mimicry. As a child Saleem played with a tin globe: "Two cheap metal hemispheres, clamped together by a plastic stand," bearing the legend "MADE AS ENGLAND" (259). The image of the globe could be a graphic illustration of Anderson's Spectre of Comparison – in the wake of the spread of nationalism, the world has been completely divided among nation-states, each defined in the same way – but instead it serves as an emblem of colonial inauthenticity. The misprint in the label, which betrays that the globe was not actually made in England, conveys at once the manufacturers' desire to be the same and the way they inevitably fall short of the original.

At the heart of Rushdie's novel is Methwold's Estate, where the Indian heirs of the colonizers affect British accents, live in houses called Buckingham, Sans Souci, Escorial, and Versailles, and play at cowboys and Indians (Sans Souci is an allusion not just to Frederick the Great's palace at Potsdam and Henri Christophe's imitation of it in Haiti, but also to the palatial mansion of Bombay's own Sassoon family [Dwivedi and Mehrotra 1995, 68]). When the Englishman William Methwold sells his houses on the eve of independence, he makes it a condition that the new Indian owners leave everything untouched until the final handover of power. The immediate inspiration for this scene in the novel no doubt came from the orders left by Mountbatten, the last Viceroy, that "everything was to be left behind; all the stern oil portraits of Clive and Hastings and Wellesley, all the sturdy statues of his great-grandmother Victoria, all the seals, the silverware, the banners, the uniforms, the diverse paraphernalia of the raj were to be left to India and Pakistan for whatever use they wanted to make of them" (Collins and Lapierre 1976, 258). The new inhabitants of Methwold's Estate must live among ceiling fans, pictures of white babies, soft mattresses, water closets, and almirahs full of clothes. Very quickly, as Methwold intended, the habits of celebrating the cocktail hour and living among other people's things transform the current residents into not-so-pale imitations of those they have supplanted.

Methwold's strategy of turning Indians into ersatz Englishmen is in the spirit of Macaulay's notorious "Minute on Education" of 1835, which argued for the creation of a "a class of persons, Indian in blood and colour, but English in taste, in opinions, in morals, and in intellect" (Macaulay 1952, 359). Such assimilation was not always European strategy. Macaulay's Minute was actually a vehement argument against the practice, current at the time, of funding native education only in Arabic and Sanskrit. In the eighteenth century the Jesuits who followed Francis Xavier to India had sought to win converts by Indianizing Christianity. It is in that ecumenical spirit that a Catholic bishop in *Midnight's Children* seeks to build "a sort of bridge between the faiths" by depicting Jesus as blue and associating him with Krishna (103). In 1947, however, such indigenization is an anachronism. Ever since Macaulay the emphasis had been not on Indianizing the colonial administration but on Westernizing Indian subjects.

Macaulay at least believed that Indians could be the equals of Englishmen (Macaulay 1957, 358) and that the educated elite would go on to "refine the vernacular dialects of the country" and "to render them by degrees fit vehicles for conveying knowledge to the great mass of the population" (ibid., 359). He foresaw that, "having become instructed in European knowledge," Indians "may, in some future age, demand European institutions" and be "desirous and capable of all the privileges of citizens," a time which, he thought, would then be "the proudest day in English history" (cited in Read and Fisher 1997, 38). In the intervening century, however, the contempt that colonizers like Macaulay felt for Indian languages and cultures was further inflected by racism. Methwold's strategy in Rushdie's novel is not, like Macaulay's, to make Indians into Englishmen but to reduce them to *mimic men*, always reminded of their failure to be Englishmen. The objects that the bewigged colonialist leaves behind – the talking budgies that echo their new owners' "imitation Oxford drawls," and Lila Sabarmati's pianola that does not need anyone at the keys in order to play "Pale Hands I Loved Beside the Shalimar," a song which can be taken as an anthem of colonial mimetic desire (Rushdie 1981, 98) – all these objects are emblems not just of Englishness but, more especially, of mimicry. The irony of colonial mimicry, as Methwold well knows, is that it is itself the mark of the mimics' distance from the imperialist original and of their continuing colonial status. When they speak like Englishmen, these Indians will prove they are not Englishmen but parrots. The colonial mimic men of Naipaul's novel of that name only pretend to be men; in reality they are adrift in the world and hopelessly crippled (Naipaul 1969).

Of course, Methwold himself has lived with the mocking presence of parrots and pianolas. His Englishness is no less mimic than that of the people who take over the Estate: a state of affairs symbolized by the fact that his hair, with its distinctive centre part in which appears to reside his power, is actually just a wig that he removes as he leaves. Postmodern theory has nothing to teach Methwold about the performative nature of cultural behaviour: now that he is departing the scene, he wants to "play his part" and "stage" the transfer of assets (97). However, he counts on the new inhabitants of Methwold's Estate being less self-aware than he is: *he* designs the roles that *they* play. Put another way, the new inhabitants will start by playing roles but will end up becoming the roles they play.

Methwold believes Indians will never be Englishmen, presumably for reasons of race. Nationalists, like imperialists, rely on the notion of mimicry to critique false modes of being, but their indictment of the colonized who mimic the colonizer is not that they failed in their imitation but that they should ever have tried. Nationalists will urge the abandonment of false roles, whose falseness is measured by racial inheritance, and a return to authenticity. In *Midnight's Children*, however, Indianness is, like Britishness, but a role to be performed. Ahmed Sinai, the businessman so westernized that he is turning white, invents a Moghul ancestry with which to impress Methwold. Inspired by Persian and Arabic lore about the wondrous song of the bulbul, he goes to buy one at the market but is sold "a talking budgie" with painted feathers (199), no different from the talking budgies Methwold left behind. The ersatz bulbul refuses to sing but repeats its new owner's refrain "in his own self-same voice: *Sing! Little bulbul, sing!*" (200). Whether inventing a Moghul ancestry or enjoying cocktail hour, Ahmed Sinai brands himself a mimic. Indians are not the only ones playing at being Indian. A young American on a train travelling to Bombay lectures his fellow passengers on Hinduism and teaches them mantras. But he does not fully understand what he is imitating or he would not fan himself with a peacock fan (434), which we are told is an emblem of ill omen (47). Nor does he realize that Saleem's cheerful cry of "Back to Bom!" is not another mantra (435).

The way to escape mimicry is not by somehow being true to the self. In *Midnight's Children* there is no authentic self betrayed by the mimicry: there is only the performance. Mimicry is not a question of the roles one plays but of the self-consciousness or lack thereof with which one plays them. Individuation in the novel is entirely a function of role-playing. In a world of mirrors and parrots, there is no way of establishing one's authenticity.

Is there nothing then but imitation? Saleem feels he is doomed to reenact the story of Cyrano de Bergerac (182): tongue-tied, he gets Sonny to speak to Evie Burns on his behalf, and predictably she falls in love with his spokesman instead of him. Marx thought mimicry the inevitable fate of the middle classes, and Saleem himself seems to concur when he says of his relation to Cyrano, "Perhaps it would be fair to say that Europe repeats itself, in India, as farce" (182). Rushdie's satire of mimicry is inevitably double-edged, however: Saleem's irreverent twist on Marx's bitter phrase from *The Eighteenth Brumaire* not only mocks his own younger lovesick self, but also effectively deflates the vaunted power of the European original. The story of Cyrano gives us a clue to Rushdie's strategy: his satire emphasizes at once the power of words and the inevitable displacement of words which can as easily be spoken by another. Those whose words they once were cannot control how those words will be received in another context.

How does Rushdie, the writer of an English-language novel modelled on Sterne and Grass, escape (or at least claim to escape) the fate of Saleem who feels himself "sucked into a grotesque mimicry of European literature" (182)? Irreverence is clearly one strategy: mimicry can mock the original as well as the mimic, for the original is always already, like Methwold, a performance. Another prong of Rushdie's strategy is explicitly to thematize mimicry: the talking budgies and pianolas are as much the author's as they are Methwold's. Thematizing mimicry, drawing attention to it by deliberately exaggerating it, allows the mimic to stand outside his performance. We are to assume that, because he knows what he is doing, Rushdie evades mimicry's connotations of debasement and proves his own mastery. Just as Methwold pulls off his wig and Saleem constantly pulls back the curtain to reveal the strings, so Rushdie keeps his distance from what he describes.

One instance of colonial mimicry receives particular prominence in the narrative: the print of a sentimental Victorian painting that hung on Saleem's bedroom wall and that was one of the few things that the Sinais kept after Methwold's final departure (127). The print, first mentioned in the novel's opening pages, stands prominently at the threshold of Book Two, supplies the name of the chapter "The Fisherman's Pointing Finger," and marks Saleem's entry as a character in the narrative of his own life. It is also very possibly the first representational object that the boy ever became aware of. Saleem does not tell us the name of the painting or the painter and may not know them. The postcolonial subject is not an innocent viewer, however, and he does know that the painting represents Sir Walter Raleigh as a boy. Everything in Saleem's description of the print points to its being a copy of a painting that exists outside the novel and that the reader may consult: "The Boyhood of Raleigh," painted in 1870 by Sir John Everett Millais, later to become president of the Royal Academy (Fig. 6). We cannot say that the print in Saleem's room *is* Millais's painting – there are slight discrepancies that either point to Saleem's imperfect memory or indicate that the painting is a variation on the original – but we can say that the print is based on Millais's tribute to empire and that Rushdie can expect readers familiar with the painting to recognize it.

Millais's painting features two aristocratic Elizabethan lads who listen raptly to a barefoot old salt telling of his voyages. As he speaks, the sailor points an outstretched finger beyond the sea to the horizon. The setting of the painting is presumably Raleigh's native Devon and

Fig. 6 John Everett Millais, "The Boyhood of Raleigh" (1870). Courtesy of the Tate Gallery

the sailor is pointing west to the New World. The painting depicts the moment when Raleigh first conceived the dream of making history: we understand that the sailor's stories of the New World will inspire the young Raleigh to go himself in search of El Dorado, in the voyage he will later record in *The Discovery of Guiana*.

This is Saleem's description of the painting:

> The fisherman's pointing finger: unforgettable focal point of the picture which hung on a sky-blue wall in Buckingham Villa, directly above the sky-blue crib in which, as Baby Saleem, midnight's child, I spent my earliest days. The young Raleigh – and who else? – sat, framed in teak, at the feet of an old, gnarled, net-minding sailor – did he have a walrus moustache? – whose right arm, fully extended, stretched out towards a watery horizon, while his liquid tales rippled around the fascinated ears of Raleigh – and who else? Because there was certainly another boy in the picture, sitting cross-legged in frilly collar and button-down tunic … and now a memory comes back to me: of a birthday party in which a proud mother and an equally proud ayah dressed a child with a gargantuan nose in just such a collar, just such a tunic. A tailor sat in a sky-blue room,

> beneath the pointing finger, and copied the attire of the English milords … "Look, how *chweet*!" Lila Sabarmati exclaimed to my eternal mortification, "It's like he's just stepped out of the *picture*!"
>
> In a picture hanging on a bedroom wall, I sat beside Walter Raleigh and followed a fisherman's pointing finger with my eyes; eyes straining at the horizon, beyond which lay – what? – my future, perhaps; my special doom, of which I was aware from the beginning, as a shimmering grey presence in that sky-blue room, indistinct at first, but impossible to ignore … because the finger pointed even further than that shimmering horizon, it pointed beyond teak frame, across a brief expanse of sky-blue wall, driving my eyes towards another frame, in which my inescapable destiny hung, forever fixed under glass: here was a jumbo-sized baby-snap with its prophetic captions, and here, beside it, a letter on high-quality vellum, embossed with the seal of state – the lions of Sarnath stood above the dharma-chakra on the Prime Minister's missive, which arrived, via Vishwanath the post-boy, one week after my photograph appeared on the front page of the *Times of India*.
>
> ……………………………………………………………
>
> Perhaps the fisherman's finger was not pointing at the letter in the frame; because if one followed it even further, it led one out through the window, down the two-storey hillock, across Warden Road, beyond Breach Candy Pools, and out to another sea which was not the sea in the picture; a sea on which the sails of Koli dhows glowed scarlet in the setting sun … an accusing finger, then, which obliged us to look at the city's dispossessed. (122–3)

The Sinais want to heed the picture's call to make history, a task which is figured in terms of repeating the heroic narrative of the past and extending that narrative into the future. The boys in the painting and the boy looking at the painting are directed to go out into the world and make history such as has already been made by other men before them. The problem is: no one in Saleem's Bombay is quite sure what the painting is pointing to. Saleem's mother and ayah dress their son in Elizabethan garb and urge him to join Raleigh *in* the painting. Young Saleem's own misreading of the Raleigh print works differently: by bringing the Elizabethan sailor into contemporary Bombay. He imagines that the sailor is pointing to something in the bedroom or visible from the bedroom window. The two readings of the painting, one which sees in the painting depths that the viewer can enter and one that locates the painting in a context that the painter could not have intended or even imagined, are at once too close and too distant, as if the colonial eye has not yet been taught to read the painting. Saleem's stereoscopic ekphrasis (the verbal representation of a visual representation) remains out of focus: we might say that in its eagerness to find three dimensions where there are only two it is overly literal.

Rushdie's own intent in hanging the painting in Saleem's bedroom is evidently satirical. The display in post-independence Bombay of a sentimental Victorian painting chosen for its heroic content rather than its aesthetic merit is comical in effect, only slightly less absurd than dressing a modern Indian boy in Elizabethan costume. The painting is at once a sign of the Sinais' desire to imitate the history-makers and the mark of their failure to do so. Donning outmoded attire and displaying kitsch art betray an improper historical consciousness: the Sinais do not appreciate their own historical moment.

We should not, however, be too quick to judge how the satire cuts. The Sinais do display a genuine insight, however confusedly expressed: the parents who want their son to enter the painting and the son who locates the painting in Bombay ignore the pastness of the painting's subject matter. They understand that the supposedly linear narrative of history retains a sense of timeless greatness, as history in the sense of the past becomes history in the sense of the narrative about the past. National history transforms time into space: the heroes of the past join each other in a national portrait gallery where they become models to be invoked by the would-be heroes of the present. The Sinais understand that Millais's painting is about the demarcation of heroic space in terms of an outer field of adventure and an inner circle where the story is told. Their response is to recentre on themselves the emblematic moment of bequest when empire's heroic legacy is bestowed upon its heirs. Saleem's ekphrasis, while seemingly respectful of the painting, is an attempt to appropriate it for himself.

In Saleem's description, the fisherman's finger does not point deeper inside the painting, but outside altogether. Saleem follows the finger as it points along the wall to another frame, containing a newspaper clipping about his own birth and the letter of congratulations that he received from Nehru. The newspaper and the state letterhead and prime ministerial signature signal that these are history-making texts. The Finger of Destiny pointing to the Writing on the Wall, like the disembodied hand that writes on the palace walls of King Belshazzar in Daniel 5:5, proclaims the end of an empire. With the fight for independence, history has ceased to be the purview of European nations and is now made by Indians. The history made by Indians may, as Benedict Anderson reminds us, look like English history – as the Indian constitution looks like Western constitutions – but it cannot *be* English history and indeed must be written against English history.

When Saleem follows the sailor's finger past Nehru's letter, it points out the window, "down the two-storey hillock, across Warden Road, beyond Breach Candy Pools, and out to another sea," the Arabian Sea and not the Atlantic. The finger is still pointing west across a sea, but no longer across a Western sea. The "sea which was not the sea in the picture" is the site of the labour of the Koli fishermen, the "dispossessed" original inhabitants of Bombay (92). The finger thus points, as cause to effect, both to the English-language text written by Nehru and to the imperialist-created topography of Bombay. Breach Candy Pool, the reader will remember, is built in the shape of British India. The two framed images that accompany the print of Millais work against each other: Nehru's letter celebrates Indian history-making, and the presence of the Koli fishermen serves to denounce all history-making. To follow the finger out the window to a real world of labour and suffering is to recognize the true meaning of Raleigh's heroic desire: British history-making led to the dispossession of millions.

The bedroom window, which seems to promise direct access to an empirical reality against which the falsehood of imperialist and nationalist representation can be judged, is itself, however, inevitably a frame. Saleem describes the view through the window in painterly terms: it is "a sea on which the sails of Koli dhows glowed scarlet in the setting sun." Why should the sun be setting except that Saleem's memories are coloured by a Romantic aesthetic shaped by paintings like Millais's? His memories are also influenced by the words of "Red Sails in the Sunset," the song popularized by Tony Brent, the Bombay-born UK crooner (230), that his nurse Mary Pereira used to sing to Saleem and still sings to his son (441). The view out the window is thus not unmediated reality on display; it has been given significance by memory, which in turn has been shaped by aesthetic experience. Memory will always pair the view out the window with the Millais print that hung beside it. Indeed the view can only be remembered because it has been encoded with aesthetic meaning.

The Millais painting is located on a wall and in a city and so recontextualized. City and wall, however, are seen from a perspective that always includes the painting. If it is true that "real life was better than the pictures, sometimes" (50–1), that is only because "real life" is preserved in memory as a narrative or a picture. Art does not hold up a direct mirror to life, but life can only be seen through the mirror of art. Bombay, to which the fisherman's finger is pointing, seems to Saleem itself "an outstretched, grasping hand, reaching westward into the Arabian Sea" (92), and he directs readers who are looking for the Koli fishermen to "follow Colaba Causeway to its tip ... and you'll find them": "Squashed now into a tiny village in the thumb of the handlike peninsula" (93–4). Indeed, the way life reflects art may be said to be the theme of Millais's painting: the discovery of the New World was conditioned by the tales of marvels that the discoverers heard before ever they set sail. The boys in the painting have their backs to the sea and do not look where the sailor's finger directs them, but see in their mind's eye whatever is being described to them. Saleem the narrator notes the way that the sailor's "liquid tales rippled around the fascinated ears of Raleigh." The sailor's mouth and the boy Raleigh's ears are linked by a space of blue that, because it does double duty and represents both sound waves and the ocean, constitutes a visual pun. Ocean and the narrative about ocean cannot be separated (though they can be distinguished).

If there is no unmediated access to reality, there is also no unstudied naturalness. An older Saleem, now an inveterate voyeur, gazes through the dirty window of the Pioneer Café at his mother's secret rendezvous with her lover. He describes the window as a cinema screen, on which Amina Sinai and Nadir Khan play out their love scene, as in an Indian movie, complete with "indirect kissing" (212), that is, with the suggestion of contact that is never realized. The comparison of the lovers to actors reflects the boy's exposure to cinema, but also betrays the lovers' own inevitable sense of themselves as performing roles. All lovers, declares Saleem, "are in a sense the avatars of their predecessors": "Radha and Krishna, and Rama and Sita, and Laila and Majnu; also (because we are not unaffected by the West) Romeo and Juliet, and Spencer Tracy and Katherine Hepburn" (252). All that marks the point where art ends and life begins is "the ineptitude of genuine amateurs" with which the lovers play their parts (212).

There is no original art, and the presence of the pointing finger in Rushdie's novel is itself dependent on prior aesthetic models. It inevitably echoes other textual fingers, notably that of the Roman figure of Allegory painted on the ceiling of Mr Tulkinghorn's rooms in Dickens' *Bleak House*. That painting is heavy with portent but "with no particular meaning" (Dickens 1981, 546) until the murder of the lawyer, at which time the finger of the Roman points at the corpse and signals "the murderous hand uplifted against his life" (ibid., 547). When it comes to pointing to scandal, be it murder or imperial history, one can always find a helping hand from the Victorian novelist at the appropriately named Scandal Point Second Hand Library (234).

Saleem the narrator cannot oppose the truth of empirical reality to the falseness of the imperialist representation any more than the sailor's finger can point outside Millais's painting. There are only representations. But that is not to say that Saleem's consciousness can never escape its colonization. If the view out the window as remembered by Saleem can itself be regarded as a landscape painting, then it is just as responsible for colouring memory as the Millais painting. It is presumably his memory of the Koli fishermen seen from the window that causes Saleem to misremember the storyteller in the painting as a fisherman mending nets (122), wearing "what looked like a red dhoti" (17). Saleem's experience is coloured by his exposure to British representation and narrative, but his perception of the British painting is shaped by his experience of Bombay.

The juxtaposition of a European painting or text with a window that promises an elusive access to empirical reality recalls the opening image of *Midnight's Children*. Occupying the same liminal position with respect to the novel as a whole that the print of the pointing fisherman occupies with respect to Book Two is the large bedsheet with a hole in the centre which Saleem declares will serve as his talisman, his open-sesame, through the entire project of writing (11). Both images, the bedsheet and the Victorian print, seem in Saleem's memory to have stood at the origin of the events that the narrative recounts and to have contained within them all that would happen afterwards. Held up as an imperfect veil before the young and ostensibly sick Naseem Ghani when Dr. Aadam Aziz is called by her father to examine her, the sheet functions as a motor of desire, much more successful than it would be to make the daughter fully accessible or completely hidden. The hole in the sheet provides only a mediated view, but that mediation is precisely what constitutes its significance. The veil could not have inspired desire without the hole which promised access to something behind, but neither could it have aroused desire had access to that something not been withheld. Had Aadam Aziz been given complete access to the patient, she would have remained metaphorically invisible: he might never have seen her as more than a patient. The veil is as necessary for the stimulation of desire as the six-inch perforation in the centre. It is the frame that makes the view meaningful.

Just as he juxtaposes the picture of Raleigh with the bedroom window, Rushdie puts the perforated sheet beside a work of European art. Ghani, the rich landowner who has hung the screen between Aadam and his daughter, is an art collector. His blindness does not pose a problem; if anything, it has sharpened his appreciation of how art works. Hung above Aziz's head as he contemplates what is revealed by the concealing sheet is a painting of Diana the Huntress displaying "wide expanses" of exposed skin (21). The bedsheet with the hole is a screen onto which the young doctor is invited to project his desire, a desire presumably whetted by the image of the naked goddess of chastity. The sheet held up before a young woman who is at least partly naked is also like a painter's canvas: Aziz is the painter and Naseem his model.

We could see in this juxtaposition of European painting and window an example of what René Girard calls triangular mediation (Girard 1965): what Aadam projects onto the screen is not some authentic expression of his own desire, but what he has been taught to desire by the proximity of the Roman goddess, mythological and white. Rushdie suggests the aesthetic quality of the scene itself when, in the screenplay he wrote of the novel, he describes the light in the bedchamber as "Vermeer-like" (Rushdie 1999B, 24). In a very real sense Aziz finds himself framed, or at least painted into a corner. It would be wrong, however, to imagine that Girardian mediation is all that is at work. The painted goddess is described as a "plain girl" with "blemished pink skin" (20–1), and arguably Aziz, just home from Europe, finds the invited comparison is to the advantage of the girl behind the veil. The young doctor in love is well on his way to becoming an Indian nationalist.

Is there nothing then but imitation? In a scene in chapter two, set in Amritsar before the Jallianwala Bagh massacre, Aadam Aziz holds a pamphlet announcing Gandhi's call for a hartal, as out of the window he sees posters proclaiming the same message. The text and the view out the window may coincide, as they do in this case, if what is outside the window is another text: "Leaflet newspaper mosque and wall are crying *Hartal!*" (33). Gandhi's text does not reflect the world but successfully calls on the world to answer his appeal.

Saleem's own strategy is different from the Mahatma's: in his ekphrasis of the Millais print as in his account of the bedsheet, he juxtaposes different frames, in effect incorporating the European work of art into a larger composition. When describing the print, Saleem removes the frame of the painting by locating it on a sky-blue wall above the sky-blue crib of the baby boy. The blue erases the horizon within the painting: there is blue not just above but all around. The solidity of the earth on which Raleigh and his friend sit, a solidity figured by the anchor in one corner of the original though not in Saleem's description, is thus relativized and the boys made to float in an uncertain space. What Saleem then does is to make the painting the left-hand panel of a triptych. There are three frames on the wall of what is in effect a miniature art gallery, something like the postcard peepshow of Lifafa Das. The first panel, the print of Millais's painting, represents Europe, high art, and empire. In the centre of Saleem's triptych is the newspaper clipping announcing Saleem's birth, accompanied by a photo of Saleem (the "jumbo-sized baby snap"), and Nehru's letter of congratulations. Together they represent the Indian nation-state opposed to the British Empire. The third frame, the window, offers a different horizon and a different sea to balance the first frame. It represents a level below that of the nation-state, the level of the local and of immediate experience.

Boyhood of Raleigh	Baby Saleem and letter from Nehru	View out of window of setting sun

How are we to read the juxtaposition of these three frames? If we read them in a linear fashion from left to right, which is the order in which they are presented and the direction in which we are reading the English-language text, then we can see that empire is to nation and to city as cause is to effect. Alternatively, the view on the right of the setting sun, suggesting as it does the decline of the empire on which the sun was never supposed to set, marks the end of the narrative whose beginning is represented in the left-hand panel. If we focus instead on the middle panel of the triptych, on the letter from the prime minister with the seal of the nation that incorporates the dharma-chakra or wheel of dharma, then the documents affirming national history may represent the hub or the still centre of the revolving universe (Lannoy 1971, 290), and the sailor's finger will be merely one spoke, one of the many paths which lead from the rim to the centre. In that case, we might see a balance among the three panels: Saleem's own identity, vouchsafed by the newspaper clipping and the prime ministerial letter which performs the office of birth certificate, stands between Europe and India, and between art and lived experience. This in-between position is the hybrid location of the postcolonial writer, who stands between European text and local context, neither one nor the other but partaking of both.

However we read the triptych, its significance is that it constitutes a reframing of the Millais painting. Millais's painting depicts a pregnant moment which purports to contain the whole of Raleigh's life and even the whole of imperial history. Saleem's narrative, in effect, displaces Millais's synecdoche and makes it a metonymic part of a larger and different whole. The container is itself contained.

A frame, however, is no more an immanent given than is the view out the window. Both must be constructed. The careful balance of

Saleem's triptych into which we have been quick to read significance actually repeats the composition of Millais's painting. The three components of the triptych – "The Boyhood of Raleigh" on the left, the Koli fishermen on the right, and Saleem and Nehru in the middle – are already prefigured in the order of Millais's three figures: Raleigh on the left, the "fisherman" on the right, and another boy of uncertain significance in the centre. Saleem's triptych reduces Millais's painting to a part of a larger whole, but the painting already prefigures and so contains that larger whole. Synecdoche returns to haunt metonymy. Saleem's alternative framing, although centred on the nation and its history rather than on empire, seems itself caught within the frame of history implied by Millais's staging of Raleigh's boyhood.

Must every attempt to reframe the whole inevitably be caught within the frames that have been rejected? Saleem's ekphrastic description of the British imperialist painting deploys two common postcolonial strategies but also undermines them. Saleem cannot point to an empirical reality to prove the falsehood of imperialist art, and he cannot reframe the imperialist painting in an original, self-validating frame. The acknowledged impossibility of the strategies does not prevent their being deployed: readers are still invited to consider the painting alongside the scene of the city's dispossessed and to contemplate the unorthodox reframing of Millais's original framing of imperial history. Nonetheless, the text does not finally rely on these strategies and even gently mocks them.

Saleem the narrator does not so much rewrite the version of history implied by Millais as draw attention to the nature of the story-telling done by both canvas and text, by both imperialist and postcolonial. If Millais's three figures form an inescapable synecdoche, if the relations between the boy Raleigh, the story-telling "fisherman," and the second boy are repeated in Saleem's bedroom gallery (and in Rushdie's novel as well), it is because the painting constitutes a meditation on the relations that story-telling establishes among the audience, the teller, and the subject of the tale itself.

"The Boyhood of Raleigh" features an emblematic scene that freezes the narrative of Raleigh's life and distills its significance. The painting does not, however, depict a heroic deed or a scene familiar from history, nor does it travel to far climes, and it features neither exotic natives nor English royalty. The moment Millais chooses to depict is not even, strictly speaking, an episode from Raleigh's life, but a fictional moment of oral narration with Raleigh as its audience. The subject of the painting is first and foremost not the building of empire but the nature of story-telling. The moment depicted in Millais's tableau, like the funnel of an hourglass, represents a point of junction between two narratives, between the completed experience of the sailor/story-teller and the adventures upon which Raleigh, inspired by that narration, will embark. What unites the events of the past and of the future is a larger story of empire that contains them both and that gives them their shape. The deeds of empire are twice repeated: first in story and then in new deeds. Yet another repetition is constituted by the painting itself as the visual representation of a verbal representation, the converse of ekphrasis. The painting does what Saleem the adult narrator himself obsessively does: it finds in every moment echoes of what came before and omens of what is to come. The painting, by reminding Victorian viewers of Elizabethan greatness, anticipates a further repetition in the deeds its viewers will be inspired to perform. The young Raleigh is portrayed in the same position of receptivity and potential as the implied Victorian viewer of Millais's painting. The viewer who looks on the rapt faces of the boys is, as it were, looking in a distant mirror.

The history that Millais is concerned with is not a question of deeds, but of the stories told of those deeds. Raleigh's significance lies not in what he did, but in the way that what he did has filled the imaginations of Englishmen ever since. As Greg Dening writes of the Mutiny on *The Bounty*, to make history is not to change the world, but to change memory (Dening 1992, 200). Raleigh is part of the mental environment in which the English locate themselves and to which they must respond. The proof that he has made history is that the painting does not have to teach viewers about Raleigh; it has only to call him to mind. The history-making spirit that joins the Elizabethans to their Victorian successors is passed down through a tradition that we might call cultural literacy. Millais's painting presumes viewers for whom Raleigh is part of their cultural equipment. To such viewers the tableau might be said to speak. Without such cultural literacy, the call issued by the painting will remain unheard.

"What nonsense," Saleem's immediate audience, Padma, might say. "How can a picture talk?" (46). The postcolonial viewer who wants to recognize himself in the boy Raleigh might well feel some self-doubts. Raleigh has a destiny pointed out for him; the Victorian boy may feel called to a similar destiny; but the postcolonial subject can never be sure of as much. Saleem takes the pointing finger as at once the guarantee of his significance and a challenge to that significance, an invitation to make history and a reminder that history has already been made by others. The moustache of Millais's sailor recalls to Saleem the walrus whiskers of Brigadier R. E. Dyer, the British commander who ordered the massacre at Amritsar witnessed by Aadam Aziz. What would it mean for Saleem to make history as Dyer had done? The Indian viewer may see in the painting an invitation to make history, but is just as likely to see a reminder that history has been made at his expense.

Saleem's ambivalence is expressed in terms of a by now familiar gender anxiety. Millais's painting features a male initiation: a man of the people inspires two young aristocrats with dreams of romantic lands waiting to be conquered. He thrusts a finger in the air to show them what they must do. The boy in Bombay who views the European painting, insofar as he feels called upon to identify with it, may find in it a promise of virility. However, that same insistent virility bears the threat of his own emasculation. The seven-year-old Saleem Sinai, who is dressed up by his mother and his ayah in a copy of the clothes worn by the boys in the painting, feels mortified to be wearing a "frilly collar and button-down tunic": "Look, how *chweet*!" exclaims his neighbour, Lila Sabarmati (142). Before the European painting, the colonized male occupies the position of woman.

In Bombay young Saleem, who feels no qualms about identifying with the imperialists in the tableau, identifies, however, not with the sailor who supplies the story nor with Raleigh whose meaning is guaranteed by the story, but with the second boy in the painting. This second boy is not dressed in the bright colours of the sailor and Raleigh. He is smaller than Raleigh, almost formless and all in black; he resembles nothing so much as Raleigh's shadow, that which is not itself there but is required to prove the solidity of Raleigh. If we imagine the story of El Dorado travelling from the sailor's mouth to Raleigh's ear, it may be said to pass directly over this second boy's head. It is this second boy, however, who occupies the very centre of the painting. All the lines of perspective – the sailor's two arms, his leg, and the central horizon between land and sea – converge on the magical space between this boy's face and the sailor's other hand, the left hand which is not pointing but holding the boy's attention in its grip. This second boy, and not the horizon pointed to by the sailor, is in the position of the painting's vanishing point, that which, at once there and not there, the eye is directed towards, even by the arm pointing in the opposite direction.

The second boy constitutes almost a Rorschach blot, at the centre of the painting. Saleem may be right to see in him a figure of the viewer, as if Millais's painting were one of those two-dimensional tableaux found at amusement parks that have a hole cut out where you are invited to put your head so as to enter the picture. The area of darkness that is the boy also corresponds to the hole in the centre of the talismanic bedsheet. In the gratuitousness of his presence, he is a sign of the real. Yet he is also a blank slate onto which a viewer like Saleem can project his desires.

Who is this second boy? The source for Millais's painting has been identified as an article by the apologist for empire James Anthony Froude, entitled "England's Forgotten Worthies" (Spielmann 1898, 124). Froude's article, a review of a new edition of *The Discovery of Guiana*, imagined Raleigh as a young boy playing at sailors with his half-brothers, Humphrey and Adrian Gilbert, and all three "listening with hearts beating, to the mariners' tales of the new earth beyond the sunset" (Froude 1852, 53). The second boy in the painting might thus represent (somewhat anachronistically given the thirteen-year age difference between the two half-brothers) the young Humphrey Gilbert, another adventurer-hero "whose boyish dreams [would] become heroic action" (ibid., 53). Yet F.G. Stephens, a contemporary art critic, assumed the second boy was intended as a contrast to Raleigh, being one "whose intelligence is not of the vision-seeing sort, but rather refers to the visions of others" (Millais 1905, 222). Stephens felt himself qualified to judge the secondary intelligence capable only of mimicry – is it not written in the boy's face, there for all to see? – but we may be permitted to doubt whether this second boy is another Raleigh, a Raleigh manqué, or a foil that represents everything that Raleigh is not.

The anonymous lad who has heard the same tale as Raleigh but who is not remembered – who is, to misquote Bhabha, almost but not quite Walter – is in the position of the colonized who have listened to and read English history, have even been inspired by the models of English history-makers, but will never be remembered in English history. He appears between the sailor and Raleigh, literally bracketed by the storyteller and his listener, in the space that is filled by the story. He thus holds a place for the non-European peoples whom Raleigh and others will transform into subject populations and who are the unspoken subject of the painting. In his own staging of the painting, in the context of a dramatic retelling of West Indian history, Derek Walcott makes the sailor the son of a Spanish father and a Taino mother, who identifies with his mother's people (Walcott 2002, 176–87).

The example of Raleigh teaches the young Saleem that for his life to have narrative shape that shape must already be implicit at the beginning and must resemble the shape of a larger heroic narrative. The significance of Raleigh's boyhood is that in retrospect it already held the whole of Raleigh's future: the child is father to the man. Writing at what he feels is the end of his own life, Saleem seeks to discern an immanent historical design in his own career. He looks back on the narrative arc of his life seeking a guarantee of significance already implicit in the beginning and fails to find one. Saleem's anxiety makes readers ask just how it was that we knew what Raleigh's significance was. Millais's title instructs viewers to regard the painting within the context of a narrative that they are already familiar with. The moment of origin depicted in the painting requires a knowledge of the end for its significance; viewers can imagine the story told by the sailor because they know the story written by Raleigh. In that sense, the origin always comes after the end and owes all its significance to the end. What we know of Raleigh the man informs how we see Raleigh the boy, who in turn is imagined as holding the seeds of the man he will become; everything is made to hold together. But whatever Millais's sailor is pointing to is not present in the painting. It is not before Raleigh's eyes; he has his back turned to the sea and the horizon. It is not the finger that directs his thoughts, but his thoughts that supply the object that is pointed to. The same can be said for the viewer.

The child Saleem reads the pointing finger as a promise of his own "inescapable destiny" (122), like Dr Narlikar's beloved tetrapod, "a kind of icon pointing the way to the future" (174). The adult, however, is no longer sure what the finger was signalling. It is perhaps "accusing," like the fingers in Mary's guilt-ridden dreams (138); rebuking, like the "mosque's long pointing finger" (320); or mocking, like the "pointing fingers" at school from which nine-year-old Saleem hides (155). Destiny and the promise of meaning may as easily be doom and the inevitability of unmeaning, and the fisherman's finger the "Moving Finger" of Omar Khayyam, as translated by Edward Fitzgerald: "The Moving Finger writes; and, having writ,/Moves on: nor all your Piety nor Wit/ Shall lure it back to cancel half a Line,/ Nor all your Tears wash out a Word of it" (Fitzgerald 1996, ll. 281–4). The adult even wonders if the fisherman was pointing to anything at all; he may have been holding up his finger to highlight the significance of one of Saleem's own digits which, when mutilated in an accident requiring a blood transfusion, reveals the secret of his identity: that he is not the genetic son of his parents (123).

The painted pointer is not just of iconic significance but also serves as a literal index, directing the eye to something beyond itself. But to what? The boy cannot be sure whether the finger in the print points to Nehru's letter and the emerging postcolonial future or out the window to the dispossessed Koli fishermen and the vestigial past (123). The finger may be pointing, like the figure of the buddha in the Sundarbans, "'That way,' and then, 'Down there'," while leading the viewer on a wild goose chase (349). We may legitimately conclude that the finger can point wherever the viewer wants it to point. Not only can the finger point to anything, but anything may have a finger pointing to it. The adult narrator sees pointing fingers everywhere:

betel juice spat in the direction of a passing British brigadier "congeals like a red hand in the dust of the street and points accusingly at the retreating power of the Raj" (44–5); a black cloud rising from a burning godown "thrusts itself westward into the heart of the old city ... pointing ... like a finger" at the site of future communal riots (74); Dr. Narlikar's "pointing finger" aims at the promenade where he dreams of reclaiming land (132); and, shortly before Gandhi's assassination, the beaches of Bombay are "littered with the ominous corpses of dead pomfret, which floated, without the ghost of an explanation, belly-side-up, like scaly fingers in to shore" (135). Where there are so many indices directing the attention to so many disparate things, how does one determine which are significant and how they fit together? The polysemy of the finger means that everything is pointed to, everything is included. The writer of a narrative, looking back in search of origins and omens, will always find signs ready to be interpreted. The finger held aloft also draws attention to the man doing the pointing, to the storyteller who prefigures Saleem's own performance as he reads his narrative aloud to Padma and as he directly addresses us his readers.

Saleem invites us to read Millais's painting as depicting not the object of desire but the making of desire. The painting is about the nature of story-telling. At the very beginning of the novel, counterpointed with the scene of Aadam Aziz's courtship, Saleem tells how Aziz as a boy sat at the feet of an old boatman, listening to his tales. The scene is related to the print that later hung on the wall of Aziz's grandson: in Saleem's memory, the sailor addressing Raleigh is identified with the old boatman Tai who fills the ears of his young acolyte with tales "fantastic, grandiloquent and ceaseless" (16): "It was magical talk, words pouring from him like fools' money, past his two gold teeth, laced with hiccups and brandy, soaring up to the most remote Himalayas of the past, then swooping shrewdly on some present detail" (17). Tai is of "an antiquity so immense it defied numbering" (16) and the repository of stories linking him to the time when Alexander and later Christ came to India. Just as Millais's sailor inspires Raleigh with the desire to make history, and William Methwold's vision of a future Bombay "set time in motion" (92), so Tai sets "history in motion" (14) by bringing Aziz the summons from landowner Ghani to attend his daughter.

As a boy, Saleem identified with the young listeners in Millais's print, but as narrator, he declares that his is "as peripheral a role as that of any redundant oldster: the traditional function, perhaps, of reminiscer, of teller-of-tales" (431). Saleem does not grow up to be Raleigh but to be the sailor. The lesson he finally learns from Millais's painting is that power does not belong to Raleigh but to the painter. In making Millais's painting the subject of his own scene-painting, Saleem usurps some of that power for himself. He writes his narrative for his son, passing on the story to the next generation.

The passing on of an oral narrative to the next generation, the archetypal moment of empire depicted by Millais, thus bears an uncanny resemblance to what is arguably the archetypal scene of postcolonial literature as well: a group of young listeners gathered around a hoary old storyteller. The difference between imperialist and the postcolonial story-telling lies in the confidence with which the imperial and postcolonial audiences receive their respective messages. Saleem imagines a rupture between the young Aadam Aziz who listened to Tai's marvellous tales as a boy and the newly minted doctor who returns to Kashmir from studies in Germany. The distinction between myth and history, between orality and literacy, is also a class distinction. Aziz's parents had always disapproved of their son's contamination by "the ragged reprobate" Tai and his "pillaging armies of germs" (17). The medical doctor returned from abroad finds his modern wisdom cuts him off from Tai, whose response is to become filthier than ever. The class distinction that Saleem observes is already present in Millais's painting where the sailor is barefoot and in a baggy shirt while the boys are finely dressed. It is part of a contradiction in the notion of making history: the sailor's account of where he has been and what he has seen somehow inspires Raleigh to become the first to travel there. Raleigh can be the first because, unlike the sailor, he will write his voyage down and his voyage will be written about by others. If to make history is to shape memory and history is made by the interpreters as much as by the actors, then the sailor who fashioned the young Raleigh's memory and imagination can also be said to have made history. The anonymity of Millais's sailor reminds us, however, that he is not remembered in written accounts and is condemned to remain outside history. The painting is of the boyhood of Raleigh, not of the wisdom of the old sailor.

But, as Saleem's own reading goes to show, the imperialist painting cannot control its own reading any more than the traditional oral story-teller can. We have been reading Millais's painting as a celebration of the continuous line of heroic narration that joins the viewer through Froude to Raleigh and, indeed, beyond, to the sailor who served as Raleigh's inspiration. We have been assuming that we knew all along what the finger in Millais's painting was actually pointing to and that Rushdie offers a disobedient reading of the imperialist painting. Saleem's ekphrasis, however, is not so much disobedient as unstable. It puts into question the possibility of a single, self-evident obedient reading that would control the inward and outward movement of meaning of the painting. The very title of Froude's article, "England's Forgotten Worthies," is a reminder that the line of narration is never unbroken, that in fact repetition is the dominant trope of imperialist narrative precisely because that narrative always fails to be repeated.

The second boy, the lightning rod for Saleem's anxiety, puts imperialist history itself in doubt. His presence makes clear how much Raleigh himself is not a figure of immanence and plenitude but a blank slate on which the viewer projects a desired narrative. In particular, the presence of a second boy makes it impossible for us to be certain which boy is Raleigh. We have been assuming that Raleigh is the boy who is more brightly dressed, but there is room for doubt and for further anxiety. If two boys listened to the sailor's tale and either one or both responded, how can we be sure to whom the sailor's finger is addressed and what significance it carries?

In Rushdie's story, there are also two boys: Saleem and Shiva, switched at birth. The exchange makes it impossible to claim that the subsequent significance of Saleem's life was always implicit at the beginning. How can one say which boy truly represents India? Saleem also has a sibling, and in Rushdie's screenplay of the novel, the print of "The Boyhood of Raleigh" dissolves into a live-action scene where Jamila, the sister, assumes the role of Raleigh, while Saleem hovers at the edge, "out of place" (Rushdie 1999B, 186). Jamila, however, will be a national heroine in Pakistan, not India. And outside the text Saleem has yet another double in the figure of Grass's Oskar Matzerath, an acknowledged model beside whom Saleem appears like a mere imitation. Millais's print in Saleem's narrative actually repeats Grass's own ekphrastic description of the plaster statue at the side-altar of a church, which is also a tableau of three figures: the Virgin with two young boys, Jesus and John the Baptist. Oskar says, in words that Saleem will echo, "I shall not dwell too long on the boy Baptist, who pointed his left forefinger at Jesus as though counting off to see who should play first: 'Eeny meeny miny mo…' Ignoring such childish pastimes, I take a good look at Jesus and recognize my spit and image. He might have been my twin brother" (Grass 1962, 135–36). Doubles within doubles; imitations of imitations.

If we cannot be confident that we know who Raleigh was, we cannot be certain of our reading of the Koli fishermen either. Saleem describes them as the "dispossessed," but, in his 1999 novel *The Ground Beneath Her Feet*, Rushdie explicitly associates the Arab dhows visible from Cuffe Parade and Apollo Bunder ("Silhouettes on the horizon, red sails in the sunset" [Rushdie 1999A, 259]) with "the feats of Elizabethan privateers" (ibid., 258). According to this reading, the Koli fishermen are pirates like Raleigh, to be admired for their lawlessness and daring. They are not history's victims but its agents. William Methwold, the novel's representative colonizer, although an object of satire, is strangely not a source of anxiety. Indeed Saleem finds himself incapable of bearing him any grudge (95). Rushdie himself goes a long way to rehabilitating Methwold in *The Ground Beneath Her Feet*, where the ex-colonial, now Lord Methwold, proves himself a student of Indian mythology and marries a Parsi widow from Bombay.

A strange thing happens in *Midnight's Children* to the objects that serve as satirical emblems of mimicry. After the satire of Book One, Methwold's Estate itself comes to be regarded with nostalgia as the place where Saleem most belongs: a kind of Brideshead in Bombay. Saleem considers it tragic that Methwold's Estate should ever be desecrated by FOR SALE signs. The destruction of the villas to make way for high-rise apartment buildings he regards as symptomatic of all that is wrong with the city and with India. Methwold's Estate, that emblem of colonial mimicry, thus becomes associated with other things that are under threat, with childhood innocence, even with the Koli fishermen. The threat to the houses of the Estate comes from the Narlikar women who represent, if not capitalism exactly, at least commodification (they buy people's homes) and the homogenization and ugliness associated with modernity (they build skyscrapers). It is as though, once the satirist has proven his distance from and superiority to the colonial mimicry represented by Methwold's Estate, the memoirist regrets that he cannot get back inside. Such is the power of artistic representation that the merely mimic becomes real when recalled by memory and itself imitated. One generation's mimicry becomes the next generation's hybridity.

Something similar happens to the toy globe that Saleem used to play with as a football, "secure in the knowledge that the world was still in one piece [...] and also at my feet" (259). The globe "MADE AS ENGLAND," originally introduced as an emblem of mimicry, becomes one more fetish representing the self. The day the Narlikar women buy up most of Methwold's Estate, Saleem's sister jumps on the globe with both feet and crushes it, marking the end of "the world of my childhood" (259). Later, when Buckingham Villa is itself sold, Saleem buries the globe, like a navel-string, in the ground. The model of the earth that is buried in the earth contains the not quite "holy relics" of Saleem's identity: the newspaper article that proclaimed his birth and the letter he received from Nehru, all that remains of his past apart from whatever is recorded in "the closed books of heaven, Sidjeen and Illiyun, the Books of Evil and Good" (296). The globe, a "long-buried world," is, unlike Saleem's navel-string, later dug up by him and finds a "yellowed ant-eaten jumbo-size baby-snap" and Nehru's letter (441). The tin globe, originally an emblem of mimicry, thus becomes associated first with the loss and then with the preservation and recovery of identity.

As Saleem the mimic becomes Saleem the memoirist, mimicry becomes representation. The globe filled with personal memorabilia is obviously an image for the text as well, at once large enough to contain the world (or at least India) and yet filled by a single person and his memories. Like the globe, the novel that might convict its creator of mimicry manages to escape its derivative status through satire. A clever alchemy then transforms bitter satire into childlike playfulness.

Saleem's fascination with "The Boyhood of Raleigh" is a satirical mark against him, but Rushdie's prolonged attention to the painting and to its potential for meaning goes a long way to redeeming the painting. This transformation in the novel's judgement of the painting is remarkable because Rushdie has nothing to gain: in contemporary critical circles Millais has no standing whatsoever. It is not just that his apologetics for empire are embarrassing; it is that Victorian representational painting now feels like kitsch, seemingly so self-confident and naïve that it forestalls satire, almost as if Millais were already mimicking Victorianness. Whatever contemporary nostalgia there may be for the Raj, about which Rushdie has written with scorn, is unlikely ever to extend to Millais. No household aspiring to middle-class culture anywhere in the world can hang a print of Millais on its walls; the French impressionists have long consigned the nineteenth-century painters of historical themes to the cultural dustbin. Yet, Rushdie accords the painting serious attention. This is part of a paradox larger than Rushdie: postcolonial writers have renewed the critical interest in imperial figures, like Kipling, even Raleigh himself, who not so long ago would have been almost entirely forgotten. Postcolonial satire of things English first hollows out England and its history and reveals its mimic nature, but then it restores England to itself as a place that derives its interest from its connection to India.

13

The Dispossessed and Romance

Midnight's Children ends with a nightmare: on the eve of his wedding to Padma, to whom he has been reading his memoirs aloud, Saleem Sinai imagines an apocalyptic scene that will erupt after the ceremony and prevent their departure by train on a honeymoon to Kashmir. He foresees a "crowd without boundaries" that will separate him from his new bride; his life will pass before his eyes; and the "numbers marching one two three, four hundred million five hundred six" will buffet him until he explodes, his bones crack, and he collapses into "specks of voiceless dust" (445–6). This annihilation by numbers is more than the nervous jitters of a prospective groom, but contrary to what most critics assume (e.g. Islam 1999, 133; Lopez 2001, 203), it is not how Saleem's life actually ends. The fact that the crowd includes everyone who has ever figured in his life is a reminder that it is but a projection. Saleem cannot report on the end, except in prophecy, because "it has not taken place" and therefore "cannot be preserved" (440). While he displays remarkable prowess and stamina as a retrospective prophet, we have no reason for trusting his forecast of the future. He may just be "cracking up" and should be taken away in a straitjacket by the likes of Doctor Baligga who cannot see the cracks he is raving about (66). Or, having come to the end of the self-imposed task of writing his life story, a story that has seemed to himself and perhaps to his readers as large as the world, Saleem may simply feel an apocalypse is a more fitting note on which to conclude than a wedding. Certainly Rushdie feels that way: his previous novel had ended with the literal death of Grimus at the hands of a mob, a death Grimus himself had planned because it is "both psychologically and symbolically satisfying": "The cataclysm being followed by a new and very similar order. It is aesthetic. It is right" (Rushdie 1989, 240). The final sentence of *Midnight's Children* is a deliberate echo of the apocalyptic conclusion of *A Hundred Years of Solitude* (García Márquez 1991).

Readers should remember, however, that the novel offers alternative endings. Before setting down the future "with the absolute certainty of a prophet," Saleem asks his readers how he should end his narrative: with happiness, with questions, or with dreams (444). Anything, it would seem, is possible. "Yet so many possibilities are open to a man of thirty," says Oskar Matzerath, coming to the end of his own narrative (Grass 1962, 576). "At thirty a man should marry" (ibid., 576). Alongside the final vision of postmodern apocalypse that most readers of *Midnight's Children* take away with them is an old-fashioned romance: even physical annihilation must wait until after the wedding. (In *Grimus* the death of the eponymous mastermind is followed by a scene of love-making cosmic in scale.) Moreover, if we consider not Saleem's actual narrative but the trajectory of his life up to the moment when he starts writing, we see yet another story-line take shape. The story of his active life in the world ends with the much-battered Saleem, abject and destitute, being recognized by and restored to the substitute mother from whom he has been separated since the age of eleven. Saleem is permitted to do what is denied to most young men: he can return to the ayah who cared for him as a child and live by her side forever more. What is this but the dream of the bourgeois child come true? Restored to his ayah's unconditional love, he enjoys the security and the calm needed to write his memoirs.

There are two conflicting principles at work in the conclusion of the novel. On the one hand, dispossession, marginalization, and even death are associated with a privileged access to truth: Saleem wields more authority at the end of his narrative because he is the world's victim. On the other hand, his worth has been recognized and rewarded by the love of his ayah and of Padma. Saleem is able to give up his cake and eat it, too. In this chapter, I will show that the principles in conflict correspond to the modes of realism and romance.

In most first-person *Bildungsromans*, including *Midnight's Children*, the perspectives of the child who experienced the world and the adult who remembers those experiences correspond to two different narratives: the young boy projects into the future a romance of which he is the hero, in which the greatness he carries inside is finally revealed and receives honour, but the adult has surrendered such fond dreams and comes to regard his life as a lesson rather than a model. As the poet A.K. Ramanujan puts it in "No Amnesiac King,"

One knows by now one is no amnesiac
king, whatever mother may say or child believe.

One cannot wait any more in the back
of one's mind for that conspiracy
....
the one well-timed memorable fish,
so one can cut straight with the royal knife

to the ring waiting in the belly,
and recover at one stroke all lost memory (Ramanujan 1995, 126)

The ring in the fish's belly is, like Saleem's spittoon, the token that guarantees the identity of the romance hero. That they are not the favoured children of providence and that their meaning is not guaranteed is, however, the bitter lesson eventually learned by the protagonists of the realist novels of Dickens, Balzac, Joyce, Kureishi, and Naipaul. Saleem's own unhappy destiny resembles theirs. He has his special powers drained from him and becomes as others are. Later, his childhood friends all meet violent, gruesome deaths, their own dreams of greatness turned to a mockery by war. All the surviving Midnight's Children (with the exception of Shiva) suffer the loss of their gifts and abandon hope in the dungeons of the Widow's state tyranny. Saleem is eventually driven to declare that "privacy, the small individual lives of men, are [sic] preferable to all this inflated macrocosmic activity" (419). After all that he has suffered – amnesia, the massacre of family and friends, a nightmare journey into madness, the horrors of war – Saleem renounces his former sense of centrality and declares that rage is now his primary motivation: he is no longer proud of being the motor of events, but resents that he has witnessed so much history. He has made the progress made by so many other young heroes of *Bildungsromans*, from "I was about to make my presence felt" (86) and "Those jerks; if they knew who I was they'd get out of my way pretty damn quick!" (227) to "It should have been me" (262), and finally to "It's not fair" (365) and "Why me?" (370). Saleem says, "it was at the house of the wailing women that I learned the answer to the question of purpose which had plagued me all my life" (410), and he has learned that the answer is that he has no special purpose. The retreat of the hero from an identification of himself with the world we may call realism.

The response of Dickens' Pip to the collapse of his great expectations is to put himself at the centre of a narrative of lost illusions. The loss of the dream of a social order that serves the self is compensated for by an artistic order that sees the social order for the unhappy and unjust world it is. Saleem is engaged in a similar project in writing the story of his life and times for his son, and must convince the reader of his neutrality as an observer of the whole. Realism, by expressing the distance between things as one wants them to be and things as they are, exposes the ideological underpinnings of romance. The world is not built around the self; the self is inescapably located within the world.

Midnight's Children, of course, differs from realist *Bildungsromans*. What makes Saleem's narrative magic as well as realist is that, although his own great expectations have come to nought and his illusions have been lost, Saleem blames the world for not meeting his expectations and not the falseness of those expectations. Saleem, unlike other heroes of *Bildungsromans*, never really believes in the worth of private activity. At the end of his active life, as he undertakes his memoirs, he is more determined than ever to show his essential link to the nation. The adult narrator draws parallels between himself and the nation that are only available to a reader of newspapers and history texts and that he never perceived as a boy. For Saleem, as for postcolonial literature in general, the injustice and alienation of the world are not just painful and soul-destroying, they are also essentially false.

Midnight's Children, which feels magical because it locates the individual and the collective on a common scale, is arguably more akin to epic poetry than to the realism of the *Bildungsroman*, where the conventions of verisimilitude prohibit such mixing of scales. Moretti argues that the classical epic, which featured a "totality that is 'living' and inseparable from individuality: a world that takes form thanks to a hero, and recognizes itself in him," is no longer possible in the modern world (Moretti 1996, 12). Classical epic may not be imaginable in twentieth-century Britain, France, or the United States, but it has flourished in the Caribbean and Latin America. Saleem's relation to the nation-state shares something of the grandiosity (if none of the sublimity) of a Pablo Neruda or an Aimé Césaire. Saleem, who can write that his country "was not only my twin-in-birth but also joined to me (so to speak) at the hip" (373), sounds like Césaire who says, "now we are standing, my country and I, hair in the wind, my hand small now in its enormous fist and strength is not within us, but above us in a voice piercing the night (Césaire 1983, 76)."

Of course, *Midnight's Children* has, like *Ulysses*, as much of mock-epic as of epic: it only looks like epic. It is actually closer to romance. Like Bombay cinema, Saleem's narrative relies heavily on the motifs of romance as listed by Frye: "stories of mysterious birth, oracular prophecies about the future contortions of the plot, foster parents, adventures which involve," as well as "narrow escapes from death, recognition of the true identity of the hero and his eventual marriage with the heroine" (Frye 1976, 4). Magic realism is commonly read as a challenge to realist conventions of uniform space and verisimilitude. This explicit relation to realism reminds us, however, that the latter mode is itself a displacement of older modes, in particular of romance (McKeon 1987). Magic realism's displacement of realism's displacement brings with it the return of eternal romance.

Romance is the literary mode of wish fulfilment, where what one wants is also recognized as what should be and even as what will be. Saleem who has many (but never enough) tokens of his status as Fortune's favourite child is confident that he is a romantic hero, someone with a destiny, without whom the world cannot be understood. He is more confident than ever of his innate significance when he sits down to write. We can apply to romance the definition that Rushdie gives of "song" in *The Ground Beneath Her Feet*: "Our lives are not what we deserve; they are, let us agree, in many ways painfully deficient. Song turns them into something else. Song shows us a world that is worthy of our yearning, it shows us ourselves as they might be, if we were worthy of the world" (Rushdie 1999A, 19–20). The key words here are "deserve" and "worthy." In romance, identity is a question of merit and its recognition. Romance presents the world as it should be because it assigns the hero the place that his merit deserves. In romance the hero's inner greatness finally receives its public acknowledgement.

But what is the moral economy that allows us to measure merit and to judge the social order according to how it rewards merit? The notion of merit presumes distinctions: some deserve recognition and others do not. As Lord Khusro Khusrovand's propaganda declares, it is a lie "that we are all Born Equal!": "Is a Crook the equal of Saint? OF COURSE NOT!!" (261). A proper social order would see the rule of the virtuous and the defeat, or at least the neutralization, of the crooked. The "lie" that "all men are created equal" is proclaimed by a Sanjay Gandhi clone, in whose mouth it is both cruelly false (some people have power and others do not) and parodically true (all are equally in thrall to the ruling family). With a display of snake-charming bravado, Picture Singh gives the lie to the assertion of equality, proving that "some persons are better, others are less. But it may be nice for you to think otherwise" (385).

It is one thing to declare that there are differences of merit that society must take into account, but quite another to declare that existing social inequalities actually reflect merit. Because it accompanies a declaration of his own moral superiority, Lord Khusro's denial of equality is suspect, and so, of course, is Saleem's. To counter some of those suspicions, Saleem constantly draws attention to his own contraventions of verisimilitude, regrets the loss of his special powers, and abjures the claims to significance that he himself has forwarded. His intention is to win the allegiance of readers by making clear the relation of his India to the world shared with others. The realist pretends that his identity is formed by the experiences he has had: "I am the sum total of everything that went before me, of all I have been seen done, of everything done-to-me" (370). He also learns that his merit will never be recognized, that indeed his sense of his own merit was a harmful illusion that interferes with his seeing the world for what it is. The individual and the social order remain irretrievably at odds.

While in realism the self is a product of the world it finds itself in and of the choices it makes, romance presumes that identity is given – the choices a hero makes are true or false depending on whether they conform to the identity that is already his. This is not to say that romance is not fraught with anxiety, only that it assuages that anxiety differently. The "structural core" of romance, Frye argues, "is the individual loss or confusion or break in the continuity of identity" (Frye 1976, 104). The hero of romance feels that experience always threatens the unmaking of the self which, as we have seen in chapter eight, is associated with female virginity. His journeys and adventures lead Saleem ever further away from where he should be. Only his return to Methwold's Estate and to his ayah's side can restore wholeness. Saleem the writer of romance stages the loss of a coherent self and the collapse of the world into chaos in order to show that the hero's true identity is never utterly destroyed but merely submerged or hidden, to be restored or revealed in the fullness of time. Romance further promises that, with the revelation of identity, the proper order of things, "a world worthy of our yearning," will also be restored.

Romance's concern with the preservation, recognition, and restoration of identity and its capacity to assuage anxiety constitute its attractions for both colonial and postcolonial literature, as Sommer has shown (Sommer 1990). In romance individuation and socialization generally proceed together: the social order should reflect the merit of the individual, and where it does not, the discrepancy is a mark of the upside down nature of the social order. Romance is therefore frequently (but not always) conservative. It is associated with aristocracy and chivalry and in modern times most commonly with race or nation. A conservative ideology, of course, may yet serve the interests of the minoritized and oppressed if what is to be recovered or preserved is an alternative to the hegemonic. In conservative romance the truth of identity is a question of parentage. Discover who your parents or ancestors were, and you also discover who you are and where you should be. Identity is inherited and able to be bequeathed to future generations because ultimately it is located in the genes or, as romance is more likely to put it, in the blood. Blood establishes identity in the form of nobility, race, or a legal claim to property or status. The hero is able to pass uncontaminated through the world, because the world does not determine character, blood does. The gentleman proves by his noble character, the necessary corollary of his noble birth, that he deserves his superior status, the churl by his actions and speech the appropriateness of his menial status. In more contemporary romances, the descendants of Africans or Jews or aboriginal peoples, who find themselves in a hostile world not of their own making, come to understand why they act and feel as they do and are ready to assume their rightful place in the world once they learn who their ancestors were. Knowledge of parentage makes judgement possible: the good can be rewarded and injustice stands exposed.

Romance expresses a truth: the anxieties it assuages and the desires it fulfils are real. The truth of romance is insufficient, however, because the anxieties are never fully assuaged nor the desires entirely satisfied. The recognition of romance's insufficiency is expressed in realism, which makes it possible to imagine a world not centred on the self but shared with others. Realism derives its authority by relinquishing claims of special merit and acknowledging a world of others whose perspective is dependent not on character but on relative position. Elizabeth Ermarth writes of the arbitrariness of point of view in realist narration: "that arbitrariness suggests a potential equality among viewpoints. Because the realistic medium of experience is neutral, the same everywhere, there is a potential continuity between the vision of the spectator and the vision of all possible spectators in the same horizon. Any position would reveal the 'same' world with as much validity; and any person could take up the position of the implied spectator. The implied spectator's privilege, that is, depends not upon qualitative distinctions between 'better' and 'worse' points of view, but rather upon quantitative distinctions, between more and less distance. It is a privilege available to anyone who is willing to travel" (Ermarth 1983, 20–1).

Saleem relies on two contradictory claims to authority: he displays the virtue of the romantic hero and the clear sight of the marginalized outsider. Prime among the romance motifs in *Midnight's Children* is the baby switch, which does not, however, prove the ineluctability of an identity based on blood, as it would in a conservative romance, but quite the reverse: it illustrates the social construction of identity. Mary Pereira, a nurse in Narlikar's Nursing Home, seeks to prove her revolutionary stripes to her communist lover, Joseph D'Costa, by switching a baby boy born into wealth with another otherwise doomed to poverty. Her confused intention is to show that social status is not based on innate qualities, that character is not written in the blood, but that the self is a blank slate to be written upon by the experience of social class. The possession of wealth and privilege is a function of inheritance all right, but the inheritance is not genetic. The baby switch, like an undergraduate psychology experiment, proves a lesson about nature and social environment: identity is not written within the body at birth but is written upon the individual after birth. In Rushdie's parody of romance, we are what we have been made. The "truth" revealed in decidedly unromantic blood tests, however scientifically absolute, is, arguably, not the truth at all. Saleem remains his parents' son, because, as he puts it, "they could not imagine me out of the rôle": "their love was stronger than ugliness, stronger even than blood" (292).

In the shadows, as it were, of Saleem's story is the muted form of a conservative romance in which a true heir, Shiva, raised in poverty and kept in ignorance of his identity by a usurper, nevertheless manages to win the attention of the ruler of the land by his deeds of prowess, and so is plucked from poverty and set among the class that was rightfully his by birth and to which he has proven that he belongs. The wicked usurper (the position Saleem occupies) is meanwhile cast down and confesses his perfidy in writing. Although Shiva's story has the shape of a romance, it is not allowed to engage readers as a romance. The hero of this parody is all libido and his desires refuse to accommodate themselves to a world of others. As Auden would say, he has been "poisoned by reasonable hate" (Auden 1991, 233). Unlike the hero of a romance, Shiva himself never fully believes that he deserves his promotion in status and is easily convinced by Roshanara Shetty that his high-class female patrons are secretly mocking him. As the true scion of wealth and privilege, he may have legitimate grievances, but readers are not anxious to see Shiva restored to his "rightful" place, which his character manifestly does not deserve. His rise in status reflects not what we want to see, but what we dread to see.

By this reading *Midnight's Children* is not a romance but a trickster story. Much later Saleem apostrophizes Shiva, his "changeling brother" (274), as a "birthright-denying war hero" and as his "mess-of-pottage-corrupted rival" (415), an allusion to the story in Genesis of Jacob and Esau. Saleem specifically accuses Shiva of selling out his fellow Midnight's Children for personal reward, but the allusion suggests that he has always seen their relationship in terms of the twins born to Isaac and Rebecca. Esau, the older twin and legitimate heir, is stronger, hairier, and his father's favourite, but he is outsmarted and cheated by the smaller, more effeminate Jacob with the help of his mother. When Esau sells his birthright to Jacob for a mess of pottage, it is not the trickster but the one bribed and tricked who is guilty of corruption and who proves his unworthiness. Similarly, even as we recognize that Saleem is the usurper and Shiva the dispossessed, readers are asked to side with former.

Saleem, the writer of these memoirs, knows very well he might have occupied Shiva's unenviable position and Shiva his. What he denies is that it might now be worthwhile to bring such a reversal to pass. Shiva points to the world and doubts whether there is purpose: "For what reason you're rich and I'm poor?" (215). Readers know even better than Shiva does the arbitrariness of the inequity, yet the menace in the slum gang leader's voice is such that readers will not want to see the contingent order overthrown in his favour. If there is no reason for one to be rich and another poor, there is, in Saleem's account at least, good reason for doing nothing about it now. Saleem knows that his genetic parentage has not made him who he is: whoever has enjoyed the privilege that he has had would display the same sensibility. He even knows that he has within himself the capacity to be Shiva: when he is taunted by his schoolmates, "the image of two irresistible knees" floats into his head and he reacts with rage and violence (228). But Saleem believes there is genuine merit in the social order as it exists, that at the very least it is superior to the risk of social disorder that its overthrow would incur.

Saleem the trickster-usurper can win our assent to his usurpation because he has learned, as Shiva has not, that he is not at the centre of the world. Before Saleem and Shiva were born, a fortune-teller had predicted the fate of Amina Sinai's son. Because the prenatal prophecy of Shri Ramram Seth proves so accurate ("Spittoons will brain him – doctors will drain him – jungle will claim him – wizards reclaim him!" [87]), and yet applies not to the child in Amina's womb but to the child who will be substituted for him, it suggests that any male child raised by the Sinai family would have had Saleem's fate. Mary Pereira's baby switch and later confession, by dividing Saleem into the middle-class boy at the centre of Methwold's Estate and the adult narrator who knows the truth about his inheritance and is therefore in some measure outside the world and able to judge it, function somewhat like the heuristic "veil of ignorance" that John Rawls argues is necessary to measure a just society. Rawls suggests that we must imagine a society designed according to principles of justice from behind a veil that makes it impossible for anyone "to design principles to favor his particular condition" because no one can predict what that condition will be: "Among the essential features of this situation is that no one knows his place in society, his class position or social status, nor does anyone know his fortune in the distribution of natural assets and abilities, his intelligence, strength, and the like" (Rawls 1972, 12). In this way it becomes possible to imagine a society that could win the consent of members *before* they are actually born into it.

What are the principles of justice that the novel's readers are asked to consent to? Rawls argues that expediency, the notion that some suffer for the greater good, cannot be such a principle for "it is not just that some should have less in order that others may prosper" (ibid., 15). There is, however, "no injustice in the greater benefits earned by a few provided that the situation of persons not so fortunate is thereby improved" (ibid., 15). Justice need not mean equality. Saleem the usurper claims to have an insight that his rival lacks: that, although class is arbitrary and does not reflect merit, democracy, accompanied by security for property, is preferable to the tyranny of might.

Because it stresses the constructed nature of identity, Saleem's narrative is not conservative. But neither is it progressive or radical. It shows that class is arbitrary and not based on blood, but then argues that order and stability are valuable. Saleem's vision of the world can best be described as liberal. Like a good liberal, Saleem argues in the parliament of the Midnight's Children Conference against the zero-sum game that is the conflict of interests and, in an echo of the "third way" that Nehru sought between Russians and Americans, urges the children to be a "third principle" beyond "the endless duality of masses-and-classes, capital-and-labour, them-and-us" (248). Saleem defends "free will ... hope [...] poetry, and art" (249), against Shiva's proclamation that there are only things: "only money-and-poverty, and have-and-lack, and right-and-left; [...] only me-against-the-world!" (249).

There is an obvious difficulty with Saleem's vantage point outside the world divided into rich and poor. The outside vantage point is also always an inside: the defender of noble ideas and ideals against Shiva's sordid materialism is himself a product of Methwold's Estate, the very world of "things things things" that Shiva lusts for (426). Saleem, who declares himself able to see beyond the struggle, actually represents one of the two principles at stake. His perorations on the duties of citizenship are actually claims to the benefits of citizenship which, in India, are privileges enjoyed only by a few. Gupta, who also defends civil society and the rule of law, admits that, in India, "the basic ethic of civil society can hardly be said to exist in any meaningful way" and "it is impossible to be civil in an uncivil society" (Gupta 2000, 186).

There is no neutral outside vantage point because the effort to stand outside inevitably determines the shape of the whole that it sees. The outside perspective from which realism imagines the world is itself but a convention, like any of the conventions of romance, and not directly accessible. Indeed, we might argue that realism fosters a romance of its own, what we might call a romance of clearsightedness, where the hero proves his merit by abjuring his centrality and claiming neutrality. The claim to be outside and so to see clearly is its own claim to personal merit: "I see more clearly and therefore am more worthy than others and deserve the rewards that my superior insight entitles me to." This special merit is related to the feminine power we discussed in the previous chapter, the power that comes from abjuring power.

Delourme argues that a "law of reversibility contaminates the novel" (Delourme 1995, 23; my translation). Certainly, Saleem understands just how contingent and undeserved is his privilege. He only keeps the truth of the baby switch from Shiva because he cannot trust that, from a similar position of understanding, his changeling alter ego will give his consent to the inequality of their condition. A Shiva who knew the truth would occupy the impossible position expressed in an "Irish bull" quoted by Maria Edgeworth: "'I hate that woman,' said a gentleman, looking at one who had been his nurse, 'I hate that woman, for she changed me at nurse'" (Edgeworth 1832, 134). The absurdity of the Irish bull arises from the fact that the "I" who speaks cannot be the same as the "me" who was changed precisely because the switch has intervened. The bull can be read as a figure for the postcolonial dilemma: the postcolonial subject cannot claim that colonialism has misshapen him before birth, for the one who protests does not share an identity with the one who has been changed. Saleem does not make the same mistake: he knows he is everything he has experienced and learned since the switch.

It is not true, however, that, had the baby switch not occurred, the son raised by the Sinais would still have had the character as well as the name of Saleem and the child raised by Wee Willie Winkie those of Shiva. Certainly, a Midnight Children's Conference forced to convene in the head of the child raised in poverty would have looked utterly different. The discovery of the hidden truth of his birth makes no difference to who Saleem is *except* insofar as he must hide that truth from his rival. That exception, however, is as large as the world. Saleem's identity is a function of the world that has made him and that he remembers, a world that includes not just Methwold's Estate and Cathedral and John Connon Boys' High School but also, as a result of the switch, Shiva himself. The baby switch does not leave the world unchanged: as Shri Ramram Seth's prophecy foretells, "There will be two heads – but you shall see only one – there will be knees and a nose, a nose and knees" (87). Saleem is who he is only because he is not Shiva *and* because he knows it. Shiva is essential to his identity. I suggested above that the baby switch proves the post-colonial self cannot be abstracted from its experience and therefore cannot logically object to what colonialism has wrought before it was born as if it had been done to itself. The self, however, is always more than its own experience: it is also all the selves it might have been and by whose images it finds itself surrounded and reflected. It is because the self receives images and a narrative from the world, even, we can say, from colonialism itself, that it will inevitably regard events of the past before it was born as things suffered by itself. The baby switch makes Saleem who he is. Saleem, who can legitimately claim to have been formed entirely by the experience of Methwold's Estate, nevertheless cannot, try as he might, abjure Shiva. He can never expel Shiva from his narrative because he needs his rival to understand himself. Saleem goes so far as to report Shiva dead at one point, but then retracts the report. Shiva cannot die before Saleem himself does.

How are we to understand the mutually imbricated social positions that Saleem and Shiva represent? Saleem is the heir of nationalists like Nehru who, as Chatterjee shows in *Nationalist Thought and the Colonial World*, accepted the hegemonic moral universe associated with modernity but not their own subordinate place in it (Chatterjee 1986). In a discussion of the Kenyan experience, John Lonsdale describes how the nationalists who sought to replace the colonizer found it galling that modernity's self-justifying promise of a rational social order was not actually fulfilled in the colonial order where, as a result of racism, their own merit went unrecognized. Lonsdale calls this class of would-be citizens "readers," which seems a good title for Saleem as well. The "readers, fired by their unrequited merit," challenge the colonizer and demand their rights (Lonsdale 1992, 355). They also, however, face rivals within the colony itself whom they despise "as spivs and hooligans" (ibid., 355). This second group of colonials, subjects rather than citizens in Mahmood Mamdani's terms, derive their status and identity from the social order displaced by modernity and mourn what feels like its unmerited loss (Mamdani

1996). Unmerited loss certainly describes the condition of Saleem's rival, Shiva, who is without a stake in the nation-state.

Shiva, of course, has little to do with tradition or a premodern social order. That position, as we have seen, is occupied by Tai the boatman, who stands not just for "changelessness" (107) but also for the dispossessed. Shiva is not Tai, but there are suggestions that at some conceptual level he is Tai's heir. His father, Wee Willie Winkie the minstrel, is an entertainer as the boatman-storyteller was, and as we have seen, Saleem even declares, somewhat mysteriously, that he has borrowed his own narrative techniques from Shiva (214). The reference to Shiva the story-teller is ludicrous, for everything else in the novel would deny him that title and make him the enemy of story-telling. Tai has no heir, and his memory is kept alive not by Shiva but by Saleem. Saleem claims to inherit from both modernity and tradition, both literacy and orality, leaving Shiva nothing to represent but motiveless irrational violence. All that Shiva has in common with Tai, who goes mad and refuses to wash, is his bottomless rage.

There is another possibility: although Shiva has no stake in the modern state, he appears nonetheless to have been generated by the same forces of capitalist modernity that produce Saleem. In moving from Book One, the record of Saleem's genealogy, subsequently proven to be false or at least invented, to Book Two, his account of growing up among the Sinais, the narrative parallels a historical shift that Michel Foucault traces from a discourse based on blood to one based on adversarial relations. Where premodern collectives had been imagined in terms of connections based on inheritance, modern society is imagined as a struggle for power. Saleem's narrative illustrates the new "biologico-social racism" that, according to Foucault, is characteristic of modern society and that is predicated on the notion that "the other race is neither one arrived from somewhere else, nor one which at a certain moment triumphed and dominated, but instead one with a permanent presence, that incessantly infiltrates the social body – that reproduces itself uninterruptedly within and out of the social fabric" (cited in Stoler 1995, 66). The nation, Foucault tells us, is engaged in an internal war "carried out not between two races, but between a race placed as the true and only one (that holds power and defines the norm) and one which constitutes various dangers for the biological patrimony" (ibid., 67). Ian Baucom has shown that, for many Victorian writers, London's poor constituted "a space of racial and cultural alterity disturbingly present in the heart of the great metropolis," "an alien nation in the centre of the great city" (Baucom 1999, 61). Shiva represents a similar alien nation at the heart of Bombay. Saleem acknowledges the possibility that Shiva is the true generator of human affairs – he "has made us who we are" (290) – but also assumes this is an unhealthy state of affairs.

Whether Shiva is a vestige of the premodern or as modern as Saleem himself, the relation of the two changelings represents a dialectical return to romance and to notions of fixed identity: a romance in which Saleem is now the hero and Shiva the villain. In the last of the novel's three books, Saleem switches places with Shiva a second time: the street apache becomes a war hero received in high society, usurping the legitimate place of the middle-class child, who is undeservedly banished to the slum but who carries with him a token of his true identity in the form of a silver spittoon whose provenance he has forgotten. Although Saleem and Shiva change fortunes, they remain at heart what they were as boys: the violent social outlaw and the mild-mannered schoolboy. In this second-order romance, it is not genetic parentage that is crucial in character and identity-formation, but the first ten years of life, generally spent with parents.

Identity in Rushdie's novel is a matter of culture (in the sense of upbringing) and not of race or blood, but culture appears every bit as ineluctable as race ever was. Those raised in poverty and those raised in privilege will perpetuate their class-determined identities through generations. You can be whatever you want, sings Mary Pereira, but she is wrong: in Saleem's world, you will always be what you were at age ten. It is as though, like a Hindu Brahman, Saleem is twice-born: the sense of self coalesces and memory first takes hold when the boy awakens to sexuality and national consciousness inside a second womb, the washing-chest, out of which he tumbles "with laundry wrapped around my head like a caul" (160). This second birth fixes his identity forever.

Saleem's ineluctable identity feeds a romance not based on blood but rather on orphanhood. Before he even learns of the baby switch, Saleem is conscious of a secret identity that has nothing to do with his parents. He appears to be the child of ordinary middle-class Muslims, but is actually of a different order of being altogether. He is the child of midnight who has more in common with the other children born within the first hour of India's independence, including his rival Shiva, than with the family that raised him. This is the romance of the superman, which Saleem declares "the most potent of all modern myths" (262). The magical midnight hour acts like a dose of radiation to produce mutations. Most of these mutants are eliminated as ill-suited to their environment – 420 die within the first ten years of life (193) – others, however, prove better adapted to their environment than are their own parents. "History is natural selection," declares the narrator of *Shame* (Rushdie 1983, 133).

This second-order romance presents all the features associated with romance listed by Jameson in *The Political Unconscious*: a heightened magical world where the scene of the action is more important than those who perform it, a struggle between representatives of good and evil which are magical forces larger than the characters themselves, and "a salvational historicity" (Jameson 1981, 148). Saleem finds in the world around him signs secretly confirming his inner greatness: the letter from Nehru, the fisherman's pointing finger, and the Kolynos Kid on the billboard advertising toothpaste. Only Saleem and a select coterie with similar powers are aware of his secret. Unfortunately the secret has been leaked to the forces of evil. At the home of his uncle the civil servant, Saleem gets a glimpse of "a black leather folder labelled TOP SECRET, and titled PROJECT M.C.C." (379). The plane above common humanity on which the superhero lives is shared with an enemy who has superpowers like his own but puts them at the service of evil.

In this romance of orphanhood rather than of blood, all that is not a confirmation of one's greatness becomes a threat to that greatness. The novel's final confrontation between the forces of good and the forces of evil, involving a conspiracy against the Midnight's Children, thousands of Sanjay Gandhi clones, and sinister forced sterilizations, is worthy of Thomas Pynchon. The mastermind behind the conspiracy is none other than the Prime Minister, Indira Gandhi, Saleem's foremost competitor for centrality (406). Gandhi herself declares that there exists a "deep and widespread conspiracy which has been growing," words which Saleem interprets to refer not to the opposition Janata Morcha but to the Midnight Children's Conference: "the truest, deepest motive behind the declaration of a State of Emergency was the smashing, the pulverizing, the irreversible discombobulation of the children of midnight" (412). In his paranoia Saleem sees paranoia everywhere.

The romance of orphanhood and cosmic struggle is, of course, just as susceptible as the romance of blood to the critique of realism, which denies the centrality of the self. In *Midnight's Children* there is not one orphan with a secret identity but several hundred. The existence of other potential centres makes it possible to imagine alternative romance narratives from whose perspective the hero's self would be on the periphery rather than at the centre. In particular, Saleem is aware that Shiva is as much an orphan as he himself is.

Indeed Shiva is more obviously heroic: witness his military prowess, his progress from gangleader to major in the army, his appeal to women. Shiva has the strongest claim to be the hero of a Darwinist narrative of the survival of the fittest. Alone of the male children of midnight, he is able to father children. He litters the land with thousands of offspring by different mothers and wins the competition for the genetic future hands down. As with the romance of blood, the juxtaposition of two romances and two children of midnight makes clear the unsustainability of romance. Rival romances cancel each other out by dissolving their respective binaries of good and evil into identity: the one I seek to overcome is the same as me, or rather I am the same as him.

Saleem is now outside and Shiva in. Where once his parents had ridden in a train to Delhi and resisted the desperate appeals to be let in, made by those without tickets hanging on the outside (67), Saleem is now himself a faredodger on the train to the capital, clamouring for admittance (426). Ermarth writes with regards to realism, "Alone, their experiences remain eccentric," but "two converging lives – like the two converging sight-lines in pictorial realism – together objectify a world and thus reclaim unity from discontinuity and confusion" (Ermarth 1983, 202). Saleem is able to see and judge precisely because he has lost his privilege and come to live among Delhi's slum-dwellers. He belongs to both worlds and to neither: "the crime of Mary Pereira had detached me from two worlds, not one" (399). This experience of two worlds with different perspectives allows Saleem to claim a fuller understanding of the whole. "The implication of realist technique," writes Ermarth, "is that proper distance will enable the subjective spectator or the subjective consciousness to see the multiple viewpoints and so to find the form of the whole in what looks from a closer vantage point like a discontinuous array of specific cases" (ibid., 35).

And what does Saleem see with his new objectivity? Like Stendhal's Julien Sorel or Balzac's Lucien de Rubempré, who come into conflict with their society even as they try to master it, Saleem learns that what originally looks like social mobility is actually independent of will or worth and merely a question of Snakes and Ladders, an ancient game, Indian in origin, that traditionally comes with small illustrations of virtue and vice being appropriately rewarded but in which progress and decline are actually determined by the roll of a die. In Saleem's narrative, however, the social order is not mere chaos, careless of the individual: the social order is actually upside down and victimizes the truly worthy. In Book Two, Shiva threatened the social order, which is assumed to be good. In Book Three Shiva's full participation in the social order is the mark of its corruption. Shiva's social mobility, the very quality that had justified the bourgeois democracy into which Saleem was born, proves society's perversion. Mary Pereira's slogan, "anything you want to be you kin be," which Saleem comes to feel is "the greatest lie of all" (445), is only a lie as far as he himself is concerned. It accurately describes Shiva's career which takes him up through the ranks of army and society. Shiva is a lower-class parvenu who gets above himself. When the wrong orphan finds a home with the prime minister, the social order is clearly upside down.

Almost all wealth in the novel is tinged with corruption and inherently unstable. Uncle Zulfikar, who built his fortune "on the miseries of fleeing Hindu families in 1947" (326) and on smuggling, Ismail Ibrahim, who bribes judges and juries, and his brother Ishaq, who is in debt to local gangsters (250), all suffer the fates they deserve, but not because they deserve them: Zulfikar is killed by his son (326), Ismail is suspended from the Bar (258), and Ishaq's hotel is burned down (258). Even worse than military generals, speculators, and stock market traders are their sons who have done nothing to earn wealth. Gauhar Ayub who runs the "enigmatic Gandhara Industries" and Sanjay Gandhi who has the "Maruti Car Company" (323) fulfil the "Bombay film stereotypes of a distinguished man's son being a buffoon" (Chakravarty 1993, 148). In his scorn for wealth Saleem makes an exception for those owners of property who actually produce things: Ahmed Sinai is happier and more likable when he manufactures towels than when he plays the stock market or buys real estate, and Mrs Braganza's pickle factory is a warm environment. Those who produce nothing and remain poor, however, like Uncle Mustafa, the sycophantic civil servant, are as scorned as investors and speculators.

Where growing up means the imbrication of self in sticky networks of money, law, and power, it is better never to grow up. Saleem never chooses a career, does not follow his father into business, and deserts the army as soon as he can. Business is corrupt, power is abuse, labour is brutish and degrading. There is one moment in the novel when Saleem "takes stock," realizes that he is without funds or education, and decides to seek a job in the civil service (376). Even then, his notion of making a career is to find a relative who can "protect support assist" him (376). Saleem cannot stomach, however, the sycophancy, the jealousy, and, perhaps most galling of all, the anonymity that characterize the civil service, and returns to the ghetto and to Parvati. His plans to save the nation are more plausible among the magicians of the ghetto who live by entertaining than in the atmosphere of deliberate mediocrity characteristic of government administration.

For Saleem it is but a short step to the feeling that his dispossession and marginalization prove his personal virtue. Saleem describes the home he finds in a Delhi ghetto as "that true inheritance of poverty and destitution of which I had been cheated for so long by the crime of Mary Pereira" (383). The Delhi slum, of course, is not the nightmare place of destitution that has originally deformed Shiva, and Saleem can move through it uncontaminated.

Saleem thinks of himself as "the good guy and natural victim" (250): in his world victimhood is a mark of goodness. He is no longer the superhero, but the gangly, lonely adolescent who dreams of being the superhero, the "perennial victim" painfully conscious of his appearance (232). He loses every contest, because he is too incapable, too weak, or just too young. As a boy Saleem imagined that his Clark Kent persona was but a mask for the Superman identity he had to hide from others. But at the meetings behind his eyebrows of the Midnight's Children Conference, where Saleem does not have to hide and can legitimately claim leadership, he continues to abjure the strongman tactics favoured by Shiva and maintain the persona of the conciliator. Saleem's hero is not the man of steel but Clark Kent himself, the mild-mannered reporter who cannot get the girl.

The claim to clear sight, the power of x-ray vision that derives in Saleem's case from the chiasmic exchange of positions with Shiva, is itself a claim to special merit: "Because I see what others see, I see more than they do." Such merit still requires, however, recognition and confirmation. Saleem finds this confirmation in the love he inspires first in Parvati and then in Padma. This love is no more than a version of the love that he first received from his ayah and that he never had to earn. Mary Pereira, the first arbiter of the two rivals Saleem and Shiva, chose Saleem, and at the end of the novel she welcomes him again.

In colonial romance, as Katie Trumpener shows, the key figure is the nurse, the woman drawn from the lower classes yet closer to the middle-class hero than his biological mother: "the native nurse is able, through her milk, her love, and her influence, to heal the colony's scars and to effect a lasting rapprochement between the colonizers and the colonized" (Trumpener 1997, 230). In Saleem's narrative, adoption is actually superior to blood relations and even to the orphan status of the superhero because the foster mother loves the child without conditions.

In spite of her would-be radical political intentions in switching the babies, Mary herself cannot resist the allures of romance, the promise that what has happened is fate and fate has purpose. She invests young Saleem, the changeling whose circumstances she is herself responsible for, with heroic status and asks to be taken on by the Sinai family as an ayah so she can watch over his fortunes. Throughout the novel Mary is wracked by guilt, which takes the shape of Joseph D'Costa's ghost. The guilt she feels, however, is not for having condemned the scion of privilege to a life of poverty, but for having concealed the truth about Saleem. It is Saleem she is worried about ruining if her secret is learned. Saleem himself, of course, is not surprised by her dedication and feels it is no more than he deserves.

Saleem declares he has two mothers: his father's wife, whose class the bourgeois child inherits, and his ayah, through whom he is linked to the lower classes. Saleem discovers that Amina, whom he had been trained to think of as his mother, is not really his mother, and his ayah, who intervened to make him who he is, has as much right as anyone to that title, indeed perhaps more right. The biological mother that Saleem eventually learns about, Vanita, who died in giving birth to him, appears to be but a version of Mary, whom she resembles in having a non-Hindu non-Muslim name and in her low status. Vanita draws off all the sexuality associated with reproduction and conveniently dies, leaving Saleem free to transfer his debt of filial allegiance to the virginal Mary.

Mary Pereira sleeps beside him every night. When his parents are not sure what to do about the child who does not share their blood and send him to spend five weeks with his Uncle Hanif and Aunt Pia, Mary follows him into exile and continues to sleep on the floor by his side (235). Saleem, like every other member of the middle classes, is forced to leave his ayah behind as he grows up. He must follow his parents to Pakistan, where he is unhappy. But the family are killed off, and Saleem eventually makes his way back to Bombay. Saleem's final secret, withheld from his readers until the last chapter, is that the "someone who cannot be named" (206), Mrs Braganza who owns the pickle factory where he is writing his memoirs, is actually Mary his ayah. At the end of the novel, having lost all the privileges associated with inherited wealth, Saleem returns to the woman of the people who raised him. When she sees him again after so many years Mary exclaims, "O Jesus sweet Jesus, baba, my son" (440). The return to the circumstances of childhood is so nearly complete that Mary's apartment actually occupies the same cube of air that once was occupied by Saleem's blue bedroom (441). There she rocks Saleem's son, as once she did Saleem, singing "Red Sails in the Sunset," while through the window red dhow sails can be seen (441). This twist resembles what Trumpener identifies as a nationalist rewriting of the colonial romance: instead of the poor boy discovering he has noble blood, the child of privilege discovers his links to the dispossessed. This fulfills a larger pattern of nationalist romance: "through their class demotion, and the loss of the lands to which they now have no 'natural' claim, the 'aristocratic' characters come for the first time to understand their own deep connection to the people" (214). Saleem magnanimously declares he has "forgiven Mary her crime" (442).

A suggestive parallel for Saleem and Shiva in the novel is the relation between Ganesh and Skanda, the two sons of Shiva and Parvati in Hindu mythology. Because Rushdie's use of the changeling motif is certainly inspired by the prominence of the double in Indian popular culture, including cinema (Nandy 1995, 224–33), and because Indian cinema borrows heavily from mythological themes, we do not have to presume an extensive knowledge of Hindu mythology on Rushdie's part in order to find this parallel. Although they are brothers, Skanda is born of Shiva's seed and merely adopted by Parvati, while Parvati fashions Ganesh out of cloth and he comes to life when he touches her breast. Kakar sees in Skanda and Ganesh "personifications of the two opposing wishes of the older child at the eve of the Oedipus stage," torn between autonomy and a return to the mother (Kakar 1990, 137). Shiva in the novel, like Skanda, is exiled from his mother's presence. Such exile means that he is able to function as an independent and virile adult. Again, like Skanda, "the great general of great power and courage" (O'Flaherty 1975, 112), Shiva fathers thousands of children and, as a military hero, becomes the darling of the nation. Saleem, on the other hand, like Ganesh to whom he explicitly compares himself, enjoys his mother's undivided attention: Mary and Amina both dedicate themselves to him completely. The price for such closeness to the mother, however, is the impotence figured by Ganesh's broken tusk and by Saleem's cut finger and literal castration. Saleem, who returns to the ayah, remains turned inward and now lives, perfectly satisfied, in a small room.

Unlike Oskar in Grass's *The Tin Drum*, who retains a child's body as he grows older, Saleem grows into an adult yet remains a version of Rushdie's boyhood self, which may explain his peculiar combination of narcissism, passivity, and sexlessness. His incestuous desire for his sister is part of a desire to return to childhood, to a world before sex. It is hard for the reader to think of the thirty-one-year-old narrator as an adult. He is always the little boy in Methwold's Estate. The people around him also have trouble imagining him as a householder or fathering a child. Upon Saleem's return to India from Pakistan at age twenty-four, his mother's age when she gave birth to him, Picture Singh still affectionately calls him "baby sahib" (374). Shiva calls him "little rich boy" when both of them are twenty-nine years old (415). Padma calls the thirty-year-old story-teller her "little princeling" (121). Durga, his son's nurse, invites him to suckle her left breast while baby Aadam feeds from her right (430).

The romance of adoption, no less than that of birth and of orphanhood, is unstable and susceptible to the critique of realism. Mary's name associates her not only with the virginal mother of Christ, but also with Miriam, the sister of Moses, responsible for arranging the switch that saw her brother adopted by the daughter of Pharaoh and raised as an Egyptian prince. In the Quran, Christ's mother and Moses's sister are the same person. Saleem, like Moses, with whom he explicitly identifies (161), eventually rejects or is cast out from his privileged world and finds his rightful place with the poor and dispossessed, the slum-dwellers of Delhi. This "return" to his people is also ultimately a return to his nurse (who in Moses's case was actually his own birth mother) and to his sister. As always, however, the presence of an alternative romance challenges the centrality of the hero. Mary, the Miriam who starts Saleem's story by switching the babies, feuds with a fellow servant called Musa, the Arabic name for Moses. Jealous of the comparative favour Mary enjoys in the Sinai household and fearful that he himself will be sacked, this Musa steals the family heirlooms, the silver spittoon and the contents of a green tin trunk, notably a perforated bedsheet (144). In other words, Musa steals the talismans of identity that Mary had earlier stolen from the boy who became Shiva and had given to the boy who became Saleem. The nature of the theft is a blow not just to the Sinais' wealth but also to their family history. As the result of a terrible oath taken to assert his innocence, Musa becomes a leper, covered in sores. He will, however, yet prove to be the "Bomb-in-Bombay" (144): his return as a leper to the household he left in disgrace will so frighten Mary, who sees in him a ghost, that she will confess her original guilt in the baby switch. In other words, Musa stands in as a figure for Shiva, serving to remind Mary that her baby switch has not just produced one Moses but made another Moses her sworn enemy. The novel ends not with Saleem's happy reunion with Mary Pereira, but with him being pursued by "the terrifying figure of a war-hero with lethal knees, who has found out how I cheated him of his birth-right" (445).

Clearly the dialectic of realism and romance is endless. Romance provides Saleem with his meaning, but for his authority he needs realism. The novel wants it both ways. My point is that Rushdie's magic realism is best understood not in terms of hybridity, a metaphor from genetics that locates identity in the blood, but in terms of a struggle between meaning and authority. If the magic realism of *Midnight's Children* is indeed well suited to describing Indian reality, it is not because India is somehow exotic and magical, but because postcolonial identity is a matter of conflicting desires and anxieties.

14

Hindu India

Saleem opposes hybridity, which is both true and valuable, to purity, neither a truth nor desirable. However, it is possible to distinguish two kinds of hybridity in the novel. The first that Saleem champions, associated with impurity and able to contain difference, is an image of himself projected onto the world. The second, which he associates with chaos and a lack of differentiation, represents a hostile world in which he is potentially submerged. The threat of dissolution is Saleem's greatest fear, greater than his fear of the hollowness of mimicry, of the final impossibility of wholeness, or of being fixed and contained.

In spite of his grand claims to significance, Saleem appears to be more a creature of his environment than its master – and I do not mean political environment. The course of Saleem's life can be plotted against the weather: in 1956 "unease was in the air" (165); in April 1965 "the air buzzed with the fallibility of sons" (323); in late 1970 irritation was "in the air" (340). The air is often laden with a miasma, the product of heat and emotion, that disturbs the perception of reality, and in particular of time: "Heat, gnawing at the mind's divisions between fantasy and reality, made anything seem possible; the half-waking chaos of afternoon siestas fogged men's brains, and the air was filled with the stickiness of aroused desires"; "What grows best in the heat: fantasy; unreason; lust" (165). The world of *Midnight's Children* thus resembles Jameson's description of romance: "the strangely active and pulsating vitality of the 'world' of romance […] tends to absorb many of the act- and event-producing functions normally reserved for narrative 'characters'," reducing the hero to "something like a registering apparatus for transformed states of being, sudden alterations of temperature, mysterious heightenings, local intensities, sudden drops in quality, and alarming effluvia"

(Jameson 1981, 112). The tropical miasma makes the air liquid and vaporizes solids in the form of smoke. It makes the human vegetable and the real fantastic. And, in the "boiling streets" and bubbling "air" (164–5), "other people's lives," Saleem finds, "are blurring together in the heat" (169).

In this world, bodies absorb, according to Lamarckian principles, the colouring and the texture of their environment. A diet of fish has "made fish-lovers" of everyone in Bombay, with the exception of Aadam Aziz's descendants who, "infected with the alienness of Kashmiri blood, with the icy reserve of Kashmiri sky," remain "meateaters to a man" (92). Aadam Aziz's eyes are "a clear blue, the astonishing blue of mountain sky, which has a habit of dripping into the pupils of Kashmiri men" (14). The "barren angularity of Marathi," one of the two most prominent languages in Bombay, was "born in the arid heat of the Deccan," while the Gujarati language manifests a "boggy, Kathiawari softness," reflecting its origins in the Kathiawar peninsula (186). Karachi is "a city of mirages": "hewn from the desert, it had not wholly succeeded in destroying the desert's power" but is beset "by illusionary sand-dunes and the ghosts of ancient kings" (299). It is precisely because he understands the effect of environment on the soul that Methwold stipulates that the Indian buyers of his houses live among the possessions of their predecessors.

Of course, as the "logic of the jungle" has it (350), even as people come to resemble their world, the world takes on the character of the people in it: when people riot, "the weather joined in the mêlée" (218), and shedding tears can make it start to rain (350). People are not separate from the world but – women especially – add their own flavours to the mix, secreting back into the environment emotions that they had first absorbed from it. Reverend Mother who takes a vow of silence is able to create around her "a bog of muteness" (54), a "marshy time without words" (55). Guilt condenses in a fog around Amina's head, "her black skin exuding black cloud" (157), from which rain drops when she weeps (159). And as her guilt grows, the fog thickens and in turn infects other people: she begins "to exude the magnetism of the willingly guilty; and from then on everyone who came into contact with her felt the most powerful of urges to confess their own, private guilts" (157). When for forty days Bombay is "besieged by dust" (264), which makes Pia weep and sneeze (265) and clogs up the Brass Monkey's spirits (266), Aunt Alia spreads "her ancient, dusty disappointment through the air" (266).

Bodies do not divide selves but link them, to each other and to the world: "Things – even people – have a way of leaking into each other," "like flavours when you cook" (39). Tai's laughter "infects"

Aadam Aziz (19), as does his anger (22). Guilt contaminates everything Mary Pereira touches and, through her chutneys, seeps into the family she cares for (169). Amina stirs her own disappointments into "a hot lime chutney which never failed to bring tears to the eyes" (173). Reverend Mother's curries fill Amina "with ancient prejudices," and especially a sense of sin (139). Padma's "down-to-earthery, and her paradoxical superstition" leak into Saleem (39), as do her "dreams of marriage and Kashmir" (392). He also absorbs Ahmed Sinai's inability to follow his own nose (73), Uncle Hanif's sadness (168), and Aadam Aziz's "vulnerability to women" (267). Saleem's own capacity for revelation and higher purpose in turn leaks into Aadam Aziz (267) and has leaked "through the osmotic tissues of history" into Indira Gandhi herself (406).

The outside penetrates the body. When their godown burns to the ground Saleem's father and his two business associates "breathed air filled with incendiarized bicycles': "Arjuna bicycles moved in and out of their lungs" (74). The "cloud of cremated Indiabikes" then settles on an entire muhalla, where "something brittle and menacing" enters the souls of the inhabitants (75). A cold wind from the north carries the heady perfume of hashish fields to the Land of Kif, "and all who breathed it became doped to some extent" (313). The "hashashin wind" (313) is etymologically related to Ayub Khan's would-be "assassin," who is "carried away by a tide of history in which sons (high and low) were frequently observed to behave exceptionally badly" (323). The jungle of the Sundarbans enters those it swallows: Saleem and his three companions drink water that, in falling through the leaves of the trees, has "acquired on its journey something of the insanity of the jungle" (351). The culmination of this loss of self and mutual interpenetration is that the four lost souls suffer the fearful fate of becoming transparent.

All this breathing and swallowing must have an end, however. His companion Farooq Rashid declares that Saleem has "so many bad things" inside that it is "no wonder he kept his mouth shut" (354). But without some means of evacuation, the body might explode, like the leaches in the Sundarbans that suck blood until they burst, "being too greedy to stop sucking when they were full" (351). As the "unspoken words inside her were blowing her up" (59) Reverend Mother swells and finally bursts (60). "Overfull of hate resentment self-pity grief," Ahmed Sinai's heart "became swollen like a balloon, it beat too hard, skipped beats, and finally felled him like an ox" (288). The "overfilled balloon" that is public optimism during the Sino-Indian War also bursts (290), as does "the great ballooning fantasy of history," deflated by "the hundred daily pin-pricks of family life" (335).

The only way a container can accommodate the world is by exhaling or excreting at the same rate as it ingests. The infant Saleem has a "healthy metabolism," for "Waste matter was evacuated copiously from the appropriate orifices; from my nose there flowed a shining cascade of goo" (124). The adolescent Saleem is still distinguished by the quantity of matter that drains from his every orifice, "voiding below" as well as "drainage-above" (336). Unrestrained drainage, however, poses a threat of its own. Despite his parents' best efforts, Saleem has trouble subduing the world of snot, shit, and pee, the control he must learn in order to take his place in the world of adults. Too much drainage spells hollowness. Amina, for instance, feels "her strength of mind and her hold on the world seeping out of her" (83). The Delhi magicians, having misplaced their "powers of retention," find that "Communism had seeped out of them and been gulped down by the thirsty, lizard-quick earth" (428–9). When they suffer diarrhoea in the Sundarbans, Saleem and his three comrades-in-arms are forced "to examine the excrement in case their intestines had fallen out in the mess" (351). They allow their dream-life to leak out of them and become as dangerously "hollow and translucent as glass" (356).

Alongside the risk of emptying is the terrible danger of the pollution that would result if what is emitted from the body were allowed to re-enter. Such pollution is sometimes hard to avoid. Amritsar, for instance, is full of excrement: "Amritsar dung was fresh and (worse) redundant. Nor was it all bovine. It issued from the rumps of the horses between the shafts of the city's many tongas, ikkas and gharries; and mules and men and dogs attended nature's calls, mingling in a brotherhood of shit" (33). In the midst of the excrement are flies, "Public Enemy Number One," which "buzzing gaily from turd to steaming turd, celebrated and cross-pollinated these freely-given offerings" (33). Saleem senses with some alarm that the shitter does not stand apart from what he excretes. The description of the mountain of shit resembles Saleem's "pellmell tumble of a brain, in which everything ran into everything else," and the flies visiting from turd to turd are like his thought processes, in which "the white dot of consciousness jumped about like a flea from one thing to the next" (210). Mary Pereira's thoughts make similar "sorts of flea-jumps" (442).

As the image of flies hovering over a mountain of shit may suggest, bodies do not just take in the world by ingestion and absorption, but also by infection. Optimism is a virus (40); so is fame (304). The whiteness disease (Rushdie's cruel play on vitiligo, an incurable loss of pigment in patches on the skin) "leaked into history and erupted on an enormous scale shortly after Independence" (45). Less dangerous contagions also mark the susceptibility of the self to takeover by the outside: Mr Kemal is "infected with the cadences of the lawcourts" (71), Mustapha and Hanif and Rashid the rickshaw boy with "the listlessness of the times" (59), Saleem with that particularly "Indian disease," the "urge to encapsulate the whole of reality" (75). The magician Chishti Khan permits his illusionist expertise to infect his real life (387).

Aadam Aziz's mother, concerned lest her son pick up germs through his exposure to Tai the boatman, vows, "We'll kill that boatman's bugs if it kills you" (17). However, the pasteurization of Saleem's India is proceeding only fitfully at best. In general, germ theory is not well understood. "The great heat of 1956," Mary believes, "was caused by little blazing invisible insects" (156). Japanese tourists in India, Saleem says slyly, wear "surgical face-masks out of politeness, so as not to infect us with their exhaled germs" (401–2).

People may do what they can to resist germs, but there can be no defence against that other form of disease transmission: genes. The diffusion of miasma and germs through space has an equivalent in the transmission of genes across generations. Atavism figures frequently as an explanation for character and behaviour in all magic realism. Think of García Márquez's Buendía family who repeat not only names but also character types over a hundred years. The magic of magic realism is not just that individuals disregard the ordinary laws of behaviour or of nature, but also that individuals blur into each other. In *Midnight's Children* genetic inheritance does not mark who one is, but rather the trace, unwelcome to someone who believes he chooses his own parents, of other people within the self. Tai's laugh, for instance, which infects young Aadam Aziz – "a huge, booming laugh that seemed macabre when it crashed out of that old, withered body, but which was so natural in my giant grandfather that nobody knew, in later times, that it wasn't really his" – is then passed on to the hearer's descendants: "my uncle Hanif inherited this laugh; so until he died, a piece of Tai lived in Bombay" (19). Saleem traces the "forbearance of my own mother and the late steeliness of Naseem Aziz" to the "long sufferings of my great-grandmother," while "my great-grandfather's gift of conversing with birds" descended "through meandering bloodlines into the veins of my sister the Brass Monkey" (106). The superstitions of her mother run "deep in the veins" of Amina (99), where they do battle with the "adventurous spark" inherited from her father (100), a spark which eventually reasserts itself (138).

Not only is the world not the self but the self may not be the self either. The unity of the self is an illusion fostered by an identification with the reflection of body in the mirror. The body appears whole, "Indivisible, a one-piece suit, a sacred temple, if you will," and able to keep the outside from merging with the inside (230–1), but that wholeness is merely an illusion. Saleem declares that he has cracks appearing all over his body which cannot be discerned by the eyes of the medical profession and which arise from the intolerable pressures put on the shell of the body by the mass of contradictions and repressions within (37): "a human being inside himself, is anything but a whole, anything but homogeneous; all kinds of everywhichthing are jumbled up inside him, and he is one person one minute and another the next" (230). There is something here of Ramanujan's sense, expressed in the poem "Elements of Composition," that the self is composed of chemical elements, of memories, and of lepers and goddesses – "I pass through them/as they pass through me/taking and leaving/affections, seeds, skeletons":

> and even, as I add,
> I lose, decompose
> into my elements,
>
> into other names and forms,
> past, and passing, tenses
> without time,
>
> caterpillar on a leaf, eating,
> being eaten. (Ramanujan 1995, 122–3)

That last line, about the eater eaten, may remind us of the soldier Shaheed, who kills ants and licks them off his palm, and who is in turn eaten by ants.

Throughout the novel, walls between inside and out prove to be disconcertingly permeable. Aunt Alia's vengeful resentment oozes into the furniture and the walls of her house and into the curriculum, the bricks, and the students in her school until it resembles a force of nature. It is part of the same energies that manifest themselves as "Bitterness, issuing through the fissures of the earth" (292). Titanic, "numberless nameless Godknowswhats" emerge when the earth cracks during a drought (40). Walls crack, not because they are poorly built, but because fissures are part of the definition of walls. History "pours out" of Saleem's 'fissured body" (39).

What if the relation between inside and outside were neither separation nor violent penetration, but rather a matter of osmosis? Remove the borders and there would be no inside or out, no otherness to be feared ... but also no self to be protected. As an adolescent,

Saleem almost succeeds in drowning the past in the "thick, bubbling scent-stew" of the present in Karachi (307). The jungle of the Sundarbans swallows the buddha (Saleem) and his three companions "the way a toad gulps down a mosquito" (350). The would-be first mover is himself the moved; the swallower is in the belly of that which he would contain.

The subjectivity of the citizen has to do with mirrors and images, with reflection and imitation. Saleem identifies with images like the painting of Raleigh, the Kolynos Kid, and the map of India. As we have seen, sight is the sense that Saleem's narrative most relies on. Sight, paradoxically, fosters an identification with the unseen, with the abstract nation read about in newspapers and history books in which the boy finds a reflection of himself. And because it establishes the viewer's distance from the object and thus consolidates his identity (must the viewer be male?), sight inspires the impulse to totalization. Whether the observer identifies with its wholeness or asserts his difference from it, he stands outside that which he observes.

The other senses, taste, smell, and hearing, however, blur the frontier between inside and outside. Smell, in particular, surrounds the perceiver and eludes totalization. As Tai tells Aadam Aziz, the nose is "the place where the outside world meets the world inside you" (19). Smell "pours" into the perceiver (307), taking him over as it were and making him part of his surroundings. Adorno and Horkheimer explain that "Of all the senses, that of smell – which is attracted without objectifying – bears clearest witness to the urge to lose oneself in and become the 'other'" (Adorno and Horkheimer 1986, 184). Smells are the most inarticulate of the senses: in his attempts to classify them, Saleem must resort to other registers such as colour, weight, and shape (308), because there are almost no words for what the nose perceives. Smells are therefore associated with the animal and the non-human, with that which lives close to the ground and has not yet distinguished itself from nature. It belongs to the dog and not the man.

The word "smell" refers not only to the perceiving sense but also to that which can be sensed as it "pours" out of the body (307). In *Midnight's Children*, strong emotion, when pent up, manifests itself as body odour: for instance, "the acrid stench" of Aziz's "mother's embarrassment" (20) and "the sharp stink of my grandmother's curiosity and strength" (52). A "strange discontent in Padma" exudes "its enigmatic spoor from her eccrine (or apocrine) glands" (121), and "vengeful odours" leak out of Alia's glands (298). Saleem's father is followed all his life by "the stink of future failure" (73), his uncle

Zulfikar by "the unmistakable scent of success" (54). Saleem is all too familiar with "the glutinous reek of hypocrisy" (298), "the fatalistic hopelessness of the slum dwellers, and the smug defensiveness of the rich" (299).

In *Midnight's Children* self is not wholly absorbed into environment. Fogs, diseases, and genetic inheritance are still subject to personal agency. An anti-Hindu riot in a Delhi muhalla begins as "something hysterical in the air" that contaminates everyone (75), but requires a spark, provided by an eight-year-old girl who starts to hurl abuse at Lifafa Das, the Hindu peepshowwallah. So, too, the optimism disease coalesces around the charismatic figure of Mian Abdullah the Hummingbird, whose powerful hum affects the wills of those around him. The hum is independent of the disease, but is what makes Abdullah such an effective carrier. It may, however, be more accurate to speak of people as poles and nodes in force fields rather than as agents. The coalescence, absorption, and radiation of emotions are determined by the virulence of the emotions rather than by the individual will. Powerful emotions, which are always negative emotions such as guilt, bitterness, or despair, radiate outwards from a strong soul or are transmitted to others through conduction. Reverend Mother and Aunt Alia transmit emotions through the foods they prepare and the clothes they make for others.

The diffusion of emotional energy in the world of the novel does not obey the first law of thermodynamics, which holds that, since there is only a fixed quantity of energy, where energy is added to one site it must be taken from another. The forces in *Midnight's Children* follow the opposite principle: expending energy actually serves to increase energy in the system. The virulent emotion of a Reverend Mother or an Aunt Alia gains in strength as it radiates outwards. Those who do not themselves spread virulent emotion are most often drained of whatever is their own and filled by others. To the one who has more will be given, while from the one who has nothing, even the little that he has will be taken away. The result of this peculiar thermodynamic principle is that, at any one moment, the quantity of energy in the system as a whole may be much larger or much smaller. An equilibrium is maintained only over time: energy cannot, it seems, increase indefinitely and nothing is more certain than that what has been gained will eventually be lost. Filling and draining constitute a tidal movement, almost predictable and soothing, beneath the seeming randomness and frenetic desperation of Saleem's style. "Dal and pistachio-nuts poured into my grandmother while salt water flooded from my aunt" (265); public opinion "puffs up" with jingoistic emotion (290), but morale soon "drains away" (293). Saleem imagines this dynamic in terms of Snakes and Ladders: what goes up must come down. "Climb a ladder (or even a staircase) and you find a snake awaiting you," often a literal one (250). In Saleem's terms, "For every snake, there is a ladder; for every ladder, a snake" (297). A ladder can sometimes even be a snake (179). Snakes and ladders are found in Pakistan (297), as in India.

Rushdie himself has described the way "in which people 'leak' into each other" in *Midnight's Children* as symbolic of "cultural hybridisation" or adulteration, which in his terms is a good thing (Tripathi and Vakil 2000, 84). In practice, however, osmosis in the novel has rarely to do with anything usually classified as cultural and almost always involves negative forces that menace the self. It is very rare that desirable emotions spread from person to person. Hope that is communicated from person to person is always mere "optimism," that is to say false hope. Amina's assiduity during her husband's convalescence, which succeeds in "pouring her strength into his body" so that he is "filled" with love (288–9), is the one exception.

Critics most often follow Rushdie's own cue and regard the hybridity that he finds in Nehru's India as a morally superior alternative to the religious purity of Pakistan and to the Orientalist and racist notions of the colonizers. According to this reading, hybridity becomes synonymous with the freedom of the individual and the liberation of the colonized. Rather than being a symbol of "cultural hybridisation," however, leaking is an image of great anxiety in the novel. Karachi is characterized less by its purity than by its indiscriminate blending of terrible smells. We could explain the anomaly by saying that Rushdie mocks Saleem's panic at losing his fragile self. But the terror generated by the Sundarbans and the threat posed by the mob that breathes poisonous air are real enough. To understand what is at stake in Rushdie's conception of the nation it is more useful to contrast his notion of cultural hybridity, not with ethnic or religious purity, but with a rival notion of hybridity. Although Rushdie himself does not acknowledge this, the novel distinguishes between two kinds of hybridity, the one based on the Sundarbans and the other on Bombay.

Through several chapters in Book Three Saleem loses his memory and, with that, his self altogether. The amnesia is not so much exceptional as exemplary. It makes clear that where the self rules, there could as easily be other selves or even no self. The culmination of the amnesia is the journey to the Sundarbans, a figurative descent into Hell. The Sundarbans, a jungle area in the Ganges delta, belong to a time before earth and sea are divided, to the "primeval world" from which selves and nations emerge, before mirrors, "before clocktowers" and time (92), before words. In the Rann of Kutch, another such area, the borders between nations and even the line dividing sea and land appear to be erased. A "chameleon area which was land for half the year and sea for the other half" (276), "this amphibian terrain, this bog of nightmare" is reputed to be the home of mermen (276) and "fish-women" (325), and certainly is a haven for smugglers who operate without regard for state boundaries. The maps drawn up in 1947 declare the Rann of Kutch to be in India (though that would be disputed by Pakistan) and the Sundarbans are divided between East and West Bengal, but in Rushdie's novel both regions are nowhere and everywhere. They represent a deep realm below the state, below individual consciousness, and below meaning.

The Sundarbans represent a "magic" that is different from the magic of oral story-telling and from the magic of literalizing metaphor, a magic that has more to do with scale than with miracle. This magic belongs to an objective world characterized by flows and currents which dwarf the individual altogether. The jungle of the Sundarbans appears as "an impossible endless huge green wall, stretching right and left to the ends of the earth!"; but, the text asks, "who builds walls across the world?" (348). In the permeable world of the jungle, the boundaries separating inside from outside, states from states, and selves from each other are rendered absurd. Saleem, amnesiac and emotionally numb when he enters the region, is terrified of becoming wholly transparent, a green thought in a green world.

Bitten by a snake, Saleem retrieves his memories and so his self, and flees the jungle: "he was reclaiming everything, all of it, all lost histories, all the myriad complex processes that go to make a man" (353). The dangerous magic of the Sundarbans must be resisted by the "realism" of memory, which knows the self to be single and whole and continuous through time. The verb "reclaiming" links this process of self-recovery to the process whereby dikes and dams reclaim land from the sea, which is also how the original Seven Isles, Bombay, "Mazagoan and Worli, Matunga and Mahim, Salsette and Colaba," were brought together as Bombay (92). The names of Breach Candy Hospital and Breach Candy Swimming Pool, directly across Warden Road from Methwold Estates, commemorate the Great Breach, the channel through which seawater once poured at high tide, drowning the Flats that separated the islands. The Great Breach was dammed in the early eighteenth century. Hornby Vellard (now called Lala Lajpatrai Marg) was part of that "sea wall" (132). The answer to the question "who builds walls across the world?" is: the British and their nationalist successors.

"Land and sea; sea and land; the eternal struggle, not so?" (133). If the Sundarbans, the jungle where river and ocean meet, represent the world that can swallow the self, then Bombay represents a model whereby the self can contain the world of others. When the original William Methwold's colonizing vision "set time in motion," "sunken piles turned the Seven Isles into a long peninsula like an outstretched, grasping hand" emerging from the sea (92). Dr Narlikar, whose ambition is to succeed the British in their reclamation projects, lectures Saleem's father: "The British joined them up. Sea, brother Ahmed, became land. Land arose, and did not sink beneath the tides!" (133). Dr Narlikar defines imperialism in terms of "reclamation" (92), a task which he now believes falls to the imperialists' nationalist successors. The tetrapods with which he hopes to accomplish this (based on the actual curious tetrapods that shore up the embankment along Marine Drive) are "four-legged conquerors triumphing over the sea" (133).

Rushdie explicitly compares his own project in writing the novel to the reclamation of land from the sea that created Bombay (Rushdie 1991, 10). The self, the text, and the city are products of the same process. All involve erecting walls to hold back the sea. To avoid being swallowed by the tidal movements, the self must channel and contain the tides.

Saleem declares from some Archimedean position above the earth that he is like "Sin, the ancient moon-god, ... capable of acting-at-a-distance and shifting the tides of the world" (172). Saleem, however, is not on the moon but on the earth, and far from being the tides' master, he is but a conduit that the tides pass through. In hindsight he realizes that "the spirit of aggrandizement which seized me" when he declared himself the mover of the tides "was a reflex, born of an instinct for self-preservation" (172). "Self-preservation," however, requires that, even if Saleem knows he is not the mover of the tides, he pretend to be: "If I had not believed myself in control of the flooding multitudes, their massed identities would have annihilated mine" (172). When "like a drugged person," Saleem's head reeled "beneath the complexities of smell" in Karachi, he tells us "my overpowering desire for form asserted itself, and I survived" (307). Self is preserved by asserting form and resisting flux.

Saleem often compares other people to the sea. Dr Narlikar's female relatives form "an enormous stream of outsize womanhood flowing up our two-storey hillock" (175). The Marathi and Gujarati language marchers, each group demanding their own language-based states and laying claim to Bombay, form a "stream of chanting humanity which flooded Warden Road more completely than monsoon water" (186). The "waves of the march" part when Saleem comes hurtling down the hill on his bicycle (188), but quickly close over him again. Language marchers kill Dr. Narlikar by casting him, still clutching one of his beloved tetrapods, into the sea, where the drowned man, "by swallowing large quantities of the sea," had "taken on the qualities of water" and "had become a fluid thing" (175).

Women are often compared to fish at home in the sea. The swim team at Walsingham School for Girls swim like "fish" (181). Amina's eyes are "wide and unblinking as a pomfret's" (86), like the "fishy eyes"of Koli fisherwomen (94), and she makes "fish-like flutterings of lips" and "fish-motions" with her mouth (157–8). When he sees her hobbling on her corn-filled feet, Saleem imagines her as a silkie: "Amma, maybe you're a mermaid really, taking human form for the love of a man – so every step is like walking on razor blades!" (156). Saleem cannot but recall the stories he knows of "fish-women" who "lay with their fishy heads underwater, breathing, while their perfectly-formed and naked human lower halves lay on the shore, tempting the unwary into fatal sexual acts, because it is well-known that nobody may love a fish-woman and live" (325).

The male self, it would seem, must resist the feminized tides that threaten to sweep him away. This he can do by registering and measuring them, by finding or asserting the presence of form. A taste or a smell can stimulate a Proustian involuntary memory and thereby restore the past to the present, creating the impression of a continuous self that transcends the flux. When "Pickle-fumes" serve to "stimulate the juices of memory" (165) and a "shimmering heat-haze" in the present recalls a previous heat wave (165), the child that the writer once was is restored to him. Meeting Dr Schaapsteker again, nine years after he cured our hero of typhoid, stirs "time like a sluggish dust-cloud" and rejoins Saleem "to my one-year-old self" (250–1). Consciousness is the product of a personal feedback loop in the eternal flow. The rediscovery of Mary Pereira's green chutney makes possible not only a return to a past self but also the very writing of the narrative, which is done in Mrs Braganza's pickle factory.

The perceived continuity between then and now has, of course, as much to do with the larger tidal flow as with the self. Instead of shoring up the self, the restoration of the past can just as easily provoke a relapse of disease, a return of the repressed. Saleem recognizes a fever that fells him: "it's come up from inside me and from nowhere else; like a bad stink, it's oozed through my cracks" (205). He "caught exactly such a fever on my tenth birthday," and "now, as my memories return to leak out of me, this old fever has come back, too" (205). The point is that Saleem's hybrid self is constituted not just by its separation from the world but also by its openness to the world. Its defence against the flux of the world is to contain the world.

It is tempting to see in the tidal flow that sweeps through the narrative something before and below the self, a primordial Indianness, a manifestation of "the ancient insanities of India" (250). Saleem, at least, finds it tempting. Where might we find outside Saleem's narrative an expression of this primordial watery world, of what we might call the Indian Ocean? Calasso explains the type of knowledge cultivated by the *rsis* or *rishis,* the ancient seers, in liquid terms:

> The mind was confined within a compound, like the Cows, like the Dawns. Whatever happened, happened inside a fence, inside the walls of a palace, inside a cave sealed by a great stone. Outside foamed the immense ocean of the world, barely audible beyond a thick wall of rock. Inside, in the compound, was another liquid, a "pond," which, however small, was nevertheless equivalent to the ocean without. The ocean was outside the mountain but inside the mountain too. By splitting the rock, Indra allowed the inside ocean, "the ocean of the heart," *hrdyá samudrá,* to communicate with the outside ocean, the palpable ocean of the world. It was a moment that opened up a new way of knowing. For the *rsis* it was knowledge itself, the only knowledge they wished to cultivate. Not the mind shut away in its airy cage reconstructing a conventional image that corresponded point by point to the vast cage of the cosmos. But, quite the contrary: the waters of the mind flowing into those of the world and the waters of the world flowing into those of the mind to the point where they become indistinguishable one from the other. (Calasso 1999, 246–7)

The image of India as fluid, filling and leaking, is a common one. Nehru also declared that India was "infinitely absorbent like the ocean" (Chakravarty 1993, 23).

This other version of India, conceived of as a sea rather than as a territory, as a flow rather than as a sovereign whole, is always present in Saleem's narrative as that which he must transcend, although he doubts that he can. This is not the India that was born in 1947, "MADE AS ENGLAND," and defined against Pakistan, but an India, as old and as large as the world, which we might identify with the Sundarbans. To keep our hydrographic metaphor and speak of what the anthropologist Valentine Daniel calls "fluid signs" (Daniel 1984), the world in *Midnight's Children* is that sea into which all rivers flow, a sea that does not mark a final rest but is filled with motion, including tides that regularly reverse the direction of the estuaries that pour into it. The tides in *Midnight's Children* belong to an "Indian world-view," with the emphasis not on "Indian" but on "world." In this world, distinctions between India, Pakistan, and England become as meaningless as the discriminations Saleem is able to make between aerated soft drinks, "sniffing out which was Canada Dry and which 7-Up, unerringly separating Pepsi from Coke" (308).

In his essay entitled *Nationalism*, Tagore defines India as "the country of the No-Nation." Tagore sought a merger of East and West, but he made a distinction between "the spirit of the West," which is valuable and universally valid and therefore belongs properly to India as well, and "the Nation of the West," which represents an anti-human, would-be scientific force harmful to Westerner and Indian alike (Tagore 1976, 11). According to Tagore, nationalists who oppose imperialism in the name of a universal principle of nationalism uphold the same inhuman principle that drives imperialism in the first place. Tagore denounces the Hobbesian state because it pretends to be self-sufficient and a law unto itself and as such knows no morality but self-interest. He declares, "This government by the Nation is neither British nor anything else; it is an applied science and therefore more or less similar in its principles wherever it is used" (ibid., 10). Tagore explains that India the civilization is not India the nation: "the history of India does not belong to one particular race but to a process of creation to which various races of the world contributed – the Dravidians and the Aryans, the ancient Greeks and the Persians, the Mohammedans of the West and those of Central Asia. Now at last has come the turn of the English to become true to this history and bring to it the tribute of their life, and we neither have the right nor the power to exclude this people from the building of the destiny of India" (ibid., 9). However, the "Western Nation acts like a dam to check the free flow of Western civilisation into the country of the No-Nation" (ibid., 13). Western and Indian civilizations are fluids and the Nation, whether it takes the form of England or India, frustrates their flow.

Tagore, whom Rushdie refers to somewhat disparagingly as "old Rabindranath" in *The Jaguar Smile* (Rushdie 1987, 56), also wrote a novel in which the hero identifies with the nation. In the protagonist of this eponymous novel, *Gora*, he created a young Brahmin nationalist who, according to his acolytes, "had taken upon his own shoulders all the faults of present-day fallen India and was going to perform penance on behalf of the whole country" (Tagore 1980, 387). When he learns, however, that those whom he thought were his parents were actually his foster parents and that he was actually born to an

English couple killed in the Mutiny, Gora feels, like Saleem in the Sundarbans, that he "had no mother, no father, no country, no nationality, no lineage, no God even": "Only one thing was left to him, and that was a vast negation" (ibid., 402). Saleem returns from the Sundarbans as from a journey to annihilation, but Gora passes through the annihilation, as it were, to a place where he finally understands that India is not based on rules of purity or on separation but is all-inclusive: "In me there is no longer any opposition between Hindu, Mussulman, and Christian" (ibid., 406). He has realized the prayer that the poet Ramanujan makes to Murugan: "Lord of solutions/ teach us to dissolve/ and not to drown" (Ramanujan 1995, 116).

I do not mean that Tagore in any way thought of the "East" as a mystical ceaseless flux. Nor do I mean that, when he wrote the Sundarbans chapter, Rushdie had Tagore in mind. He may have been thinking of a more general pattern of Hinduism: Sujala Singh suggests that the Sundarbans episode be read as a Vanaprastha, literally a journey through the forest, the stage in life when a man renounces his worldly connections and prepares his soul for leaving. If so, then Saleem is someone who refuses to renounce and "is condemned to the Hindu cycle of birth and re-birth" (Singh 2000, 172). My point is that the novel features two kinds of hybridity weighted differently. Saleem sings the body eclectic but fears a fluid hybridity associated with the Sundarbans and with personal extinction. The contrast in *Midnight's Children* is not between what Bakhtin calls the closed body of classical sculpture and the open, grotesque body of popular culture (Bakhtin 1968, 320). Instead the novel features two kinds of grotesque: the glorious giant self that would swallow the world and the terrifying world that would mutilate and swallow the self. Bakhtin believes the grotesque is a celebration of the transindividual body of humanity that dies to be reborn: "Actually, if we consider the grotesque image in its extreme aspect, it never presents an individual body; the image consists of orifices and convexities that present another, newly conceived body. It is a point of transition in a life eternally renewed, the inexhaustible vessel of death and conception" (ibid., 318). In the world of *Midnight's Children*, such grotesqueness, Bakhtin's "inexhaustible vehicle of death and conception," belongs not to Saleem but to Shiva, violent destroyer and profligate inseminator. Saleem's own grotesque physicality, a function of protuberances and orifices, is not transindividual but inseparable from all that make him unique. He fears that which Bakhtin celebrates: being "swallowed by the world" (ibid., 317) and being dependent on the cycles of death and procreation. According to Bakhtin, "grotesque imagery constructs what we might call a double body" (ibid., 318), but the doubled body at the centre of Rushdie's novel is precisely what Saleem most fears. Saleem fears death, which will mean not new life but the loss of self. The preservation of the self is not guaranteed by new bodies, not even that of his son (fathered by Shiva): it is rather secured by memory and art. Saleem preserves the form of his life by writing it down for his son.

Saleem is that seeming contradiction: someone who revels in his own grotesqueness yet remains terrified of losing his precious self if he cannot maintain the distinctions between inside and out. Rushdie is a true descendant of Forster, who also could not decide if India was a window onto a different ontology (magic) or if what appeared to be a different ontology was but a projection of otherness onto a common humanity best understood by liberal humanism (realism). Forster's solution was to make the Muslim Aziz someone with whom the liberal Englishman Fielding could have a dialogue and to make the Hindu Godbole and the Marabar Caves occupy a genuinely alternative metaphysical space only understood, if at all, by the mystic Mrs Moore. The force of *Midnight's Children* derives from a similar contradiction. Either India must be regarded as a nation in the same way as England is a nation, or there are no nations, only a terrifying flux which casts up flotsam in the form of nations and then reabsorbs them, a flux perhaps best understood in Hindu terms.

I do not mean to reinstate a notion of magic as particularly Indian and realism as modern and Western. The magic of the Sundarbans is as large as the world, as we can understand if we compare it to what Hardt and Negri call Empire, a postmodern world beyond the "spatial configuration of inside and outside" (Hardt and Negri 2000, 186) and best described as "smooth": "It might appear to be free of the binary divisions or striation of modern boundaries, but really it is crisscrossed by so many fault lines that it only appears as a continuous, uniform space": "In this smooth space of Empire, there is no *place* of power – it is both everywhere and nowhere. Empire is an *ou-topia*, or really a *non-place*" (190). By such a reading, the division into realism and magic would not be between the modern West and traditional India but between a modern world, divided into inside and out and into nation-states, and a postmodern world without such divisions.

The contest in *Midnight's Children* between Bombay and the Sundarbans is between competing versions of the human, each, by virtue of being universal, claiming to contain the other and each, inevitably, excluding that which it cannot contain. What is excluded by each version of the universal returns, however, to disrupt it.

Saleem is performing what Chakrabarty would call "yet another attempt, in the long and universalistic tradition of 'socialist' histories, to help erect the subaltern as the subject of modern democracies, that is, to expand the history of the modern in such a way as to make it more representative of society as a whole" (Chakrabarty 2000, 94). This attempt is based on excluding that which it fears, yet it has the very real virtue of providing "at least a glimpse of its own finitude, a glimpse of what might constitute an outside to it" (ibid., 93). By preserving the traces of the political struggle between alternative universals, *Midnight's Children* is both as large as the world and constrained to testify to where its own world ends.

15

Cosmopolitanism and Objectivity

Magic realism, whether in Rushdie, Grass, García Márquez, or Okri, always involves magic or fantasy in a twentieth-century context where one would not expect to find it. It is post-realist as much as anti-realist. Brian McHale makes a useful distinction between modernism, where uncertainty is a function of epistemology – nothing can be known for sure – and postmodernism, where uncertainty is a matter of ontology: there are different worlds which obey different rules (McHale 1987). Most magic realism, by this definition, is postmodernist. *Midnight's Children*, however, is unusual in retaining strong elements of modernism: it questions ontology and epistemology both. Kumkum Sangari describes the juxtaposition of the ontological and the epistemological in *Midnight's Children* as modernist: "The totalizing yet open epic structure exists cheek-by-jowl with an epistemological mode (based, like Western modernism, on an acknowledged yet decentred realism) that privileges faulty sight, peripheral or incomplete vision, limited perception, deliberate fallibility, and the splinter effect – in short, with a covertly totalizing quasi-modernist aesthetic of the fragment. To some extent the narrative finds its dynamic in the modernist challenge to premodern forms and vice versa" (Sangari 1987, 178). Like the modernists Conrad, James, Faulkner, and Ford, Rushdie depicts a single consciousness whose commentary on events we are not allowed to trust, but the limits of whose perspective we read as a metonymic symptom of the historical moment.

The juxtaposition of modernism and postmodernism is another way of expressing what is by now a familiar contradiction: is the novel about an India where ordinary rules of verisimilitude do not apply, or does it reflect Saleem the individual with a limited perspective, an unreliable memory, and an agenda of his own that readers must be suspicious of? Is the magic of the novel a function of India's spiritual nature or of Saleem's madness?

Unlike most magic realist narrators, Saleem displays an awareness that his narrative strains credibility. A common refrain of his is "believe me, don't believe, but this is what it was like!" (345, 368, 393, 443) and "It happened that way because that's how it happened" (443). He does not treat the extraordinary with the nonplussed familiarity of a García Márquez narrator. Saleem knows what his readers are prepared to believe and how much he is asking of them. He meets his readers on their ground before inviting them to join him on his. Saleem presumes both the conventions of verisimilitude and an extratextual narrative, that of modern Indian history, which can be described as realist, and he deliberately measures his own story against them. Where he deviates from the established narrative of Indian history, he signals the deviation: "If you don't believe me, check" (48). He will also draw attention to his own errors, thereby invoking a standard of factuality inapplicable to the timeless and mapless worlds of García Márquez or Okri, where it would be meaningless to question the reliability of the narration. Readers unfamiliar with Colombian history will not suspect that behind García Márquez's account of the civil war and the massacre of striking banana workers lies a historical reality. Saleem not only invokes an extratextual history but goes so far as to tell us that he has got the date of Gandhi's death wrong (164). Most critics quote Saleem's confession to prove that he is indifferent to factual history, but the confession has exactly the opposite meaning: he deliberately draws our attention to history.

Saleem does not tell us when Gandhi was assassinated. The narrative sequence of events culminating in the public announcement of the assassination includes for the most part undated family events. Without his confession of the error most of the readers who need Saleem's translations of Hindi-Urdu would not even pick it up. So what does Saleem mean when he says he got the date wrong? Presumably he means that his narration has already so filled 1948 with "events piled upon events" (136) that there is not enough room left for the assassination on January 30th. In January of that year Dr. Narlikar first approached Ahmed Sinai with his land reclamation schemes (132). The businessman's investment in the project unfortunately attracted the attention of the government, which, in the aftermath of Partition, was suspicious of Muslims moving cash and froze his assets. The need for money to challenge the freeze in the courts sent Amina Sinai to the Mahalaxmi Racecourse to gamble. Yet all this is supposed to have happened before the family hears that

Gandhi was killed. Moreover, when she goes to the racetrack, Amina is "weighed down" by a baby (165), conceived in January (139), which will be born on September 1st (284). Amina's gambling spree therefore appears to take place at least several months after January, and the news of Gandhi's assassination arrives "in the midst of her racing days" (141). Again, the logic of the narration pushes the assassination a few months back; how many remains unclear. Only one date, however, explicitly contradicts historical chronology: the Sinai family survived the freezing of assets by renting out an upstairs room to Dr Schaapsteker, who, Saleem tells us, moved in at the end of February (136), although at this point in the narrative we have not yet been told the news of the assassination. All that would be required to accommodate the date of Gandhi's assassination would be to backdate the freezing of the assets and the renting of the apartment to late 1947. Yet, having discovered the supposed mistake in dating Gandhi's death, Saleem declares that he will not go back: "But I cannot say, now, what the actual sequence of events might have been; in my India, Gandhi will continue to die at the wrong time" (164).

There are several explanations possible for the discrepancy. Syed Manzurul Islam excuses the narrative's "faulty memory" on the grounds of "imaginative truth," modernist "epistemological uncertainty," and the migrant's right "to be a legitimate subject of enunciation" (Islam 1999, 129). Although Syed Islam celebrates all these deviations from factuality and the novel blurs them all, they are not equivalent and even contradict one another. Epistemological uncertainty and imaginative truth operate on wholly different principles: the first presumes that Saleem cannot be certain of anything and the second that he really does know something, even if what he knows is not the facts. The latter is the explanation offered by Saleem and most favoured by critics: his infidelity to history is a measure of his faithfulness to memory, which, while possibly counterfactual, possesses "the authentic taste of truth" nonetheless (444). Saleem patiently explains to Padma that memory "selects, eliminates, alters, exaggerates, minimizes, glorifies, and vilifies also; but in the end it creates its own reality, its heterogeneous but usually coherent version of events; and no sane human being ever trusts someone else's version more than his own" (207). This last phrase, quoted approvingly by Rushdie himself (Rushdie 1991D, 25), implies that memory supplies, if not the truth about what happened, at least the truth about the self's understanding of itself and its place in the world. Rushdie says that he found himself remembering what it was like to be in India during the war with China, even though he could not possibly have been there at the time (ibid., 24). A particular narrative can become so integral to one's sense of self that it cannot be surrendered without damage to the self.

We should, however, be suspicious of the supposed truth of memory. Saleem himself accuses India of being a "nation of forgetters" (38), implying that the past is a sacred trust that can be betrayed by faulty memories. How does he reconcile this with his notion that memory allows one to doctor and enhance, even falsify the past in the interests of a personal truth? Fidelity to this kind of memory is not necessarily, whatever Saleem might say, the mark of a "sane human being." It presumes that the self is solely a function of personal memory, however warped, and is therefore already known: "I know what I know and no one can tell me different." This is not the self discovered or recovered by historicizing.

Moreover Saleem (like Rushdie) does not actually remember or even misremember hearing the news of Gandhi's death – he was less than six months old at the time. The error here is not the truth of personal memory. What seems to be at stake in the case of the Gandhi assassination is the narrative that older members of the Sinai family have told the next generation. Such a narrative, if not true to the facts or even to memory, can, of course, like memory, still be integral to the idea that individuals have of themselves. The chronological incompatibility presumably arises through the conflation of two stories current in the Sinai family: How We Survived the Great Freeze and How We Learned of Gandhi's Death. But if the version of events given by Saleem represents family lore that he grew up with, it is difficult to see why the canonical story should be so specific about the date at which Schaapsteker moved in upstairs. Precision in chronology is, after all, rare in most family lore. Normally in ancestral stories, accounts of concurrent events avoid explicitly contradicting each other.

Saleem's retention of the error suggests that his sense of self requires a narrative link between the historical cataclysm that was Gandhi's death and the coming of Schaapsteker. The chapter title "Snakes and Ladders" suggests the link. The presence of Schaapsteker, the director of a scientific institute doing research into venoms and anti-venoms who is gradually becoming like the snakes he studies, introduces the motif of snakes, which then becomes the frame used to present Gandhi's assassination. According to Saleem, who was not there, the family was attending the premiere of Uncle Hanif's new film when they heard the news. *The Lovers of Kashmir*, whose title echoes the courtship of Aadam Aziz and Naseem Ghani, was, Saleem tells us, notable for its pioneering of the technique of the indirect kiss.

Rather than kiss each other, which the censors and public morality would not have permitted, the screen lovers kiss apples and mangos that they then exchange. The chaste and fruit-filled romantic idyll is brought to a halt by the news of the assassination, which ever afterward is recalled as a fall, the violent intrusion of a Serpent into a garden (142). The novel's report of Gandhi's assassination – "Some madman shot him in the stomach" (142) – deliberately echoes the hole left in Aadam Aziz by his loss of faith when he fell from the Edenic innocence associated with Kashmir. The death of the Mahatma also marks the irruption of the real into the safe, conventional, and hermetic world of Uncle Hanif's film, a reminder of a real world of pain and danger on the other side, as it were, of the artistic screen.

We have therefore an explanation for the presentation of Schaapsteker, the snake doctor, before the news of the assassination but still no explanation for why Schaapsteker should move in specifically in February and Gandhi's death must be postponed. We cannot escape the conclusion that Saleem retains the strangely precise chronology, not *in spite of* its inaccuracy but *because* it is inaccurate. Saleem's highly stylized account of how the news of the assassination disrupted Hanif's film manages to fit disruptive reality back into his own art, ostentatiously subordinating Gandhi's death to the needs of his narrative. The news bulletin becomes one of a series of snakes, juxtaposed with a series of ladders. The supposed error about Gandhi makes the point that the real can never actually erupt into art; reality is always mediated. The assassination is not, as it would be for most people alive at the time, the linchpin around which the Sinais order their memories – where were you when you heard the news? – but can be fitted into a narrative that already has its own shape.

The supposed error is of a piece with Rushdie's strategy in all his novels, from *Grimus* to *The Ground Beneath Her Feet*, of insisting that fiction creates an alternative dimension or a "parallel universe" (Rushdie 1983, 65). In *Shame* the narrator declares that he builds "imaginary countries" and tries "to impose them on the ones that exist" (ibid., 92). In *Midnight's Children* a host of small errors, especially those that involve dates that Rushdie must have looked up, are clearly deliberate and underline the distance of the fiction from the historical record. In the novel Sheikh Mujib-ur-Rahman proclaims the state of Bangladesh on March 25th, 1971 (344), and Pakistani troops respond by massacring university students. In history the massacre actually occurred first, and Independence was proclaimed by Major Zia in Mujib's name on the following day, the 26th. The Pakistani Lieutenant General A.A.K. Niazi surrenders to the Indian army on December 15th in the novel (367), when it was the 16th on which he surrendered and the Indian Army marched into Dacca. Niazi surrenders to Sam Manekshaw in the novel, when he actually surrendered to Lieutenant General Aurora (not Arora as Rushdie writes [Rushdie 1991D, 22]). In 1944 Subhas Chandra Bose invaded eastern India from Burma with a Japanese-backed army of Indian soldiers but, "drenched by the returning rains," his advance was fatally delayed by the monsoons (60). Saleem says this happened in August 1945 (59), implying perhaps that Bose in the jungle had not yet heard of the end of the war.

Saleem declares himself indifferent to errors in the service of a higher truth, but that indifference is mere bravado. He actually needs errors so much that he is prepared to invent them. Critics often quote Saleem's confession of error about Gandhi's death and agree with him about the value of experience and of memory, however doctored, without noting that what he says is the product neither of experience nor of memory, not even of the collective memory passed on through family lore, but of prophecy and of an artistic reconstruction that is a form of prophecy cast backwards. Saleem's narration is from the perspective of a "new, all-knowing memory, which encompasses most of the lives of mother father grandfather grandmother and everyone else" (88). Saleem's version is not partial but total. His prophetic memory partakes of what he calls "the illusion of the artist," which is that "I can find out any damn thing!" and "There isn't a thing I cannot know!" (172).

Saleem's "memory," therefore, does not reflect personal experience. There may well be "as many versions of India as Indians" (323), but it is not true that Saleem's is as valid as any other. Saleem's truth is closer to Syed Islam's "imaginative truth," the artist's vision of the world to which he must be faithful, than to the truth of memory. A strong case can, of course, be made for imaginative truth. Syed Islam argues that, if the migrant author is to speak, his narrative cannot be "subjected to the law of constative proposition" but must be considered "an object of ethico-political investment" (129). In the article "Errata" Rushdie readily confesses to an error of historical fact concerning an event that occurred long before he was born: the novel depicts the soldiers with Brigadier Dyer who mowed down the crowd at Amritsar in 1919 as "white" when they were, in fact, Indian (Rushdie 1991D, 36). The "wrongness," however, "feels right" (ibid., 23); in other words, it is faithful to a larger historical truth about colonialism.

My point, however, is that fidelity to artistic vision is not the same as fidelity to memory, and their truth claims differ. Saleem wins his reader's assent to the partial truth of memory – this is but one man's version of events – and then passes off a totalizing vision of the world, complete with apocalyptic end, as if it were memory. Saleem's version readily admits it is but a metonym, one part of the whole, and as such its truth, because partial and subjective, cannot be questioned. Yet the authority derived from the limited truth claims then appears to underwrite a vision of the whole that goes unsubstantiated. To the extent that Saleem explicitly claims only to be remembering, his confession of error is actually a smokescreen. Artistic license, of course, may legitimately be claimed by Rushdie who has invented both Saleem and his story. He can be excused his totalizing, for by definition he knows the complete truth of this world he has created. Saleem, however, cannot be so easily excused.

Saleem's confession suggests that his error regarding Gandhi was unintentional and that he only realized it after the fact, but this is clearly disingenuous. As Saleem fills 1948 with events, he postpones the cataclysmic event that readers at all familiar with Indian history are expecting and even makes them doubt if he will remember to include it at all. The omens of disorder in the universe – "They – we – should have known something bad would happen. That January, Chowpatty beach, and Juhu and Trombay, too, were littered with the ominous corpses of dead pomfret, which floated, without the ghost of an explanation, belly-side-up, like scaly fingers in to shore" (135) – are deliberately and ludicrously read as pointing to Ahmed Sinai's financial woes. Moreover, other events that occur after January are still referred to as "omens": in February the snakes escape from the Schaapsteker Institute (136), yet religious leaders at the time read the snakes as collective "punishment," not for Gandhi's assassination, which in Saleem's narrative has not happened yet, but for secularism (136). This narrative teasing is the reverse of the suspense built up by the countdown in Book One: the inevitable and already known is deliberately misread and defused.

The confession of error hides the nature of the error. We are told that the Sinais and other Muslims did not dare to leave their homes for forty-eight hours after the terrible news of Gandhi's assassination was first announced, for fear of anti-Muslim violence (142). Rushdie himself told David Sheff that this was the story as he heard it from his parents (Sheff 2000, 196). However, according to Collins and Lapierre's *Freedom at Midnight*, which we know Rushdie read (Cundy 1996, 36), the news of the assassination was actually withheld from the public for forty-five *minutes* until it could be confirmed that the assassin was a Hindu. At six p.m., 30 January 1948, at the same time as the news of Gandhi's death, All-India Radio broadcast the name and the religion of his killer (Collins and Lapierre 1976, 508–9). In other words, Gandhi's death was not the moment of great fear that Saleem records. It was instead a time of great mourning, perhaps especially for Muslims, since it was the Mahatma's efforts towards post-Partition reconciliation between India and Pakistan that had so offended the militant Hindus who killed him. To misremember the event is to misunderstand the nature of Gandhi.

The discrepancy in chronology is so minor, however, that it is not reproduced in Rushdie's screenplay of the novel, where Gandhi dies in January. More significant than the error is the confession which draws attention to the error. Saleem's need to confess is such that he is prepared to admit to errors that are hardly errors at all and to invent them where they do not exist. He is quick to admit that he has depicted the elections of 1957 as taking place after his tenth birthday in August when they actually took place in March (217), an error whose only significance is that it can be confessed.

Critics tend to see in Saleem's and Rushdie's admissions of error proof that author and narrator are unconcerned with positivist history. However, Saleem's confessions of error actually prove how much the narrative is aware of an extratextual national history and deliberately deviates from it. The proof that the narrative is concerned with an extratextual India is that, while some errors can be excused as compatible with a truth larger than history, others, it seems, cannot. In "'Errata'," Rushdie declares that he has deliberately made Saleem an unreliable narrator. In other words, the author expects readers to have some sense of how Saleem deviates from the truth and to judge him accordingly. When Saleem tells us Valmiki dictated the *Ramayana* to Ganesh (149), he proves how little he knows about Hinduism (Valmiki dictated the *Ramayana* to Rama's twin sons, Lava and Kusa; Vyasa dictated the *Mahabharata* to Ganesh). Readers who catch the error are not to assume that in Saleem's India, just as "Gandhi will continue to die at the wrong time" (164), so, too, Valmiki will continue to dictate to Ganesh. No, Rushdie asks the reader to recognize that "Saleem is wrong" (Rushdie 1991D, 22). There is an extratextual India to which readers must hold the narrator accountable. It is possible to imagine an India in which Gandhi dies on the wrong date, but not an India in which Valmiki and Vyasa change places.

Rushdie wants it both ways: he expects that readers will tolerate errors – it is only a novel, folks – and will catch Saleem's errors and "maintain a healthy distrust" (ibid., 25). Sometimes Rushdie asks readers to see around Saleem's unreliable narration, and sometimes Saleem speaks, in a voice very much like Rushdie's, of the truth of the artist's vision which cannot be questioned. The two kinds of errors, the permissible and the inexcusable, correspond to two extra-textual Indias, one which artistic license is free to invent, the other which cannot be reimagined because it is needed to establish artistic authority. In general, it is contemporary politics that Saleem can play fast and loose with. The second India, in which mistakes are not allowed, concerns religion, pre-colonial history, and Bombay life. Ignorance of these, because it casts doubt on whether Saleem is inside India at all, severely compromises his authority. The point of the error in chronology concerning Gandhi is that the Mahatma is one of the things Saleem can afford to be mistaken about: readers are forced to concur that Gandhi is not integral to India in the way that Ganesh or the *Ramayana* are. Saleem's India is pried loose from Gandhi.

Permissible and inexcusable errors – Saleem can be wrong about Gandhi but not about Ganesh – are distinguished by their presentation: the former are confessed to, the latter are not. Saleem expects that he can be forgiven any error he confesses to; Rushdie insists that errors that go unconfessed can be held against Saleem. Confession works to forestall criticism: others cannot accuse you of a sin you have already accused yourself of. Saleem fully expects to have hostile readers and "venom-quilled critics" (349), but he boasts that he has already twice survived snakebite and emerged stronger.

The power of confession is more than prophylactic. The purpose of the confession is to establish Saleem's sincerity – he is someone who tells the truth as he knows it and if he makes mistakes, he can at least be trusted not to be deceiving us. Because he admits he lies, Saleem must be telling the truth. The confession of error, by scaling back truth claims, is actually a claim to authority. Moreover, the confession wins the reader's assent to much more than the speaker can actually claim. Saleem's confessions say, in effect, "my errors do not matter because you and I, reader, both know what does matter." He then proceeds to tell readers what matters, having flattered them that they already know it. Confession has the paradoxical power of making an error or a lie true: you can say anything and retain the trust of the listener as long as you admit you are not telling the truth. By confessing to error, Saleem appears to be saying that what happened is less important than what one remembers, but what he believes is that "what actually happened is less important than what the author can manage to persuade his audience to believe" (263). To err is human, but confession can fix that.

Saleem has always taken delight in "admission-of-guilt, revelation-of-moral-turpitude, proof-of-cowardice" (349). Ever since a boy, there has been a "confession, trembling just beyond my lips" (257). He is ever ready to hang his head "before the inevitability of his guilt" (354;

167, 339, 350, 419, 427). Saleem the adult regards his narrative as a confessional or a therapy session: "I swore to confess everything" (310); "So permit me to criticize myself" (345); and "To all my readers, I should like to make this naked-breasted confession" (349). He twice begins a chapter by offering a critique of the previous one, declaring he will "own up" (349) and "To tell the truth, I lied" (427). Saleem apologizes for his past behaviour – "I confess: what I did was no act of heroism" (252) – as well as for the shortcomings of his narrative, including the cliché of telepathy (166), the cheap melodramatic "gimmick" of amnesia (339) and even the absurd prevalence of confession itself: "Enough confessions"(39).

An abashed Saleem is the first to admit that his lapse in chronology marks the extent to which he is "prepared to distort everything – to re-write the whole history of my times purely in order to place myself in a central role" (164). He joins his readers in their criticism of his narcissism. He refers to his younger self in the third person, describing how sixteen-year-old "Saleem Sinai came to terms with himself": "I will not say he was not sad; refusing to censor my past, I admit he was as sullen, often as uncooperative, certainly as spotty as most boys of his age" (306–7). At the same time, confession confirms the sinner in his centrality – "Yes, it was my fault (despite everything)" (115); "Nehru's death: can I avoid the conclusion that that, too, was all my fault" (271); "Jamila's fall was, as usual, all my fault" (381). Saleem is so eager to confess because confession is the most powerful form of that magic which brings a world into being by speaking it. Confession appears to be constative, a statement about the state of affairs, but is actually performative (Austin 1962).

Confession can also be a way of making the hearer of the confession complicitous in the crime. In the Alfred Hitchcock film "I Confess," which Saleem knows well (105), a murderer confesses to Fr Michael Logan, who does not betray the sanctity of the confessional even when he is himself charged with the crime. Confession is a trick Saleem learns from women. Mary Pereira loves confessing so much she goes to the confessional even when she has as yet done nothing that needs absolution. When she finally confesses her crime of switching the babies to the Sinai family, "the dream-world she invented when she changed name-tags," which had come to seem an intolerable lie, is of a sudden rendered acceptable and even inevitable (272). The Sinais find that Mary's confession changes nothing. History, it seems, has "the power of pardoning sinners" (319).

Rushdie, who, in his own person, has confessed to some errors and blamed all the others on Saleem, plays the same game as his narrator. He expects readers to forgive because he has confessed. The confession, however, hides as much as it reveals, and is rhetorical in purpose. Of course, Rushdie has not always been successful in winning readers' assent. His disavowal of Saleem's narrative did not prevent him from being successfully sued by Indira Gandhi for libel, and he was forced to remove from all subsequent editions of the novel the following offensive sentence: "It has often been said that Mrs Gandhi's younger son Sanjay accused his mother of being responsible, through her neglect, for his father's death; and that this gave him an unbreakable hold over her, so that she became incapable of denying him anything" (406). *The Satanic Verses* has notoriously posed a similar conundrum: the author claims his fictional world is at a remove from history and therefore should not offend anyone, yet, when it suits him, he will also insist on the novel's relevance and even prescience.

Certainly both Saleem and Rushdie have a great deal to confess. Faulkner's, Conrad's, or Ford's unreliable narrators reveal something about themselves when they present the world askew, but Saleem's errors do not derive from character and location. They are quite simply not functions of memory, at least not of the memory of someone who has lived all his life in India and Pakistan. It is implausible that a man who currently lives in Bombay among Bombayites should not know that Mumbadevi has a special day. It is inconceivable that Padma to whom he reads his narrative should not correct him. The only explanation for the narrator's unreliability is that Rushdie must have someone to blame for the inevitable errors that result from his own outsider status. In an interview he gave shortly after publication and in which he prides himself on including "probably" as many Eastern sources as Western sources in his novel, Rushdie explains that Ganesh is "the god who, according to legend, sat down at the feet of India's Homer, the poet Valmiki, and copied down the *Ramayana*" (Ross 2000, 2). In other words, the mistake that Rushdie would later call a "howler," that supposedly betrays Saleem's "narratorial pomposity" (Rushdie 1991D, 25) is actually his own! Saleem's egregious errors serve as a cover for the fact that Rushdie does not know what he himself believes that the author of *Midnight's Children* should know.

Some errors are readily excusable. Saleem seems to think that the number 420 has been "associated with fraud, deception, and trickery" since "time immemorial" (193), but the number is actually a reference to section 420 of the Code of Criminal Procedure promulgated by the British, which covers small-scale fraud and confidence tricks (Aravamudan 1989, 7). Mary Pereira supposedly goes to confession in St Thomas's Cathedral, but Mary is Catholic and the cathedral is Anglican. She would not go there, and they would not hear confession. Although Saleem went to St Thomas's every Wednesday with his class (225), he never paid much attention. Other errors, however, are more egregious. In "Errata" Rushdie mocks readers who query minor details like the bus route that Saleem takes to school (Rushdie 1991D, 23). But the error in the bus route does not reflect a small lapse of memory on Saleem's part, but rather an ignorance of the topography of the city. It is impossible that, in travelling from Warden Road to Cathedral and John Connon Boys' High School in the Fort district, the bus would turn left off Marine Drive and pass "Victoria Terminus towards Flora Fountain, past Churchgate Station and Crawford Market" (153). Such a journey would mean going around in widening circles. The error reveals an ignorance that belonged perhaps to a young boy who was only an inattentive passenger in a bus *and who left Bombay at age fourteen*, but is wholly implausible in Saleem who is supposed to be living in Bombay even as he writes.

Trivedi shows that Rushdie makes mistakes in Hindi-Urdu that put in doubt the novel's use of non-English words as markers of authenticity. Saleem supposedly speaks "classy Lucknow-type Urdu" (340), and he mocks the language spoken by Deshmukh who claims to have "a magical belt which would enable the wearer to speak Hindi": "I am wearing now, my sir, speak damn good yes no?" (360). The novel's hybrid language does not, however, reflect a bilingual or multilingual consciousness so much as the vagaries of English as it is spoken in the subcontinent. Almost all the Hindi-Urdu words in the novel can be found in Ivor Lewis's *Sahibs, Nabobs and Boxwallahs*, subtitled "A Dictionary of the Words of Anglo-India" (Lewis 1997). One word not listed in Lewis's dictionary nor in *Hobson-Jobson*, its famous precursor, is *funtoosh*, which Saleem uses to mean "kaput" but which, according to Trivedi, does not have that meaning at all, but derives from the 1956 Chetan Anand film with that title about a comical mimic-man figure. Rushdie's error (Trivedi convinces us that it is not Saleem's alone) proves that he does not know what *funtoosh* means and so shows how much he is himself a proper funtoosh. Trivedi is too quick, however, to pounce on this error. It is surely possible that *funtoosh* was a slang term belonging to Malabar Hill, to schoolboys of a certain era, or to the Rushdie family, a word of private significance such as Saleem says *dubash* was (129).

I am less interested in the question of Rushdie's authority than in the way narrative authority is itself of overriding concern in the novel. Trivedi accuses Rushdie of being outside the national culture, a location to which Trivedi attributes not special knowledge but unfortunate ignorance. By all that he does not know, Rushdie proves he is not Indian. My point, however, is not Trivedi's: that Rushdie is merely a funtoosh figure. Trivedi understandably resents that so many readers have read the novel's version of India as authoritative, but he assumes that to explode the novel's authority is to remove its interest. Like many of the novel's admirers, Trivedi reads the novel as a version of India, with the difference that he proves the version to be false. It is important to appreciate the novel's inaccuracy, but I presume that readers should still want to read and to understand the text even after its authority as a version of India has been exploded. Rushdie is, as Brennan says, a cosmopolitan intellectual, writing for an international rather than a national audience. But to dismiss Rushdie because he is not a national writer is as shortsighted as to applaud him for being one: it is not the superior authenticity of the nationalist writer but the relation of the cosmopolitan to the nationalist that should matter to critics. Both those who celebrate Rushdie as the voice of a continent and those who denounce the cosmopolitan intellectual presume that national writers are somehow superior or more authentic. What is most interesting is that *the author of* Midnight's Children *feels the same way* (or else why would he hide his errors behind Saleem's unreliability?). Rushdie the cosmopolitan wants some of the authority that belongs properly to nationalists.

In *Midnight's Children,* there are two rival sources of authority: the insider's and the outsider's. When the boy Saleem is comfortably enshrined in Methwold's Estate, his rival Shiva is outside in the cold. As we saw in chapter thirteen, however, the outside poses a challenge to the legitimacy of the inside. Shiva has a powerful Manichaean view of a world divided into rich and poor, me and you, winners and losers, that poses a direct challenge to the nation with which Saleem identifies. Saleem seeks to overcome this terrible binary that would fix him at one pole by locating himself outside the binary and so containing Shiva. Saleem shifts the ground of opposition and posits a third way. The memoirist is able to rise above the struggle between rich and poor by dividing himself into two selves: one, Saleem the convenor of the Midnight Children's Conference, who is inside, and the other, Saleem the narrator, who is out. From his superior vantage point, the second Saleem is able to mock the fears of Saleem the protagonist and so to contain Shiva.

The narrator's freedom does not extend to the point where he can invent a death for Shiva. When the memoirist does so, he must retract that scene in the next chapter. But, as we have already noted, a confession of a lie is still a claim to authority: the confession that he is not free to act on his wishes and to eliminate his rival is implicitly a claim for the faithfulness of his portrait of Shiva: Saleem cannot get away with lies, so he must be telling the truth.

Cronin writes that Saleem possesses knowledge without power, while Shiva represents the power he lacks (Cronin 1985). As Saleem himself puts it, "A nose will give you knowledge, but not power-over-events" (298). In order to know you must be outside and therefore cannot act; to act you must be inside and therefore cannot know. But Saleem the memoirist both knows more than Saleem the protagonist and is more powerful than Shiva. His knowledge may appear powerless, but Saleem the narrator controls how much air time Shiva is allowed: "throughout this narrative I've been pushing him, the other, into the background (just as once, I banned him from the councils of the Children)" (393). As we have repeatedly seen, Saleem's impotence is a ruse with power of its own. The real division in the novel is between the self who knows, because he is inside, and the self who sees, because he is outside.

The result of the split in Saleem is both a radical objectivity and a radical subjectivity. Thomas Nagel argues that, in modern times at least, all people split themselves this way: "To acquire a more objective understanding of some aspect of life or the world, we step back from our initial view of it and form a new conception which has that view and its relation to the world as its object. In other words, we place ourselves in the world that is to be understood" (Nagel 1986, 4). At the end of the novel, in a scene that took place just before he started to write, Saleem looks up into an overhead mirror and sees himself from outside and from above, "transformed into a big-headed, top-heavy dwarf" (430). The "mirror of humility" achieves the division into body and soul usually associated with "the Black Angel of death" (431). Saleem the memoirist has, as Ramram Seth prophesied, died "before he is dead" (87) and achieved a transcendental understanding: he can look at himself from outside as it were. On the night before he finishes writing for good, Saleem dreams of "floating outside my body" and being able, like "the ghost of Reverend Mother," to look down on the world "through the hole in a perforated cloud" (444). The novel that began with Saleem "clutching at the dream" of a "holey, mutilated square of linen" through which Aadam Aziz had looked on Naseem Ghani (11) ends with him joining Naseem in looking down on himself. He can look from both sides of the sheet.

Nagel argues that the modern self develops a capacity to regard itself from the outside, as part of the world it is viewing. This objective self seeks a centreless view of the world, free of perspective and therefore able to contain all perspectives, those which it receives directly (from the sense impressions of the self) as well as those it receives indirectly (from observation of others). The objective view, the view from nowhere belonging to no one or anyone, is always, however, attached to and developed from the perspective of a particular person. This modern subject is always "both the logical focus of an objective conception of the world and a particular being in that world who occupies no central position whatever" (ibid., 64). The result is an existential dilemma: "The same person who is subjectively committed to a personal life in all its rich detail finds himself in another aspect simultaneously detached; this detachment undermines his commitment without destroying it – leaving him divided. And the objective self, noticing that it is personally identical with the object of its detachment, comes to feel trapped in this particular life – detached but unable to disengage, and dragged along by a subjective seriousness it can't even attempt to get rid of" (ibid., 210). The problem that Nagel examines without resolving, "how to combine the perspective of a particular person inside the world with an objective view of that same world, the person and his viewpoint included" (ibid. 3), is precisely the subject of Rushdie's novel.

It is not certain that this combination of subjectivity and objectivity is only modern. The self that is larger than the world yet in the world can be related to the *ātman* of Hinduism, which Calasso describes as "the Self that observes the I" (Calasso 1999, 46): "Between Self and I there is but one difference: the Self watches the I, the I does not watch the Self. The I eats the world. The Self watches the I eating the world" (ibid., 225). Calasso explains, "The first words the Self said were: 'I am.' Nothing existed as yet when the Self said: 'I am.' The I owes its existence solely to the fact that it was pronounced by the Self" (ibid., 225). Saleem makes a passing reference to "the Lotus calyx, which grew out of Vishnu's navel, and from which Brahma himself was born" (192), which is also an allusion to the Self and the I: Vishnu contemplates Brahma sitting on the lotus, while Brahma contemplates the supine body of Vishnu whence rose his own world, "each believing he was everything" (Calasso 1991, 401).

Saleem's self is, however, explicitly modern. The division between inside and outside that makes the novel possible is a symptom of an alienation created in a particular class by its experience of school and the world. Saleem's peculiar combination of radical objectivity and radical subjectivity was already prepared for, when, as a boy, he retreated to the washing-chest in order to travel the nation. The binary division between inside and outside can therefore be folded back into the inside: it is a product of the world it sees. "The only people who see the whole picture," says Sir Darius Xerxes Cama in *The Ground*

Beneath Her Feet, while staring out a window at a view of the Arabian Sea much like that from Saleem's bedroom, "are the ones who step out of the frame" (Rushdie 1999A, 43). But Sir Darius is a notorious Anglophile. The superior vantage point that he claims remains locatable in the world and therefore vulnerable. There is no outside.

When Saleem the narrator positions himself outside the original binary opposition between the first two Children of Midnight in a location from which he can contemplate both, he does not escape the binary opposition but creates another one, between then and now, inside and outside. In escaping the confines of "he-and-I," that is, Shiva and Saleem (222), the narrator has risen to a level where "He and I, I and he" refers to Saleem the magical child and to the adult memoirist (165). The binary opposition returns, however, because it is integral to the constitution of Saleem. We should not therefore be surprised to see a figure like Shiva return in the present of the narrative to challenge Saleem's claim to a privileged position above the fray. The anxieties of Saleem the memoirist coalesce around the illiterate female factory worker, Padma, to whom he reads each chapter as he completes it. As Brennan notes, "Saleem's occasional revulsion for Padma's smells and habits carries to the cultural and personal level the same class tensions found between Saleem and Shiva" (Brennan 1989, 103).

Saleem says Padma's "ignorance and superstition" are "necessary counterweights" to his own "miracle-laden omniscience" (149), and by a "show of erudition" and by "the purity of [his] accents," Saleem can shame Padma "into feeling unworthy of judging me" (208). He browbeats her into conceding his authority: "I never said I didn't believe," she wept. "Of course, every man must tell his story in his own true way; but …" (207). There is, however, a great deal of anxiety on Saleem's part here. The master is dependent on his slave for confirmation of his mastery, and Saleem is at a loss when Padma rebels. Eventually the two are to be married, but that marriage will be insufficient to relieve the middle-class writer's anxiety about his own authority. When Saleem, engaged to be married, imagines the future, Padma disappears and Shiva returns, having "found out how I cheated him of his birth-right" (445).

Nagel explains that there is no such thing as absolute objectivity and the process of locating ourselves and our old view in a new, larger view that contains them can always be repeated, "yielding a still more objective conception" (Nagel 1986, 4). Saleem tries to escape what Brennan calls the impossible "contradiction between *chamcha* and people" (Brennan 1989, 107) by once more dividing himself, this time rising above Saleem the story-teller and possible husband for

Padma and assuming the vantage of a metafictional commentator, who addresses unseen and unnamed narratees above Padma's head as it were. Padma is illiterate and unable to appreciate Saleem's postmodern English-language novel in the way that another audience, directly addressed throughout the narrative, is presumed to be able to. Once he finishes each chapter Saleem reads it aloud to Padma, but then he rewrites the chapter to include her reactions. These rewritten chapters are all we readers have. We know that they differ from his original versions because at one point Saleem quotes directly from what he read to Padma, a boast about having won her love, and then tells us how she reacted with anger (121). The offensive passage is no longer part of the chapter except insofar as it is quoted and inserted into a narrative about the circumstances in which he is writing. In the rewritten chapters that we read, there are things that he has not told Padma. For instance, he pretends to go along with her plans for marriage even though he has no confidence they can be realized: "how am I to tell her about death? I cannot; instead meekly and with every appearance of gratitude, I accept her proposal" (428). The fact that each chapter is written twice belies the urgency with which Saleem claims to be writing and his self-declared inability to go back and edit.

One can hear the voice of the metafictional commentator in a sentence like "I seem to be stuck with this radio metaphor" (221) or in a passage like the following, which I have already had reason to quote: "With some embarrassment, I am forced to admit that amnesia is the kind of gimmick regularly used by our lurid film-makers. Bowing my head slightly, I accept that my life has taken on, yet again, the tone of a Bombay talkie; but after all, leaving to one side the vexed issue of reincarnation, there is only a finite number of methods of achieving rebirth" (339). Like the division between hero and narrator, the distinction between narrator and metafictional commentator constitutes a claim to the truth of the insider's experience and, at the same time, to the clearsightedness of the outsider. We can also hear the metafictional commentator when Saleem the narrator is divided into two voices that argue over how to proceed: "No, that won't do [...] Oh, spell it out, spell it out" (11), and later, "Stop this; begin. – No! – Yes" (407). One part of Saleem feels a personal pain at the memory; the other can stand outside and insist the truth must be told. This second Saleem (or rather third) describes how he must jerk "my narrator's eyes away from the described past" and force him to face the "as-yet-undescribed future" (307).

Book Two opens with Padma having left, and she is absent for five chapters. During this stretch of narrative, all of Saleem's authorial comment is directed to his narratees who replace her as his primary audience. Even after her return he continues to address "future exegetes" of his narrative directly (287). Saleem speaks to Padma of "Our Bombay" (93), even of "our hero" (369), but to his narratees, presumed to be more on his own level, he can patronizingly speak of "our Padma" (66, 88, 149), and "our plump Padma" (25).

This third-order Saleem, the metafictional commentator, appeals to readers who know about Scheherazade, the Quran, and Indian history and who understand the conventions of postmodern narration. He regularly flatters his narratees that they can see (and hear) more than Padma can: "I wish, at times, for a more discerning audience, someone who would understand the need for rhythm, pacing, the subtle introduction of minor chords which will later rise, swell, seize the melody; who would know, for instance, that although baby-weight and monsoons have silenced the clock on the Estate clock-tower, the steady beat of Mountbatten's ticktock is still there, soft but inexorable, and that it's only a matter of time before it fills our ears with its metronomic, drumming music" (101). He lets readers in on the rhetorical tricks he has used with Padma and Mrs Braganza: "How I persuaded them: by talking about my son, who needed to know my story; by shedding light on the workings of memory; and by other devices, some naïvely honest, others wily as foxes" (207). Of course, letting his audience in on his strategy is precisely Saleem's strategy. His preferred manœuvre, with his narratees no less than with Padma, is to pretend to draw back a veil that he himself has drawn over the narrative. He will readily confess, "I am, perhaps, hiding behind all these questions. Yes, perhaps, that's right. I should speak plainly, without the cloak of a question-mark: our Padma has gone, and I miss her. Yes, that's it" (149). Saleem declares himself an "incompetent puppeteer" forever revealing "the hands holding the strings" (65). But Saleem only reveals the hands with which he holds the strings in order to draw attention away from the other pair of hands with which he pulls back the curtain.

Saleem tries to win the confidence of his narratees by anticipating their reactions to his account: "'A cook?' you gasp in horror, 'A khansama merely? How is it possible?'" (38), and the reply is "I am not, you see, one of your 200-rupees-a-month cookery johnnies" (38). His assumptions about what his readers will believe are not too different from the assumptions he makes about Padma. He weighs his audience's likely reaction to his story just as he weighs Padma's: "I don't know how much you're prepared to swallow" (176). Lest his readers find it difficult to credit Amina's winning streak at gambling, Saleem flatters his readers on their scepticism and their forensic skills:

"You ask: how is it possible? How could a housewife, however assiduous, however determined, win fortunes on the horses, day after racing day, month after month? You think to yourself: aha, that Homi Catrack, he's a horseowner; and everyone knows that most of the races are fixed; Amina was asking her neighbours for hot tips! A plausible notion; but Mr. Catrack lost as often as he won [...] So it was not the Parsee who was behind it – but perhaps I can offer another explanation [...]" (140).

The significance of this metafictional commentary is not that Saleem actually convinces his narratees of his explanation, but that he establishes common ground with them. He is ever ready to confess to error and acknowledge implausibility: "Telepathy, then; the kind of thing you're always reading about in the sensational magazines. But I ask for patience – wait. Only wait. It was telepathy; but also more than telepathy. Don't write me off too easily" (166). Saleem admits to personal failures as well, joining the narratee outside the narration and describing himself in the third person:

> Despite the many vital uses to which his abilities could have been put by his impoverished, underdeveloped country, he chose to conceal his talents, frittering them away on inconsequential voyeurism and petty cheating. This behaviour – not, I confess, the behaviour of a hero – was the direct result of a confusion in his mind, which invariably muddled up morality – the desire to do what is right – and popularity – the rather more dubious desire to do what is approved of. Fearing parental ostracism, he suppressed the news of his transformation; seeking parental congratulations, he abused his talents at school. This flaw in his character can partially be excused on the grounds of his tender years; but only partially. Confused thinking was to bedevil much of his career.
>
> I can be quite tough in my self-judgements when I choose. (170)

Saleem's comic confessions of impotence and of anxiety are intended to win his audience's confidence. As Suleri has argued with regards to *Shame*, authorial intrusion "documents the writer as writer in order to erase his sense of connectedness to the plot itself: the writer is invoked to enable him to disappear" (Suleri 1992, 188). The metafictional commentator treats his narratees much as the narrator treats Padma and as the hero treats his Midnight's Children's Conference – he is the leader but does not want to be called chief: "just think of me as a ... a big brother, maybe" (222). At the same time Saleem warns readers against those "whose personal cast of mind is too inflexible" (194) and castigates "the unperceptive" (443). This Big Brother brooks no dissent.

The movement from inside the narrative to outside is a Houdini manœuvre. Saleem is a master of distracting patter and of legerdemain, waving a pointing finger at what he is doing in order to direct his readers' attention away from it. As a boy he escaped from the boot of his mother's car (another small confining space) by carefully choosing a moment "when all eyes turned to watch the passing of a second car" and using a pink piece of plastic that Sonny has given him. He "had been looking through several pairs of eyes to help me choose my moment" (211). Saleem is lucky, however, that his mother has not engaged a boy to watch the car. How could he have gotten out of the car, he asks, "under the eyes of a guardian-urchin" (210)?

An undistracted guardian-urchin set to watch over the narrative would no doubt spot the novel's error about Valmiki and the *Ramayana* or the error about Mumbadevi. The metafictional commentator is ultimately no more able to establish his authority with his narratees than the protagonist was in the Midnight's Children Conference or the narrator was with Padma. The author who makes Saleem an unreliable narrator has seen to that. The novel necessarily implies yet another level of self, a fourth order, that of the implied author, let us call him "Rushdie." "Rushdie" is explicitly related to the author of the same name who has written articles inviting readers of the novel to join him in regarding the narration from a vantage point superior to Saleem's.

The problem with all narrative authority is that the writer finds himself the written. The capacity to stand outside and write the world always involves putting oneself in paper where one can be read oneself. Saleem's terror at finding himself written and thus read is indirectly expressed through the nightmares of his mother, Amina, who, when pregnant, dreams of being trapped "like a fly" in flypaper, an image which corresponds to nothing that happens in the narration and seems instead to have to do with her prescient awareness of being in a book: "she wanders now, as before, in a crystal sphere filled with dangling strips of the sticky brown material, which adhere to her clothing and rip it off as she stumbles through the impenetrable papery forest; and now she struggles, tears at paper, but it grabs her, until she is naked, with the baby kicking inside her, and long tendrils of flypaper stream out to seize her by her undulating womb, paper glues itself to her hair nose teeth breasts thighs, and as she opens her mouth to shout a brown adhesive gag falls across her parting lips …" (109). To stand outside and write is to have power over those who are trapped inside the writing. But how can the writer himself escape being written?

The irony that allows implied author and reader to exchange winks over Saleem's head is, as we have already suggested, much less stable than "Rushdie" pretends. Any reader who knows enough about both Bombay and Hinduism to catch the unreliable narrator's errors may be forgiven for wondering, as Trivedi does, whether the errors are Saleem's or "Rushdie"'s. After all, the English-language reader to whom Saleem addresses his commentary will quite possibly miss the supposedly giveaway errors about Valmiki and Mumbadevi. "Rushdie" insists too much on the distance between himself and Saleem. Even as he invites others to join him in a community of the like-minded, the clear-sighted "Rushdie" remains afraid of being caught out by a reader who, with the benefit of hindsight, we might call "Trivedi."

Brennan argues that the author of *Midnight's Children* is a cosmopolitan intellectual who reveals the falseness of the nation-state, in which "the lower classes are deceived, the upper classes deceive" (Brennan 1989, 108–9). But, as I have tried to show, all these anxiety-filled binaries, Saleem and Shiva, Saleem and Padma, Saleem and his narratee, "Rushdie" and "Trivedi," are versions of the nationalist cosmopolitan's own complicated position, whose authority requires him to be both inside (so he can speak the truth) and outside (so he can see the whole), but who is always vulnerable to the charge that he is outside (and therefore cannot know) and ultimately inside (and can himself be known). Saleem the narrator, Saleem the metafictional commentator, and "Rushdie" the implied author all claim a vantage point outside and above. But "Cosmopolitanism must take place somewhere," says Ackbar Abbas (772). "If you are outside, you are not one of us," says Shiva to Saleem, says Padma to the narrator, says the narratee to the metafictional commentator, says "Trivedi" to "Rushdie." The narrator, metafictional commentator, and implied author all retort, "I see that outside is a location of its own and, because I see it, am outside it. I am outside the outside and therefore I see more of the inside than you do."

It is possible to discern yet a further level beyond the implied author, a level which we might identify with the later Rushdie who has achieved fame as the writer of *Midnight's Children*. When interviewed shortly after publication, Rushdie denied that his book was pessimistic and insisted that "although the possibility that Saleem represents is finished, a new and tougher generation is just beginning" (Pattanayak 2000, 19). Since then, however, Rushdie has revisited his characters in later novels and revised his opinion of them. Eighteen years after his birth, Aadam Sinai, Saleem's adopted son for whom he is writing his memoir, makes an appearance in *The Moor's Last Sigh* (Rushdie 1995) as a corrupt businessman, drug and arms-dealer, money-launderer, and procurer. The later novel expresses the pessimism of a proscribed writer living in hiding, writing about a Bombay that has seen the rise of Hindu fundamentalism and gangster rule. It is also a retrospective comment on the optimism of *Midnight's Children*. Rushdie describes Adam Sinai (sic) thus: "It seems he was originally the illegitimate child of a Bombay hooligan and an itinerant magician from Shadipur U.P., and had been unofficially adopted, for a time, by a Bombay man who was missing-believed-dead, having mysteriously disappeared fourteen years ago, not long after his allegedly brutal treatment by government agents during the 1974–77 Emergency" (Rushdie 1995, 342). This is the same ironic gesture made by Joyce when he undermines the hero of *A Portrait of the Artist* in the later novel *Ulysses*. There could be no more damning critique of Saleem's version of events. It would seem that, as Saleem had warned, "Reality is a question of perspective; the further you get from the past, the more concrete and plausible it seems" (164), and, he might have added, the smaller and more fixed it seems.

In an essay entitled "Outside the Whale" Rushdie takes issue with the quietism expressed by George Orwell in "Inside the Whale." We are not, argues Rushdie, inside but outside, and moreover, "there is no whale" (Rushdie 1991D, 99). We must position ourselves outside the system of power in order to denounce the system's lies. We must take sides. An outside position allows one to diagnose what is wrong and take a stand for rights and freedom. Rushdie goes on to say, however, that we must also abandon all hope of knowing the absolute truth: "Outside the whale the writer is obliged to accept that he (or she) is part of the crowd, part of the ocean, part of the storm, so that objectivity becomes a great dream, like perfection" (100). So, although we may be outside the whale, we are still inside the ocean. But this is a return to Orwell's point: those who imagine they are outside are nonetheless part of the beast. Both Rushdie and Orwell are suspicious of any will to power or to knowledge.

My point is neither to defend Orwell nor to criticise Rushdie. I suspect the two are much more alike than Rushdie will admit, and the difference between them is less a question of politics than of temperament: Orwell, writing in 1940, was less optimistic than Rushdie was in 1984. My point is that Rushdie's imagination works by claiming to be at once inside and out. He says that we must step outside the lies of power in order to denounce them, but the surest sign that something is a lie is that it claims actually to know. We can only prove that we ourselves are not lying when we abandon our truth claims. The confusion between inside and outside is shared by Orwell, who writes that Henry Miller's attitude is "Let's swallow it whole" (Orwell 1946, 219) and that he "has performed the essential Jonah act of allowing himself to be swallowed, remaining passive, *accepting*" (ibid., 245). Orwell's Miller somehow both swallows and is swallowed.

Rushdie positions himself outside and above in order to be able to see that he is inside. This is a version of the familiar liberal paradox: we must denounce in absolute terms any claims to absolute knowledge. We cannot tolerate intolerance. All knowledge is contingent and relative, except the relativity of knowledge. I am less concerned with the tenability of this position than with the world it implies. Rushdie the liberal imagines himself outside the whale, and outside the nation. He is the individual who stands apart. At the same time he denies that there is an outside; every point is in the same ocean. This combination of inside and outside produces both the cosmopolitan nationalist (Saleem) and the nationalist cosmopolitan (the author of *Midnight's Children*).

Conclusion

Brennan discusses Rushdie as a cosmopolitan intellectual, one who poses as transcending all nations and identifies with the universal, but whose position is easily located as itself particular and privileged. Brennan applauds Rushdie's humanism, but argues that, compared to Fanon or Cabral, he does not sufficiently appreciate "the necessity of national struggle": "'Discipline,' 'organisation,' 'people' – these are words that the cosmopolitan sensibility refuses to take seriously" (Brennan 1989, 166). Brennan does not make the same mistake. He himself is a nationalist on behalf of other people's nations because, he argues, such nationalism is the form that resistance to American imperialism takes. In a later book, *At Home in the World*, he argues against forms of cosmopolitanism current in the American academy, arguing that they only find America wherever they look and therefore are really forms of nationalism masquerading as cosmopolitanism. Cosmopolitanism's strategy of transcending nationalism by making the self congruent with the world actually reduces the world to the self: the world looks curiously like a version of liberal America. By this argument, because it denies its own location, cosmopolitanism is a kind of false consciousness, and the nationalist, who declares that the world that most matters coincides with the self, is more clear-sighted. But where does Brennan himself stand when he judges? Although Brennan does not say this, it is clear that the nationalist on behalf of all nations but his own is the true cosmopolitan, able to judge the value of both nationalism and pseudo-cosmopolitanism. We might call Brennan a metacosmopolitan intellectual.

In a curious echo of the relationship of Aadam Aziz to Naseem Ghani and of Saleem to Padma, Brennan says he himself fell "in love with another culture" (Brennan 1989, xiv). He sounds like no one so much as Rushdie himself, who calls his relation to India an "unrequited, unbearable love" (Rushdie 2002, 181). Brennan does not, however, write about the culture he loves but about Rushdie, the cosmopolitan intellectual distanced from that culture. In order to justify the attention he lavishes on Rushdie and distinguish himself from the latter's bourgeois humanism, Brennan must locate Rushdie in a binary that he transcends. The American academic sees the "advantages and limitations" of the cosmopolitan intellectual (Brennan 1989, 165) and so is in a position to declare Rushdie's political vision inferior to those of "Roque Dalton, June Jordan, Obi Egbuna" (ibid., 166) or to the "larger political aesthetic" of Farrukh Dhondy (ibid., 150). Brennan's relation to Rushdie is as Rushdie's to Saleem the narrator and as the narrator's to Saleem the protagonist. Saleem, Rushdie, and Brennan each set up such a binary in order to stand outside it. Each relinquishes authority so that it will be given back to them. Any attempt to transcend the boundary by standing outside will, however, reproduce the binary, as certainly as outside implies inside.

My point is not that Brennan's politics are false – quite the opposite: I agree with them – but that Brennan is unfair to Rushdie's novel. Rushdie's novel neither flatters its cosmopolitan audience nor confirms them in their sense of the world, but genuinely measures itself against the world and, in setting itself that Herculean task, makes new discoveries about the world possible. Indeed, there is a real sense in which all critics are inevitably caught in the endless reframing implied by Saleem's narrative. Ashis Nandy and Partha Chatterjee follow a strategy that is the inverse of Rushdie's cosmopolitanism. They argue that nationalism is inherently Western, either because the Indian state is a form of "derivative discourse" (Chatterjee 1986) or because Hindu fundamentalism is Western in its will to power (Nandy 1994). The true India is outside both cosmopolitanism and nationalism. Any attempt to transcend the divide between nationalism and cosmopolitanism results, however, in contradictions between inside and out along the lines of those we have been exploring in *Midnight's Children*. Nandy and Chatterjee rely on a distinction between Western modernity and Indian authenticity that echoes the distinction that they denounce as false.

The attempt to pry nationalism and cosmopolitanism apart is like trying to separate rhetoric and hermeneutics. When Trivedi denounces Rushdie for participating in something called Western culture, identified with the English language and British literary history but more particularly with privilege, he expresses the belief that culture in the sense of *self,* who you declare you are, determines culture in the sense of *mental framework,* what you know and how you see the world. Self is a function of the community one identifies with and the audience one is writing for. Because Rushdie is writing for the West, he can only purvey, Trivedi feels, an Orientalist version of India. If he were writing for an Indian audience, he would write very differently. Self is therefore primarily rhetorical, appealing to certain symbols and narratives in order to establish common cause with a community of others. Brennan argues that Rushdie is more interested in hermeneutics than in rhetoric, in analysing and interpreting the mental framework of others, the total complex of norms, values, ideas, and patterned behaviour shared by citizens of the nation. Hermeneutics implicitly claims to transcend self by interpreting the rhetoric that creates and defines the selves of others. As Brennan also reminds us, however, hermeneutics cannot be separated from location and itself participates in a rhetoric of objectivity. The cosmopolitan intellectual who sees through the rhetoric of the nationalist self can easily be returned to the political field by those who disagree with him.

Nationalists will legitimately argue that the cosmopolitan's hermeneutics is itself merely rhetorical. The cosmopolitan Rushdie claims to see around the rhetorical divisions between inside and outside that constitute identity, but the nationalist Trivedi declares that the cosmopolitan who stands outside proves by his own mouth that he is not inside. The cosmopolitan retorts that, because he is better able to see the whole, he is in a position to know those who make insidious moral distinctions between inside and outside better than they know themselves. The nationalist might reply by asking, "Who is making invidious claims to superiority now?"

Nationalism is a rhetoric that implies a hermeneutics, and cosmopolitanism a hermeneutics that is inevitably rhetorical. Because of an essential symmetry, the clash between nationalism and cosmopolitanism suggests a third space where two would-be universals can be located, have their measure taken, and perhaps be put in dialogue. However, any dialogue between two putative universals that each seeks to contain the other will inevitably resemble Saleem's address to his narratees, as much a site of contest and sly deception as a potential meeting ground. Arriving at any such third space requires seeing through and around Saleem, as well as recognizing one's own imbrication in the world of the novel.

The first thing I wrote about *Midnight's Children* was the discussion of allegory that is now Chapter Three of this study. It constituted an attempt to get at the whole of the novel. I soon came to realize, however, what has no doubt also struck my reader: that the attempt was in vain. I catch myself doing what Saleem himself does, attempting to summarize the whole and then opening up my account to the world that was left out of the summary. Is this systole and diastole of summary and openness some kind of Indian disease? "Worse: am I infected, too?" (84). Why does the book do this to the reader?

Like Saleem, who, when possessed by a two-headed demon, sends an anonymous note to Commander Sabarmati, I have cut the text up in small pieces and pasted it back together in a different order with a message of my own. Like Ahmed Sinai with his ambition to rewrite the Quran in chronological order, I have tried to bring order to chaos, although without such a simple principle as chronology to guide me. Arguably, all that I have revealed thereby is my own conception of form. Moreover, acknowledging my inevitable complicity even as I reach for meaning is also a trick borrowed directly from the narrator of *Midnight's Children*. Precisely because my text is bound up in the same struggle to contain and not be contained it cannot serve as a substitute for Rushdie's novel. The novel contains me.

In putting the two would-be universals of nationalism and cosmopolitanism side by side and discussing their limits and their symmetries, I have adopted a position that is itself best termed cosmopolitan in the sense that it stands outside and sees around nationalism. My own study values hermeneutics, the study of culture in the sense of mental framework, above rhetoric, the appeal to culture in the sense of identity. If there is anything we can conclude from Saleem's narrative, however, it is that the quest for an outside vantage point from which the whole can be seen complete, when not an expression of bad faith, is inevitably quixotic. My desire for detachment and objectivity can be read for what it reveals of my own location and my own allegiances. To locate cosmopolitanism and nationalism in a common frame is not to escape the conflicts of inside and outside.

Inside and outside, native and non-resident, nationalist and cosmopolitan, are defined against each other. The nation is a function of the guilt, anxiety, and insecurity roused in the nationalist by the cosmopolitan and in the cosmopolitan by the nationalist. The novel's anxiety cannot be assuaged by inviting a reader to a higher vantage-point, explicitly more cosmopolitan, because any vantage point, *including, I confess, this one*, that claimed to see beyond the binary between the cosmopolitan and the national would conjure another perspective called national against which it would be defined.

Midnight's Children is the object of critical disagreement, but also provides the grounds where the disagreement is staged. The emphasis in postcolonial literary criticism is frequently on the heroism of subversion or the guilt of complicity. Rushdie is lionized or execrated according to how his political message is read. Those who champion him and those who denounce him often espouse the same politics of resistance: where they differ is in their interpretation of how Rushdie measures up to those values. I hope I have shown that *Midnight's Children* does not fit simply into a world already assumed to be known. Rushdie's novel is larger than its critics, larger than the themes of mimicry and hybridity that are its ostensible message, and larger, too, than this attempt to contain it.

The superimposition of two fields, the nationalist and the cosmopolitan, accounts for the novel's capacity to speak to and for so many readers around the world. The novel does not, however, control all the energies it generates. We are reminded that we are in the presence of different, perhaps irreconcilable cultural frameworks when, in the Sundarbans, Saleem's hybridity is opposed not by purity but by another hybridity. As I argued in chapter fourteen, Saleem's own efforts to contain the world inevitably bring him hard up against a world that threatens not just to situate and fix him but to sweep him away altogether. The grounds of Saleem's self cannot be separated from all that he fears. In the final analysis, the greatness of Rushdie's novel does not lie in all that it can contain but in all that escapes its control: in the anxieties it unleashes that resist containment and threaten to disrupt the narrative, and in the energies it must generate in order to assuage those anxieties.

Glossary for Salman Rushdie's *Midnight's Children*

Rushdie embeds within the novel definitions for most of the Hindi-Urdu words he uses. I have included many of these words here because, although definitions are not necessary, it may be useful to see at a glance all the non-English words he includes and how he translates them. I have put his definitions in quotation marks and noted the pages on which they occur in parentheses.

"Aad and Thamud we also destroyed"	a line that occurs several times in the Quran, spoken by Allah who boasts of destroying these two tribes that would not heed his prophets
Aadam	the first man whom Allah created, first fashioning clay into clots of blood and the blood into flesh. When the devil tempted him and Eve to eat the fruit of the forbidden tree, he and Eve were cast out from Paradise.
aap	formal second-person pronoun (see *tu*)
Aarey Milk Colony	a model dairy outside Bombay
Abdullah, Sheik [Muhammad]	"The Lion of Kashmir" (253); President of the National Conference, founded in Kashmir in 1939 to agitate for democracy in the princedom and for accession to India. Abdullah promoted *kashmiriyat* or Kashmiri particularity. In 1953, he was dismissed as Chief Minister of Kashmir and arrested on charges of seeking independence for the province. He spent many years in Indian prisons.
abracadabra	as Saleem says, a "cabbalistic formula" of the Basilidean (note spelling) gnostics, heretical Christian mystics in the second century CE. The formula contains "the number 365, the number of the days of the year and of the heavens" (442), and is related to Abraxas, a name for the Supreme Being.

Abubakr or Abu-Bakr	Muhammad's first convert to Islam and his successor as leader, the first caliph
achar-chutney	see chutney
acharya Sankara	see Sankara Acharya
Ahmad [Fakhruddin Ali]	President of India 1974–77, who supported Prime Minister Indira Gandhi's declaration of a state of emergency in June 1975
Ahuramazdah	creator-god of Zoroastrianism (see Parsis)
Aksai Chin region	region claimed by both India and China, of strategic importance to the Chinese, who built a road through it linking Xinjiang and Tibet
Aladdin or Alaudddin	he of the "fabulous cave" (152), the "lamp" and the "genie" (303), whose story is told in the *Arabian Nights*
Alexander, A.V.	First Lord of the Admiralty, member of the Cabinet Mission
Ali	"nephew of the prophet Muhammad" (61), actually his cousin and son-in-law
Ali Baba	he of the "forty thieves hiding in the dusted urns" whose story is told in the *Arabian Nights* (152)
Ali-Baba	perhaps the 1954 French film or the 1952 film *Son of Ali Baba* with Tony Curtis (253)
Liaquat Ali	see Liaquat
Al-Lah	Saleem is engaged in debunking Islam when he says that the name Allah comes from the goddess Lah, "a carved idol in a pagan shrine" (283).
Allah-tobah	"heaven forfend" (81)
All-India Radio	national broadcaster in India whose signature is *Ye Akashvani hai*: "This is All-India Radio" (164), literally "Here is the Voice from the sky" [Should be written "yeh" (singular) not ye (plural)]
almirah	cupboard, chest of drawers
Alpha and Omega	the first and last letters of the Greek alphabet; a title of Jesus, indicating he was there at the beginning and will be at the end
"Amar Sonar Bangla"	"My [not Our] Golden Bengal" (344), song by Tagore adopted as Bangladeshi national anthem
Amritsar	"holy city" of the Sikhs, site of the "Golden Temple" (33)
Amul Dairies	Gujarati dairy cooperative
Annadurai, C.N. [Kanchipuram Natarajan]	Tamil leader

Ananda Marg	"notorious extremists" (387): a violent right-wing party founded in 1955 (literally "Path of Eternal Bliss")
Anarkali	the name of a courtesan at Akbar's court with whom Prince Salim, later emperor Jehangir, was in love and the title subject of a 1952 movie. Her name means "pomegranate-bud" (366).
Anglepoised	brand name of an adjustable, hinged desk lamp
anna	16th of a rupee, in use until 1957
Anna-D.M.K. party	Dravida Munnetra Kazhagam, party founded to defend the interests of South Indian Dravidians
apsaras	celestial girls or nymphs for the pleasure of the spirits of Hindu sages after death
Arabian Nights	see Scheherazade
archangels	"Michael, Anael, Gabriel, Cassiel, Sachiel, and Samael" (166). Islam recognizes four archangels (including Azrael, Gabriel, and Michael), Judaism and Christianity traditionally recognize seven, but there is no agreement on their names beyond Michael, Gabriel, and Raphael. The names on Rushdie's list are all angels.
Arjuna or Arjun	"a hero of Hindu mythology" (74): great archer and one of the Pandavas, he fought against Karna in the war of the Kauravas and Pandavas.
arré	Hey!
arré baap	See here!
astrakhan	lamb wool from Astrakhan, an area of Russia on the Caspian Sea
Atharva-Veda	"the Brahmins' 'Secret Book'" (388), the last of the four Vedas and not always accepted as such, for it contains popular magic spells. The spells Padma recites to cure Saleem's impotence come from the Atharva-Veda: "Thou potent and lusty herb! Plant which Varuna had dug up for him by Gandharva! … Give heat like that of Fire of Indra. Like the male antelope, O herb, thou hast all the force that Is, thou hast powers of Indra, and the lusty force of beasts" (190). So, too, the spell that Parvati recites: "Garudamand, the eagle, drank of poison, but it was powerless; in a like manner have I deflected its power, as an arrow is deflected" (388). The "sraktya" (388) is a tree from which a powerful talisman is created.

Attlee, [Clement]	Labour Prime Minister of Britain who succeeded Sir Winston Churchill and had promised to negotiate India's independence
Aung San [not Sam]	Burmese national leader who won independence from British (65)
Aurangzeb	the son of Shah Jehan and last of the great Mughal Emperors, he died in 1707. He fought a debilitating war against Sivaji (q.v.).
auto-rickshaw	three-wheeled motorized vehicle used as a taxi
Awami League	political party in East Pakistan dedicated to Bengali interests.
ayah	nanny (from Portuguese)
Ayub Khan, [Muhammad]	Pakistani commander-in-chief and later president who came to power in the 1958 coup. He is the general with the globe-shaped head whose plotting Saleem witnesses. He resigned in March 1969, handing power over to the commander-in-chief of the army, General Yahya Khan.
Ayub, Gauhar	Gohar, son of Ayub Khan, acquired a General Motors assembly plant and called it Gandhara Motors (323).
Azad, Abul Kalam	the most prominent Muslim leader in the Congress Party, he died on February 22, 1958.
baap-re-baap	exclamation of surprise or grief (literally Father-O-Father!)
baba	title of respect for grandfather, father, and child
Babar	Babur (note spelling) conquered India in the sixteenth century and founded the Mughal dynasty.
babu	derogatory slang for an educated Bengali
Back Bay	the large bay skirted by Marine Drive
badmaash	rogue
Mohun Bagan	Calcutta-based football team
Bandung	conference of African and Asian nations in Bandung, Indonesia in 1955, which eventually led to the non-aligned movement in which Chou Enlai and Nehru were very prominent
Barilwi, Syed Ahmad	Sayyid Ahmad Barelvi (note spelling) led a jihad in the early nineteenth century against Sikh rule in North-West India.
Baroda	now called Vadodara
bas	"Enough" (369)
Basic Democracy	in the 1964 Pakistani election, Ayub Khan had limited the franchise to 80,000 Basic Democrats, chosen

	from among his supporters, to represent the 80 million citizens.
Bassein Road	Vasai Road, north of Bombay Island
Batman	DC Comics superhero created in 1939
bearer	domestic servant, valet
begum	Muslim Indian lady
Bellasis Road	now called J. Boman Behram Marg
Benares	now called Varanasi, formerly Kasi
Benarsi	from Benares
Bergerac	see Cyrano
bhaenchud	"sister-sleeper" (310)
Bhagwan	God; an epithet of Shiva and Vishnu
bhai	brother
bhang	cannabis
bhangi	"dirtyfilthyfellow" (381); caste addicted to drugs
Bharat-Mata	Mother India
bharatanatyam	(properly two words, the first capitalized) a popular system of South Indian classical dance (literally Bharata's dancing). Bharata was the author of a dance manual.
Bhave, Acharya Vinobha	follower of Gandhi who "spent ten years persuading landowners to donate plots to the poor in his bhoodan [gift of land] campaign" (253). With Jayaprakash Narayan he founded the Sarvodaya movement of self-help. The title *Acharya* means "spiritual guide."
bhelpuri	snack mixture of puffed rice, deep fried vermicelli, chopped onions, and potatoes
Bhima	one of the Pandava brothers in the *Mahabharata*
Bhutto, Zulfikar Ali	founder of the Pakistan People's Party (PPP), which in the general elections in December 1970 won a large majority in West Pakistan but failed to reach an agreement with Sheikh Mujib-ur-Rahman, the majority winner from East Pakistan. Following the 1971 war and the separation of East Pakistan, Bhutto took over as President and Chief Martial Law Administrator on December 20, 1971. He was deposed in a coup in 1977 by Zia ul-Haq and executed in 1979.
bibi	Muslim lady
Bilal	"Muhammed's muezzin" (284), chosen for his beautiful voice
bimbi	"navel" (405)
biriani	dish of rice cooked with meat and vegetables
biris	(or bidis) Indian cigarettes made of tobacco rolled in dried leaves

Birla, [Ghanashyamdas]	great industrialist who made his fortune in textile and paper mills
Birla House	the house belonging to G.D. Birla, located at 5 Albuquerque Road, New Delhi, where Gandhi was assassinated
bitch-in-the-manger	from the phrase "dog in the manger": Aesop tells the tale of a dog in a manger who, although he cannot eat the hay himself, prevents the ox from eating it. Padma cannot read and resents those who can (25).
Black Hole of Calcutta	overnight on June 20, 1756, Siraj-ud-Daula, Nawab of Bengal, locked up British prisoners in the brig at Fort William. According to British mythology, more than a hundred died of suffocation or heat exhaustion, although the actual figures were much lower.
black-money	undeclared, untaxed money
black stone god	Shiva, whose lingam (q.v.) is worshipped as a black stone (13). Saleem also calls the Qa'aba in Mecca "the shrine of the great Black Stone" (283). Linking these two deities this way suggests that Saleem subscribes to a theory that meteorites (black stones) were common objects of worship in pagan times. (see Qa'aba)
Blanco	brand name of bleach
bodhi tree	peepul tree, the tree under which the Buddha attained enlightenment
bodhisattva	a person capable of attaining enlightenment but who delays doing so out of compassion for suffering beings
Bombeli's the Confectioners	Freddi Bombelli, a Swiss, had a restaurant on Churchgate Road (Veer Nariman Road).
Borivli	suburb north of Bombay
Bose, Subhas Chandra	Nationalist who led a Japanese-backed army of Indian soldiers against the British, invading eastern India from Burma in 1944. However, his army was "drenched by the returning rains" (60): the monsoons delayed his advance until the British could bring in reinforcements. He died in a plane crash over Taiwan in August 1945.
Bovril	brand name of beef extract
box-wallah	shopkeeper
Catherine of Braganza	Portuguese princess who married the newly restored English king Charles II in 1662. Bombay was part of her dowry.
Brahma	the creator god of the Hindu triad: he is called "lotus-born" (192).
brahmin	member of the upper, priestly caste

Brabourne Stadium	Bombay's premier cricket pitch from 1937 to 1975
Braz	Braz Gonsalves, alto saxophonist and one of "those great jazzmen" (235) who played at the Venice Restaurant in the sixties
Breach Candy	the Great Breach was a channel through which seawater poured at high tide, drowning the Flats that separated the islands that later formed Bombay. It was dammed in the early eighteenth century.
Breach Candy Swimming Club	still exists directly across Warden Road from Windsor Villa where Rushdie lived. The pool is reputedly shaped like British India (94), but the shape is very stylized and not immediately recognizable.
Brent, Tony	Bombay-born UK crooner
brinjal	eggplant (Portuguese)
Buckingham Villa	based on Windsor Villa, where Rushdie grew up
Buddha	Siddhatta Gotama (or Gautama Siddhartha) attained enlightenment under a bodhi tree in Gaya in Bihar and started his teaching in the deer park at Sarnath, outside Benares.
bulbul	"Indian nightingale" (199)
burqa	strict purdah gown enveloping face and form of Muslim women in public
Butt, S. P.	Butt was Rushdie's mother's maiden name (Hamilton 1996, 90)
Cabinet Mission Scheme	The Cabinet Mission was sent by Attlee to negotiate with Congress and the Muslim League in 1946. It proposed a federated India with a weak central government.
Caliban	the earthbound native in Shakespeare's *The Tempest*, whose island has been taken over by Prospero
camphor garden	in Surah 76 of the Quran, the virtuous are promised they shall drink a cup from the Camphor Fountain
Cantonment	"where the army was based" (61); a military station
Cape Comorin	now called Kanyakumari, the southern tip of India where "three seas meet" (171): the Bay of Bengal, the Arabian Sea, and the Indian Ocean
Carnac Road	now called Lokmanya Tilak Road
Cathedral and John Connon Boys' High School	elite school attended by Rushdie, founded by the Anglo-Scottish Education Society and located in the part of central Bombay called the Fort
chadar	"the curtain or veil" (304)
chaloo-chai	sweetened spiced tea with milk
chambeli	jasmine
chamcha	"literally a spoon, but idiomatically a flatterer" (378)

chand-ka-tukra	"piece of the moon" (107)
Chandela	a dynasty in Central India whose capital was Khajuraho, which survived from the ninth to the fourteenth centuries
Chandni Chowk	the market area of Old Delhi
channa	nuts of various kinds, e.g. groundnuts or garbanzos
chapati	"thin cakes" (32) of unleavened whole wheat bread
chappals	sandals
chaprassi	messenger (hotel doorman on page 33)
charas	marijuana
charpoy	light "bed" with string mattress (73)
chatterjees	a slur making use of the common Bengali name Chatterji
chavanni	"four-anna" coin (73)
chawl	"tenement building" (83), especially in Bombay
chaya	"time of afternoon when the shadow of the Friday Mosque fell across the slum" (374); shade or shadow
cheroot	cigar
Chhamb	right on the border of Pakistani-controlled Azad Kashmir
chhi-chhi!	"Filthy!" (154) "how dirty!" (289)
chick-blinds	screen blind made of split bamboo which can be rolled up or down
chinar	Oriental plane tree
Chindits	Allied Special Forces in World War II, formed and led by Major General Orde Wingate. The Chindits waged hit-and-run jungle warfare against Japan deep behind enemy lines in North Burma.
chiriyas	"birds" (also "clubs" in "cards") (366)
chitties	a letter or certificate (now obsolete, replaced by chit)
Chor Bazaar	second-hand market (literally Thieves Market), where Ahmed Sinai is cheated by "some crook" (199)
chota pegs	small measure of spirits
Chou En-lai	prime minister of China 1949–1976 (now usually written Zhou Enlai)
Chowpatty Beach	popular beach along Marine Drive
chugha	"chugha-coat" (28), a loose, sleeved coat-like garment of Turkish origin
Chup!	Be quiet!
Churchgate Station	terminus for the Western Railway (trains going to Delhi)
chutneys	relish made of condiments, fruits, coconut, lime juice, garlic, chillies, etc., the whole ground into a paste.

	British chutney is milder and a sort of pickle, which Indians would call *achar.*
Civil Lines	area of town reserved for government officials during colonialism
civil-list	privy purses accorded by Parliament to former princes, abrogated in 1970
"The Clouds Will Soon Roll By"	1932 song recorded by Tony Brent in 1958. It includes the line: "Each little tear and sorrow only brings you closer to me" (128).
Cobra Woman	1944 film about the jungle queen of a cobra-worshipping cult and her evil twin sister (224)
Coconut Day	festival held by Hindus at full moon in the month of *Shravana* (Aug-Sept), "a few days" before Saleem's birthday (93), to mark the end of the rough monsoon seas
coir	fibre of coconut husks for making matting
Colaba	southernmost peninsula of Bombay
Colaba Causeway	now called Nanabhai Moos Marg
compère	master of ceremonies
Congress Party	the Indian National Congress, the party of Nehru and Gandhi that had won independence, split in 1969 and then again in 1975, becoming increasingly personalized as Congress I (for Indira), whose election symbol was not the "cow- suckling-calf" (384) but the open hand.
Connaught Place	the hub of Delhi located between Old Delhi and New Delhi and divided into blocks with letters for names
Constitution of 1956	see Mirza
Cooch Naheen, Rani of	*khutch naheen* means "nothing." A rani is a princess. Her name sounds like that of the Maharajah of Cooch Behar, who made a big impression when he travelled to England around the turn of the nineteenth century. Cooch Behar is in Bengal. There is also a less well-known Maharajah of Kutch, the swampy area in Gujarat (see Rann of Kutch).
"The Cow"	the first surah in the Quran
Crawford Market	now called Mahatma Phule Market
Cripps, Stafford	Clement Attlee's Chancellor of the Exchequer, a socialist with close ties to the Congress Party. He chaired the Cabinet Mission sent in 1946.
crorepati	billionaire (a crore is 100 lakh or 10 million)
CUTIA	(*kutiya*) "bitch" (338)
Cyrano de Bergerac	seventeenth-century French writer, chiefly remembered for his large nose. In the 1897 play of that name

	by Edmond Rostand, Cyrano recites love poetry to the woman he loves on behalf of his friend who does not have his facility with words, a loose parallel to Sonny whom Saleem asks to sing his praises to Evie (182).
Cyrus the Great	king of Persia (where Parsis originally come from) in the sixth century BC
Dadar	suburb north of Bombay
dahi	curds
Daily Jang	Pakistani newspaper in English and Urdu
Daisy gun	brand name of an air-gun
Dal and Nageen Lakes	Dal Lake, east of Srinigar, is actually a series of lakes, including Nagin Lake.
Dalda Vanaspati	brand name
Dalhousie, [James Ramsay, Marquess of]	Governor-General of India 1848 to 1856
Dange, [Shripad Amrit]	leader of the Communist Party faction loyal to Moscow after the split in the party in 1964
Dawoods, Saigols, Haroons	wealth in Pakistan has been concentrated in the hands of twenty-two families, among them the Dawoods, led by Seth Ahmad Dawood, originally from Bombay; the Saigol group founded by Amin Saigol; the family of Sir Abdullah Haroon, one of the few originally from Karachi; and the Valibhais, also known as Valikas (302).
Dee, Sandra	made her film debut in 1957. Saleem may have seen *Until They Sail* (1957) or *The Reluctant Debutante* (1958) with the Sabarmatis (252).
Deo	variant of *dev*, meaning God
deodar	cedar trees from the Himalayas
"Deputy E-Pak Speaker"	Shahid Ali, the Deputy Speaker of the East Pakistan Assembly, died September 25, 1958 (not August [253]) from wounds suffered two days before when disorder broke out inside the assembly.
Desai, Morarji	"Chief Minister" of Bombay from 1952 to 1956 (172), later "Finance Minister" in Nehru's cabinet (317). Engaged in a power struggle with Indira Gandhi, Desai split from the Congress Party in 1969. He went on a fast unto death, demanding new elections after president's rule was declared in 1974. He was Prime Minister 1977–79. He wrote a book about the healthiness of the Brahmin custom of drinking a litre of one's own urine every day (172).

Dev	Dev Anand was the star of such films as *Mr Funtoosh* and *The Guide.*
Devi	"the goddess … who slew the buffalo-demon" Mahisa. Among her many manifestations are "Kali Durga Chandi Chamunda Uma Sati and Parvati" (393).
Devi, Bano	"the famous lady wrestler" (126); I have not been able to confirm this.
dharma-chakra	wheel of dharma (the cosmic principles by which all things exist). The dharma-chakra was the sign the conquering warriors of Ashoka, founder of the Hindu empire, bore upon their shields and is now part of the seal of India.
dhoban	"washerwoman" (429)
dhobi	washerman
dhoti	loin-cloth worn by all respectable Hindu castes of northern India
dhows	vessels of "Arab" build with one mast and lateen rig (92)
dia-lamps	a *diya* is a lamp, especially an "earthenware" vessel holding the oil for a light (114).
Diana the Huntress	Roman goddess of hunting, chastity, and the moon, associated with the Greek goddess Artemis. When Actaeon came across her bathing, she changed him into a stag and he was torn to pieces by his own hounds.
Dilli-dekho	"Come see Delhi" (75). A Dilli-dekho man appears in Satyajit Ray's 1955 film *Pather Panchali.* In *Samskara,* Anantha Murthy's 1965 Kannada novel, a similar peepshow is called a Bombay Box.
Divali	Hindu festival of lights (October-November)
Diwan-i-khas	Hall of State used for a "private audience" (306)
djelabbah	"loose flowing garment" worn by Arab men in North Africa (364)
djinn	in Islam, an intelligent spirit lower than the angels, able to appear in animal or human form. In English, often written "genie"
doctori-attaché	(*daktari*: doctor of Western medicine)
Dravidian	member of the original peoples of South India conquered by the Aryans
dubash	an interpreter or a broker. In Gujarat, a man reputed to act like Bunyan's Mr Two Tongues (Lewis 1997, 105)
Dulles, [John Foster]	US secretary of state (1953–9) who forged a chain of military alliances, including with Pakistan, to contain communism (252)

dugdugee drum	(*dugdugi*), a two-faced drum
Dunya dekho	"see the whole world" (74) (spelled "*Duniya*" in Hindi, "*Dunya*" in Arabic)
dupatta	"muslin [scarf]wound around [a woman's] head" (43); "the cloth of modesty" (57)
Dupleix Road	just south of the Rajpath, New Delhi
durbar	public levee held by ruler
Durga	Devi in her fierce aspect; often has a quiver of "arrows" (430).
Dyer, Brigadier [Reginald Edward Harry]	ordered the firing at Jallianwala Bagh in 1919.
East India Company	incorporated in 1600 with a monopoly of British trading in India. Its ships first arrived in Surat in 1615. It received Bombay from Charles II in 1668 and transferred its main base of operations there.
Eid-ul-Fitr	celebration to mark the end of Ramadan, signalled by the sighting of the new moon
ek dum	immediately, "double-quick time" (368)
El Cid	1961 film with Charlton Heston and Sophia Loren about Rodrigo Diaz de Bivar, the Christian warrior with the Muslim title, who led an army of Christians and Muslims to defend Spain against North African Moorish invaders and who, even when dead, was tied to his horse and "led an army into battle" (312). It is difficult to imagine this film ever having been shown in Pakistan.
Elephant	"who is also the rainbow, and lightning" (192): the god Indra carries a thunderbolt and a rainbow and rides a milk-white elephant, Airavata, whose name means rainbow.
Elephanta	an island in Bombay harbour noted for its "caves" and "carvings," accessible by "motor-launch" from the Gateway of India (206)
Elphinstone, [Mountstuart]	Governor of Bombay 1819–1829
Escorial	named after the palace of Philip II of Spain
falooda	farinaceous sweet drink
fauj	army
Feldman, Herbert	Englishman (not American, as Saleem says [308]) who lived most of his life in Karachi in the decades after independence and wrote a chronicle of his times in several volumes
fenugreek	seeds used in curry powder

Ferdy	Xavier Fernandes played piano with Braz Gonsalves (see Braz).
feringhee	term applied by Indians to persons of Portuguese descent or Europeans
feronia elephantum	also called wood apple
Filmfare	magazine started in 1952
filmi	film music
Filmistan Talkies	a film company formed in 1942
Flora Fountain	modern Hutatma Chowk
420	"the number of trickery and fraud" (193); a reference to section 420 of the Code of Criminal Procedure, originally promulgated by the British: "Whoever cheats and thereby dishonestly induces the person deceived to deliver any property to any person, or to make, alter, or destroy the whole or any part of a valuable security, or anything which is signed and sealed, and which is capable of being converted into a valuable security, shall be punished with imprisonment..." "Section 420," frequently the abbreviated explanation of an arrest in Indian newspapers, alludes to those who attempt small-scale fraud and confidence tricks (Aravamudan 1989, 7).
St Francis Xavier	Jesuit missionary (1506–1552) who arrived in Goa in 1541. Although he died in China, his body, which remained uncorrupted, was brought to Goa in 1553, where it is under protective covering in the Church of Bom Jesu. When it was first displayed to the public in 1554, Dona Isabel de Caron, a Portuguese lady, bit off the fifth toe of the right foot.
Francis the Talking Mule and the Haunted House	properly *Francis in the Haunted House*, 1956 film with Mickey Rooney
French cricket	road cricket
Friday Mosque	the Jamal Masjid, Delhi
Frontier Mail	train that travels between Amritsar and Bombay, passing through Delhi, which is why Aadam Aziz takes it from Amritsar to Delhi (31) and Ahmed Sinai takes the same train from Delhi to Bombay (91)
funtoosh	Rushdie uses the word to mean "finished," but it usually means "crazy"
Gabriel	see Jibreel
Gai-Walla	literally "Cow-boy." Rushdie jokes about this Indian Western film in *Shame*: "An unusual fantasy about a

	lone, masked hero who roamed the Indo-Gangetic plain liberating herds of beef-cattle from their keepers."
Gama, Vasco da	Portuguese explorer, the first European to arrive in India. Da Gama sailed around the Cape of Good Hope and arrived on the Malabar Coast in 1498.
Gandhara	area of the upper Indus valley now lying within the borders of Pakistan and Afghanistan
Gandharva	minor deity, the servant of Varuna
Gandhi, Feroze	Indira's husband, himself elected to Parliament where he was "a ferocious critic of the Nehru government, exposing the Mundhra scandal" (406) in 1957, which involved a businessman, Haridas Mundhra, and the Finance Minister. He died in 1960.
Gandhi, Indira Priyadarshini	Nehru's daughter, born on November 19, 1917, married Feroze Gandhi in 1942 (not 1952 [406]), elected President of the Congress Party in 1959 (not 1958 [253]), became prime minister in 1966. Expelled from Congress in 1969, she formed her own Congress party. After she was found guilty of campaign malpractice on June 12, 1975 (402), she declared a State of Emergency at dawn on June 26, 1975 (not midnight June 25 [405]). She was defeated in the election of March 1977.
Gandhi, Mohandas K.	assassinated January 30, 1948
Gandhi, Sanjay	Indira's younger son, who became powerful during the Emergency as head of the Youth Congress and as his mother's heir-apparent. His vigorous slum clearance around the Friday Mosque in old Delhi alienated working-class Muslims. Appointed head of India's car manufacturing industry, he started the Maruti Car Company (Maruti is another name for Hanuman). He died in the crash of an airplane he was flying in 1980.
Ganesh	"the elephant-headed god" (15), son of Parvati and stepson of Shiva, who cut off his head and replaced it with an elephant's
Ganpati Baba	another name for Ganesh
Ganesh Chaturthi	Ganesh's feast day, in August or September, "when huge processions are 'taken out' and march to Chowpatty bearing plaster effigies of the god, which they hurl into the sea" (93)
Ganga	the Ganges, a goddess which Vishnu sent to earth and which "streamed down to earth through Shiva's hair" (417)
garam	legumes

garibi	poverty. *Garibi hatao*, "Away with poverty," was the slogan of the Congress (I) Party in 1971.
Garudamand	"the eagle" Vishnu rides (388) (usually Garuda, occasionally Garutmant)
Gateway of India	triumphal arch in Bombay completed in 1924 to commemorate the visit of George V in 1911
Gautama	see Buddha
Gaylord's	the original restaurant is on Churchgate Road (Veer Nariman Road).
ghat	steps or landing on a river, the site of cremations in Benares; also either of two Mountain Ranges running parallel to the coasts on either side of the Deccan Plateau
Ghaznavids	rulers of Ghazni (see Mahmud)
ghee	clarified butter used in cooking
Ghosh, Dr Prafulla Chandra	leader of the Praja Socialist Party in 1959
Goa	Portuguese colony on the West Coast of India. A Goan Liberation Committee was established in 1954 and launched several *satyagraha* campaigns (252). The Indian army entered and took over in 1961.
godown, gudam	"warehouse" (71)
Godse, Nathuram	member of the R.S.S.S., assassin of Gandhi, executed in 1949
Golden Temple	Sikh holy shrine in Amritsar
"Good Night Ladies"	traditional English song
Goojar Tribal	(properly Gujar) a nomadic group in Kashmir
goondas	"troublemakers" (36), "hooligans or apaches" (394)
Gowalia Tank Road	now August Kranti Marg
gram	chick-pea
gramdan	(properly capitalized) literally free gift of a village for the good of a community
green medicine	herbal medicine
Grundrisse	huge manuscript written by Karl Marx in preparation for what would become *A Contribution to the Critique of Political Economy* (1859) and *Capital* (1867) and not intended for publication
gulab-jamans	gulab is rose-water; jamans are fried dough balls
Gulmarg	large meadow southwest of Srinigar
gulmohr	flamboyant or flame tree
gur	coarse sugar from cane
Gurkhas	the majority group in Nepal, from whom the British recruited soldiers

Guru Mandir	district of Karachi
Guru Nanak	founder of Sikhism
haddi-phaelwan	"skin-and-bone wrestler" (210) (*haddi* means "skinny")
Hadith	any of the approved accounts of the life and words of Muhammad
Hai Ram	Alas! Rama! These were supposedly Gandhi's last words.
Haji Ali's tomb	at the end of Warden Road, where it intersects with Pedder Road, is the causeway leading to the mausoleum of this Muslim saint, a site of pilgrimage for Bombay's Muslims. The causeway is submerged at low tide.
Hajis	"men who had made the pilgrimage to Mecca" (15)
hakimi	physician in India and Muslim countries practising a medicine called Unani (meaning "of Greek origin")
halal	"permitted parts" of meat, "drained of their redness, their blood" (59)
hamal	servant
Hanging Gardens	Sir Pherozeshah Mehta Gardens, called the Hanging Gardens because of their location on top of a hill
Hanuman	"the monkey god who helped Prince Rama defeat the original Ravana," who had abducted Sita and taken her to Lanka (84). When Ravana captured Hanuman he had his tail padded with cotton soaked in oil and set on fire, but Hanuman ran about Ravana's capital, setting fire to all the buildings and destroying it.
Hardwar	Haridwar, located where the Ganges emerges from the Himalayas and so considered holy
Haroon	see Dawoods
Haroun al-Raschid	"Caliph" of Baghdad who figures prominently in the Arabian Nights and who wandered anonymously "cloaked through the streets of Baghdad" (369)
hartal	a day when shops are voluntarily shut (from the Hindi meaning to lock doors). In protest against the Rowlatt Acts, Gandhi declared on April 7 1919 a hartal, when shops and schools would be closed.
hashashin	Indian hemp
Hatim Tai	Arab king, famous for his alms-giving, whose adventures are collected in the *Qissa*
Hayworth, Rita	Hollywood star, married Prince Aly Khan in 1949 (301), divorced in 1953
Hazratbal Mosque	shrine in Kashmir, which houses a quartz vial five inches long in which is stored a single strand of hair

	known in Persian as the Moe-e Muqaddas, "the Sacred Lock" of the Prophet. It made its way from Medina to Srinigar 300 years or more ago. At 4:45 AM on Friday, December 27, 1963 (not Saturday the 28th [269]) Mohammed Khalil Ghanai noticed the relic was missing. Abdul Rahim Bande, the relic's custodian, was arrested. The relic was recovered on January 4, 1964.
Hero and Leander	in Greek mythology, Leander swam every night across "the Hellespont toward Hero's burning candle" (252), until one night, when a storm had put out the candle and he drowned.
Hijra	"transvestite" (82): hijras constitute a distinct community in North Indian Hinduism, living in groups and often dancing and playing music to earn money.
Hindustan car	Indian company which started manufacturing cars in 1942 and began producing the Ambassador in 1957
Hindustani	Muslim lingua franca from which Urdu derives, based on Hindi with many Arabic and Persian elements
Mount Hira	site just north of Mecca where Muhammad received his revelation
Holi	"paint-festival" (445); spring festival in honour of Krishna, when passers-by are drenched with paints
Hooghly	river in Calcutta
hookah	waterpipe
Hornby Vellard	now called Lala Lajpatrai Marg; built along an original dam holding back the sea
houris	virgin companions awarded to the virtuous in Paradise, described as "untouched by man or djinn" (335) in Surah 55 of the Quran, which also asks rhetorically, "Which of your Lord's blessings would you deny?" (329).
"How Much is that Doggie in the Window"	hit song for both Lita Roza and Patti Page in 1953
Humayun	fell mortally ill in 1530 as a result of a curse on his father, Babur, for the massacre of the Dutt clan (110). He was healed when two surviving members of the clan gave their blessing in return for as much land as their horses could cover in 24 hours.
Hyderabad	princely state whose ruler, the Nizam, was reputed to be the richest man on earth as a result of the state's gold and diamond mines

I Confess	a 1951 Alfred Hitchcock film, in which Father Michael Logan (Montgomery Clift) hears the confession of a murderer. He does not betray the sanctity of the confessional even when he is himself charged with the murder.
Ibn Sina	"master magician, Sufi adept" (295); the great eleventh-century philosopher Avicenna, more famous for medicine and rationalism than magic
Ibn Sinan	see Maslama
Ibrahim	Arabic and Koranic form of Abraham, the original patriarch in both Judaism and Islam, and the father of Ishmael and Isaac, or Ismail and Ishaq. Ishmael is the ancestor of the Arabs.
ichneumon	mongoose
Id-ul-Fitr	see Eid-ul-Fitr
Illustrated Weekly of India	popular journal
Iltutmish, [Shams ud-Din]	Turkish general in the service of Qutbuddin Aibak who founded the Delhi Sultanate in 1206
Indra	foremost among the gods of the early Vedic Age. Using a mountain as a churning-stick and with the help of the gods and demons, Indra churned the oceans, producing a great fire, which he put out (191). The great labour produced heavenly bodies, gods, creatures, and finally the desired goal: ambrosia. He carries a Hook or *anka* (393), and rides a white elephant.
Iqbal, [Muhammad]	Urdu poet who put forward a proposal for a Muslim state in northwestern India at the 1930 session of the All-India Muslim League in Allahabad. He was still thinking at the time of a Muslim state in an Indian federation.
Ira	"queen consort of Kashyap" (192), one of ten such consorts, who gave birth to elephants
Isa	Jesus "Christ" (17). Ahmadiyya Muslims believe Christ escaped from the cross and travelled to Kashmir.
Iskandar the Great	Alexander of Macedon who, in his conquests, crossed the Indus into India in 327 BCE
Ismailis	Muslim sect, headed by the Aga Khan, many of whose members came to India in the nineteenth century when they had to flee Persia. Jinnah was born into an Ismaili family.

itr	attar; fragrant "essence" (375) from flowers used for perfume
Jahannum	"Hell" (437)
Jai	Long live!
jail-khana	jail
Jain	member of an ancient religion (origin in sixth century BCE) preaching ahimsa or non-violence toward all living things. Jains try "to avoid stepping on an ant, or even a fly" (33).
Jaisalmer	the Golden City in Rajasthan, a tourist destination famous for its "fortress" (171)
Jallianwala Bagh	"The largest compound in Amritsar" and site of the massacre April 13, 1919 (36). According to official estimates 379 people were killed and 1,200 wounded.
Jamuna River	see Yamuna
Jan or Jana Sangh	"Hindu-sectarian" party (387), the political arm of the R.S.S.S., that promoted Hinduism, the Hindi language, and protection for cows (the forerunner of today's BJP)
Janata Morcha	literally People's Movement, formed in 1977 as coalition in opposition to Indira Gandhi
Jang	see *Daily Jang*
Jantar Mantar	"Mughal observatory" of Maharajah Jai Singh II, built in 1725 in Delhi (416)
janum	beloved
Jat	a community in northern India that might be described as a caste, a tribe, and an ethnic group
jawan	private soldier in Indian army
Jehangir	Mughal emperor whose name meant "Encompasser of the Earth" and who built the Shalimar Gardens in Kashmir (18). His last words were "Only Kashmir."
Jesus	"Gentle Jesus meek and mild" (247) is a hymn by Charles Wesley. (see Isa)
Jhansi, Rani of	Lakshmibai, the widowed Rani of Jhansi, died in 1858 in Gwalior, fighting the British while disguised as a man, in what was the last major action in the Great Indian Rebellion.
Jibreel	archangel Gabriel who dictated the Quran to Mohammad
Jinnah, Fatima	Jinnah's sister, called "mader-i-millat or mother of the nation" (312), led the Combined Opposition Parties against Ayub Khan in the Pakistani elections of 1964.
Jinnah, Muhammad Ali	leader of the Muslim League, first prime minister of Pakistan, called Qaid-i-Azam (or Quaid), meaning

	"the great leader" (305). He died a year after taking office, in 1948. (see Pakistan)
Jinnah Mausoleum	Saleem calls it "eternally unfinished" (309) because plans were first made for its construction in Karachi in 1956, construction started in 1960, and it was completed only in 1970.
John Company	nickname for the East India Company
jooloos	(properly *julus*) "procession" (411)
Jor-El	see Superman
juggernauts	from *jagannath*, Master of the World, the name of a statue of Krishna dragged through the city of Puri, under whose wheels devotees were said to have thrown themselves and been crushed
Juhu Beach	beach north of central Bombay where one can find the Sun-n-Sand Hotel (93)
Jung, C.G. [Carl]	psychologist who believed causality could not explain certain improbable coincidences. Instead he saw another principle at work that he called "synchronicity" (192).
junglee	"wild" (103), inhabiting the jungle
kabaddi	vigorous chasing game between two teams of nine
kachcha	"mud" used for "homes" (32)
Kailash, Mount Kalaisa	Himalayan mountain considered the "home of gods" (94), especially of Shiva, Parvati, and Ganesh
Kala Pul	"the black bridge" in Karachi (299)
Kali	"black dancing goddess" (355), avatar of Durga, goddess of death and destruction
Kali-Yuga	at the end of each eon (Maha-Yuga) the world will be destroyed by fire while Brahma sleeps, until he creates it anew. A Maha-Yuga, each of which is 4,320,000,000 years long, consists of four ages, named after the four throws of the dice. The fourth is the Kali-Yuga, when virtue is at its lowest ebb and the human life-span is shortest, which lasts 432,000 years. The current Kali-Yuga began, as Saleem says, on Friday February 18, 3102 BCE. The Maha-Yuga is imagined allegorically as a cow standing on the four legs of dharma. With each age it loses one, until at the end of the Kali-Yuga it is left with none (191).
kameez	loose shirt
Karamstan	in Calcutta (not Benares [109]), Swami Mandanan-and cast the new state's horoscope and found "From midnight August 14 through August 15, Saturn, Jupiter and Venus would all lie in the most accursed site

	of the heavens, the ninth house of Karamstahn (sic)" (Collins and Lapierre 1976, 197).
Karna	see Arjun
kasaundy	spicy condiment with a mustard seed base
Kashmir	princedom to the north of India. The only state in India with a majority Muslim population, the Hindu ruler chose to accede to India rather than Pakistan in 1947. Kashmir is claimed by both Pakistan and India and currently divided among occupation forces from India, Pakistan, and China.
Kashyap	"the Old Tortoise Man, lord and progenitor of all creatures on the earth" (192); first of the seven great rishis created by Vishnu
Kasi	see Benares
Kaul, General [Brij Mohan]	the defeat of the Indians in the 1962 border war with China has been attributed to Kaul's incompetence and political interference by Nehru and Menon. (Kaul was Nehru's relative by marriage).
Kelim rugs	flatweave or pileless carpets from Turkey and Iran
Kell antibodies	if an embryo has Kell antigens and the mother does not, the mother may develop antibodies that fight these antigens, resulting in serious complications.
Kemp's Corner	where once stood Thomas Kemp and Co (Chemists) (181) and where there is now a flyover (540)
kemo-sabay	what the Lone Ranger (q.v.) was called by Tonto
Kerala	see Namboodiripad
Khadija	Muhammad's first wife
Khajuraho	site of many temples in Madhya Pradesh
Khan, Aly	son of Aga Khan III (see Hayworth, Ismailis)
Khan, Ayub	see Ayub
Khan, Tikka	military governor of East Pakistan who led the Pakistani forces in the 1971 war
Khan, Ustad Changez	combination of the names of Ustad Bismillah Khan, a famous shehnai player, and Genghis Khan
khansama	"cook" (38), chief table-servant and purchaser of food
khichri	kedgeree; dish of rice, dhal, onions, etc.
Khichripur	"hotch-potch-town" (416), site of a resettlement camp in East Delhi
Kif, Land of	kif is marijuana
King's Evil	"European curse" (31), scrofula, a swelling of joints and lymph glands, so-called because the touch of the king was supposed to cure it

Kind Solomon's Mines	misprint (140) for *King Solomon's Mines,*1885 adventure novel by H. Rider Haggard set in Africa
Kismeti	"Lucky" (375) (kismet is lot or fate in Hindi and Arabic)
Kissinger, Henry	Secretary of State under President Richard Nixon. The US was allied with Pakistan. Kissinger relied on the Pakistani connection to arrange Nixon's state visit to China in 1972 (363).
Koli fishermen	Dravidian fishing people, the first inhabitants of Bombay. Their name still survives, not only in "Colaba" but also in the word "coolie," the western Indian term for any labourer.
Kolynos toothpaste	toothpaste now owned by Colgate
korma	mild curry
Krishna	an avatar of Vishnu, depicted with blue skin. As a child he was transferred from one womb to another and raised by foster-parents. This has been regarded as a parallel to Jesus, as the bishop says (103), and resembles Saleem's own case as well. Radha, a gopi or cowgirl, was Krishna's mistress, and theirs is an example of perfect love (252).
Krishna's Birthday	Janmashtami, in July or August
Krishnamachari, T.T.	"Finance Minister" resigned in 1958 (406)
Krypton	see Superman
kulfi	milk-rich ice cream
Kundalini	in Tantra, the divine power coiled like a snake at the root of the spine that can be aroused and channelled to aid in the liberation from rebirth
Kurla	suburb north of Bombay which is not on the Western Railway line coming into Churchgate Station (206), but on the Central Railway line
kurta	loose-fitting tunic or shirt
Kurus and Pandavas	the Kauravas and Pandavas, the two sets of brothers whose epic war is recounted in the *Mahabharata*, are both descended from the Kurus
Kwality's	restaurant at Kemp's corner
laddoo	sweet confection of balls of sugar, ghee, wheat and gram flour mixed with rasped coconut
Laika	"first and still the only dog to be shot into space" (208), launched in the Soviet satellite Sputnik II in 1957
Laila and Majnu	(Majnun: preferred spelling) lovers from different Arab nomad clans who were prevented from marrying by her family. Driven insane, Majnun wandered in the desert with wild animals and eventually died

	of love-sickness. The Persian Sufi poet Nizami retold the folk story in a narrative poem near the end of the twelfth century.
lalas	shopkeepers (derogatory, meaning unwarlike)
langoors	"Long-tailed and black-faced … monkeys" (84), commonly identified with Hanuman
lassi	aerated buttermilk
lathi	metal-tipped "stick" (144), five feet long, carried by policemen
Laughing Buddha	frequent image of the Buddha as a fat, jolly monk
Leghorn	the name of the military operation in 1962 intended to push China back to the McMahon line which was the border declared by the British but not recognized by the Chinese
Lenin	in the 1902 pamphlet *What is to be Done?* the revolutionary vanguard needs to lead the proletariat
Lent	forty days of fasting observed by Catholics before Easter
Liaquat Ali Khan	Jinnah's "assassinated friend and successor," the first prime minister of Pakistan (305), killed in 1951
Lilith	in Jewish and Islamic tradition, Lilith was the original wife of Adam; she was turned out of Eden and replaced by Eve because she refused to submit to his authority. In Islamic tradition, she subsequently slept with the devil and gave birth to the djinn.
lingam	phallic symbol of Shiva worship
lok sabha	lower house of "parliament" (221), literally people's assembly
The Lone Ranger	1956 film starring Clayton Moore as the hero and Jay Silverheels as his Indian sidekick, Tonto
loowind	(usually two words: loo wind) hot wind from the desert that sweeps across central northern India in June
Lost Horizon	1937 Frank Capra movie about the paradise of Shangri-La, a secret colonial outpost high in the Tibetan Himalayas, where Europeans find they retain their youth and live very long lives; however, a beautiful woman who left immediately "shrivelled" and showed all the marks of her true age (297).
lotah	small brass pot
Lucknow-work	embroidery
lungis	cloth wrapped around the hips
Lutyens, [Sir Edwin]	architect who designed New Delhi when the British Raj moved its capital there (a move completed in 1931)

Madrasi	from the state of Madras (now Tamil Nadu)
Mahalaxmi	goddess of wealth. A shrine to her on a rocky outcrop by the Great Breach was destroyed before the British came but later rebuilt.
Maharaj, Maharajin	king, queen
mahaseer trout	found only in Indian rivers
Mahatma	"Great Soul," a title accorded Gandhi
Mahim	suburb north of central Bombay
Mahisha	"buffalo-demon" (393): demon with the head of a buffalo and the body of a man slain by Devi
Mahmud of Ghazni	Sultan of Ghazni in modern Afghanistan who conquered parts of northern India in the eleventh century, bringing with him Arabic which has three forms of the letter S (301)
Mahratta	Maharashtrian, a speaker of Marathi
maidan	open space, parade-ground
Malabar Hill	Bombay's ritziest neighbourhood, right beside Warden Road
mali	gardener
mamu	maternal uncle in Urdu (Hindi would be *mama*)
Manekshaw, [Field Marshal] Sam	chief-of-staff of the Indian Army who, according to Wolpert, "personally" accepted the surrender of Pakistani General Niazi (Wolpert 1989, 390) – the source of Rushdie's error. (Niazi actually surrendered to Lt. General Jagjit Singh Aurora.)
Mangeshkar, Lata	playback singer who was the most powerful woman in Indian film through the fifties, sixties, and seventies
Mangharam, J.B.	biscuit manufacturer
Manikarnika-ghat	"the place of funerals," the main site of cremation in Benares (176)
Mankad, Vinoo	famous cricket all-rounder
Manolete	the name used by the most famous twentieth-century Spanish bullfighter, well-known for his use of the "muleta," or red cape (152)
mantra	sacred Vedic text used as prayer or incantation
Marine Drive	seaside boulevard whose string of lights at night has earned it the nickname the "Queen's Necklace." Saleem describes it as "a great arcing necklace" (295). It is shored up by cement tetrapods.
Markandaya	there are many stories of sexual change in Hindu mythology and folklore, including Narada (q.v.), Vishnu himself, King Ila, Amba, and Manahsvamin, but I have not been able to identify a story where the famous rishi, Markandaya, changes sex.

Marvé	beach area north of Bombay, at the mouth of Manori Creek
Mary	the virgin mother of Jesus, in the Quran as in the Bible. Joseph was her husband. "Hail-Mary-full-of-grace" (247) is the first line of a Catholic prayer.
masala	spicy mixture
Maslama	Rushdie lists "other prophets" in Arabia at the time of Muhammad, Maslama, Hanzala ibn Safwan, and Khalid ibn Sinan (296), a list he takes almost word for word from Maxine Rodinson's biography *Mohammed*.
mata	mother
maulvi	"religious tutor" (43), doctor of the Law; teacher of Arabic and Persian; a learned man
maund	Anglo-Indian form of weight (about 40 kg)
mausi	"little mother" (143), usually the title for a mother's sister
Maya	"dream-web of the world" (207): illusion, especially the illusory nature of the phenomenal world
Mecca Sharif	*sharif* or *shareef* means "noble, exalted"
[Shri] Meenakshi Temple	in Madurai, named after a wife of Shiva, and the destination of many pilgrims
mehndi	ornate henna patterns on the hands and feet
Menon, Krishna	"Defence Minister" 1957–62 (286); leader of India's delegation to the UN, 1952–57
methuselah	very old (the patriarch Methuselah in the Book of Genesis lived 969 years)
Metro cinema	at the corner of Mahatma Gandhi Road and First Marine Street (Anandilal Podar Marg)
Methwold, William	from 1633 he was the East India Company president at Surat; when he returned to Britain in 1639 he was a director and later deputy-governor of the East India Company till he died in 1653. Rushdie was probably inspired by A.R. Ingram's 1938 history *The Gateway to India: The Story of Methwold and Bombay.*
Methwold's Estate	based on Rushdie's childhood home, Westfield Estates
Minto, Dom	"Bombay's best-known private detective" (254), also mentioned in *The Moor's Last Sigh*. I have not been able to confirm this information.
Miranda, Carmen	"European actress with a mountain of fruit on her head" (75); actually Brazilian, who made Hollywood movies with fruit-covered hats in the 1940s
Mirza, Iskander	as Governor-General, he ruled Pakistan, imposing and deposing "four-prime-ministers-in-two-years"

	(279): Chaudhuri Muhammad Ali from the West Wing held the post from 1955 until September 1956; Huseyn Shaheed Suhrawardy, leader of the Awami League of East Pakistan, succeeded him in 1956, but was forced to resign after slightly more than a year; Ismail Ibrahim Chundrigar headed a coalition government for two months before being succeeded by Firoz Khan Noon, leader of the Republican Party in Pakistan. On March 2, 1956, a new constitution had declared Pakistan an Islamic Republic and Mirza had become President. With the support of Ayub Khan, commander-in-chief of the Armed Forces, he proclaimed martial law and dissolved the National Assembly on "October 7, 1958," the night Saleem witnesses the generals plotting a coup. October 27, "three weeks" later, Mirza was himself deposed at gun point by Ayub Khan (281).
Mishra, L.N. [Lalit Narayan]	"the railway minister," involved in licensing scandals, who was killed in a bomb blast at Samastipur Railway Station, January 2, 1975 (400)
Mohammed, [Malik] Ghulam	governor-general of Pakistan 1951–5. His deteriorating health led to his succession by Iskander Mirza (q.v.).
monkey-nut	nut similar to the cashew
Montague and Capulet	(properly Montagu) the families of Romeo and Juliet (324)
moon	popular superstition has it that it is bad luck to see the "new moon … through glass" (47)
Moore, Clayton	see Lone Ranger
Moplas of Malabar	Muslim inhabitants of Kerala, descended from Moors and Arabs who married local Malabar women
Morarji	see Desai
Mountbatten, Louis	the last British viceroy, who oversaw the transfer of power. He was named an Earl on August 14, 1947.
Mountbatten, [Edwina]	Saleem calls her a "chicken-breast-eater" (108) because, upon first arriving at the Viceroy's House and asking for food for her two dogs, she was amazed when servants brought in roasted chicken breasts. Appalled at this decadence she took the chicken and retired to the bathroom where she ate it herself (Collins and Lapierre, 1976, 85).
Mubarak	"He who is Blessed" (112)
mucuna pruritus	actual herbal ingredient of medicine against male impotence

muezzin	Muslim crier who calls to prayer
mufti	civilian clothes, from the Hindi and Arabic word for an expounder of Muslim law
Mughal Empire	Muslim rulers of India who conquered the Delhi sultanate in 1526. In decline after 1739, the empire came to an end in 1858.
Mughal Gardens	same as Shalimar
muhallas	"Muslim neighbourhoods" (69)
Muhammad	an "orphan" (66), at age forty he received the Quran from the angel Jibreel on Mount Hira (161). He is called the "Last-But-One" (161) because his is the final revelation before the end of the world. Mahound (161) is a disrespectful name applied by medieval Christianity (and used by Rushdie in *The Satanic Verses*).
Muhammed bin Sam Ghuri	Muslim conqueror from Ghur, in modern Afghanistan, in the late twelfth century. He had no sons (301), but his lieutenant who succeeded him, Qutbuddin Aibak, made Delhi his capital and established the Delhi Sultanate (not Caliphate [301]).
mujahideen	warriors on behalf of Islam
Mujib-ur-Rahman, Sheik	leader of the Awami League in East Pakistan and first Prime Minister of Bangladesh. He was assassinated in 1975 and succeeded by General Ziaur Rahman, "called by the same name" as Zia ul-Haq, the Pakistani general who executed Prime Minister Z. A. Bhutto (305).
Mukti Bahini	"guerrillas" in East Bengal fighting against Pakistanis (346) (literally Liberation Forces)
mullah	learned man, teacher
mumani	maternal aunt in Urdu (Hindi would be mami)
Mumbadevi	Mother Goddess of Bombay (92). A local deity, an aboriginal personification of the Earth Mother, Maha-Amba-Aiee or 'Mumba Devi,' for whom Bombay may be named; worshipped in conjunction with Navaratri, the ten-day festival in September-October to honour the goddess Durga
Mumtaz Mahal	see Shah Jehan
Murree Hills	just north of Rawalpindi
Musa	Moses, who, according to the Quran and the Bible, first heard God's voice on Mount Sinai speaking from a fire, directing him to "put-off-thy-shoes" (295). Later, leading the journey of the Israelites out

	of Egypt, Moses received the Ten Commandments on Mount Sinai, but found the Israelites had built themselves an idol in the form of a "golden calf" to worship (295).
Muslim League	political party founded in 1906 that sought to defend the interests of Muslims. Until a very late date, it favoured a loose federation rather than a separate nation-state.
"My Red Dupatta of Muslin"	wedding song (a red dupatta is worn by the bride)
Naga	snake "god" (136); a cobra, often represented around Shiva's neck
Naga dialects	languages spoken by tribes in Nagaland, easternmost India
Nagaraj	"great snake" (385)
nakkoo	"the nosey one" (17); more accurately, someone who has his nose in the air (Kashmiri)
namaskar	Hindu greeting with bowed head and hands joined together
Namboodiripad, E.M.S.	Chief Minister of first democratically elected Communist government in the world, in Kerala in 1957. Political discord fomented by the Congress Party led Nehru to dismiss the government and call new elections that were won by Congress (252). Namboodiripad split from the Communist Party and formed the CPI(M) in 1964 (386).
Nanga-Parbat	Himalayan peak
Narada	sage famous for his asceticism, who asked Vishnu to be shown Maya. Vishnu instructed him to bathe in a tank, and he emerged transformed into a woman who had forgotten her past.
Narayan, Jaya-Prakash	Very active in nationalist politics before independence, he later renounced party politics and joined Vinobha Bhave (q.v.). His criticism of Indira Gandhi in 1974 made him a figure of opposition, and he was arrested in 1975. Although the spiritual guide of the Janata Party, he did not take up formal leadership.
nargisi kofta	meatballs
nasbandi	"sterilization" (414), vasectomy
Nasser, [Gamal Abdel]	President of Egypt 1956–70, he nationalized the Suez Canal, the main shipping route from Europe to India, in 1956, bringing war with Britain, France, and Israel. He "sank ships" in order to block the canal (149).

Nastaliq script	cursive Persian script used for Urdu
nautch girl	dancing girl
nawab	"Prince" (310), high-ranking political-military official
Naxalite	originally an anti-landlord movement among peasants in Naxalbari, West Bengal, later a radical Communist group (Marxist-Leninist) espousing violence that broke away from the other two groups of Communists
Nehru, Jawaharlal	India's first prime minister. He sought to retire in 1958 (252) but a storm of protest forced him to continue as prime minister. He died in office on May 27, 1964.
Nell [Gwyn]	orange-seller turned actress who became Charles II's mistress (92)
Nelson, [Admiral Horatio Lord]	reported to have said before the Battle of Copenhagen in 1801, when disregarding a signal: "I have only one eye – I have a right to be blind sometimes" (66)
Nepean Sea Road	now called Laxmibai Jagmohanda Marg
New Empire Cinema	near Victoria Terminus
Niazi, A.A.K. [Ameer Abdullah Khan] "Tiger"	Pakistani general in the East Wing at the time of the Bangladeshi War. After the war, he spent two years as a POW, and upon his return to Pakistan was dismissed from the army and jailed. (see Manekshaw)
nibu-pani	lemonade (more commonly nimbu-pani)
nikah	"the wedding proper" (401); Muslim marriage
nipa palms	stemless palm trees found in the Ganges delta
Nizam of Hyderabad	see Hyderabad
Noor Ville	name of actual villa in Westfield Estates (see Methwold's Estate). Others were Windsor, Sandringham, Glamis, and Balmoral.
Oakley, Annie	US sharpshooter, one of the star attractions of Buffalo Bill's Wild West show and the subject of a 1935 movie with Barbara Stanwyck
Oberoi-Sheraton	hotel owned by M.S. Oberoi at Nariman Point, "on land reclaimed … from the sea" (436)
Ohé	watch out
Old Fort, Delhi	see Purana Qila
Old Fort district	(properly just called "the Fort") area of Bombay, north of Colaba on the site of the British fort
OM	mystic syllable used as a mantra
open-sesame	password used by Ali Baba
O.S.S. 117	title of a series of French spy films inspired by James Bond. The Office of Strategic Services was the precursor of the CIA.

"Our Golden Bengal"	see "Amar Sonar Bangla"
Outram Road	modern Purshottamdas Thakurdas Marg
paan	"paste of the betel … folded in a leaf" for chewing (38)
Padma	Padma means lotus and is another name for Sri Laxmi, who is also called "The One Who Possesses Dung" (*karisini*), because, when she asked the cows if she could live among them, she was given permission to live in their urine and dung. Her two sons are Moisture and Mud (192).
Padma River	the name of the Ganges in East Bengal
Pakistan	like India, Pakistan was born at midnight between August 14 and August 15, 1947, but it celebrates Independence Day on the earlier date. Perhaps this is because in South Asia the day begins not at midnight but at dawn.
Pakola	soft drink made by Mehran Bottlers in Karachi, along with Bubble-Up and Vimto
pakora	dish of diced or chopped vegetables coated with batter and stuffed into pastry
"Pale Hands I Loved Beside the Shalimar"	poem by Laurence Hope in *Love Lyrics of India*, set to music by Amy Woodforde-Finden
pallu	border on the width of sari that hangs over the shoulder
Panjim	Panaji, the capital of Goa
parahamsa	"mythical bird," the Gander (218), a Hindu symbol of the unity of the self and the other
paratha	pancake of unleavened bread
Parsees (or Parsis)	Zoroastrians who settled in India after the Arab conquest of Persia in the seventh century CE
Parvati	wife of Shiva, mother of Ganesh
pasanda	curry with meat cooked in a creamy yogurt sauce
pashmina	wool from the necks of goats in Kashmir
patchouli	kind of perfume distilled from the plant of the same name
Patel, [Sardar Vallabhbhai]	Deputy Prime Minister and Home Minister in the first government after independence
Vallabhai Patel Stadium	off Hornby Vellard by Mahalaxmi racecourse
Pathan	a people in North-West Frontier Province famous as warriors
Patil, Boss [S.K.]	Member of Parliament who wanted Bombay to be a city-state not associated with either Maharashtra or Gujarat

peacock-feather	in many parts of the world considered to be "bad luck" because of the eye, resembling the evil eye, at the end (47)
Pedder Road	now called Gopalrao Deshmukh Marg
Pereira, Mary	based on Mary Manezes, a worker in the hospital where Salman Rushdie was born, who became his ayah (Hamilton 1996, 90)
Pethick-Lawrence [Lord]	Secretary of State for India
phaelwan	*pahlwan*, professional wrestler
"physician heal thyself"	ancient proverb quoted by Jesus in Luke 4:23
pice	copper coin, a quarter anna
Picts	people in ancient Scotland reputed to paint themselves blue
pie-dog	(usually pye-dog) stray dog
Pied Piper	a piper who rid the town of Hamelin in Germany of rats but, when he was not paid, lured away all the town's children
Pinocchio	wooden puppet in Carlo Collodi's 1883 story whose nose grew when he told lies and who wanted to become a real boy; subject of 1940 Disney film
pista-ki-lauz	pistachio sweetmeat
P.K.	chewing gum made by Wrigley's (253)
playback singer	in Indian movies a singer or musician who substitutes for an actor or actress
plimsolls	rubber-soled canvas "shoes" (211)
pomfret	fish commonly caught in bag or trawl nets
Poppy	I cannot identify this reference (235).
P.P.P.	see Bhutto
puja	religious "rite" (174) offering flowers or food to a god
Punchinello	the chief character in an Italian puppet-show, with a long nose and chin (in English: Punch)
"Prima in Indis"	Bombay is often called "Urbs Prima in India," meaning the First City in India. The "old tune" "Prima in Indis,/ Gateway to India,/ Door [not Star]of the East/ With her face to the West" (92) is actually the school song of the Cathedral and John Connon Boys School (q.v.).
Purana	eighteen major collections of stories about the lives of the gods, 300–1000 CE
Purana Qila	literally "Old Fort": "that blackened ruin … of an impossibly antique time" (81), built in the sixteenth

	century by Sher Shah, an Afghan ruler who briefly captured Delhi from Humayun (q.v.)
purdah	"housebound" (14); literally curtain or veil
puri	small, round wheat cake
Pushtu	language of the Pathans
Qa'aba	the "shrine of the great Black Stone" (283). Embedded in the Qa'aba in the Great Mosque in Mecca is "a giant meteorite." As Saleem explains, it was worshipped by pagans before it was conquered by Muhammad. (see black stone god)
queen-of-the-night	cereus
Quentin Durward	1955 film with Robert Taylor
Quit India	August 8, 1942, Gandhi issued a call for the British to Quit India. As a result the Congress leaders were all imprisoned and the Muslim League, which declared its support for the British War effort, formed the government, as the Rani of Cooch Naheen complains (46).
Quran	the 114 chapters or surahs of the Quran are organized in terms of length, the longest first and the shortest last. A project like Ahmed Sinai's to rearrange the Quran in the order in which the chapters were composed would put Surah 96 first, the surah in which the angel Jibreel orders Muhammad to "Recite: in the Name of the Lord thy Creator, who created Man from clots of blood" (162).
Qutb Minar	tower of victory erected in Delhi, starting in 1193, to celebrate defeat of the last Hindu kingdom and the establishment of the Delhi Sultanate
Radha	see Krishna
Radhakrishnan, [Dr Sarvepalli]	"President of India" 1962–1967 (293)
Raffles, [Sir Thomas Stamford]	entrepreneur responsible for establishing a British trading post at Singapore in 1818
raga	classical Indian song
Rajpath	New Delhi boulevard, "between India Gate and the Secretariat buildings," the former "Kingsway" (377)
Rajputana	the land of the Rajputs; another name for Rajasthan
Rajputs	warrior clans who provided many of the soldiers for the Mughal and British armies
rakshasa	demon
Raleigh, Sir Walter	Elizabethan adventurer, subject of the painting, "The Boyhood of Raleigh" by Sir John Everett Millais

Ram, Jagjivan	"most powerful of the untouchables" (317), he quit Congress to form his own party in 1974 and joined the Janata Party in 1976.
Rama and Sita	Rama is an avatar of Vishnu. He married the lovely Sita, who was abducted by the wicked Ravana (q.v.). Their story is the central tale of the *Ramayana.* He did not just "draw the undrawable bow" of Shiva (196), he broke it in two.
D.W. Rama Studios (Pvt) Ltd.	an invented film studio which appears again in *The Satanic Verses*
Ramayana	see Rama, Hanuman, and Valmiki
Ramzàn	Ramadan, "the month of fasting" (178)
Ranji	famous cricketer who played for England
Rann of Kutch	a Rann is a salt marsh regularly submerged by monsoon rains. The Rann of Kutch is in Gujarat.
rasgullah	spongy Indian sweetmeat, made from milk, sugar, various flavours, and soaked in syrup
Rashtrapati Bhavan	"President House" (257)
ratel	honey badger
Ravana	"many-headed demon" (71) who stole Sita from Rama (q.v.) and carried her away to Lanka (see Hanuman)
Ray, A.N.[Ajit Nath]	"Chief Justice," hand-picked by Indira Gandhi in 1973. He was almost assassinated in 1975 (402).
Reader's Paradise	bookstore that still exists on Warden Road across from Breach Candy Swimming Pool
reccine	(usually spelled rexine) synthetic "leather cloth" (42)
Red Fort	Lal Qila, "at the top of Chandni Chowk," "where Mughals ruled" (80). Its "infinitely extending walls" (376) are 2 km long.
"Red Sails in the Sunset"	1935 song
Republican Party	Pakistani political party formed by Khan Sahib from dissenters of the Muslim League in 1956. President Iskander Mirza depended on Republican Party support to retain office, and he was afraid of losing that support when Suhrawardy of the Awami League made an alliance with Noon of the Republican Party (282).
rhesus	antigen occurring on red blood cells of most humans; Saleem is rhesus negative, meaning he lacks these antigens.
rishi	seer, sage
Rite of the Tree	see Atharva-Veda

RK Films	(RK Studios) owned by the famous film-maker Raj Kapoor
Rowlatt Act	(should be plural) acts passed in 1919 by the British "Against political agitation" (34), including imprisonment without trial
Roy, Pushpa	Rushdie's invention (125); the first Indian to swim the English Channel was actually Mihir Sen in 1958.
R.S.S.S. party	Rashtriya Swayam Sewak Sangh (National Self-Service Society), "extremist" Hindu nationalist party whose symbol is the swastika (75)
rutputty	dilapidated
Sabarmati, Commander Vinoo	Rushdie's invention, inspired by the case of Kawas Nanavati, a naval officer who killed the lover of his English wife Sylvia in 1959, was acquitted by the jury, but then sentenced to prison by the judge. Sabarmati is the name of a river on the banks of which Gandhi founded his ashram near Ahmedabad upon his return to India from South Africa.
sabha	council
Sabkuch ticktock hai	(should be *thik thak*) "Everything's just fine" (97)
Sachivalaya	"State Secretariat" (173)
sadhu	recluse or saint
sahib	lord
sahibzada	crown prince
Saint Joan	1923 play by George Bernard Shaw about Joan of Arc, who is presented as the prophet of the new force of nationalism
St Thomas's Cathedral	the oldest British building in Bombay (actually Anglican, not Catholic)
salan	creamy gravy
salwars	loose trousers tied with drawstrings
salwar kamees	pyjama-like outfit
Aung Sam	see Aung
Samachar	"Widow's own news agency" (412); Indira Gandhi forced the amalgamation of the Press Trust of India and United News of India into a single news agency to facilitate government control.
samosas	triangular envelope of pastry, fried in oil, and stuffed with meat or vegetables
Samson	Biblical hero whose strength, like Methwold's (113), lay in his hair and who was tricked by his wife Delilah into revealing his secret
Sangeet Sammelan	annual "All-India Radio music festival" (239), first held in 1954

Sankara Acharya	hill outside Srinigar on which is a temple dedicated to Shiva, "the black stone god" (12). Muslims call the hill Takht-e-Sulaiman or "Seat of Solomon" (31).
Sans Souci	named after the Potsdam palace of Frederick the Great of Prussia and the palatial Bombay mansion of the Sassoon family
Santa Cruz Airport	Bombay's international airport
sarangi	stringed musical instrument resembling a violin
Sarasvati	holy subterranean river that reappears to join the confluence of the Ganges and the Yamuna
sarkar	the state or government
Sarnath	site of the deer park where Buddha gave his first sermon and where an ancient sculpture with four lions facing four different directions was found, a sculpture now on the seal of India
sarod	stringed musical instrument
sati	self-immolation by widows as a sign of fidelity
Satyagraha	Gandhi's strategy of non-violent civil disobedience (literally insistence on truth)
Scandal Point	area on Warden Road, probably named after the Scandal Point in Shimla, which earned its name because of its popularity with courting couples
Scaramouche	1952 swashbuckler directed by George Sidney
Schaapsteker	a kind of snake (the name derives from Afrikaans: sheep piercer)
Scheherazade	in the frame tale of the *Thousand and One Nights*, Shahriyar, the ruler of India and China, having been deceived by his queen, kills her and then every day marries a new bride whom he kills the next morning. This continues until Scheherazade marries him and staves off her own execution by telling him stories which she leaves "hanging in mid-air … night after night" (25).
Scindia-ghat	see ghat
Screen Goddess	I cannot identify this reference (235)
seers	Indian weight
seven-tiles	game in which seven tiles are piled up. The object is to knock them down with a ball and then to pile them up again before the other side can retrieve the ball and hit you with it.
Shah Jehan	Mughal emperor "whose name meant 'king of the world'" (58) and who built the Taj Mahal as a mausoleum for his wife Mumtaz Mahal who died in 1630

"Shahbaz Qalandar"	*"Dam-a-dam mast Qalandar"* a Punjabi-language song about the Sufi mystic saint Lal Shahbaz Qalandar. The song was sung by Noor Jehan (the probable model for Jamila Singer's career) in 1968 and was associated with Bhutto's Pakistan People's Party. The song is a *qawwali*, a rhythmic song accompanied by drums whose prime purpose is to attain spiritual ecstasy but which is often performed at modern weddings.
shahi-korma	lamb dish
Shahryar, Prince	see Scheherazade
Shaitan	the "Devil" (212)
Shakti	"cosmic energy"; the female principle, especially when personified as the wife of a god (392)
Shalimar Bagh or Gardens	Garden of Love planted by Jehangir for his wife Noor Jehan
Shankar, Uday Dance Troupe	Shankar was largely responsible for reviving classical dance in India in the 1930s.
Shastri, Lal Bahadur	compromise choice for Prime Minister 1964–6
shatranj	"chess" (132)
shehnai	oboe-like musical instrument
shikara	Kashmiri "small boats" (14)
shikara-wallah	one who poles a shikara
Shiva	the destroyer in the Hindu divine triad; husband of Parvati and father of Ganesh (but not biological father)
Shroff, Anand, "Andy"	name means money-changer
Sidjeen and Illiyun	according to Surah 83, the record of sinners is Sijjin, that of the righteous is 'Illiyyun (296).
Sikander But-Shikan	Sultan of Kashmir whose name means "the Iconoclast," much hated for his destruction of Hindu temples "at the end of the fourteenth century" (301).
silkie	Sea-Faerie, able to discard her seal-skin and come ashore as a beautiful maiden. If a human can capture this skin, the silkie can be forced to become a wife. However, should she ever find her skin, she immediately returns to the sea.
Silverheels, Jay	see Lone Ranger
Baroness Simki von der Heiden	I cannot identify this reference.
Sin	"the ancient moon-god" (172), originally of Mesopotamian origin but planted in Arabia (Hadhramaut), where he became the major god. His name is related

	to Sinai. Saleem is clearly influenced by those who seek to debunk Islam by arguing that Sin was the precursor of Allah, which explains the prominence of the crescent moon in Islam.
Sin	letter S in Arabic (see Mahmud of Ghazni)
Mount Sinai	see Musa
Sinai, Ahmed	Rushdie's father's name was Anis Ahmed Rushdie (Hamilton 1996, 90)
Sinbad	mariner whose voyages are recounted in the *Arabian Nights*
Singh, Dara	famous wrestler who became a film actor, playing, among other roles, Hanuman
sitar	Indian guitar
Sivaji	"Mahratta warrior-king" in the late seventeenth century, the rival of Aurangzeb. His "equestrian statue" (93) is near the Gateway of India. He is often now invoked as the historical defender of Hinduism against the Mughals (and the night ride of his statue through town is therefore menacing to Muslims).
Slave Kings	first dynasty (1206–1290) of the Delhi Sultanate, which established Muslim rule in the heartland of India
Sputniks	Russian satellites
sraktya	see Atharva-Veda
States Reorganization Commission	(not Committee) appointed in 1953 to suggest ways of demarcating state boundaries along linguistic lines. Following its report in 1955, India was divided into 14 states and 6 territories, including Kerala, Karnataka where "you were supposed to speak Kanarese" (or Kannada), and Tamil Nadu (186). Bombay was divided into Maharashtra and Gujarat in 1960.
Sufi	Muslim ascetic mystic
Sundarbans	world's largest mangrove forest, located in the Ganges-Brahmaputra delta, half in India, half in Bangladesh; flooded by tides, which regularly cut new channels and shift the sands, it takes its name from the sundri trees, very tall mangrove trees (351).
Superman	Superman's father Jor-El, like Adi Dubash, a scientist, knew about the coming "explosion of the planet Krypton," so he and his wife Lara "dispatched" their infant son Kal-El "through space" in a "rocket-ship" to Earth, where he was found by "the good, mild Kents" (262).

surahi	long-necked water pot
Surat	British trading post before Bombay
swastika	"ancient Hindu symbol of power" (75), associated with the R.S.S.S.
Swatantra	founded in 1959 as a secular but conservative party
tabla	pair of small kettle-drums
Taj Bibi	name of Mumtaz Mahal, wife of Shah Jehan (q.v.)
Taj Hotel	built beside the Gateway of India by the Parsi industrialist Jamsethji Tata to avenge the snub of being excluded from "whites only" hotels
Taj Mahal	see Shah Jehan
takalluf	"formality" (280), trouble, inconvenience
takht	chair
Takshasa	"the snake god" (388)
Talaaq	"I divorce thee" (62) (Arabic)
tamasha	"tomfoolery" (30), public spectacle, display, show that attracts spectators; fuss, commotion
tandori nan	flatbread baked in a clay oven
Tanjore River	Tanjore (Thanjavur) is on the holy river Kauvery (114)
Tannenbaum	"old German tune" (40): "O Christmas Tree," as foreign a song as can be imagined
Tantric	belonging to the Tantras, Sanskrit mystical and magical writings of relatively recent date
Tardeo roundabout	now called Naik Chowk
Tata, [J.R.D.]	heir of a family fortune going back to the nineteenth century, based on textiles, chemicals, steel, hotels, hydroelectric power generation, locomotives, motor vehicles
Taylor, Robert	Saleem would have enjoyed watching him as a Roman in *Quo Vadis?* (1951), as Ivanhoe in the 1952 film, as Lancelot in *Knights of the Round Table* (1953), and as Quentin Durward in the 1955 film.
Teen Batti	Rushdie's private joke: Teen Batti is a tenement area on Walkeshwar Road, Malabar Hill. Although the name means "three bright lights" (53), Teen Batti is so called because it is at the junction of three roads.
teetar	partridge
Telefunken	German electronics company (55)
Tenzing Norgay	sherpa who, together with Sir Edmund Hillary, climbed Everest in 1953 (154)
thali	metal dish on which food is served
Thousand and One Nights	see Scheherazade

thunderbox	commode; a box with a seat with a hole placed over a receptacle that was removed, cleaned, and replaced by a member of the sweeper caste (Lewis 1997, 235)
tick tock	along with its other connotations, "ticky-tock" is a rhythmic refrain used by Indian musicians accompanying the dance movements of nautch-girls (Lewis 1997, 236): (*thtai thtai thaka thtai thtai*).
tiffin	light midday meal
tineachloris	ringworm
tola	Indian weight, about 12 grams
tongas, ikkas, gharries	"horse-drawn" two-wheeled carriages (33)
Tote	betting window
Tower of Silence	where Parsis expose their dead, in Bombay between the Hanging Gardens and Kemp's Corner, but not in Delhi at all
Trombay	site of the Homi Bhabha Atomic Research Centre, visible from Bombay
tu	informal second-person pronoun
tubriwallah	"a Bengali snake-charmer" (136)
Tughlaq, [Muhammad]	most prominent member of a fourteenth-century Muslim dynasty of the same name originally based in Delhi (301)
Turner, Lana	starred in *Peyton Place* (1957), *Another Time, Another Place* (1958).
Umrigar, Polly	cricketer who starred for India in the forties and fifties
Umayyad	name of the first caliphs, the successors of the Prophet. In 711CE, Haijaj bin Yusuf, the Umayyad governor in Baghdad, dispatched Muhammad bin Qasim with a small army to India (301).
Valika	see Dawoods
valima	"consummation ceremony" (402); wedding banquet
Valmiki	Valmiki composed the Ramayana and dictated it not to Ganesh (149), but to Rama's own twin sons, Lava and Kusa, who in turn recited it to their father who became the first reader of the epic as well as its hero.
vanaspati	vegetable ghee
Varuna	one of the earliest Vedic gods, associated with the sky, celestial order, and therefore law and justice; see Atharva-Veda
Venice Restaurant	in the Astoria Hotel on Churchgate Road (modern Veer Nariman Road)

Versailles	Louis XIV's palace
Vera Cruz	1953 film, starring Gary Cooper and Burt Lancaster, about two soldiers of fortune in Mexico in 1866, chasing shipments of gold (224)
Verandah, Carmen	see Carmen Miranda
Victoria Terminus	modern Chatrapathi Shivaji Terminus, built in 1888
Vimto	soft drink
vina	Indian lyre: musical instrument with seven strings and a gourd at each end, played by plucking
Vishnu	the preserver in the Hindu triad; husband of Laxmi; he is traditionally said to have ten avatars, including Rama, Krishna, and the Buddha.
Vishwanatham, Roxy	I cannot identify this reference (236).
Vorwärts	a daily newspaper, the central organ of the German Social-Democratic Party, published in Berlin from 1891 to 1933
Vyjayantimala	Tamil actress who starred in such films as *Bahar* (1951), *Nagin* (1954), *Devdas* (1955), and *New Delhi* (1956)
Walkeshwar Reservoir	Saleem is probably thinking of Malabar Hill Reservoir, located under the Hanging Gardens. The Walkeshwar temple has a sacred pool whose waters sprang up when Rama shot an arrow into the ground. It is one of the oldest sites in Bombay but not the city's water supply (219).
wallah	suffix meaning "someone who performs an action or is associated with a profession"
Walsingham School for Girls	Walsingham House School, located in Breach Candy from 1950 to 1965. Originally for British children, it eventually opened its doors to Indians.
Warden Road	modern Bhulabhai Desai Road
Wavell, [Sir Archibald]	Viceroy of India, replaced by Mountbatten
Willingdon [Sports] Club	cricket grounds and golf course, located where Warden Road and Hornby Vellard meet
Wingate, Orde	see Chindits
Wee Willie Winkie	title of a 1937 film, starring Shirley Temple and inspired by a Kipling story of the same name. Shirley Temple plays an American girl visiting her British grandfather, who happens to be a Colonel commanding a fort in India. Cesar Romero plays a shifty Indian guerilla leader. The implication is that America inherits responsibility for the Raj. Upon her arrival in India Shirley Temple confuses Indians with native Americans, just as Evie Burns does (180).

witch's nipples	moles
yaar	interjection meaning friend or pal
Yahya Khan, General [Agha Muhammad]	came to power in Pakistan in 1969 and resigned after the defeat in the Bangladeshi War in 1971.
Yaksa genii	forest godlings prominent in Indian mythology (192)
Yamuna River	where Krishna bathed
yara	see yaar
Xavier	see Francis Xavier
zafaran	Arabic for "saffron" (113)
zamindar	"landlord" (353)
zenana	secluded women's quarters in an upper-class Muslim home
Zulfikar	"two-pronged sword carried by Ali" (61)
zygosity	determines whether two twins are identical (monozygotic) or fraternal (dizygotic). This, of course, has nothing to do with Saleem's case (230).

References

Abbas, Ackbar, 2000. "Cosmopolitan De-scriptions: Shanghai and Hong Kong." *Public Culture* 12.3, 769–86.

Adorno, Theodor and Max Horkheimer, 1986. *The Dialectic of Enlightenment* (1944). Trans. John Cumming (1972). London: Verso.

Ali, Tariq, 1985. *An Indian Dynasty: The Story of the Nehru-Gandhi Family.* New York: Picador.

Alter, Joseph S., 1992. *The Wrestler's Body: Identity and Ideology in North India.* Berkeley: University of California Press.

Anderson, Benedict, 1991. *Imagined Communities.* London: Verso.

– 1998. *The Spectre of Comparisons: Nationalism, Southeast Asia and the World.* London: Verso.

Anderson, Quentin, 1971. *The Imperial Self.* New York: Knopf.

Appadurai, Arjun, 1996. *Modernity at Large: Cultural Dimensions of Globalization.* Minneapolis: University of Minnesota Press.

Appiah, K. Anthony, 1996. "Cosmopolitan Patriots." In *For Love of Country: Debating the Limits of Patriotism*, ed. Joshua Cohen, 21–9. Boston: Beacon Press.

– 2001. "Cosmopolitan Reading." In *Cosmopolitan Geographies: New Locations in Literature and Culture*, ed. Vinay Dharwadker, 197–227. New York: Routledge.

Aravamudan, Srinivas, 1989. "Being God's Postman Is No Fun, Yaar: Salman Rushdie's *The Satanic Verses.*" *Diacritics* 19.2, 3–20.

Armstrong, Karen, 2001. *Buddha.* New York: Penguin.

Auden, W.H., 1991. *Collected Poems*, ed. Edward Mendelson. New York: Vintage.

Austin, J.L. 1962. *How to Do Things With Words.* Cambridge, Mass.: Harvard University Press.

Bakhtin, Mikhail, 1968. *Rabelais and His World.* Trans. Helene Iswolsky. Cambridge, Mass.: Massachusetts Institute of Technology Press.

Ball, John Clement, 1998. "Pessoptimism: Satire and the Menippean Grotesque in Rushdie's *Midnight's Children*." *English Studies in Canada* 24.1, 61–81.

– 2000. "An Interview with Salman Rushdie." In Reder, 101–9.

Balzac, Honoré de, 1976. *Illusions Perdues*. Paris: Presses de la Renaissance.

Batty, Nancy E., 1999. "The Art of Suspense: Rushdie's 1001 (Mid-)Nights." In Mukherjee 1999, 95–111.

Baucom, Ian, 1999. *Out of Place: Englishness, Empire, and the Locations of Identity*. Princeton: Princeton University Press.

Berlant, Lauren, 1991. *The Anatomy of National Fantasy*. Chicago: University of Chicago Press.

Bhabha, Homi, 1994. *The Location of Culture*. London: Routledge.

– 1996. "Unsatisfied Notes on Vernacular Cosmopolitanism." In *Text and Narration*, ed. Peter C. Pfeiffer and Laura García-Moreno, 191–207. Columbia, S.C.: Camden House.

Birch, David, 1991. "Postmodernist Chutneys." *Textual Practice* 5.1, 1–7.

Bongie, Chris, 1998. *Islands and Exiles: The Creole Identities of Post/Colonial Literature*. Stanford: Stanford University Press.

Brennan, Timothy, 1989. *Salman Rushdie and the Third World: Myths of the Nation*. London: Macmillan.

– 1997. *At Home in the World: Cosmopolitanism Now*. Cambridge, Mass.: Harvard University Press.

– 2001. "Cosmo-Theory." *South Atlantic Quarterly* 100.3, 659–91.

Brooks, David, 2000. "Salman Rushdie." In Reder 57–71.

Brooks, Peter, 1993. *Body Work: Objects of Desire in Modern Narrative*. Cambridge, Mass.: Harvard University Press.

Brubaker, Rogers, 1998. "Myths and Misconceptions in the Study of Nationalism." In *The State of the Nation*, ed. John Hall, 272–306. Cambridge: Cambridge University Press.

Butler, Judith, 1987. *Subjects of Desire: Hegelian Reflections in Twentieth-Century France*. New York: Columbia University Press.

– 1993. *Bodies That Matter*. New York: Routledge.

Calasso, Roberto, 1999. *Ka: Stories of the Mind and Gods of India*. Trans. Tim Parks. New York: Vintage.

Carey, John, 1973. *The Violent Effigy: A Study of Dickens' Imagination*. London: Faber.

Césaire, Aimé, 1983. "Cahier d'un Retour au Pays Natal." In *The Collected Poetry*, 32–85. Trans. Clayton Eshleman and Annette Smith. Berkeley: University of California Press.

Chakrabarty, Dipesh, 2000. *Provincializing Europe: Postcolonial Thought and Historical Difference*. Princeton: Princeton University Press.

Chakravarty, Sumita S., 1993 *National Identity in Indian Popular Cinema 1947–1987*. Austin: University of Texas Press.

Chatterjee, Partha, 1986. *Nationalist Thought and the Colonial World: A Derivative Discourse.* London: Zed Books.

– 1993. *The Nation and its Fragments.* Princeton: Princeton University Press.

– 1995. "History and the Nationalization of Hinduism." In *Representing Hinduism*, ed. Vasudha Dalmia and H. von Stietencron, 103–28. New Delhi: Sage.

Cheah, Pheng, 1998. "Given Culture." In *Cosmopolitics: Thinking and Feeling Beyond the Nation*, ed. Pheng Cheah and Bruce Robbins, 290–328. Minneapolis: University of Minnesota Press.

Clark, Roger Y., 2001. *Stranger Gods: Salman Rushdie's Other Worlds.* Montreal: McGill-Queen's University Press.

Cocks, Joan, 2002. *Passion and Paradox: Intellectuals Confront the National Question.* Princeton: Princeton University Press.

Collingwood, R.G., 1961. *The Idea of History* (1946). London: Oxford University Press.

Collins, Larry and Dominique Lapierre, 1976. *Freedom at Midnight.* New York: Avon.

Cooper, Brenda, 1998. *Magical Realism in West African Fiction: Seeing With a Third Eye.* London: Routledge.

Cronin, Richard, 1999. "The Indian English Novel: *Kim* and *Midnight's Children*." In Mukherjee 1999, 134–48.

Cundy, Catherine, 1996. *Salman Rushdie.* Manchester: Manchester University Press.

Daniel, Valentine, 1984. *Fluid Signs: Being a Person the Tamil Way.* Berkeley: University of California Press.

Dell'Aversano, Carmen, 1999. "Worlds, Things, Words: Rushdie's Style from *Grimus* to *Midnight's Children*." In *Coterminous Worlds: Magical realism and contemporary post-colonial literature in English*, ed. Elsa Linguanti et al., 61–70. Amsterdam: Rodopi.

Delourme, Chantal, 1995. "L'Un pour l'autre dans *Midnight's Children* ou notes sur une substitution inaugurale." *Ateliers* 2, 21–32.

Dening, Greg, 1992. *Mr. Bligh's Bad Language.* Cambridge: Cambridge University Press.

Desai, Anita, 1980. *The Clear Light of Day.* London: Penguin, 1980.

– 1995. "Introduction" to Salman Rushdie, *Midnight's Children*, vii-xxi. New York: Knopf.

Devy, G.N., 1992. *After Amnesia: Tradition and Change in Indian Literary Criticism.* London: Sangam.

Dickens, Charles, 1981. *Great Expectations.* New York: Bantam.

– 1993. *Bleak House.* Hertfordshire: Wordsworth.

– 1996A. *David Copperfield.* London: Penguin.

– 1996B. *Oliver Twist.* London: Penguin.

Dostoevsky, Fyodor, 1960. "Notes from the Underground." In *Three Short Novels of Dostoevsky.* Trans. Constance Garnett. New York: Doubleday.

Dumont, Louis, 1970. *Homo Hierarchicus*. Trans. Mark Saintsbury. Chicago: University of Chicago Press.

Durix, Jean-Pierre, 2000. "Salman Rushdie." In Reder, 8–16.

Dutheil, Martine Hennard, 1998. "Rushdie's Affiliation with Dickens." *Dickens Studies Annual* 27, 209–26.

Dwivedi, Sharada and Rahul Mehrotra, 1995. *Bombay: The Cities Within*. Bombay: India Book House.

Edgeworth, Maria, 1832. "An Essay on Irish Bulls." In *Tales and Novels*. Vol. 1, 121–289. London.

Eksteins, Modris, 1989. *Rites of Spring: The Great War and the Birth of the Modern Age*. Toronto: Lester & Orpen Dennys.

Eliot, T.S., 1975. "*Hamlet*." In *Selected Prose of T.S. Eliot*, ed. Frank Kermode, 45–9. London: Faber.

Ellison, Ralph, 1995. *Invisible Man* (1952). New York: Vintage.

Embree, Ainslee T., 1980. *India's Search for National Identity*. Delhi: Chanakya.

Ermarth, Elizabeth Deeds, 1983. *Realism and Consensus in the English Novel*. Princeton: Princeton University Press.

Fanon, Frantz, 1967. "On National Culture." In *The Wretched of the Earth* by Frantz Fanon. Trans. Constance Farrington, 166–99. Harmondsworth: Penguin.

Featherstone, Michael, Scott Lash, and Roland Robertson, eds., 1995. *Global Modernities*. London: Sage.

Fitzgerald, Edward, 1996. "The Rubáiyát of Omar Khayyám of Naishápúr." In *The Norton Anthology of Poetry*, ed. Margaret Ferguson, et al., 866–78. New York: Norton.

Forster, E.M., 1979. *A Passage to India* (1924). Harmondsworth: Penguin.

Friedman, Jonathan, 1995. "Global System, Globalization and the Parameters of Modernity." In Featherstone et al., 1995, 69–90.

Froude, James Anthony, 1852. "England's Forgotten Worthies." *Westminster Review* (July-October), 32–67.

Frye, Northrop, 1976. *The Secular Scripture*. Cambridge, Mass: Harvard University Press.

Gandhi, Mohandas K., 1957. *An Autobiography: The Story of My Experiments with Truth*. Boston: Beacon.

García Márquez, Gabriel, 1991. *One Hundred Years of Solitude*. Trans. Gregory Rabassa. New York: Harper & Row.

Gellner, Ernest, 1997. *Nationalism*. London: Weidenfeld & Nicolson.

Girard, René, 1965. *Deceit, Desire, and the Novel: Self and Other in Literary Structure*. Baltimore: Johns Hopkins University Press.

Gogol, Nicolai, 1957. "The Nose." In *Tales of Good and Evil* by Nicolai Gogol. Trans. David Magarshack, 203–32. New York: Doubleday.

Gorra, Michael, 1997. *After Empire: Scott, Naipaul, Rushdie*. Chicago: University of Chicago Press.

Grass, Günter, 1962. *The Tin Drum*. Trans. Ralph Manheim. New York: Pantheon.

Guha, Ranajit and Gayatri Chakravorty Spivak, eds., 1988. *Selected Subaltern Studies*. New York: Oxford University Press.

Guibernau, Montserrat, 1996. *Nationalisms*. Cambridge: Polity.

Gupta, Dipankar, 2000. *Culture, Space and the Nation-state*. New Delhi: Sage.

Haffenden, John, 2000. "Salman Rushdie." In Reder, 30–56.

Hamilton, Ian, 1996. "The First Life of Salman Rushdie." *The New Yorker* (December 25, 1995 and January 1, 1996): 90–113.

Hardt, Michael and Antonio Negri, 2000. *Empire*. Cambridge, Mass.: Harvard University Press.

Harter, Deborah A., 1996. *Bodies in Pieces*. Stanford: Stanford University Press.

Heffernan, Teresa, 2000. "Apocalyptic Narratives: The Nation in Salman Rushdie's *Midnight's Children*." *Twentieth Century Literature* 46.4, 470–91.

Hogan, Patrick Colm, 2001. "*Midnight's Children*: Kashmir and the Politics of Identity." *Twentieth-Century Literature* 47.4, 510–44.

Hutcheon, Linda, 1988. *A Poetics of Postmodernism*. London: Routledge, Chapman & Hall.

– 1989. *The Politics of Postmodernism*. London: Routledge.

Islam, Syed Manzurul, 1999. "Writing the Postcolonial Event: Salman Rushdie's August 15th, 1947." *Textual Practice* 13.1, 119–35.

Jameson, Fredric, 1981. *The Political Unconscious*. Ithaca: Cornell University Press.

– 1986. "Third-World Literature in the Era of Multinational Capitalism." *Social Text* 15, 65–88.

– 1992. *The Geopolitical Aesthetic*. Bloomington: Indiana University Press.

Jenkins, Richard, 1996. *Social Identities*. London: Routledge.

Joyce, James, 1964. *A Portrait of the Artist as a Young Man*, ed. Richard Ellmann. New York: Viking.

Juraga, Dubravka, 1999. "'The Mirror of Us All': *Midnight's Children* and the Twentieth-Century *Bildungsroman*." In *Critical Essays on Salman Rushdie*, ed. M. Keith Booker, 169–87. New York: G.K. Hall.

Kadzis, Peter, 2000. "Salman Rushdie Speaks." In Reder, 216–27.

Kakar, Sudhir, 1978. *The Inner World*. Delhi: Oxford University Press.

– 1990. *Intimate Relations: Exploring Indian Sexuality*. New Delhi: Penguin.

– 1995. *The Colours of Violence*. New Delhi: Penguin.

Kamra, Sukeshi, 1996. "Replacing the Colonial Gaze: Gender as Strategy in Salman Rushdie's Fiction." In *Between the Lines: South Asians and Postcoloniality*, ed. Deepika Bahri and Mary Vasudeva, 237–49. Philadelphia: Temple University Press.

Kanaganayakam, Chelva, 2001. "Midnight's Grandchildren: A Poetics of Contemporary South Asian Writing." In *Sharing a Commonwealth*, ed. C.S. Lim et al., 191–203. Kuala Lumpur: Association for Commonwealth Language and Literature Studies (ACLALS).

Kane, Jean M., 1996. "The Migrant Intellectual and the Body of History: Salman Rushdie's *Midnight's Children*." *Contemporary Literature* 37.1, 94–118.

Khilnani, Sunil, 1997. *The Idea of India.* London: Hamish Hamilton.

Kipling, Rudyard, 1987. *Kim.* London: Penguin.

Kureishi, Hanif, 1990. *The Buddha of Suburbia.* London: Faber and Faber.

Lamming, George, 1983. *In the Castle of My Skin* (1953). New York: Schocken.

Lannoy, Richard, 1971. *The Speaking Tree: A Study of Indian Culture and Society.* London: Oxford University Press.

Laxman, R.K., 1988. *The Eloquent Brush.* New Delhi: Times of India.

– 1990. *The Best of Laxman.* Vol. I. New Delhi: Penguin.

– 1993. *The Best of Laxman.* Vol. II. New Delhi: Penguin.

Lazarus, Neil, 1999. *Nationalism and Cultural Practice in the Postcolonial World.* Cambridge: Cambridge University Press.

Lewis, Ivor, 1997. *Sahibs, Nabobs and Boxwallahs: A Dictionary of the Words of Anglo-India.* Delhi: Oxford University Press.

Lipscomb, David, 1991. "Caught in a Strange Middle Ground: Contesting History in Salman Rushdie's *Midnight's Children.*" *Diaspora* 1.2, 163–89.

Lonsdale, John, 1992. "The Moral Economy of Mau Mau: Wealth, Poverty and Civic Virtue in Kikuyu Political Thought." In *Unhappy Valley* by Bruce Berman and John Lonsdale. Book II, 315–504. London: James Currey.

Lopez, Alfred J., 2001. *Posts and Pasts: A Theory of Postcolonialism.* Albany: State University of New York Press.

Macaulay, Thomas Babington, 1952. "Minute on Education." In *Speeches*, ed. G.M. Young, 345–61. London: Oxford University Press.

Mamdani, Mahmood, 1996. *Citizen and Subject: Contemporary Africa and the Legacy of Late Colonialism.* Princeton: Princeton University Press.

Marais, Eugene N., 1937. *The Soul of the White Ant.* Trans. Winifred de Kok. London: Methuen.

McClintock, Anne, 1996. "'No Longer in a Future Heaven': Nationalism, Gender, and Race." In *Becoming National*, ed. G. Eley and R.G. Suny, 260–84. Oxford: Oxford University Press.

McCrone, David, 1998. *The Sociology of Nationalism.* London: Routledge.

McHale, Brian, 1987. *Postmodernist Fiction.* New York: Routledge.

McKeon, Michael, 1987. *The Origins of the English Novel, 1600–1740.* Baltimore: Johns Hopkins University Press.

Meer, Ameena, 2000. "Salman Rushdie." In Reder, 110–22.

Merivale, Patricia, 1999. "Saleem Fathered by Oskar: Intertextual Strategies in *Midnight's Children* and *The Tin Drum.*" In Mukherjee 1999, 116–33.

Millais, John Guile, 1905. *The Life and Letters of Sir John Everett Millais.* London: Methuen.

Mohammed, Patricia, 1997. "Midnight's Children and the Legacy of Nationalism." *Callaloo* 20.4, 737–52.

Monti, Alessandro, 1999. "Representing the Worlds: Sanskrit poetics and the making of reality." In *Coterminous Worlds: Magical Realism and Contemporary*

Post-colonial Literature in English, ed. Elsa Linguanti et al., 71–82. Amsterdam: Rodopi.

Moretti, Franco, 1987. *The Way of the World: The Bildungsroman in European Culture*. London: Verso.

– 1996. *Modern Epic*. Trans. Quintin Hoare. London: Verso.

Moss, Laura, 1998. "'Forget those damnfool realists!' Salman Rushdie's Self-Parody as the Magic Realist's 'Last Sigh'." *ARIEL* 29.4, 121–39.

Mukherjee, Meenakshi, 1985. *Realism and Reality: The Novel and Society in India*. Delhi: Oxford University Press.

– ed., 1999. *Rushdie's Midnight's Children: A Book of Readings*. Delhi: Pencraft International.

Nagel, Thomas, 1986. *The View from Nowhere*. New York: Oxford University Press.

Naipaul, V.S., 1969. *The Mimic Men*. Harmondsworth: Penguin.

– 1973. *Mr. Stone and the Knights Companion*. Harmondsworth: Penguin.

– 1976. "Indian Autobiographies." In *The Overcrowded Barraccon* by V.S. Naipaul, 60–6. Harmondsworth: Penguin.

– 1979A. *A Bend in the River*. London: Andre Deutsch.

– 1979B. *India: A Wounded Civilization*. Harmondsworth: Penguin.

– 1981. *Among the Believers*. London: Andre Deutsch.

– 1983A. "A Foreword to this Edition." In *A House for Mr. Biswas* by V.S. Naipaul, vii-xii. New York: Knopf.

– 1983B. *A House for Mr. Biswas* (1961). New York: Knopf.

Nair, Rukmini Bhaya, 1999. "History as Gossip in *Midnight's Children*." In Mukherjee 1999, 49–68.

Nairn, Tom, 1977. *The Break-up of Britain*. London: NLB.

Nandy, Ashis, 1994. *The Illegitimacy of Nationalism: Rabindranath Tagore and the Politics of the Self*. Delhi: Oxford University Press.

– 1995. "An Intelligent Critic's Guide to Indian Cinema." In *The Savage Freud and Other Essays on Possible and Retrievable Selves*, by Ashis Nandy, 196–236. Princeton: Princeton University Press.

Narayan, R.K., 1981. *Waiting for the Mahatma*. Chicago: University of Chicago Press.

Needham, Anuradha Dingwaney, 2000. *Using the Master's Tools: Resistance and the Literature of the African and South-Asian Diasporas*. New York: St. Martin's Press.

Nehru, Jawaharlal, 1981. *The Discovery of India* (1946). New Delhi: Oxford University Press.

Nussbaum, Martha, 1996. "Patriotism and Cosmopolitanism." In *For Love of Country: Debating the Limits of Patriotism*, ed. Joshua Cohen, 2–20. Boston: Beacon Press.

O'Flaherty, Wendy Doniger, ed., 1975. *Hindu Myths*. London: Penguin.

Okri, Ben, 1992. *The Famished Road.* London: Vintage.

Orwell, George, 1946. "Inside the Whale." In *A Collection of Essays*, by George Orwell, 210–52. New York: Harcourt Brace Jovanovitch.

Parameswaram, Uma, 1988. *The Perforated Sheet: Essays on Salman Rushdie's Art*. Delhi: Affiliated East-West Press.

Patel, Sujata and Alice Thorner, eds., 1996A. *Bombay: Metaphor for Modern India*. Bombay: Oxford University Press.

– eds., 1996B. *Bombay: Mosaic of Modern Culture.* Bombay: Oxford University Press.

Pateman, Carole, 1988. *The Sexual Contract.* Cambridge: Polity Press.

Pattanayak, Chandrabhanu, 2000. "Interview with Salman Rushdie." In Reder, 17–9.

Pollock, Sheldon, Homi K. Bhabha, Carol A. Breckenridge, and Dipesh Chakrabarty, 2000. "Cosmopolitanisms." *Public Culture* 12.3, 577–89.

Premchand, 1968. *The Gift of a Cow.* Trans. Gordon C. Roadarmel. London: Lokamaya.

Quilligan, Maureen, 1979. *The Language of Allegory.* Ithaca: Cornell University Press.

Ramanujan, A.K., 1995. *Collected Poems.* Delhi: Oxford University Press.

Ramazani, Jahan, 2001. *The Hybrid Muse: Postcolonial Poetry in English.* Chicago: University of Chicago Press.

Rao, Raja, 1963. *Kanthapura.* New York: New Directions.

– 1987. *The Serpent and the Rope.* Woodstock: Overlook.

Rawls, John, 1972. *A Theory of Justice.* Oxford: Clarendon Press.

Ray, Sangeeta, 2000. *En-Gendering India: Woman and Nation in Colonial and Postcolonial Narratives.* Durham: Duke University Press.

Read, Anthony and David Fisher, 1997. *The Proudest Day: India's Long Road to Independence.* New York: Norton.

Reder, Michael, ed., 2000. *Conversations with Salman Rushdie.* Jackson: University of Mississippi Press.

Rée, Jonathan, 1998. "Cosmopolitanism and the Experience of Nationality." In *Cosmopolitics: Thinking and Feeling Beyond the Nation*, ed. Pheng Cheah and Bruce Robbins, 77–90. Minneapolis: University of Minnesota Press, 1998.

Ricœur, Paul, 1988. *Time and Narrative.* Vol. 3. Trans. Kathleen Blamey and David Pellauer. Chicago: University of Chicago Press.

Robbins, Bruce, 1993. *Secular Vocations: Intellectuals, Professionalism, Culture.* London: Verso.

Rohlehr, Gordon, 1992. *The Shape of That Hurt and Other Essays.* Port of Spain: Longman.

Rose, Charlie, 2000. "*The Moor's Last Sigh.*" Interview with Rushdie. In Reder, 199–215.

Ross, Jean W., 2000. "*Contemporary Authors* Interview: Salman Rushdie." In Reder, 1–7.

Rushdie, Salman, 1981. *Midnight's Children*. New York: Knopf.
– 1983. *Shame*. New York: Knopf.
– 1985. "*Midnight's Children* and *Shame*." *Kunapipi* 7.1, 1–19.
– 1987. *The Jaguar Smile: A Nicaraguan Journey*. London: Pan.
– 1988. *The Satanic Verses*. London: Penguin.
– 1989. *Grimus* (1975). London: Paladin.
– 1991A. *Imaginary Homelands*. London: Granta.
– 1991B. "Attenborough's Gandhi." In *Imaginary Homelands*, 102–6.
– 1991C. "Dynasty." In *Imaginary Homelands*, 47–52.
– 1991D. "'Errata': or, Unreliable Narration in *Midnight's Children*." In *Imaginary Homelands*, 22–5.
– 1991E. "Imaginary Homelands." In *Imaginary Homelands*, 9–21.
– 1991F. "'In God We Trust'." In *Imaginary Homelands*, 376–92.
– 1991G. "Outside the Whale." In *Imaginary Homelands*, 87–101.
– 1991H. "The Riddle of Midnight: India, August 1987." In *Imaginary Homelands*, 26–33.
– 1991I. "Thomas Pynchon." In *Imaginary Homelands*, 352–7.
– 1992. *The Wizard of Oz*. London: British Film Institute.
– 1994. *East, West*. Toronto: Vintage.
– 1995. *The Moor's Last Sigh*. Toronto: Knopf, 1995.
– 1999A. *The Ground Beneath Her Feet*. London: Jonathan Cape.
– 1999B. *The Screenplay of Midnight's Children*. London: Vintage.
– 2001. *Fury*. Toronto: Knopf.
– 2002A. *Step Across This Line: Collected Nonfiction 1992–2002*. Toronto: Knopf.
– 2002B. "A Dream of Glorious Return." In *Step Across This Line*, 180–209.
– 2002C. "Step Across This Line." In *Step Across This Line*, 347–81.

Sangari, Kumkum, 1987. "The Politics of the Possible." *Cultural Critique* 7, 157–86.

Scarano, Tommaso, 1999. "Notes on Spanish-American Magical Realism." In *Coterminous Worlds: Magical realism and contemporary post-colonial literature in English*, ed. Elsa Linguanti et al., 9–28. Amsterdam: Rodopi.

Schreiner, Olive, 1993. *The Story of an African Farm*. New York: Bantam.

Shaw, George Bernard, 1924. *Saint Joan*. London: Constable.

Sheff, David, 2000. "*Playboy* Interview: Salman Rushdie." In Reder, 175–98.

Shell, Marc, 1993. *Children of the Earth*. New York: Oxford University Press.

Singh, Sujala, 2000. "Secularist Faith in Salman Rushdie's *Midnight's Children*." *New Formations* 41, 158–72.

Sommer, Doris, 1990. "Irresistible Romance: the Foundational Fictions of Latin America." In *Nation and Narration*, ed. Homi Bhabha, 71–98. London: Routledge.

Spielmann, M.H., 1898. *Millais and his Works*. Edinburgh.

Srivastava, Sanjay, 1998. *Constructing Post-Colonial India: National Character and the Doon School*. London: Routledge.

Stallybrass, Peter, and Allon White, 1986. *The Politics and Poetics of Transgression*. Ithaca: Cornell University Press.

Stoler, Ann Laura, 1995. *Race and the Education of Desire*. Durham: Duke University Press.

Suleri, Sara, 1992. *The Rhetoric of English India*. Chicago: University of Chicago Press.

Suri, Manil, 2001. *The Death of Vishnu*. New York: Norton.

Tagore, Rabindranath, 1976. *Nationalism*. Delhi: Macmillan.

– 1980. *Gora* (1924). Delhi: Macmillan.

– 1985. *The Home and the World* (1915). London: Penguin.

Taussig, Michael, 1997. *The Magic of the State*. New York: Routledge.

Taylor, Charles, 1989. *Sources of the Self*. Cambridge: Cambridge University Press.

– 1998. "Nationalism and Modernity." In *The State of the Nation*, ed. John A. Hall, 191–218. Cambridge: Cambridge University Press.

Tharoor, Shashi, 1998. *India: From Midnight to the Millennium*. New Delhi: Penguin.

Tiffin, Helen, 1996. "Plato's Cave." In *New National and Post-Colonial Literatures: An Introduction*, ed. Bruce King, 142–63. Oxford: Oxford University Press.

Todorov, Tzvetan, 1975. *The Fantastic: A Structural Approach to a Literary Genre*. Trans. Richard Howard. Ithaca: Cornell University Press.

Tomlinson, John, 1999. *Globalization and Culture*. Chicago: University of Chicago Press.

Tripathi, Salil and Dina Vakil, 2000. "Angels and Devils are Becoming Confused Ideas." Interview with Rushdie. In Reder, 79–86.

Trivedi, Harish, 2000. "Salman the Funtoosh: Magic Bilingualism in *Midnight's Children*." In Mukherjee 1999, 69–94.

Trumpener, Katie, 1997. *Bardic Nationalism*. Princeton: Princeton University Press.

Tuan Yi-fu, 1996. *Cosmos and Hearth*. Minneapolis: University of Minnesota Press.

Tutuola, Amos, 1961. *The Palm-Wine Drinkard*. London: Faber.

Uprety, Sanjeev Kumor, 1997. "Disability and Postcoloniality in Salman Rushdie's *Midnight's Children* and Third-World Novels." In *The Disability Studies Reader*, ed. Lennard J. Davis, 366–81. New York: Routledge.

Vanaik, Achin, 1997. *The Furies of Indian Communalism: Religion, Modernity and Secularization*. London: Verso.

Walcott, Derek, 2002. "Drums and Colours." In *The Haitian Trilogy*, by Derek Walcott, 109–294. New York: Farrar, Straus and Giroux.

White, Edmund, 1993. *Genêt*. London: Chatto & Windus.

White, Hayden, 1973. *Metahistory: The Historical Imagination in Nineteenth-Century Europe*. Baltimore: Johns Hopkins University Press.

Wolpert, Stanley, 1989. *A New History of India* (1977). New York: Oxford University Press.

Young, Crawford, 1994. *The African Colonial State in Comparative Perspective.* New Haven: Yale University Press.

Zola, Émile, 2001. *Nana.* Paris: L'Aventurine.

Index